Case Studies in Organizational Communication

Case Studies in Organizational Communication

Ethical Perspectives and Practices

Edited by

Steve May

University of North Carolina at Chapel Hill

SAGE Publications
Thousand Oaks ▪ London ▪ New Delhi

For information:

Sage Publications, Inc.
2455 Teller Road
Thousand Oaks, California 91320
E-mail: order@sagepub.com

Sage Publications Ltd.
1 Oliver's Yard
55 City Road
London EC1Y 1SP
United Kingdom

Sage Publications India Pvt. Ltd.
B-42, Panchsheel Enclave
Post Box 4109
New Delhi 110 017 India

Printed in the United States of America.

Library of Congress Cataloging-in-Publication Data

Case studies in organizational communication: ethical perspectives and practices/edited by Steve May.
    p. cm.
Includes bibliographical references and index.
ISBN 0-7619-2983-5 (pbk.)
    1. Communication in organizations—Case studies. 2. Communication in organizations—Moral and ethical aspects. I. May, Steve (Steve Kent), 1961–
HD30.3.C37155 2006
302.3'5—dc22

                                        2005026094

This book is printed on acid-free paper.

06   07   08   09   10   10   9   8   7   6   5   4   3   2   1

Acquiring Editor:	Todd R. Armstrong
Editorial Assistant:	Deya Saoud
Project Editor:	Astrid Virding
Copy Editor:	Teresa Herlinger
Typesetter:	C&M Digitals (P) Ltd.
Indexer:	Juniee Oneida
Cover Designer:	Michelle Lee Kenny

Contents

Accountability

Courage

To Geriel
Whose integrity is constant.

Preface

I first considered editing a case study book on organizational ethics several years ago. As an instructor of organizational communication, I was frustrated by two features that were lacking in most textbooks in the field. First, I found that many of the primary textbooks in organizational communication included few, if any, case studies. By contrast, business and management programs had a long and successful history with case-based teaching and, as a result, cases were widely available. Yet, they did not necessarily offer the range and variety of perspectives I wanted my students to learn.

Although I had developed many of my own cases over the years, including a semester-long consulting case, I wondered why there was such a lack of cases in organizational communication textbooks. Most textbooks included discussion questions and even the occasional homework or fieldwork assignment, but these features never quite provided the extensive application of organizational theory that cases provided for my students. When cases were included in textbooks, they were typically short and general in their description of organizational phenomena. Until recently, there was even a lack of supplemental case study books to use in introductory or advanced organizational communication courses. I wanted more for my students.

Second, it also became clear that few, if any, textbooks included an extensive discussion of organizational ethics. Given the range and scope of organizational misconduct over the last several decades, it struck me as a glaring omission in our teaching. Based on conversations with other colleagues around the world, I knew that many instructors were, at least implicitly, discussing organizational ethics in their classrooms. But, I found that many were reluctant to explicitly identify organizational ethics as an issue in their courses. Textbooks were not much help. When they included ethics, it was often relegated to a concluding chapter. Business ethics books have been available for years, but they seemed to define "organizations" and communication very narrowly. For example, rarely were nonprofit organizations, government agencies, universities, churches, or other collectives discussed in them. In addition, they often included classic, historical cases of ethics rather than recent, emerging ethical issues most relevant to today's students.

The confluence of these two pedagogical frustrations was further set in motion with the series of organizational scandals (e.g., Enron, Arthur Andersen, Tyco, WorldCom) that have received such attention in the last five years. For years, my former students had contacted me about their own personal ethical dilemmas in organizations, but now my current students were asking important but challenging questions: What went wrong with these organizations? Why? How common are such unethical practices in organizations? Is this a new phenomenon? What should I do if I belong to an organization that engages in unethical behavior? What if I observe a boss or coworker engaging in such behavior? What changes are necessary in order to improve the ethical conduct of organizations and the people in them? What can I do to help?

Their questions led to informative, instructive, and wide-ranging discussions of organizations and ethics, but I wanted a framework for discussing ethical issues with them in both a theoretical and a pragmatic way. This book, then, is an attempt to focus and structure a meaningful and productive dialogue about organizational ethics with students. It is designed to integrate ethical theory and practice in order to strengthen students' ethical awareness, judgment, and action in organizations by exploring ethical dilemmas in a diverse range of cases.

❖ USES FOR THE BOOK

The book may be used in a variety of ways. Ideally, its availability will prompt some instructors to begin teaching courses on organizational ethics. In such courses, it may be used as a primary textbook. Or, it may be used as a supplemental text for an introductory or advanced course in organizational communication. The book will serve as an excellent companion to a primary textbook in order to bring ethics to the foreground of students' attention. As such, the book not only includes discussions of ethical perspectives and practices, but the case studies also cover a range of topics typical of many organizational communication courses such as leadership, teamwork, organizational culture, work/family balance, gender, new technologies, organizational change, crisis communication, decision making, power/resistance, and conflict, as well as emerging topics such as telecommuting and offshoring, among others. In addition, instructors will notice that many of the cases can be easily applied to common theories of organizational communication such as classical management, human relations, interpretive theory, systems theory, critical theory, and postmodern theory.

❖   WHY TEACH ORGANIZATIONAL ETHICS?

This ethics case study book is based on the belief that organizational theory and practice have become increasingly wide-ranging and diverse in the last two decades. Similar to the emergence of new, diverse theories to understand organizations, organizations themselves are growing more and more complex. Their size, mission, function, structure, and processes all seem increasingly fluid, as organizations become more "emergent" and adaptable. As a result, books on organizational dynamics cannot necessarily present singular, simplistic explanations of "the way organizations are." Rather, they must provide students with a range of organizational examples that best approximate the current and future evolution of organizations—and the practices among and between them.

One of the most recent shifts in organizations is a renewed interest in ethics, partly in response to recent scandals but also in response to the desire to rethink the role of organizations in our lives. Members of organizations are asking themselves questions like the following: What are our mission, vision, and goals? What do we value? What principles should guide our behavior with our multiple stakeholders? No longer is it accepted wisdom that "business ethics" is a contradiction in terms. Instead, questions of ethics are being taken seriously by many organizations around the world, particularly now that executives and boards of directors have realized that ethics may actually enhance individual and organizational performance. Rather than being viewed as merely a compliance or crisis issue, ethics is now seen as part of the bottom line.

The intent of this book, then, is to raise students' awareness regarding ethics and to provide them with the tools to evaluate situations and conduct themselves ethically. It introduces students to a broad, yet context-specific range of ethics-oriented issues in organizations that will supplement and extend their understanding of organizational communication. The book is based on the belief that students are best engaged when they can directly address the challenges and opportunities they will encounter in their own organizational lives. Often, these challenges and opportunities converge around ethical dilemmas that workers experience as they seek to negotiate their interests with those of their organization.

As a pedagogical tool, this book is designed to encourage students' critical thinking skills about ethics through analysis, reflection, and dialogue. Organizational ethics cases do not present easy, linear answers to organizational problems and, as a result, students will learn to explore complex, contextual, and conflicting questions about organizational life in ways that integrate theory and practice. A primary purpose of the book, then, is to further develop students' understanding of organizations by stimulating analysis and discussion of specific organizational practices that enable or constrain ethical action, thereby provoking multiple alternatives or solutions that are made more accessible to them. Additional features of the book include the following:

- An introductory chapter that explores multiple perspectives of ethics
- An innovative discussion of the most common practices of ethical organizations
- Timely case studies that examine a range of ethical dilemmas in diverse organizations
- Discussion questions at the end of each case study to prompt dialogue regarding the opportunties for, and challenges of, ethical behavior in today's organizations
- An afterword that raises new, challenging questions for ethical behavior in today's organizations

❖ WHY USE CASE STUDIES?

All too often, I have overheard students in the buildings and on the sidewalks of universities describing courses in the following fashion: "It's a theory course" or "It's a practical course." On the one hand, students are dissatisfied when courses belabor what is common sense. On the other hand, they are even more dissatisfied when courses have no clear bearing on everyday life. One of the ways to bridge this dichotomy is to recognize that understanding is the joint product of theory and common sense. As Karl Weick aptly explains, "theory and research should focus on what people routinely overlook when they apply common sense. Theory should not be redundant with common sense; it should remind people of what they forget."

Ideally, then, this book should combine theory and practice as it relates to organizational ethics. My assumption is that the two are mutually dependent. For instance, we all use implicit theories of the world around us to guide our behaviors. When those theories do not seem applicable to everyday life, then we adjust them accordingly. The same should hold true for the theories and practice of organizational ethics. Through this book, students will examine various theories of organizational ethics. Yet, each ethical perspective should also be judged according to its applicability to the cases in this book. By studying these specific organizational cases, students should develop the critical-thinking skills to determine which theories are applicable and which theories are not. They should also gain an appreciation for what "works" and what "doesn't work" in organizations when it comes to ethics.

Yet, this appreciation—and the knowledge that derives from it—cannot simply be told in a lecture. It is based on doing. According to Thomas Donaldson, the "case method," as it is often called, builds on the Socratic method of teaching, which involves the active involvement of students who explore, question, and discover in the give and take process with an instructor and fellow students.

In my teaching career, I have found that one of the primary teaching challenges is to provide students with concrete, context-specific knowledge that will supplement their past work experiences, which vary widely from student to student. Many college students often need supplemental materials that ground their theoretical understanding in a practical understanding of organizational life. This is particularly true in terms of ethical challenges that students may face once they enter (or re-enter) the full-time work force.

Many instructors draw upon their own research or consulting experience to help supplement students' work experiences. Or, they utilize the short, limited case studies that are often found at the end of chapters in textbooks. However, many instructors complain that such cases provide neither the detail nor the full range of organizational opportunities/ challenges that will develop the critical-thinking skills necessary for students to comprehend the complexities of organizations. Finally, instructors often question whether a primary text, alone, allows students to confront—in a safe, classroom environment—the ethical dilemmas that many workers face in their careers.

In the future, then, I believe that students will need to understand both the theoretical developments in organizational communication and how those developments are enacted in ethical organizational practice. This book, then, is designed to address this focus on praxis in a manner that clarifies the rapidly changing organizational environment—as well as the diversity of organizational practices that has followed these changes. In short, students need an explicit mechanism by which they can compare and contrast a growing number of developments in organizations. In addition, students need to understand, and appropriately act upon, the various ethical dilemmas and challenges they will confront in the workplace. Case studies of ethical and unethical organizational practices are one of the primary means to accomplish these goals.

Through case studies, students and instructors are able to directly assess ethical and unethical decision making in a rich, diverse, and complex manner that moves beyond merely theoretical discussions of ethics (e.g., duty, rights, utility, virtue, relationships). In short, this case study book explores "ethics in action" and, as a result, is both theoretical and practical in its focus.

❖ OVERVIEW OF THE BOOK

The first section of the book includes two chapters that provide the context for organizational ethics and an overview of ethical perspectives and practices. The first chapter explores current and past examples of ethical and unethical conduct in organizations. It also introduces students to some of the most important challenges for enhancing the ethics of organizations, as well as a means for analyzing ethical dilemmas they may face in organizations. The second chapter provides the theoretical foundation for students and is divided into two primary sections: ethical perspectives and ethical practices. The section on ethical perspectives gives students an overview of common ethical theories such as duty, rights, utility, virtue, and relationships. These theories provide one means for students to assess the case studies. Any—or all—of the theories may be applied to each case study, although students may find that one theory is either more prominent or more relevant in a case. The section on ethical practices explores several behaviors that are most common among ethical organizations, including alignment, dialogic communication, participation, transparency, accountability, and courage. Each practice is then applied to both ethical and unethical organizations.

The second section of the book includes 21 case studies that represent a range of organizational types and ethical dilemmas. Cases include not only businesses but also nonprofit organizations, universities, churches, and government agencies. The cases are organized according to the ethical practices discussed in the second chapter. However, students may find that several of the ethical practices may be relevant to each case. As a result, instructors should use the structure of this section only as a preliminary guide for exploring the case studies. For example, the cases could also be discussed according to topic (e.g., leadership, organizational culture, decision making) or according to theory (e.g., classical management, human relations, systems theory). At the least, though, students should be prepared to discuss each case according to the ethical perspectives (e.g., duty, rights, utility, virtue, relationships).

The final section of the book includes an afterword that reminds students why our discourse around ethics matters. It also extends ethics to broader organizational and cultural issues and proposes a revised ethical theory. Finally, it offers several alternative directions for students interested in further pursuing organizational ethics.

My hope is that the book will stimulate not only dialogue about, but also action on, issues of organizational ethics. The recent scandals have brought public attention to the practices of both unethical and ethical organizations and, as a result, we have a rare opportunity to help our students create organizations of the future that are simultaneously productive and ethical. Whether as employees, citizens, consumers, or shareholders, our students will, hopefully, make that difference in their own organizational lives.

Acknowledgments

As in the case of all scholarly endeavors, this book could not have been completed without the guidance, assistance, and support of numerous other individuals. So, although I take full responsibility for any of the limitations of the book, I also recognize that its strengths are the culmination of many conversations with friends, family, colleagues, and students over the course of several years.

At the least, the book is a creative collaboration that required the contributions of many colleagues who produced the cases contained in it. Although I will not name each of the case authors here, I do want to acknowledge their efforts to produce cases that, hopefully, will stimulate students' ethical awareness, judgment, and decision making. The case authors' own varied interests and perspectives have helped represent an incredibly wide-ranging and diverse set of ethical dilemmas in today's organizations.

I am also grateful for the strong support of Sage Publications in the development of this book. In particular, I want to thank Todd Armstrong, senior acquisitions editor, for his encouragement, insight, patience, and good humor. He is, in many respects, the ideal editor. I also want to thank Deya Saoud, senior editorial assistant, for her professionalism, promptness, and thoroughness throughout the process. Copyeditor Teresa Herlinger provided thorough and valuable edits to the book. I also appreciate the helpful and constructive suggestions provided by the following reviewers: Cheryl Cockburn-Wooten, University of Waikato; Joy Hart, University of Louisville; Guowei Jian, Cleveland State University; Barbara Lieb, George Mason University; and Heather Zoller, University of Cincinnati.

The early stages of the book emerged while I served as a Leadership Fellow at the Institute for the Arts and Humanities at the University of North Carolina at Chapel Hill. Ruel Tyson's direction of the institute and his advocacy of ethical academic leadership served as a motivator for me to follow through with the project. In addition, the

2003 Leadership Fellows offered continual encouragement and support regarding the relevance and the significance of the book. A year later, I served as an Ethics Fellow at the institute, supported by the direction of Martha Crunkleton. My participation in that program further strengthened the intellectual and theoretical foundations of the book. I would like to acknowledge the 2004 Ethics Fellows for their engagement with the project and for their feedback regarding the teaching of case studies on organizational ethics.

I would also like to thank the Kenan Institute for Ethics at Duke University for ongoing opportunities to both discuss organizational ethics and to put theory and research into action through ethics training in a range of organizations. I am especially grateful to Alysson Satterlund who first established my connection to Kenan and who championed my work to them. Elizabeth Kiss graciously accepted my offer to make a praxis-oriented contribution by entering into an already productive and thought-provoking dialogue with members of the institute. Noah Pickus has extended and expanded that role in a manner that continues to stretch and challenge those of us committed to ethical organizational change. Finally, members of the Ethics at Work team—John Hawkins, Deborah Ross, Catherine LeBlanc, Amy Podurgal, Kathy Spitz, Morela Hernandez, and Doris Jordan—have played an integral role in my own ethical learning and development as we tested theory "in the field." I would like to acknowledge that Chapter Two of the book is based not only on my own research and teaching, but also on a series of conversations with my friends and colleagues at Kenan.

Similarly, many students in my organizational ethics and corporate social responsibility courses offered feedback on the first two chapters, as well as the cases themselves. Their willingness to assist me and their insightful suggestions consistently affirmed my faith in public higher education. In particular, I would like to thank Stephanie Evans, who gathered and synthesized much of the material that became the foundation for Chapter 2. Her dedication and professionalism helped move the project forward.

I would be remiss if I didn't also acknowledge, albeit briefly, my own teachers—each of whom motivated my interest in producing organizations that are not only productive but are also ethical. Those ideas first emerged at Purdue University under the guidance of Linda Putnam, Cynthia Stohl, Phil Tompkins, and Jennifer Slack. Later, my interest and expertise in the topic were further developed and honed at the University of Utah through the intellectual support of Len Hawes, Mary Strine, Connie Bullis, Buddy Goodall, and Jim Anderson. At each of my academic homes, I was fortunate to have many thoughtful and thought-provoking mentors. I can only hope that I have motivated my own students in the same manner.

My closest colleagues, at the University of North Carolina at Chapel Hill, have always provided an enriching scholarly community that fosters intellectual engagement, collegiality, and mutual respect. I am particularly indebted to Bill Balthrop, whose leadership of the Department of Communication Studies combined wisdom, wit, and commitment. Bill and other faculty members there have created a context for both intellectual curiosity and rigor. My colleagues in Organizational Communication have also been long-standing sources of ideas and support. Ted Zorn, now at the University of Waikato in Hamilton, New Zealand, has been my model editor. He taught me the art and grace of editing while I served as the forum editor under his guidance as the editor of *Management Communication Quarterly.* His thoroughness, sense of humor, integrity, and compassion for authors and their work is an ethical template in its own respect. Dennis Mumby and Patricia Parker, always generous with their time and kind with their words, have been wonderful colleagues who have been willing to further stimulate and stretch my thinking.

Finally, and most importantly, I could not have completed this book without the enthusiastic and loving support of my family. In so many respects, my parents provided the early and solid ethical foundation for me. They taught me the lessons of hard yet honest work, fairness, and respect. I hope this book will, in some small measure, serve as a testament to their care of our family. My wife, Geriel, has been a steadfast source of support, a sounding board, an analytical guide, a practical problem solver, a tension-reliever, and a loving companion. In addition, her business sense has frequently served as a reality test for my work. She, more than any other person, helped bring this project to its completion. During the final stages of the project, our daughter, Arcadia, was born. Her birth has brought me boundless joy and wonder and has provided me with a new and broader sense of perspective. Ultimately, her entry into the world has also produced a sense of urgency and a profound commitment to further strengthen ethical conduct in our "organizational society."

Steve May
University of North Carolina at Chapel Hill

1

Ethical Challenges and Dilemmas in Organizations

A Case Study Approach

The business of the modern world, for better or worse, is business. Unless we learn to conduct business in ways that sustain our souls and the life supporting web of nature, our future as a species is dim.

Peter Barnes
President, Working Assets Long Distance

❖ THE CHALLENGE OF ORGANIZATIONAL ETHICS

If ethics were easy and straightforward in our organizations, there would be no need for books such as this one. However, this is rarely the case. Ethical decision making and practice are fraught with difficulties and challenges. Ethics often stretches us and moves us to think beyond our own self to consider others: our family, our work group, our organization, our country, our culture. At the least, when we consider our own ethics, we have to ask ourselves: What is my own ethical position or stance? How is that similar to, or different from, others'? Will my actions have the intended consequences? What unintended consequences might arise from my actions?

These are challenging questions to ask at a personal level. We must consider what we deem appropriate and inappropriate, acceptable and unacceptable, right and wrong for ourselves—but also in relation to others. At an organizational level, such issues can become complex, if not daunting. Given the rise of organizational power and influence, the potential impact of decisions is, in some cases, profound and far-reaching. Stan Deetz (1992) reminds us that, by many standards, the business organization has become the central institution in modern society, often eclipsing the state, family, church, and community in power. Organizations pervade modern life by providing personal identity, structuring time and experience, influencing education and knowledge production, and directing news and entertainment. From the moment of our birth to our death, organizations significantly influence our lives in ways that often go unnoticed.

That is, over time, we have developed naturalized, taken-for-granted ideas about how organizations should function and the role that they should play both in our personal lives and in our culture. One of the goals of this book, then, is to raise your awareness regarding many of our commonsense assumptions about organizations, particularly when it comes to ethics. After you have read this book, I hope that you will have developed the awareness to pursue ethical questions and establish your own views on organizational ethics. A second goal of the book is to strengthen your ethical reasoning and decision making. It is not enough to be aware of organizational ethics; it also requires strong critical-thinking skills to understand ethical situations and possible courses of action. After you have read this book, you will have developed these skills as you learn about ethical theories, in general, and ethical practices, specifically. Hopefully, you will have greater confidence in your own decision making and you will better understand the decisions of others. Finally, a third goal is to motivate you to respond to, and proactively confront, ethical dilemmas that may arise in your organizational life. Overall, it is my hope that, after reading this book, you will believe that "organizational ethics matters" and that you will use your knowledge, skill, and motivation to enhance the ethics of our organizations today—and in the future.

The stakes in organizational decisions can be particularly high: How safe is a particular product or service? Does it have negative effects on its users? How should employees be hired, trained, developed, compensated, or fired? How should wealth be developed and distributed? What effect does the accumulation of wealth have upon social, economic, political, and technological disparities with others? How do organizations impact our values, our families, and our communities? Whose definition of ethics is dominant in an increasingly global economy? These questions are certainly not exhaustive and you may come up with many others that are relevant to you.

Regardless of the question, it is clear that the consequences of organizational actions can be great for all of us. Yet, at the same time, the ethical demands on organizations are neither extraordinary nor excessive, according to Al Gini (2005):

> A decent product at a fair price; honesty in advertisements; fair treatment of customers, suppliers, and competitors; a strong sense of responsibility to the communities [they] inhabit and serve; and the production of a reasonable profit for the financial risk-taking of its stockholders and owners. (p. x)

It is worth noting, however, that not all organizations seek to produce a profit for stockholders and owners. Others are more interested in the social welfare of citizens across the world (Bonbright, 1997; Bornstein, 2004). For example, Ashoka, founded by Bill Drayton, is a non-governmental organization that operates in 46 countries and has assisted over 1,400 social entrepreneurs interested in improving human rights, education, environmental protection, rural development, health care, and poverty, among others.

It is also important to remember that our "organizational lives" are not separate or distinct from other realms of our lives. For example, it is increasingly difficult to distinguish between our public and private lives, work and family, labor and leisure (May, 1993). As a result, it is crucial that we keep in mind that organizations are a part of life. They are not silos that function in a vacuum without direct effects on all of us. For better or worse, they are part and parcel of us.

❖   THE CURRENT STATE OF ORGANIZATIONAL ETHICS

In an era of widespread organizational scandals, it is appropriate that we study organizational ethics more closely. This edited volume is not the first to explore organizational ethics (see, for example, Conrad,

2003; Donaldson & Gini, 1996; Malachowski, 2001; Michalos, 1995; Parker, 1998; Peterson & Ferrell, 2005; Seeger, 2002) nor will it be the last (Cheney, in progress). But it is a volume that seeks to capture a unique historical moment as citizens have begun to seriously rethink and reevaluate the role of organizations in their lives.

Even a limited list of recent organizational misconduct should be enough to raise concerns:

- Former WorldCom CEO Bernard Ebbers was convicted of fraud and conspiracy charges for his role in a massive accounting scandal estimated at $11 billion.

- Adelphia founder John W. Rigas and his son, Timothy Rigas, were accused of looting the company and cheating investors out of billions of dollars. Both were convicted of conspiracy, bank fraud, and securities fraud.

- Martha Stewart was convicted of conspiracy, obstruction of justice, and making false statements about her sale of ImClone Systems stock.

- Tyco International CEO Dennis Kozlowski and CFO Mark Swartz were convicted of stealing millions by accepting illegal bonuses and abusing company loan programs. Both received 25-year prison terms.

- Enron executives—former CEO and chairman Ken Lay, former CEO Jeffrey Skilling, and Chief Accounting Officer Richard Causey—are scheduled to be tried on fraud and conspiracy charges in January 2006.

- Former Qwest CEO Joseph Nacchio and six other executives face charges of orchestrating a massive financial fraud that concealed the source of billions of dollars in reported revenue.

- Freddie Mae and Freddie Mac, both government-assisted entities (GAEs), face scrutiny regarding questionable accounting practices that could place millions of mortgages of United States homeowners at risk.

- Several pharmaceutical companies, including Merck and GlaxoSmithKline, have had to withdraw drugs that have been deemed unsafe for public use, in some cases. In addition, the Food and Drug Administration is facing questions that its regulatory control over drug safety has been jeopardized by close relationships with the industry.

Even this limited list does not include scandals among nonprofit organizations, the military, churches, athletic teams, journalists, and the United States government. For example, the director of the Boy Scouts of America has been charged with receiving and distributing child pornography. U.S. military guards at Abu Ghraib prison in Iraq have been accused of engaging in physical and mental abuse of prisoners. Congress is currently conducting hearings on steroid use in baseball, although its use appears common in many other sports, as well. Individuals in the Catholic Church were not only aware of child sexual abuse among some of its priests, but they also covered it up. Several well-known journalists have recently plagiarized articles, and the Bush administration has "purchased" favorable reporting from journalists in order to "sell" its programs to the public.

Reconsidering organizations and their place in our lives affords us the opportunity to even reflect on some of our common beliefs about organizations as we know them: choice of consumers; the value of market mechanisms; the benefits of free trade; and the desire for ongoing growth and development (Cheney & Frenette, 1993).

Undoubtedly, there is growing, if not renewed, interest in organizational ethics. For a time, the recent scandals intensified the media scrutiny of organizations and their leaders. Each new scandal seemed to produce additional clamor for organizational change, with strategies that included improved legal compliance, stronger sentencing penalties for white collar crime, more rigorous professional codes of conduct, and more stringent government oversight and regulation. The scandals also raised serious questions about our trust in corporate America, in particular (Lorsch, Berlowitz, & Zelleke, 2005), and have produced lawsuits, criminal trials, and legislation (e.g., the Sarbanes-Oxley Act). In several cases, the scandals have produced the decline, if not the destruction, of several well-known organizations—most notably Arthur Andersen.

However, even as I prepare this volume in mid-2005, I wonder whether media coverage of the scandals—and the organizational ethics issues related to them—has begun to wane. Has the public's interest in organizational ethics already faded? Will the highly visible scandals overshadow less overt misconduct, as well as some of the more subtle but substantive ethical questions of today about market forces, consumerism, and globalization?

Over the years, attention to such ethical scandals "appears to ebb and flow between the well-publicized, most egregious acts of misbehavior and the mundane, naturalized, and often overlooked practices of everyday organizational life" (May & Zorn, 2003, p. 595). Recently, however, several authors have noticed a renewed focus on organizational ethics, among them Lynn Sharp Paine (2003), a noted Harvard professor of business ethics. In her book, *Value Shift*, Paine explains that ethics has found its way back onto the agenda of organizational leaders. Executives at businesses, for example, have launched ethics programs, mission-driven strategies, values initiatives, and cultural change efforts. In addition, companies have created ethics officers, high-level ethics committees, ethics ombudspersons, codes of ethics, and ethics task forces. Finally, companies have attempted to strengthen their relationships with various stakeholders, developing programs on the environment, human rights, work–family balance, corporate volunteerism, community assistance, product safety, customer service, and philanthropy, among others.

This shift in focus has left many observers asking, what is happening? Why the recent emphasis on ethics? The obvious answer is that organizations have realized that a lack of legal compliance can produce disastrous results, similar to many of the scandals mentioned earlier in this chapter. But organizational scandals alone don't explain the change. According to Paine (2003), there are several additional reasons for the shift in focus toward ethics among organizational leaders:

- Reasons related to risk management
- Reasons related to organizational functioning
- Reasons related to market positioning
- Reasons related to civic positioning (p. 7)

In effect, many leaders have learned that ethics improves organizational performance and, ultimately, the bottom line. Still others have decided that it is the right thing to do; they have concluded that organizations should be fair, honest, respectful, responsive, trustworthy, accountable, and responsible, regardless of whether it serves the organization's self-interest.

I hope that this edited volume of case studies—and others like it—will produce a visible and sustained re-commitment to organizational ethics, as Paine has noted. Although ethical scandals are not unique to our time, the confluence of ethical misconduct in so many different realms and institutions provides a rare opportunity for organizational change. To create such change, though, requires that we delve deeper into the fundamental issues that enable and constrain the opportunities and challenges of creating organizations that are simultaneously productive and ethical. What can we learn from past eras of organizational misconduct? What, if any, relationship exists between organizational ethics and broader conceptions of ethics in our culture as a whole? What are the prospects and limitations of changing organizational ethics? To what extent are ethical failures based on individual, group, organizational, or cultural phenomena? This volume is hopefully a first, incremental step toward answering some of these questions.

❖ HAVE WE LEARNED ANYTHING FROM THE PAST?

Occasionally, it can be helpful to consider some of these questions by learning from ethical and unethical behavior of the past. In many respects, the recent organizational scandals may seem to be different from those of the past. They seem larger, more significant, and of greater consequence. Yet, in fundamental ways, they are similar in that they involve greed, corruption, arrogance, and power. In the 1950s, it was the wealth and power of corporations to create domestic oligopolies prior to international competition. In the 1960s, it was the rise of unwieldy and often mammoth conglomerates that expanded without regard to consumers' needs. Hostile takeovers were the ethical concern of the 1970s. By the late 1980s, figures such as Ivan Boesky and Michael Milken became icons as a result of the insider trading scandals. In the 1990s, executive compensation, downsizing, and the transition to global labor concerned us. The most recent "corporate meltdown," according to Charles Conrad (2003), was the result of "massive financial and status-related incentives combined with declining external constraints combined to create a fraud-inducing system, which in turn provided organizational actors with ready rationalizations/legitimations of practices that 'pressed the envelope' or worse" (p. 16). Somehow, each decade seems to have its own ethical crises. Is history repeating itself? Have we learned anything from the past?

Charles Redding, considered by many to be a central figure in modern organizational communication, may help us answer these questions. Back in 1982, he noted that "the preponderance of everyday problems that plague all organizations are either problems that are patently ethical or moral in nature, or they are problems in which deeply embedded ethical issues can be identified" (p. 2). Prominent author Robert Jackall (1983, 1988) argued in his book *Moral Mazes* that businesses (bureaucracies, in particular) are vast systems of "organized irresponsibility." Similarly, two social psychologists, Sabini and Silver (1982), claimed that businesses have a "genius for organizing evil." These comments came at a time when prominent business authors were extolling the importance of ethics, and numerous centers and institutes for business ethics were emerging around the United States. One observer even called ethics "the hottest topic in corporate America" (Sarikelle, 1989).

Redding also bemoaned the fact that there seemed to be no sustained interest in organizational ethics. He likened the lack of attention to organizational ethics to "wandering in a lonely desert," asking the question of any interested observers who might listen: "When will we wake up?" At that time, over two decades ago, Redding explained that he noticed increased talk about the ethical dimensions of organizational life, as managers and executives were attending numerous conferences, seminars, and workshops that focused on ethical problems in organizations. Yet, he wondered whether all of the ethical talk was backed up by ethical action.

Redding's question regarding an ethical "awakening" could be asked today, as well. No doubt, many persons have awakened to issues related to organizational ethics. One can hardly pick up a newspaper or listen to the evening news without some new ethical scandal in the business world. Ethics centers and institutes have proliferated in the last two decades. The conferences and training programs that Redding noted in the early 1980s still continue today and, in many respects, have grown. Yet, organizational scandals—in both the for-profit and not-for-profit sectors—appear rampant. Hopefully, this time, we will learn from our mistakes and misdeeds.

❖ ETHICAL DILEMMAS

One of the ways to learn from the past—and also to enhance our ethical action in the future—is to think about the nature of ethical dilemmas that organizations and their members have faced. Throughout my discussion of organizational ethics in these first two chapters—as well as the rest of the book—it is important to remember that it is *people* who make decisions in and about organizations. Organizations don't make decisions, per se. People do, albeit within the accepted norms and standards of organizations. At one level, then, any book on organizational ethics needs to account for the actions of individuals. So, although I frequently refer to organizational ethics, it is merely a shorthand way of referring to the numerous individual and collective decisions that are made within and between organizations.

In an accessible and popular book, *How Good People Make Tough Choices: Resolving the Dilemmas of Ethical Living*, Rushworth Kidder (1995) explores the personal dimension of ethical decision making. Each of us faces a multitude of ethical decisions throughout our lifetime, even if they are not readily apparent to us. Those decisions shape our sense of self, as well as others' sense of us.

Kidder (1995) explains, though, that some of our attention to ethics is misdirected. He claims, for example, that right/wrong ethical dilemmas gain much of the public attention. On the one hand, we denounce persons who have engaged in organizational misconduct. On the other hand, we praise the courage and integrity of those persons who have engaged in "right action." The former are often shunned while the latter are sometimes idolized. But, in the end, right/wrong dilemmas tend to be fairly clear-cut and straightforward. By contrast, Kidder argues that "right/right dilemmas" are much more challenging and merit more attention. He explains his premise this way: "The really tough choices . . . don't center on right versus wrong. They center on right versus right. They are genuine dilemmas precisely because each side is firmly rooted in one of our basic core values" (p. 18).

Although any number of right/right dilemmas is possible, Kidder (1995) notes that several are most common:

- Justice versus mercy
- Truth versus loyalty
- Individual versus community
- Short-term goods versus long-term goods

According to Kidder (1995), each of the preceding dilemmas—and others like them—pose the most difficult challenge for us since they represent pairs of values, both of which we tend to accept. For example, in organizational terms, should a boss show mercy to an employee who has made a costly blunder, or should the employee be punished? When an employee finds out that a significant downsizing is imminent and a friend will be fired, should he or she tell the friend the truth or remain loyal to the company? When an employee conducts a safety study that suggests a product is unsafe for public use, should the employee remain loyal to the company by staying silent or inform the public? Should a company executive make a financial decision that will benefit stockholders and employees in the short term but may have a negative impact in the long term? We struggle with such ethical dilemmas because we are torn between two values, both of which seem right, but we are forced to decide between them.

In most cases, we choose the action that is "the nearest right"—the one that best fits our own ethical perspective on the world. As you will see in Chapter 2, we may be more or less oriented to duty, rights, utility, virtue, or relationships when it comes to ethics. However, Kidder (1995) also encourages us to explore whether there is a third way that might enact both values, the "trilemma solution":

> Sometimes that middle ground will be the result of a compromise between the two rights, partaking of each side's expansiveness and surrendering a little of each side's rigidity. Sometimes, however, it will be an unforeseen and highly creative course of action that comes to light in the heat of the struggle for resolution. (p. 167)

Ideally, though, the resolution is not so much a compromise or middle ground position as it is a creative means to move beyond the ethical dilemma by appreciating the tension between the two values.

❖ COMMUNICATING ABOUT ETHICS

Since organizations are so close to us, it can be challenging to talk about the ethical dilemmas that arise from them. Before we continue further, then, we should explore how we talk about ethics and how ethics is structured within our culture (see, for example, Willmott, 1998).

For example, it is worth considering how ethical issues are communicated in contemporary life. Are ethical issues framed in a particular way? Are there particular persons or groups who have greater (or fewer) opportunities to speak regarding ethical issues? Are there ethical issues that are rarely, if ever, discussed publicly? That is, are some ethical issues marginalized? How do persons tend to respond to ethical violations of the law or cultural norms and expectations? How do persons who have violated them explain their behavior? Noticing such patterns of discourse should provide you with interesting insights regarding the place of ethics in our culture today.

For anyone interested in constructive conversations regarding organizational ethics, it is important to consider the distinctions between descriptive ethics, normative ethics, and analytical ethics (Goodpaster, 1995). The goal of descriptive ethics is to represent, in a neutral and empirical manner, the "facts" of an ethical situation, as well as the values of the persons and organizations involved. There is no attempt to make an ethical judgment regarding the situation since the emphasis is on attaining accuracy, as much as possible. In effect, the purpose of descriptive ethics is to "map the terrain" of the ethical situation. No personal judgment is presented.

Normative ethics, by contrast, according to Kitson and Campbell (2001), "seeks to develop and defend judgments of right and wrong, good and bad, virtue and vice" (p. 11). It involves exploring points of view and presenting one's position. It introduces the question: Given the situation, what is my ethical judgment about it? As an extension of the first two, analytical ethics is interested in whether an ethical judgment is appropriate, in comparison to other ethical judgments. It functions at a meta-ethical level by comparing and contrasting different ethical perspectives, decisions, and practices. Therefore, analytical ethics provides the justifications for a normative ethical judgment.

During discussions of ethics-based case studies of organizations, it is important to distinguish the type of statement being made. How is the ethical situation in the case being described? Is a normative position or point of view presented in response to the case? Or, is a position or point of view being analytically argued that is in contrast to others? In everyday conversation, it is all too common for us to describe situations in a normative or analytical manner, reflecting our own personal values or biases. However, it can often be a helpful exercise to bracket our comments in these three steps (i.e., descriptive ethics, normative ethics, and analytical ethics), beginning with description and moving to defense of a position, based on an evaluation of multiple points of view. However, we should keep in mind that the assumption that we can accurately describe an ethical situation rests on the belief that the factual content can be separated from our values (Willmott, 1998). While descriptive ethics claims to describe "what is," some critics question whether such an approach actually privileges one way of viewing an ethical situation over another—in effect, presenting what is ultimately a value-laden description of a situation as if it is natural or taken for granted. As you discuss these cases with others, you may find, for example, that what you consider to be clear-cut and factual may be questioned by others.

Using the concepts of descriptive, normative, and analytical ethics as a conversational guide, class discussions of organizational ethics may be conducted around some of the following questions:

• How should organizational ethics be defined? That is, what constitutes responsible and irresponsible action?

• Why should students, owners, employees, consumers, and citizens be interested in organizational ethics?

• What are the prominent meanings and discourses surrounding ethics, in general, and organizational ethics, specifically?

• How has ethics evolved, historically?

• What is the relationship between organizational ethics and specific social, political, economic, ideological, and technological conditions?

• How, if at all, has ethics changed the nature of management and organizational communication?

• What is/should be the role of ethics in our emerging, global economy?

• How, if at all, has ethics changed organizing processes?

• From your perspective, how does ethics enable or constrain today's organizations?

• How might a renewed emphasis on ethics change management and organizational communication in the future?

• How, if at all, has recent attention to ethics affected management practices?

• What are the agendas for research, teaching, and practice that are relevant to persons interested in organizational ethics?

❖ BENEFITS OF CASE STUDIES

Case studies are one of the best ways to talk about the real, day-to-day ethical dilemmas in organizations. They are also an ideal way to apply theories learned in the classroom, whether they are ethical theories or organizational theories (for examples, see Donaldson & Gini, 1996; Keyton & Schockley-Zalaback, 2004; Sypher, 1997). This case studies book is based on the assumption that you need to not only understand the theoretical developments in organizational studies (for a more extensive discussion of organizational communication theories, see May & Mumby, 2005), but you also should know how they are enacted in ethical organizational practice

This book, then, is designed to address this focus on praxis in a manner that clarifies the rapidly changing organizational environment—as well as the diversity of organizational practices that has followed these changes. In short, you need an explicit mechanism by which you can compare and contrast a growing number of developments in organizations. In addition, you will need to be prepared to understand, and appropriately act upon, the various ethical dilemmas and challenges you may confront in your organizational lives. Case studies of ethical and unethical organizational practices are one of the primary means to accomplish these goals.

Case studies, in general, offer several benefits:

- Case studies provide an opportunity to explore the real-world functioning of organizations in context.

- Case studies stimulate reflection on others' actions.

- Case studies provide exemplars of appropriate and inappropriate, productive and unproductive, useful and irrelevant behaviors.

- Case studies prompt lively discussion regarding alternative courses of action.

- Case studies provide an opportunity to apply theoretical knowledge to practical situations.

- Case studies serve as an impetus for future action.

More specifically, the case studies in this book may also be used to develop skills in three primary areas:

- Ethical engagement—You should develop the desire to pursue ethical issues in greater detail and establish your own independent thinking about ethics.

- Ethical reasoning and decision making—You should develop greater confidence in your judgments and in your ability to understand and appreciate others' points of view regarding ethics.

- Ethical practice—You should develop the ability to respond to and proactively address ethical challenges that may arise in your life.

Case studies, then, should increase your motivation and interest in ethical issues, should improve your analytical and critical thinking skills around ethical challenges, and should provide you with a foundation for making organizations more ethical.

❖ CASE STUDIES OF ORGANIZATIONAL ETHICS

My hope is that this book will motivate you to think more critically about organizational ethics in your own life and also in the lives of others. More specifically, the book will 1) introduce you to a range of ethical theories based on duty, rights, utility, virtue, and relationships; and 2) explore case studies of organizations that either enable or constrain common elements of ethical practice such as alignment, dialogic communication, participation, transparency, accountability, and courage.

One of the reasons I was motivated to edit this volume is because many organizational case study books tend to be both atheoretical and ahistorical in their focus and, typically, marginalize ethics. By contrast, this book seeks to conceptualize and historicize ethics-oriented cases by 1) providing a theoretical foundation of ethical perspectives that can be applied to them; 2) identifying sets of ethical practices that might serve as examples for future organizational behavior; and 3) drawing upon their relationship to other cases (e.g., within an industry, a nation-state, a profession) within a particular period of time. The contributors to the book were encouraged to utilize their own scholarly strengths and expertise to develop fuller, richer cases, while supplementing their expertise with additional historical and current resources. As such, the cases should be seen merely as a starting point for a more thorough and complex understanding of the cases themselves—and others that may be related to them by topic, issue, ethical perspective, or practice.

The cases in this volume were selected because they focus on organizations that have confronted challenging ethical dilemmas and, as a result, have acted ethically or unethically in response to them. That is, the cases in the book represent a full range of organizational practices, from overt violations of the law to exemplars of responsible behavior. Each case, however, is written to direct you to ethical dilemmas that present tensions, contradictions, challenges or opportunities for the organization and others that it affects. You will also notice that, in contrast to some other case study books, these cases are about real—rather than hypothetical—organizations. I believe it is important for such organizations to be included in a case study book, first to present you with a realistic account of organizational life and second, to hold unethical organizations accountable and to praise ethical organizations.

As you will see when you read the cases, contributors were asked to define "organization" broadly to include not only businesses but also other types of organizations (e.g., educational institutions, religious institutions, political organizations, not-for-profit organizations) and organizing, in general. This is in stark contrast to most business ethics case study books that focus exclusively on corporations. Contributors were also encouraged to write cases that examined broader cultural constructions of work (e.g., work and identity, work–family balance, welfare-to-work programs, health care and work, globalization) that are so relevant to our everyday lives. The book, then, not only explores ethical issues within organizations, but also within the social, political, economic, ideological, and technological contexts that affect, and are affected by, organizations.

Each case also examines a unique dimension of organizational communication. Some cases focus on the communication response of organizations after a product or service has failed. Other cases in the book explore the communication strategies of leaders who have produced ethical or unethical organizations. Or, in some cases, communication is discussed as a means to frame organizational decisions. Still others explore how gender, race, and family are constructed in and through communication within organizations.

You will also notice that a variety of sources were used in constructing these cases about organizational ethics, including observations, interviews, questionnaires, and documents (e.g., company documents, media coverage, legal materials, legislative hearings, professional association studies/reports, etc.). As a result, some cases are organized chronologically to follow a time line of events while others are structured in a narrative form.

Regardless of the structure of each case, though, you should first identify the ethical dilemmas that are raised in the case. Once you have identified the ethical dilemmas, use the ethical perspectives and practices from Chapter 2—in combination with outside resource materials—to fully understand, appreciate, and discuss their complexities. You should be able to understand the context of the case, the evolution of the ethical dilemmas, and the key actors facing them. Finally, as you develop your own opinions about the cases, be sure to consider alternative views that may be presented by your instructor or by other students. Doing so strengthens your "ethical agility" and better prepares you for the variety of ethical dilemmas you may confront in the future.

Although I will not recount all of the cases here, you will find a wide array of organizations and ethical issues in this volume. Some of the cases include the following:

- Wal-Mart—The case examines claims that the company's economic impact "limits the ability of local businesses to survive." The case study also examines how Wal-Mart has responded to charges that it negatively affects local businesses.

- Coca-Cola—The case explores a history of racial discrimination at the company, which constructed "a corporate hierarchy in which African American workers were clustered at the bottom of the pay scale, averaging $26,000 a year less than White employees." According to the case, the hostile work environment created "unusually high rates of stress-related illnesses, such as depression," among African American workers.

- Mitsubishi—The case addresses a class action sexual discrimination lawsuit by several female employees of the company and explores their claims, as well as the company and union responses to them.

- Hewitt and Associates—The case considers the degree to which single and married employees with families should be treated similarly or differently.

- The Catholic Church—The case traces the chronology of the church's sexual abuse scandal, displaying the degree to which the church was candid with the general public and its parishioners regarding the extent of abuse.

- The Bush Administration—The case identifies several criteria for a "just war" and compares them to the justifications for, and practices of, the war in Iraq.

- NASA—The case reflects back on the communication and decision-making processes prior to the shuttle Columbia launch, based on lessons that should have been learned from the Challenger disaster.

It also explores NASA's public response to the explosion of Columbia, which occurred during re-entry.

- U.S. Forest Service—The case discusses the moral judgments made by the Forest Service when it blamed wildland firefighters for their own deaths in the Storm King Mountain fire. It also examines the use of fire codes in assigning blame and avoiding responsibility.

- College Athletics and Integrity—The case examines scandals and fraud in several university athletic departments, including the University of Colorado, the University of Georgia, and St. Bonaventure.

As students of organizations, it is particularly important that you be able to first identify current trends regarding ethics and second, to intervene in the emergence, development, and acceptance (or rejection) of those trends. The case studies should help you in that process. Before we move to the cases themselves, though, it is important for you to have some additional background information regarding a range of ethical perspectives and ethical practices. Chapter 2 will provide that theoretical and practical foundation for you to thoroughly explore the case studies. That chapter should give you the tools to understand, critique, and apply theoretical and practical material to the cases and, ultimately, to consider alternative ethical futures for organizations.

❖ REFERENCES

Bonbright, D. (1997). *Leading public entrepreneurs.* Arlington, VA: Ashoka.

Bornstein, D. (2004). *How to change the world: Social entrepreneurs and the power of new ideas.* Oxford: Oxford University Press.

Cheney, G. (in progress). *Professional ethics: Talk about who we are at work and why it's important.* New York: Oxford University Press.

Cheney, G., & Frenette, G. (1993). Persuasion and organization: Values, logics, and accounts in contemporary corporate public discourse. In C. Conrad (Ed.), *The ethical nexus* (pp. 49–74). Norwood, NJ: Ablex.

Conrad, C. (1993). *The ethical nexus.* Norwood, NJ: Ablex.

Conrad, C. (2003). The corporate meltdown. *Management Communication Quarterly, 17*(1), 5–19.

Deetz, S. (1992). *Democracy in an age of corporate colonization.* Albany: State University of New York Press.

Donaldson, T., & Gini, A. (Eds.). (1996). *Case studies in business ethics,* (4th ed.). Upper Saddle River, NJ: Prentice Hall.

Gini, A. (2005). *Case studies in business ethics* (5th ed.). Upper Saddle River, NJ: Prentice Hall.

Goodpaster, K. E. (1995). Commentary on "MacIntyre and the manager." *Organization, 2* (2), 212–216.

Jackall, R. (1983). Moral mazes: Bureaucracy and managerial work. *Harvard Business Review, 61*(5), 118–130.

Jackall, R. (1988). *Moral mazes: The world of corporate managers.* New York: Oxford University Press.

Keyton, J., & Schockley-Zalaback, P. (Eds.). (2004). *Case studies for organizational communication: Understanding communication processes.* Los Angeles: Roxbury.

Kidder, R. (1995). *How good people make tough choices: Resolving the dilemmas of ethical living.* New York: Fireside.

Kitson, A., & Campbell, R. (2001). Case studies in business ethics. In A. Malachowski (Ed.), *Business ethics: Critical perspectives on business and management* (Vol. IV, pp. 7–12). London: Routledge.

Lorsch, J. W., Berlowitz, L., & Zelleke, A. (2005). *Restoring trust in American business.* Cambridge, MA: American Academy of Arts and Sciences.

Malachowski, A. (Ed.). (2001). *Business ethics: Critical perspectives on business and management* (volume IV). London: Routledge.

May, S. K. (1993). *Employee assistance programs and the troubled worker: A discursive study of knowledge, power, and subjectivity.* Unpublished doctoral dissertation, University of Utah.

May, S. K., & Mumby, D. (Eds.). (2005). *Engaging organizational communication theory and research: Multiple perspectives.* Thousand Oaks, CA: Sage

May, S. K., & Zorn, T. (2003). Communication and corporate social responsibility. *Management Communication Quarterly, 16,* 595–598

Michalos, A. C. (1995). *A pragmatic approach to business ethics.* Thousand Oaks, CA: Sage.

Paine, L. S. (2003). *Value shift: Why companies must merge social and financial imperatives to achieve superior performance.* New York: McGraw-Hill.

Parker, M. (Ed.). (1998). *Ethics and organization.* London: Sage.

Peterson, R. A., & Ferrell, O. C. (Eds.). (2005). *Business ethics: New challenges for business schools and corporate leaders.* Armonk, NY: M.E. Sharpe.

Redding, C. W. (1982). *Ethics and the study of organizational communication: When will we wake up?* Lecture presented to The Center for the Study of Ethics in Society. Kalamazoo: Western Michigan University.

Sabini, J., & Silver, M. (1982). *Moralities of everyday life.* New York: Oxford University Press.

Sarikelle, P. (1989, February). Going by the book. *BFG Today,* 4–5.

Seeger, M. W. (2002). *Ethics and organizational communication.* Cresskill, NJ: Hampton Press.

Sypher, B. D. (Ed.). (1997). *Case studies in organizational communication 2: Perspectives in contemporary work life.* New York: The Guilford Press.

Willmott, H. (1998). Toward a new ethics? The contributions of poststructuralism and posthumanism. In M. Parker (Ed.), *Ethics and organizations* (pp. 76–121). London: Sage.

2

Ethical Perspectives
and Practices

❖   ❖   ❖

We live in hard times. The era of "jobs, jobs, jobs" and all that slogan implies is over. We suggest that if justice depends on employment and the good life depends on the rewards of hard work, there can be no justice, and the good life may be relegated to a dim memory. If jobs are the answer to our cultural problems, then we are in big trouble.

Stanley Aronowitz and William DiFazio
The Jobless Future

Employees are being asked to work harder and to be more committed to the company objectives while at the same time being told, and shown, that there is no such thing as job security. Historically, one of the characteristics of an effective business manager has been the ability to live with ambiguity. In the years ahead, all employees will need to develop that special ability. Whether employees and managers realize it or

*not, they are forming new social contracts to govern their
places of work.*

Kenneth Chilton and Murray Weidenbaum
Center for the Study of American Business

T he preceding quotes suggest that the historical social contract
between employers and employees has changed in recent years,
raising a series of ethical questions regarding the role of organizations—
and businesses, in particular—in our culture. In the era of corporate
mergers, downsizing, restructuring, and temporary work, it is now
common to observe that the old social contract, which guaranteed or
implied lifetime employment in exchange for employee competence
and good behavior, has expired. Taking its place is a new social contract
in which employees are sent a mixed message, aptly summarized by
Brian O'Reilly in *Fortune:*

> You're expendable. We don't want to fire you, but we will if we
> have to. Competition is brutal, so we must redesign the way we
> work to do more with less. Sorry, that's just the way it is. And one
> more thing—you're invaluable. Your devotion to our customers is
> the salvation of this company. We're depending on you to be inno-
> vative, risk-taking, and committed to our goals. (1994, p. 44)

This new social contract is the result of multiple cultural forces,
including global competition, domestic deregulation, and technological change, as well as executive mismanagement and corruption. Regardless of the reasons for the change, however, the impact will be especially
profound on management and labor relations in the years ahead. For
example, the dramatic changes in the workplace are being blamed for
escalating workplace violence, exploding workplace litigation, and
growing numbers of employees seeking medical and psychological
help for work-related stress.

The range and scope of these organizational changes and the ones
presented in Chapter 1 pose serious questions for persons interested in
ethics. Can, in fact, organizations be ethical? If not, what social, political, economic, and technological conditions limit this possibility? If so,
what would constitute an ethical organization? Do our organizations

have a unique ethical responsibility to employees? Customers? Shareholders? Citizens? The environment? What ethical perspectives and best practices within organizations might assist us in developing and sustaining ethical organizations? In order to produce a dialogue about these responsibilities and their implications for "managing" a new ethical agenda in organizations, this book includes case studies that are drawn from diverse types of organizations. It is my hope that these diverse readings will further your understanding of the multiple ways that organizations address (or do not address) ethics.

As a means to further stimulate discussion regarding the cases in the book, this chapter should provide you with additional background to raise ethical questions about the cases. It explores two primary ethical tensions (e.g., foundational/situational and individual/organizational) that are common in many organizations. It also briefly summarizes some of the primary ethical perspectives. Finally, it identifies several "best practices" of ethical organizations, providing both positive and negative examples of each organizational practice.

The purpose of this chapter is not necessarily to provide a comprehensive overview of ethical theory and practice. Several other books (Dienhart, 2000; Donaldson & Werhane, 1999; Gini, 2005; Johannesen, 1996; Shaw & Barry, 2001; Snoeyenbos, Ameder, & Humber, 2001; Velasquez, 1998) may serve that purpose. Rather, it is to provide you with an additional foundation for analyzing the cases, reflecting on them, and discussing them with your instructor and your fellow students. Hopefully, the result will be that your ethical competencies will be improved and that you will be better able to confront and respond to ethical dilemmas that you face in your own organizational life.

❖ ETHICAL TENSIONS

Different ethical perspectives lead to quite different conclusions regarding what constitutes ethical behavior. These differences are based on fundamental assumptions about the character of reality, the nature of individuals, and the obligation of individuals to one another (Anderson & Englehardt, 2001). The differences in these ethical perspectives may be described as tensions—or oppositions—and can be plotted on axes in order to locate one's own perspective. These tensions are likely to either enable or constrain ethical action, and the most commonly noted tensions, according to Anderson and Englehardt, include foundational/situational, individual/community, and essence/existence. However, we could also consider any number of additional tensions that are found in most organizations such as centralization/decentralization, collaboration/ competition, control/autonomy, strategies/tactics, specialization/ differentiation, and flexibility/structure, among others.

For our purposes, the most relevant tensions are 1) foundational/ situational, and 2) individual/community. Briefly exploring these tensions will allow us to not only apply them to the case studies, but it will also enable us to better understand our own ethical assumptions.

Foundational/Situational Tension

The first tension considers whether ethics is foundational or situational. As you read the case studies, you should consider whether you believe that ethical behavior is based on a set of actions that are constant or whether it is based on actions that are context-specific. Foundational—or universal ethics—persists while situational ethics shifts over time.

Foundational ethics suggests that reality is given, self-evident, objective, and neutral, while situational ethics views reality as socially constructed, subjective, and interpreted.

If, for example, you were to develop ethics training for an organization from a foundational approach, you might argue for a core set of values that the organization and its members must adhere to in order to be ethical. Most likely, these values would be long-standing and widely accepted (e.g., telling the truth, respecting others). In my experience, ethics training for organizations often draws on a foundational approach, since it frequently focuses on a core set of principles that are applied to every organization, regardless of size, structure, or industry.

For example, professional codes of ethics are expected to create a degree of stability and consistency regarding ethical behavior across organizations in a profession such as medicine, accounting, psychology, or journalism.

As you think about this approach, ask yourself these questions: Are there any foundational values or principles that you believe all organizations should follow? If you were working with an organization to improve its ethics, would you be willing to accept your client's values even if they contradicted your own? The answers to these questions may help you determine if you take a foundational approach to ethics in your organizational life.

If, by contrast, you developed ethics training from a situational approach, you might prefer to tailor ethics services to the specific needs of a particular organization. You might argue, for example, that it is not enough to only "follow the rules" of legal compliance or a formal code of ethics. Instead, you might focus on the distinct organizational culture of your client and seek to adapt your training to meet the needs of that organization. As a result, you might try to learn as much as possible about the organization itself, drawing on member knowledge and experience, before you offer recommendations for improving the organization's ethics. Such an approach would attempt to facilitate organization members' development of their own ethical behaviors, based on a collaborative process.

Individual/Community Tension

The second tension considers whether the individual (libertarian approach) or the community (communitarian approach) should be primary. For our general purposes, we may define community in terms of the organizations in the cases. To better understand this tension, we may ask three questions. First, is the advancement of the individual good for the organization or is the advancement of the organization good for the individual? Second, is the individual the source of ethics or is the collective wisdom of the organization the basis of ethical judgment? Third, is ethics better served by justice or by compassion? (Anderson & Englehardt, 2001, p. 47).

To extend the ethics training example a bit further, an ethics training program might integrate personal and organizational ethics. However, a more individual-oriented ethics initiative might focus more exclusively on the ethical reasoning and action of organizational members. As a trainer, you might ask yourself the following: How can I best develop ethics-based skills that are relevant and useful to every member of the organization? You might assume that individual change among the members is likely to produce organizational change.

Or, by contrast, you might develop training tools that extract the collective wisdom of the organization, since it is considered the basis of ethical judgment. For example, you might be more focused on the advancement of the organization by improving its ethical culture. In effect, you would be assuming that the organization and its leaders should be the ethical guides for members of the organization, setting the ethical tone for personal behavior.

As you consider the differences between the individual and community approaches when you read the cases, also think about how the tension raises some challenging questions for all organizations. What happens when there are contradictions between the interests of the individual member and the organization? How can you best negotiate the needs of the individual and the organization? Are their needs and interests inherently divergent or are there ways to find convergence among them?

❖ WHAT IS THE ETHICAL RESPONSIBILITY OF AN ORGANIZATION?

Thinking about the preceding ethical tensions leads us to a broader, more practical question. What *is* the ethical responsibility of an organization? How should it behave toward its various stakeholders such as members, customers, suppliers, distributors, governing/regulatory agencies, and its community? Can/should an organization be separated from its members when ethical matters are considered?

To begin thinking about these questions in more depth, it may be helpful to refer to one of the best-known and widely cited commentators on organizational ethics, Milton Friedman. Although there is widespread debate regarding whether Friedman's classic 1970 essay, "The social responsibility of business is to increase its profits," is an appropriate or an inappropriate guide for ethical action, his views are still widely accepted and used within the curriculum of many business schools.

Friedman was interested in exploring duties and, in his essay, he considers the responsibilities of business. Given the recent corporate scandals and a renewed interest in organizational ethics, Friedman's essay is very timely. His essay was in response to a growing interest at that time in a new term, *corporate social responsibility*. Taking a largely economic perspective on business responsibility, Friedman critiques arguments of the time that businesses have responsibilities beyond making money. Because of their increasingly significant role in political, social, and economic realms, critics had raised questions about the broader role of businesses in society. According to Friedman (1970), the doctrine of corporate social responsibility required accepting that "political mechanisms, not market mechanisms, are the appropriate way to determine the allocation of scarce resources." For Friedman, such an approach was more firmly grounded in socialism than capitalism and, therefore, he was highly critical of expanding the responsibilities of business beyond making money.

Friedman, then, was primarily concerned with the economic outcomes of business decision making. He believed that the greatest good would occur for all if businesses made decisions based on increasing shareholder value. His essay has been widely used to support the common business adage that one's first duty is to increase shareholder value. For example, in the case of Enron, Friedman might argue that its executives' mistakes were not that they misled employees but that they misled the shareholders—who should have been their primary responsibility. Friedman (1970) does suggest, though, that an executive should try "to make as much money as possible, while conforming to the basic rules of society, both those embodied in the law and those embodied in ethical custom." Aside from this minor caveat, though, he explains that acting in a socially responsible manner—at the expense of shareholders—is akin to spending someone else's money for the social interest. The person is, in effect, imposing a tax of his or her choice in the process.

He argues that it is best to trust market mechanisms when making decisions. A focus on social responsibility, according to Friedman, is a "fundamentally subversive doctrine" in a free society.

While accepted by many in the business world, Friedman's arguments have also garnered widespread criticism. According to some, his essay raises many unanswered, but important, questions. What criteria should executives use in deciding which actions are acceptable and which actions are unacceptable? Is a cost–benefit analysis of responsible behavior the only way to decide how to act in a business? What about the role of companies in creating (e.g., lobbying) and resisting (e.g., violations, paying fines) laws? That is, to what extent does Friedman address the relationship between economics and politics in today's society? How are we best able to determine the rules of society, based in "ethical custom?" Have ethical customs changed enough since 1970 to support corporate social responsibility? How would Friedman respond to corporate volunteerism? Philanthropy? Do executives only have a duty to serve their shareholders? If shareholder value is improved by reducing labor costs through downsizing, outsourcing, or offshoring, is that a responsible decision?

❖ ETHICAL PERSPECTIVES

Beyond Friedman's well-known and oft-repeated arguments, a more extensive understanding of the following ethical perspectives will allow us to understand that Friedman's arguments themselves are based on ethical perspectives: in this case, duty-based and utilitarian ethics. That is, he is speaking from a particular perspective. Regardless of whether one agrees or disagrees with his views, it is important to understand the basis for his arguments. However, Friedman's arguments are not the only ones of value here. Your own views are important as well. So, a brief exploration of ethical perspectives will allow you to better identify your own assumptions regarding ethics as you read the cases in this book and as you move forward in your own careers.

Duty (Religious Systems, Immanuel Kant)

In general, a duty perspective is concerned with the individual's obligations to others (often, the collective). Duties are often viewed as natural, universal, rational, and self-evident. In some examples of duty ethics—such as moral law—one performs an action because of an obligation to follow a set of standards or rules. From this perspective, persons have a duty to obey moral guidelines and, therefore, it is often considered to be a form of foundational ethics.

In other examples of duty ethics—such as deontology—actions are judged on the intrinsic character of the act rather than on its effects. Kant, for example, uses the *categorical imperative* to specify the universal character of duty. Roughly translated, he states that one ought only to act such that the principle of one's act could become a universal law of human action in a world in which one would hope to live. In effect, if an action is right for one person, then it should be right for everyone. In addition, he states that one ought to treat others as having intrinsic value in themselves and not merely as means to achieve one's ends. Thus, Kant argued that "right actions" should be those that are done without qualification. From this perspective, even some seeming "goods" such as intelligence and happiness can be suspect because they can have negative effects for others, in some cases. He believed that the categorical imperative was within the grasp of all rational humans to discover and, ultimately, come to agreement—causing one's own good will and rationality to benefit the collective as a consensus develops on the right actions.

As an Enlightenment philosopher, Kant also believed that a good action is one done by free will and motivated by the right reasons. Thus, reason should guide the will of a person, and intentions are considered a part of ethical decision making. When reason guides the will, the actions are done from duty, despite one's personal inclinations. In effect, "good will" is everything for Kant. In that respect, Kant is suggesting that an ethical action is one that lies in the worth of the act itself and not in the consequences or outcomes of the act—even if they are positive. Ethical decisions, from a Kantian perspective, then, require each of us to have respect for other rational humans. As a result, he focuses on the quality—or intrinsic merit—of others in order to develop his universal principles of ethics. Following religious rules or government laws, for example, is not ethical if the inherent dignity and free will of others are harmed in the process.

From this perspective, improving the ethics of an organization might require developing ethical, universal principles—rationally derived—that are enacted out of a sense of duty or responsibility. Members of an organization might ask themselves: What universal, ethical principles would I be willing to follow that would also become guides for behavior throughout the entire organization? What are the "right actions" in this organization that should be done without qualification? What behaviors are inherently "good," without considering their outcome or effect on the organization and its members? Organizations that tend to focus on these questions seem most likely to address acceptable and unacceptable behavior by a universal code of ethics since such documents often explicitly identify duties to various stakeholders. At a more personal level, this perspective would encourage organizational members to also choose the right action, even when their inclination (often out of self-interest) is to do otherwise.

Rights (Thomas Hobbes, John Locke, John Rawls)

A rights perspective focuses on the obligation between self and other, based on the duty that the collective owes the individual. The duty of the collective is owed to the individual in the form of rights (e.g., equality). Similar to the duty perspective, a rights approach also universalizes ethics and, as a result, rights are often considered inalienable, such as in the United States Constitution. From this perspective, then, the rights of all humans are granted, naturally, and cannot be altered because they are rationally self-evident. The goal is to establish a social compact, or contract (hence, often called the *contractarian* alternative to deontology), of rights that are maintained between individuals and the community.

This covenant creates agreed-upon behaviors that are derived from natural law, according to Thomas Hobbes. For Hobbes, all humans are bound to such agreements because they can be understood through human reason, which itself is a fundamental part of human nature. Natural law, according to Hobbes, reminds us that our behaviors—and our laws—should be consistent with our nature as reasoning persons. Similarly, John Locke claims that all persons are born with, and possess, basic natural rights. They are possessed by everyone equally and, therefore, cannot be taken away. Rights, then, become the basis by which we judge not only the action of others but also those of institutions. The social contract between people, he argued, can only be preserved if human rights are developed, maintained, and preserved.

For John Rawls, in contrast to Locke, the standard for ethical action is based on a "reasonable position." Rights, for him, can be determined by placing persons behind a "veil of ignorance" or in "the original position," where persons have a limited sense of past, present, and future. In this position or behind this veil, one cannot anticipate how a person might be affected by his or her own actions. For example, no person can expect to either benefit or be harmed any more than others. From this perspective, then, an ethical person can uphold the basic rights necessary to maintain a minimum level of dignity and justice that, for example, produces fairness for all. Organizations, from this perspective, are obligated to address injustices and resolve inequities. Regardless of the differences between them, though, both Locke and Rawls seek to create principles and practices of justice through rights. No society can be just if it is devoid of rights for its people, according to them.

From this perspective, improving the ethics of an organization might involve an emphasis on compliance and legally sanctioned rights such as EEOC guidelines, the Americans with Disabilities Act, the Family Leave Act, and the National Labor Relations Act, among others. These laws—as well as company policies—might be used to create equity or fairness in organizations as a means to preserve human rights. For example, ethics training could be devoted to issues such as gender equity, diversity, or the fairness of performance appraisal processes. Members of an organization might ask: How can we best preserve the human rights and dignity of employees, owners, shareholders, suppliers, distributors, customers, and communities? How might the diverse rights afforded to each group be protected? What policies and procedures are just in this organization? Unjust? What is our current social contract between one another and how can it be improved? How might organizations behave so that no particular group benefits at the expense of others?

Utility (Jeremy Bentham, John Stuart Mill)

A utility perspective is based on the outcomes or consequences of an action and, therefore, is considered *consequentialist*. Ethical actions should be judged according to whether they produce positive effects, often in relation to other alternatives. Jeremy Bentham, for example, noted that a principle of utility is necessary in order to evaluate whether an action creates the greatest pleasure or happiness in relation to other alternatives. He also believed that any actions should be considered in terms of not only their immediate consequences, but also their long-term effects. What produces benefits in the short term, for example, may not produce positive consequences over a longer period of time.

A utility perspective also suggests that the good of the collective is primary. According to John Stuart Mill, the purpose of ethical action is to achieve "the greatest overall happiness for the greatest number" and actions are evaluated by the extent to which they contribute to that end. However, not all pleasures are necessarily considered equal, and he valued intellectual pleasure over physical pleasure. In addition, the good of an individual may be sacrificed for the good of many. By extension, then, followers of a utilitarian perspective are also interested in the long-term consequences of any action, as noted above.

Other (pluralistic) utilitarians do not necessarily equate good with happiness and focus on other goods, such as knowledge, maturity, and friendship. In addition, *act* utilitarians believe that every specific, individual action should be measured according to whether it maximizes good. Finally, *rule* utilitarians believe that one must weigh the consequences of adopting a general rule that would follow from that action.

From this perspective, improving the ethics of an organization might mean creating change that will have positive consequences for the organization and its stakeholders. An organization would need to have tools or mechanisms in place to evaluate its effects on others. However, an ethical approach to utility would require moving beyond traditional economic models of cost–benefit analysis to consider which decisions benefit the greatest number with the greatest good. As a result, organizations might have to consider the unintended and long-term consequences of their actions. Members of an organization drawing on utility-based ethics may ask: Have we considered all alternative actions and selected the one that produces the greatest good or pleasure? How can we best serve the ends of the collective rather than the individual? What specific actions or general rules will either maximize or minimize "good"?

Virtue (Socrates, Plato, Aristotle, David Hume, Augustine, Buddha)

In some respects, virtue ethics represents a middle ground between duty and rights. Persons have the duty to self-actualize and, therefore, should be granted the right to accomplish that self-actualization. This perspective suggests that all humans are born with inherent potential and, as a result, human development is the struggle for self-actualization. An action is judged based on whether it allows for expression of full potential, thus creating benefits for both the individual and the community. Ethical virtue focuses on realizing one's social, spiritual, and intellectual potential—or other habits that are considered important to society. The development of virtue, then, requires the cultivation of good habits. These habits occur within a social realm because humans are, according to Aristotle, "social animals," thereby suggesting that ethics involves being a contributing member of a community. Doing so satisfies one's natural constitution, particularly when we use our intellect and contemplate before we make decisions. Society, then, has an obligation to develop educational and learning opportunities for citizens to develop their full potential.

A virtue (e.g., prudence, temperance, justice, fortitude) is often seen as an internal feature of humans that produces ethical behavior. For the Greeks, virtue included not only individual attributes but also societal attributes. Aristotle, for example, argued that virtue should be connected to the good of a society and can be developed not by following principles, but by living a harmonious, balanced life. In the *Nicomachean Ethics,* he described ethics as the process of both doing good works and living well and, therefore, he also connected virtue to happiness.

Plato, a student of Socrates, is perhaps best known as an advocate for virtue-based ethics. He identified courage, temperance, wisdom, and justice as the most important virtues. However, Plato considered justice to be the central virtue and, as a result, a primary question in *The Republic of Plato* is: What is the nature of justice? Ultimately, Plato's aim was to create social and political stability on a foundation of moral and spiritual absolutes by which every person might live. Plato, for example, suggested that the shepherd's responsibility is to consider those under his or her care, thereby articulating an early principle of ethics and authority. For Plato, authority is always used for the benefit of the subordinate. Authority, properly understood, serves as a trustee for the interests of those over whom authority is wielded. In this respect, Plato has been used to better account for the multiple stakeholders that any one leader—or organization—might serve. Implied in his comments is the belief that "reluctant leaders" tend to be more virtuous in that decent people accept power "because they can find no one better than themselves, or even as good, to be entrusted with power."

From this perspective, an organization's ethics might be improved by strengthening personal and institutional virtues in order to maximize human potential—both within and outside the organization. The organization would need to address the unrealized potentials of others. Or, more specifically, members might focus on improving the organization's culture or strengthening a person's character—particularly the ability to learn. Appropriate questions might include the following: What personal and organizational values are most important to us? Can they be aligned? How can we infuse the organization's culture with ethics and facilitate the full potential of its members? What are the best means to help others self-actualize and develop to the best of their abilities? How can we emphasize responsibility, reflection, courage, collaboration, and commitment, among other virtues? What is the most virtuous way to use one's authority in an organization? Should the authority of a particular person or group be presumed in an organization? What strategies might be used to develop balanced, harmonious, and happy lives among the collective?

Relationship (Martin Buber, Mikhail Bakhtin, Carol Gilligan)

As a relatively new perspective, relationship ethics focuses on the care that emerges in and through communication. Proponents of this perspective believe that dialogue is the basis of successful relationships and that, ultimately, productive relationships are the foundation for ethical action among individuals and within (and across) cultures. Via communication, organizational relationships among various stakeholders (e.g., employees, stockholders, executives and managers, customers, suppliers, community members) are built, developed, maintained, transformed, repaired, and, on occasion, dissolved. This perspective is interested in the processes that enable productive and satisfying relationships, such as a willingness to listen and engage others in interaction and a desire to establish trust through openness. Ongoing care and attention to relationships, then, is important to consider from this perspective. Attention is focused on the evolution and negotiation of relationships—and the adaptations that may be necessary to successfully sustain them. Further, relationship ethics seeks to create a dialogic community that uses power *with* others rather than power *over* others. As a result, our attitudes toward each other become an important foundation for ethical action.

This emphasis on the "other" is important in the work of Martin Buber. He suggests that interaction with others provides the opportunity for the development of personality, self, and reflection. In effect, our "self" arises in and through our dialogue with significant others such as family, friends, and coworkers. Each person in a communicative situation, then, should be cognizant of his or her effect in the development of others. Such attention requires a sense of responsibility for others through respect, honesty, spontaneity, and genuineness. It also requires that all of us engage in "perspective-taking" as we seek to fully understand and appreciate another person's views and experiences. Ethical practice, then, emphasizes authentic communication that fosters a sense of equality, interest, and commitment between people. In addition, each participant in a conversation is expected to be fully present.

Mikhail Bakhtin also suggests that, through dialogue, persons produce centripetal (change) or centrifugal (stability) forces in a relationship. That is, the specific speech acts of each person may either sustain or alter the status quo in a relationship. These micro-practices of communication may also have an iterative effect; they are repeated, expanded, and altered in new relationships with others. This partially explains why some organizations find it difficult to change their ethical cultures since sets of communicative practices become embedded and sedimented in everyday talk.

As a related ethical perspective that focuses on relationships, feminists such as Carol Gilligan propose an *ethic of care*. Drawing on the female voice and critiquing traditional notions of moral development, she suggests that interdependence is central to ethical behavior. As a component of interdependence, people should nurture others and be compassionate toward them. In an ethic of care, then, mutuality and reciprocity become central principles. Ethical actions sustain the caring relationship between self and others and, as a result, bonds of trust, loyalty, affection, and engagement are essential to an emphasis on care.

Efforts to create positive ethical change in organizations, from this perspective, would focus, not surprisingly, on relationships of all types: superior–subordinate, employee–customer or client, owner–worker, coworker–coworker, and so on. However, relational dimensions of ethics and care would not be limited to employees within an organization; they would also likely include relationships with regulators, government agencies, and communities, among others. From this ethical point of view, an organization might emphasize the importance of dialogue, participation, and collaboration in order to build and strengthen relationships. In addition, an organization might shift its focus from engaging in dialogue *about* stakeholders to engaging in dialogue *with* stakeholders. Members of such an organization might ask: With whom do we have important relationships? How can we foster those relationships to the benefit of all? In what ways can we develop perspective-taking regarding others' points of view and experiences? How can we best care for others in and through dialogic communication? (See Figure 2.1 below, which illustrates the relationship between the ethical tensions and the ethical perspectives.)

Figure 2.1   Ethical Tensions and Ethical Perspectives

Each ethical perspective may be plotted on two axes, based on the foundational/situational and individual/organizational tensions:

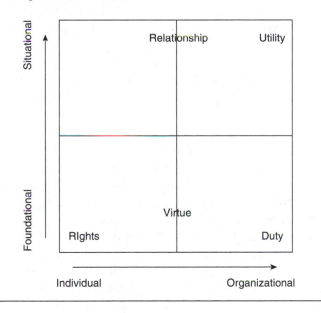

❖ ETHICAL PRACTICES

I suspect that your reaction to many of the questions at the end of each theoretical perspective is that they seem overly idealistic and unrealistic. While I may agree with you to a certain extent, the seeming irrelevance of some of the questions merely confirms how far many of our organizations have drifted from ethics. As you read through the case studies, seriously consider how the actions of the organization—and its members—might be changed if one or more of the ethical perspectives were applied in a rigorous manner.

Hopefully, the preceding brief summary of the various ethical perspectives helps you to better understand and evaluate the ethical dilemmas common to organizations and their members. But, it is also important to consider how we act in response to those dilemmas. In many respects, each of the cases in this book is designed to test the strengths and limitations of the ethical perspectives. As you read the cases, you should also think about how decisions were made—or might have been made—based on the perspectives. You may find, for example, that a particular ethical perspective is presented in a case. You may discover that several seemingly contradictory ethical perspectives can coexist in a single case. Or, you may realize that an ethical perspective raises a set of questions that cut across cases.

However, you should not feel limited to merely applying the perspectives to the various cases in the book. You should also feel free to evaluate your comfort (or discomfort) with the ethical perspectives themselves, as a result of reading the cases. That is, how can we rethink the appropriateness of each ethical perspective, based on the current organizational issues discussed in the cases? Are there some perspectives that are more or less suited to today's organizational life? Turning to the future, we might also ask: Which ethical perspective provides the best opportunity for ethical behavior for the future? The cases, then, can also serve as a means to "test" the appropriateness of the ethical perspectives, while simultaneously taking into account the past, present, and future of organizations and their members.

This book—and the cases in it—should be read, then, not as an argument for either a foundational or a situational approach, or a community or individual approach—to organizational ethics. Rather, I hope that reading about both general principles and specific behaviors will allow you to think about both the foundational (i.e., ethical perspectives) and the situational (i.e., specific cases) dimensions of ethics, as well as the community and the individual. Keeping both of the tensions in mind, simultaneously, means that the cases may be used to evaluate and adapt the perspectives and, in turn, the perspectives may be applied in specific situations or cases. This integration of theory and practice—often referred to as *praxis*—provides a more thorough (and challenging) method for both evaluating others' actions and considering our own actions (see Cheney, 2004).

Ultimately, then, although each of you will have a different view of the ethical perspectives and the cases, you share at least one common ethical challenge: All organizations and their members must balance a variety of competing demands and conflicting values in determining how to negotiate a range of common ethical dilemmas, such as justice vs. mercy, individual vs. community, cost vs. quality, competition vs. collaboration, flexibility vs. structure, and long term vs. short term, among others. Balancing these demands and managing these values requires not only ethical vigilance but also ethical insight, combining ongoing analysis and reflection.

Although I have suggested that ethics, as presented in this book, should be viewed neither as singular nor relativist, I would be remiss if I did not offer at least some ideas regarding practices that seem common to most ethical organizations. Without attempting to necessarily create a universal list, we should then ask, what practices do ethical organizations share in common?

In my experience, an ethical organization

- *Aligns* personal, professional, and organizational aspirations and behaviors
- Fosters *dialogic* communication
- Encourages *participation* in decision making
- Establishes *transparent* structures, policies, and procedures
- Emphasizes *accountability* for anticipating and responding to ethical crises
- Promotes *courageous* efforts to identify and resolve ethical dilemmas.

Alignment

One of the common practices among ethical organizations is that they tend to align formal policies and procedures (e.g., ethics code, employee handbook, training and development, performance appraisal) with the organization's informal culture (e.g., norms, rituals, narratives). While the former prescribes an organization's ethics, the latter describes the day-to-day experience of the organization's ethics. In order to develop, maintain, and refine ethical practice, an organization—and its members—will need to, in effect, walk the talk. In order to sustain a culture of ethics, an organization needs more than an ethics code. It needs the will to engage in the myriad behaviors that keep informal and formal dimensions aligned, ethically. For example, Enron had a widely accepted, formal code of ethics:

Enron
Our Values

Communication

We have an obligation to communicate. Here, we take the time to talk with one another . . . and to listen. We believe that information is meant to move and that information moves people.

Respect

We treat others as we would like to be treated ourselves. We do not tolerate abusive or disrespectful treatment.

Integrity

We work with customers and prospects openly, honestly, and sincerely. When we say we will do something, we will do it; when we say we cannot or will not do something, then we won't do it.

Excellence

We are satisfied with nothing less than the very best in everything we do. We will continue to raise the bar for everyone. The great fun here will be for all of us to discover just how good we can really be.

In retrospect, however, we now realize that such formal and very visible features of Enron's culture hid an informal set of unethical practices. Similarly, Tyco's code of ethics also masked a reality different from its public image:

Tyco

Why We Exist and the Essence of Our Business

We will increase the value of our company and our global portfolio of diversified brands by exceeding customers' expectations and achieving market leadership and operating excellence in every segment of our company.

What We Seek to Achieve

Governance: Adhere to the highest standards of corporate governance by establishing processes and practices that promote and ensure integrity, compliance, and accountability.

Customers:

Fully understand and exceed our customers' needs, wants, and preferences and provide greater value to our customers than our competition.

People:

Attract and retain, at every level of the company, people who represent the highest standards of excellence and integrity.

Operating Excellence:

Implement initiatives across our business segments to achieve best-in-class operating practices and leverage companywide opportunities, utilizing six sigma measurements.

Financial Results/Liquidity:

Consistently achieve outstanding performance in revenues, earnings, cash flow, and all other key financial metrics. Establish a capital structure that meets both long- and short-term needs.

In each of these ethics codes—and many others like them—the question is whether the code's prescribed practices are deeply embedded in the everyday life of the organization's members—whether they "stick" ethically. That is, ethical organizations have both high aspirations and realistic, practical means to meet those aspirations.

Aligned work—work that is both excellent and responsive to the needs and wishes of the broader community in which it takes place—is most readily carried out when an organization's mission, its members, and its various constituencies share some common ground, work collaboratively, and engage in activities that advance mutual goals. Or, at the least, they acknowledge differences and seek to negotiate their competing interests in ways that will benefit all. In contrast, when there are wide disparities within and across these groups, aligned work is elusive. As a current example, some of the recent scandals among journalists (e.g., plagiarism, contrived stories, accepting money to "sell" government programs to the public) indicate that their personal and professional goals often conflict with their employers'. Given the competitive nature of the information and news business today, journalism is faced with a credibility crisis as it seeks to balance objectivity with profits—particularly since the industry is increasingly dominated by media conglomerates.

To successfully align the formal and informal dimensions of organizational life, then, ethical organizations find ways to keep ethics "alive."

Beyond ethical alignment, ethical organizations do so by fostering dialogic communication; confronting difficult realities by promoting participation to meet the highest ethical standards; establishing trust through transparent operations; emphasizing accountability for anticipating and responding to crises; and promoting the ethical courage to identify and resolve ethical dilemmas.

Dialogic Communication

Alignment is best facilitated by dialogic systems in which communication is open and decentralized. A dialogic organization values the perspective of all employees and facilitates their ability to voice their opinions and concerns. It also promotes the ability of all stakeholders to have a substantial influence on the organization's decisions. Employees of dialogic organizations understand the perspective of others in ways that promote understanding among different departments, make managing diversity possible, and acknowledge the need for *collective mindfulness.* In order to establish dialogue, all parties understand that they are interdependent and, therefore, are responsible for effective, responsible communication. Leaders are better able to communicate their goals to employees and, in turn, employees are better able to provide useful feedback to leaders. A dialogic organizational culture also limits employees' desire to take concerns to the media, courts, or others outside the organization.

There are a number of organizations that foster dialogic communication, including Levi-Strauss, Hanna Andersson Clothing, and Patagonia, among others. However, one company has developed an ethics training program that is quite extensive and might be considered dialogic, BellSouth. For example, the company has integrated its ethics and compliance training materials into multiple delivery sources to demonstrate to employees that ethics is integral to every part of the business and to leverage existing infrastructure. Using media such as CD-ROMS, videos, and the company's intranet, BellSouth has blended its ethics and compliance training into new-employee orientations, general management courses, sales training, and other learning modules. The ethics and compliance team sees human resources as a key partner in its work, and continually looks at ways to include ethics and compliance topics in other employee-training programs. In addition, each operations unit has a compliance executive and a coordinator responsible for ethics and compliance oversight in that operating division. These managers draw information "from the bottom up," conduct risk assessments, and report back to the compliance office when gaps in training or communication are discovered. If the subject can best be handled on a small scale, the compliance coordinator will take care of it. However, if the corporate compliance office sees that many areas are addressing similar issues, time and money can be saved by creating cross-departmental programs. Examples of this include compliance and environment training. While the company uses technology to deliver the message, it believes that the most productive work comes from face-to-face meetings, where employees are given the time to sit and discuss the nuances of various ethical dilemmas.

By contrast, there are many organizations that still suffer from monologic communication that limits candor, fosters secrecy, and manages communication and information in a top-down manner. One well-known example is the Sears Auto scandal in the early 1990s. In June of 1992, the California Bureau of Auto Repairs (BAR) revoked the operating permits of 72 auto centers in that state. The decision was based on 18 months of undercover investigation into repair practices at 35 centers. The California BAR accused Sears of fraud and willful departures from accepted trade standards and launched a sting effort in 1990 after receiving 250 customer complaints. According to BAR, in 42 of 48 visits, Sears employees performed unnecessary services or repairs. On average, customers were bilked of $250, by replacing new parts that were not necessary and, in some cases, cars emerged in worse condition. The problem was caused by the company's efforts to improve lagging profits after the recession of the 1980s that had hurt Sears. As a result, a new compensation policy was created to give commissions to auto mechanics, which in effect provided an incentive for the mechanics to provide additional services. Employees were instructed to sell a certain number of services in an 8-hour day. If they failed to meet the goals, employees received a cutback in their hours or were transferred. When confronted with the allegations, however, Sears communicated an angry denial. It was not until the story became news that the company began to communicate more directly and honestly with its customers, placing full-page ads to apologize to them. Even then, though, the chairman of Sears only admitted that "mistakes may have occurred." Similar claims might be made about Nike and secrecy surrounding its sweatshops in Asia, as well as both Ford and Firestone in the case of the rollover deaths of drivers of Ford Explorers, which involved each company blaming the other.

Participation

Ethical organizations are, by their very nature, participatory—both internally and externally. Participatory organizations empower their employees to engage in decision making through delegation. Such organizations develop skills among employees by enabling and motivating them. They produce organizational commitment by encouraging a culture of trust that rewards and recognizes high performance and responsibility. As a result, participatory organizations are well-known for their ability to recruit, develop, and retain talented employees. Externally, participatory organizations listen to their stakeholders' concerns and are responsive to their feedback, using their knowledge and skills to improve organizational performance. In response to the opportunity to participate, stakeholders tend to be particularly loyal to, and invested in, such organizations.

One of the classic examples of a participatory organization is W. L. Gore and Associates. Best known as the maker of GORE-TEX, Gore is well-known for its ability to motivate its employees through participation. Gore has developed a variety of rules that focus on providing the resources and opportunities for a work environment in which employees participate and, as a result, take greater responsibility for their work. For example, Gore has become a successful innovator in its field by requiring managers to act more like coaches than bosses by 1) listening to employees' concerns; 2) avoiding close supervision; 3) trusting employees to work within a framework of clear direction; and 4) being responsive to employees' feedback. In addition to Gore, companies such as 3M, the Grameen Bank, the Donnelly Corporation, Ashoka, Working Assets Long Distance, and the Mondragon cooperatives in Spain have been praised for their participatory workplace cultures.

As noted in one of the cases in this book, NASA has been less successful in its efforts to involve employees in important decisions, even those that affect the safety of its astronauts. For years, NASA was well-known for a variety of its successes, particularly the Apollo missions. However, in recent years, they have been better known for the visible, public failures in the Challenger and Columbia disasters. Although NASA has blamed technological problems (e.g., the O-rings) for the disasters, oversight commissions have indicated that a lack of participation in decision making is at least one of the causes. Still fairly hierarchical in its structure, NASA employees were aware of the technical problems with both shuttles. However, there were few, if any, mechanisms in place for persons with the knowledge to fully participate in launch decisions. This lack of participation at all levels of NASA is particularly troubling since the Rogers Commission (in its review of the Challenger disaster) had noted that experienced engineers were discouraged from providing negative feedback about the O-rings. The Columbia disaster suggests that, although feedback mechanisms were later put in place, they were not used. Other well-documented cases include the Ford Pinto and its exploding gas tanks and AH Robins and its Dalkon contraceptive IUD, which apparently produced various illnesses in the women who used it.

Transparency

Ethical organizations engage in decision making that is transparent to their employees and other stakeholders. Transparent organizations have clear and visible governance, missions, policies, procedures, and guidelines. The actions of transparent organizations allow others to fully comprehend processes such as hiring, performance appraisal, and promotion, among others. In addition, transparent organizations are candid, thereby producing greater trust, respect, and fairness. Employees of transparent organizations better understand the rationales for decision making and, as a result, more fully support them and learn to make effective decisions themselves. As a result, employees of transparent organizations are more likely to accept the decisions of leaders, even when the decisions do not necessarily benefit the employees themselves. Such benefits are particularly common in industries or organizations with strained labor–management relations. For other stakeholders—such as shareholders—transparency provides greater confidence that the organization is being managed effectively, thereby increasing its perceived value.

Although companies such as Ben and Jerry's, Free Trade Coffee, and Tom's of Maine are best known for their transparency, there are less visible examples, as well. One example is Baxter International, which is discussed later in one of the cases. The company's medical therapies are used by health care providers and their patients in more than 100 countries. Because Baxter's 40,000 employees are located throughout the world (with more than half outside the United States), the company has approached the challenge of communicating its business practice standards to a global workforce by decentralizing its ethics training programs. All new employees—and in many cases, prospective employees—are given a copy of the company's business practice standards, which have been translated into 14 different languages. Each new employee takes part in mandatory training conducted by managers who have been designated as ethics trainers. Additional training programs and training schedules are left up to each region and business unit, with headquarters providing resources. For example, the team responsible for the company's Asian operations has developed a yearly training program, based on real-life scenarios, that is designed to encourage group discussion and participation. In Latin America, the company's employees develop and present their own scenarios as part of the training. In addition to the large library of case studies, Baxter is developing Web-based vehicles to supplement existing communication channels for ethical standards. These efforts suggest that, at least internally, Baxter is seeking to infuse ethics in a transparent manner.

A much more visible case, Enron, is evidence of the risks of a non-transparent organization when it comes to ethics. The level of secrecy (and related risk) upon which Enron was built, and upon which it failed, cost the jobs and retirement incomes of thousands, contributed to a slump in the stock market, and may have exacerbated California's 2000–2001 energy crisis. The collapse of the company, the largest bankruptcy in U.S. history, was followed by several criminal and civil lawsuits against the executives of the company. These lawsuits have suggested that the arrogance and greed of Enron's leaders was related to the lack of transparency in decisions made at the highest level of the company. In short, since rank-and-file employees did not necessarily realize their jobs and the company were at risk, they could not hold leaders accountable for their decisions. It appears that they had limited information about the specific decisions that were being made and, when criticisms were raised within the company, employees were reprimanded for making their concerns public. Similar, related examples include R. J. Reynolds and the tobacco industry, the Catholic Church, and WorldCom.

Accountability

Ethical organizations are accountable to their multiple stakeholders in a responsible and responsive manner. This accountability is evident in the high quality of products/services offered by such organizations. Accountable organizations view legal and industry compliance as important, but minimum, expectations. Rather, they also accept direct responsibility for any actions that negatively affect their stakeholders, and they seek to maximize their positive contributions to those stakeholders. Ethical organizations are also accountable to broader sets of stakeholders, including both local and global communities. Employees of accountable organizations take "automatic responsibility" for ethical challenges and strive to promote aspirational, ethical opportunities. Accountable organizations have a bias toward action that prompts member involvement and learning. As a result, employees develop better problem-solving skills and are less likely to blame others for mistakes. Employees in such organizations are less likely to view business units as "silos" that operate independently of one another. They learn how their decisions affect others in the organization.

The Body Shop, created by Anita Roddick, is known for its accountability to its employees, its suppliers and, ultimately, the environment. The Body Shop has grown worldwide and is an example of a company that "does good business by doing good." Believing that both employees and customers are tired of high-pressure sales tactics, the Body Shop seeks to educate both employees and customers, producing greater accountability for decision making. In addition, The Body Shop is well-known for its stewardship of the environment and its support of local, indigenous groups through programs such as "Trade Not Aid." Through a series of interrelated programs, Roddick has sought to be responsible to various stakeholders throughout the supply chain. As a result, employees are also able to hold one another accountable for their actions and to hold the company accountable for its decisions, as well. As she explains, "I think you can trade ethically. . . . It's showing that you forsake your values at the cost of forsaking your work force."

Arguably the worst corporate disaster provides a stark contrast to the Body Shop. In 1984, the Union Carbide pesticide plant in Bhopal, India, released a dangerous chemical, methyl isocyanate gas (MIC), creating the worst industrial accident in history. As a result of the accident, at least 10,000 people were killed, over 300,000 became ill, and nearly 500,000 were displaced. In time, it became clear that the plant was neither safe nor efficient and had been located in India to take advantage of cheap labor and limited regulations. In addition, most employees and citizens had not been told that they would be working and living amidst toxic chemicals. Once among the top 50 companies in the United States, Union Carbide's reputation was further tarnished when it fought lawsuits against it to compensate the victims of the disaster. Although the lawsuits have been settled, the Indian government and citizens still seek the full compensation required under the law. Another example during the 1980s was the Manville Corporation's use of asbestos in various products and consistent denial of accountability for its negative health effects on persons exposed to it. A more recent example of a lack of executive accountability, in particular, can be found in Adelphia, which filed for bankruptcy after its founder, John Rigas, and others were accused of looting the company and cheating investors out of billions of dollars. Rigas and his son, Timothy, were convicted of conspiracy, bank fraud, and securities fraud.

Courage

Ethical organizations have employees who have the courage to identify, assess, and resolve ethical dilemmas that may negatively affect the organization or its stakeholders. Courageous organizations have the courage to admit mistakes, reject conformity, respond to injustice, and defy standard industry practices or laws that may be unethical. In addition, courageous organizations seek not only to respond to ethical challenges but also to anticipate them; they exhibit the courage to be ethical. Such an organization facilitates effective problem identification and problem solving in ways that also foster innovation and creativity. They also produce cultures that are safe and supportive for employees, thereby strengthening organizational identification. The result is that employees are more likely to identify problems when they arise and communicate those concerns to their superiors. They are also more likely to offer new ways to resolve the problems.

Johnson & Johnson is perhaps best known for its ethical courage. In response to the discovery of tainted Tylenol capsules, Johnson & Johnson strengthened its standing as one of the leading health care companies by pulling the capsules off the shelves and addressing consumers' concerns about the capsules, truthfully and quickly, via the media. Although the company suffered short-term financial losses, it also affirmed its commitment to patient health and consumer safety, which have remained features of its organizational culture. As a result, it has been lauded as one of the country's most ethical and successful companies. Similarly, the owner of Malden Mills suffered financial loss in order to retain jobs for his employees. In addition, various whistle-blowers at Enron, in the tobacco industry, in the FBI and CIA, and in numerous attorneys general offices across the country have shown ethical courage to protect the public.

As a contrast to Johnson & Johnson, accounting firm Arthur Andersen made one of the quickest and most devastating falls from grace in corporate history. Despite a long-standing reputation as one of the most objective and responsible accounting firms, Arthur Andersen employees signed off on earnings statements for Enron (and other clients such as Waste Management) that were, according to industry observers, aggressive and unique at best, misleading or irresponsible at worst. The failure of Arthur Andersen came after a series of reports in the 1990s by the Government Accounting Office that noted the growing conflicts of interest among auditor–client relationships in the accounting industry. In response to numerous concerns expressed over auditor independence, Arthur Andersen argued before the SEC that "a broad scope of practice" was necessary and that "the future of the accounting profession is bright and will remain bright—as long as the commission does not force us into an outdated role trapped in the old economy." Court documents filed in a 2002 trial for "deceptive practices" indicated that Arthur Andersen had been warned about its practices and that many employees were aware of the practices and the warnings. The response of many mid-level managers was to shred company documents. The result has been the unexpected and incredibly fast decline of one of the most well-known and successful companies in the United States. Additional examples, as of this writing in 2005, include new pressures placed on the pharmaceutical industry and the Food and Drug Administration to come forward with more details regarding drug risks for patients.

❖ THE FUTURE OF ORGANIZATIONAL ETHICS

There is no question that, over the last 20 years, there have been a growing number of organizations that have sought to foster the ethical practices noted above. The following are some prominent examples:

- The Ford Motor Company has developed initiatives in South Africa to fight HIV/AIDS.

- UPS has established welfare-to-work programs, in partnership with various government, social service, community, and nonprofit organizations.

- BankBoston has established a community banking group that focuses on economic development efforts that target an entire community of moderate income and inner-city markets, while avoiding industry norms for predatory lending.

• Levi Strauss and Company has sustained a long-standing anti-racism initiative.

Certainly, each of these organizations may not meet stringent standards of ethical practice in all areas but, at the least, they have sought to make a positive impact on local and global communities.

In addition, in a speech to the United Nations in 2004 titled "Globalization's Next Frontier: Principled Codes of Conduct that Bolster the Rule of Law," Deloitte CEO William G. Parrett challenged multinational organizations to establish codes of behavior that go beyond minimum legal compliance, through principled ethical behavior that bolsters the rule of law and would, therefore, create expanded economic opportunities around the world. Speaking to global business executives, representatives from non-governmental organizations (NGOs), and academic scholars, he claimed that globalization and world security itself could be jeopardized unless multinational organizations develop ethical practices that adhere to values and principles rather than merely the law. Although his comments may be self-serving, Parrett nevertheless identifies the potential stakes for organizations that do not think about and practice business ethics. So, even within the context of post-9/11 security concerns, ethics is located as a pivotal international issue.

At the same time, it seems that a growing number of organizations also fall short when it comes to ethical practices. In Chapter 1, I noted some of the recent examples of organizational scandals such as Enron, WorldCom, Adelphia, and Tyco, among others. In some respects, then, there appears to be a bifurcation among organizations that pride themselves on their ethics and social responsibility and organizations that seek to mislead employees, stockholders, and the public for short-term profit.

I hope these introductory chapters have prepared you for the realization that our ethical challenges are significant but that our ethical opportunities are perhaps even greater. Given the widespread influence of today's organizations, there is tremendous potential for rethinking, reframing, and reproducing organizations that can be not only productive but also ethical. It is my hope that this book—and the cases included in it—will cause you take a long, hard look at organizational practices and the positive or negative effects they have on various groups.

George Cheney (2004) aptly challenges us to consider the future of organizational ethics and our own responsibility within it:

> Today we should consider an ethics of being and not just an ethics of regulation; an ethics that embraces how we are and who we are with others; an ethics that engages pressing and compelling issues of today; an ethics that challenges people yet begins with the tensions they experience in everyday life; an ethics that joins personal happiness with public integrity; and an ethics that recognises the role of public discourse in extending or pulling back our ethical horizons. (pp. 35–36)

It is my strong conviction that the ethical scandals of recent years provide both the motivation and the means to expand our ethical horizons. I think all of the contributors to this book would agree that, as future leaders of organizations—for-profit or otherwise—we expect you to fully engage with, and participate in, the important ethical issues of the day. It is time to remove organizational ethics from the margins and to stimulate broader public dialogue about the often difficult and challenging questions regarding the role of organizations in our culture. Whether it is as an organizational owner, employee, stockholder, customer, or concerned citizen, we hope that this book will encourage you to do so.

❖ REFERENCES

Anderson, J. A., & Englehardt, E. E. (2001). *The organizational self and ethical conduct.* Fort Worth, TX: Harcourt.

Aronowitz, S., & DiFazio, W. (1994). *The jobless future: Sci-Tech and the dogma of work.* Minneapolis: University of Minnesota Press.

Cheney, G. (2004). Bringing ethics in from the margins. *Australian Journal of Communication, 31,* 35–36.

Chilton, K., & Weidenbaum, M. (1994, November). *A new social contract for the American workplace: From paternalism to partnering.* St. Louis, MO: Center for the Study of American Business.

Dienhart, J. W. (2000). *Business, institutions, and ethics: A text with cases and readings.* New York: Oxford University Press.

Donaldson, T., & Werhane, P. H. (1999). *Ethical issues in business: A philosophical approach.* Upper Saddle River, NJ: Prentice Hall.

Friedman, M. (1970, September 13). The social responsibility of business is to increase its profits. *The New York Times Magazine.*

Gini, A. (2005). *Case studies in business ethics* (2nd ed.). Upper Saddle River, NJ: Prentice Hall.

Johannesen, R. J. (1996). *Ethics in human communication* (4th ed.). Prospect Heights, IL: Waveland Press.

O'Reilly, B. (1994, June 13). The new deal: What companies and employees owe one another. *Fortune*, 44–47.

Shaw, W. H., & Barry, H. (2001). *Moral issues in business* (8th ed.). New York: Wadsworth.

Snoeyenbos, M., Ameder, R., & Humber, J. (2001). *Business ethics* (3rd ed.). Amherst, MA: Prometheus Books.

Velasquez, M. U. (1998). *Business ethics: Concepts and cases* (4th ed.). Upper Saddle River, NJ: Prentice Hall.

The Ethics of the "Family Friendly" Organization

Challenges and Tensions
Related to Multiple Life Perspectives

Caryn E. Medved and David R. Novak

This case considers the degree to which single and married employees with families should be treated similarly or differently in organizations. It raises questions regarding what, if any, ethical responsibility organizations have to help their employees manage work and family responsibilities. As a result, it explores the degree to which personal, professional, and organizational goals should be aligned. It also addresses whether 1) the virtue of self-actualization among employees should be managed by an organization; 2) organizations have a specific duty to consider the private lives of employees in decision making; and 3) single and married employees should have different rights and, therefore, different policies regarding flexibility and work hours.

> *If two people want the day off . . . if it's a married person and a single person, preference is almost always given to the married people just because their reason for taking the day off somehow becomes more justified.*

> Rob, employee at Hewitt Associates

During the past quarter century, organizations in the United States have adopted various policies designed to assist employees with balancing work and family (Galinsky & Friedman, 1991). The "family friendly" organization comes complete with flexible working hours, daycare subsidies, maternity/paternity leave, lactation rooms, and even summer camps for school-aged children of working parents. This array of work and family benefits is economically advantageous for the organization (Baylin, Fletcher, & Kolb, 1997) and is celebrated as a long overdue victory for working women. Public support for work and family benefits has remained relatively unchallenged since their inception in the 1980s (Burkett, 2000). But what are the implications of "family friendly" policies for those employees whose significant relationships in life (friends, partners, close relatives) are not covered under organizational definitions of "family"? How are single or married employees without children affected differently by work and family organizational policies than those with children? What are the organizations' responsibilities in implementing and executing such "family friendly" policies? And, how is the employee accountable when the individual's family life has an impact on his or her work life? The immense value of helping employees through work–family policies is not the focus of this case study. Rather, the ways in which work and family policies and practices influence differently the various employee populations are the ethical dilemmas considered below in Rob's[1] story.

Rob began his career at Hewitt Associates, an employee benefit outsourcing company, as a business analyst in September 2001, shortly after graduating from college. Many changes in Rob's life have occurred during these last few years. Since beginning his first job, he got engaged, promoted, bought a house, and was married. As a result, Rob has experienced Hewitt Associates from a number of different life perspectives: as a single employee, a married employee, and a childless employee; he has experienced different tensions in relation to these life perspectives. As a single person, Rob has experienced challenges trying to balance his work responsibilities with his friendships, personal time, girlfriend, and immediate family members. After getting married, additional struggles emerged between time spent at work and taking care of his new responsibilities as a homeowner and husband. These tensions have been played out in his interactions with coworkers, managers, friends, and family members over the past few years. We will begin our case study of Rob's experiences just prior to his engagement in 2001; but first, let's describe briefly the business of Hewitt Associates.

❖ HEWITT ASSOCIATES: THE ORGANIZATION

Hewitt Associates was founded in 1940 as an insurance brokerage firm in Lake Forest, Illinois, a northern suburb of Chicago.[2] Today, Hewitt states that they are the world's leading provider of outsourced human resource (HR) services including benefits (health insurance, pension, 401k retirement savings plans), payroll, and workforce management, along with a full complement of HR consulting services. The main line of its business is Total Benefits Administration™ (TBA), which is an integrated technology platform allowing client organizations to outsource the daily tasks of managing their employee benefit programs. Hewitt currently employs over 15,000 people and counts one half of the Fortune 500 as well as over one third of the Fortune Global 500 as its clients. In the fiscal year 2003, Hewitt provided services to more than 2,600 organizations and generated nearly $2 billion in net revenues. Of this revenue, 63% was generated through its outsourcing business and 37% was generated by its consulting business. From its formation until 2002, Hewitt was privately owned. On June 27, 2002, the third CEO in Hewitt's history, Dale Gifford, brokered Hewitt's Initial Public Offering (IPO) and company shares became publicly traded on the New York Stock Exchange.

One of Hewitt's corporate hallmarks is its company code of conduct that "serves as a guideline for how we work with our clients, each other, and our business partners and communities." This guiding set of principles outlines the ethical standards of Hewitt regarding legal and regulatory issues as well as company values such as honesty, trust, and integrity. Included in this code is one of Hewitt's cornerstone principles: to enhance *associate engagement*. Hewitt pledges to find ways of matching employees' interests, backgrounds, and goals with comparable career opportunities at the organization. The company also tries to develop employee commitment through providing associates with a comprehensive benefits package that includes, but is not limited to, health, dental, and vision care; life insurance; retirement savings; health care spending accounts; profit sharing; 16 days of paid time off in the first year; a volunteer program; and a tuition reimbursement plan. Hewitt is also well-known for providing on-site food services where associates can eat meals at work free of charge. Finally, Hewitt is dedicated to diversity. For example, the company claims a commitment to hiring and promoting a diverse workforce, recognizing the range of their clients' workforces, and promoting company diversity by engaging many community organizations, particularly those who are financially disadvantaged. They also maintain a large number of diversity programs, from recruiting practices to supplier diversity to associate network groups (ANGs). Among these ANGs are Gay, Lesbian, and Allied Associates; Latino and Hispanic Associates; and Working Parents. Now that you know a little bit more about what Hewitt Associates is formally about, we turn to an insider's view of work and life at the organization from Rob. We begin his story during a conversation over dinner with his coworker, Craig.

❖ WORK AND LIFE AT HEWITT: ROB'S STORY

December 1, 2002

It is a Tuesday night in Lincolnshire, Illinois, a suburb of Chicago and the home of Hewitt's international offices. Rob and Craig are in the Hewitt cafeteria having dinner together for the second night in a row. Both of them began working at Hewitt just over a year ago after graduating from college. Rob has a degree in finance and Craig has a degree in communication studies. Rob and Craig have had similar jobs since their arrival at Hewitt and their career paths have mirrored each other to a large degree. Both are single, but Rob recently became engaged to be married. A few weeks prior, Craig gave his 2-weeks' notice because he was headed to graduate school and would be leaving Hewitt. It is 8:30 at night and their team meeting has just ended. Exhausted, they decide to have a quick hamburger at work because it's easier than cooking at home and it's free.

"Craig, man, I can't believe you're quitting. You're really getting out of here."

"Yep, this week is it. I'm looking forward to going back to school. But hey, I *am* leaving you my stapler. It's the least I can do." Rob smiles just a bit, puts some ketchup on his fries, and shakes his head.

"Oh, come on Rob, what keeps you here? Why don't you look around a bit?"

Rob sighs, "Now's just not the time. I've got my wedding coming up and it's not so bad. You know what's interesting though? Before I got engaged, it was like everyone assumed that I didn't have a life. Do you know what I mean?"

"Yep, they just expect you to work late nights because you're single, like you've got nothing else to do," Craig says.

"Yeah," Rob says, "I was just expected to do stuff, right off the bat. There was no prior thought as to what my schedule was like. No matter what was going on before I was engaged, it didn't make any difference. Everything defaulted to me. But, now they are starting to take into account that I've got all of this stuff to do to get ready for the wedding and moving into the house. It's just strange."

Craig replies, "You're right. Most of the people on my client team are single, but I've always noticed that the married people with kids leave pretty regularly at 4:30 or 5:00 while the rest of us are here working late. Sometimes I need to leave work, but I don't have a *legitimate* reason to go. What am I supposed to say? I need to get home and see my mom and dad?"

Rob agrees, "Yeah, the idea that I had things to do never entered anybody's mind when I was single. But it's like when you get married or engaged, it trips something in your manager's head that there may be other responsibilities that these people have to deal with now. And those are the only responsibilities that they respect. They don't respect the responsibilities of the single people. A lot of people think those responsibilities can be shrugged off or moved around!"

"You're right, Rob. Should be interesting to see how you are treated after you get married!"

After finishing their dinner and getting ready to head back to their desks, Craig says, "Well, Rob, take care. I won't be too far away at school and I'll be back here to Chicago regularly. We'll get together for that White Sox game we talked about."

"You bet," says Rob. "Take care, man. And good luck with school."

❖   A SUMMER REUNION: REVISITING ROB

July 11, 2004

It is about a year and a half later and Craig has gone home to Chicago for part of the summer break. Craig and Rob have stayed in touch, largely via e-mail. They decide to go to a baseball game and out for dinner in Chicago to catch up on Rob's experiences during the past year. After watching the White Sox lose to the Mariners 4–3, they head to Craig's favorite bar on the North Side of Chicago, the Irish Oak, and eventually the conversation turns from baseball to Rob's recent work experiences.

"So how's work been, Rob? What does Hewitt have you doing lately? How'd that transfer to the investment side work out?" Craig asks.

"Pretty good. For the most part I like what I'm doing now. I analyze mutual funds and conduct meetings or conference calls with fund managers to help clients decide what to include in their 401k retirement savings plan. I've been doing that for about 3 months or so. And the hours are a little bit more reasonable. I don't work until 9 or 10 anymore," Rob laughs.

Craig laughs back, "That's always a good thing. It has been a busy few months for you, eh? Switching jobs, the wedding . . ." says Craig.

"Don't forget we just closed on the new house, too."

"Wow. You've been busy! Good thing the new job is less stressful, huh?"

"Yeah, but one of our four group supervisors is leaving in a week. So, they are in the process of chopping up his responsibilities among the rest of us and, at least for the short term, they aren't planning on any replacements. So that is looking like it might be a decent increase in workload for the rest of us," Rob sighs.

"You'll still be busy."

"It's always hectic. That's one thing that hasn't changed. You know, when Maria and I were still planning the wedding, we had to fit everything in on the weekend. And there was a lot of work, picking out flowers, finding a DJ . . ."

"I bet," says Craig. "It's a lot of work planning a wedding, I'd imagine."

"Yeah, and by the time I get out of work, manage the long commute home, and eat dinner, there isn't any time to do much of anything. Even if I leave work on time, usually around 5:30, I don't get home until 7:00 PM. Maria and I only have one car between us, so since we've been married and living in our new house together, I have had to leave work at a certain time to pick her up from the train station each day."

"Oh, well, that works out kind of nice then. If you have to leave work at a certain time to pick up Maria, they can't really tell you to work late then, can they? That's got to help," Craig notes.

"Usually it's good, but it can cause problems, too. I have to be at the train station at a certain time to pick her up, so if work is busy or traffic is bad, I'm late sometimes to pick her up. There was one time in particular when I was late to pick her up because I had to work and it caused an argument. In the end, we both know that it wasn't my fault, but it is frustrating. And again, one of the supervisors is leaving next week which I don't think will help."

"Probably not," Craig replies.

"You know, being in this new job *is* hard in some respects. I don't feel 100% comfortable saying, 'Hey, this isn't cool how at 5 minutes to 5:00 you always ask me to do something else and I have to go pick up my wife.' They're still forming impressions of me and how I react in certain situations. I don't want to make a bad impression by saying, 'Hey the work life balance here isn't good.' A few of the supervisors seem to understand. One just had a baby so he is constantly going to the doctor or things like that. He just wants to spend time with his new daughter. I understand what he's going through but a lot of people don't get it. They want things done a.s.a.p.," Rob explains.

"Yeah, back when I was with Hewitt, my supervisors didn't really get it either. Some of them didn't understand that not everyone wants to work 50 hours a week. There are other things that are important to people and giving them time to do them might actually make them more productive, plus even commuting takes time," Craig replies.

"I think the biggest thing that an employer, any employer, can do is to be understanding. They need to remember that you have a life outside of work and that work isn't your life. Letting you have a life makes you a better employee. If you can't do things other than work, you just get bitter."

"Hewitt does that to some extent, but I think it comes down to the individual supervisor and how willing he or she is to accept that you have other things to take care of. If you have somebody who just toes the company line, you aren't going to get a lot of flexibility. But if you have somebody who *gets it*, you'll have some chance of having a life!" Rob says, exasperated.

"You're right" Craig replies.

"You know, some supervisors love working at Hewitt and supposedly they do a great job. In reality, they aren't doing a great job. The people working under them aren't happy. You get supervisors that expect everyone under them to be like them. But the people who work really hard—too hard, sometimes—and spend a lot of time at work are the people who get into the supervisory positions. They need to get supervisors that know everyone might not be like them."

"Man, being the manager isn't easy. I don't know if I would want to be in that kind of a position. It would be hard. You've got people on your back pressuring you. And, if you've got one employee who wants to leave early to go to a Cubs game and another who needs to take a sick kid to the doctor's office, what do you do? How do you say that one excuse is legitimate but the other isn't?" Craig wonders.

"You're right. I have personal stuff that I have to do and want to do. I like taking care of the new house. I like that I have the greenest lawn on the block. Getting married refocuses you to your personal life a little. You have a lot of stuff outside of work that you can concentrate on. Work is just a means to an ends. In the end, what you've got is your family and your personal life. Your work can't be the thing that dominates your life," Rob argues.

"I hear you, man. Well, don't you think we should probably be heading home?"

"Probably. Gotta get home to Maria!" Rob chuckles.

"All right, let's get out of here."

❖ THE DILEMMA: THE ETHICAL TENSIONS
    IN FAMILY FRIENDLY ORGANIZATIONS

The challenges and tensions of managing our personal and our professional lives take many different forms over our lifetimes. Rob's story provides you a glimpse into his struggle as both a single employee and a married employee without children. His experiences are not unique. Numerous organizations today have reported experiencing backlash from single or childless employees who argue they perceive a bias in work and family policies favoring workers with children (Flynn, 1996). To illustrate, the Conference Board, a research organization in New York, recently reported the findings of a survey of 300 human resource professionals in which over 25% of respondents agreed that single employees in the United States carry more of the workload than their coworkers with children (Burn, 1998). In response to recent employee backlash, many organizations have changed their previously named benefit programs from Work-*Family* to Work-*Life*. Single and childless employees as well as activist groups, however, do not believe that such changes go far enough. Changing to the language of work-life is too often simply "code" or just used to mask the same set of "family friendly" benefits (Bowles, 2004). At times, employees who do raise concerns about equity between single/childfree employees and their coworkers who are parents report being labeled "anti-child" or uncaring (Burkett, 2000). In addition, legal recourse is not available to single employees when they feel they are treated unfairly. Federal law, like that in most states, does not prohibit marital status discrimination in the organization. Similarly, union employees find grievance procedures less than helpful because many bargaining agreements do not address this issue (Single Friendly

Workplace Campaign, 2004). As a result, workplaces striving to be "friendly" to certain employees can be perceived as unwelcoming environments by other members of the organization.

Rob's story asks you to consider the problems and tensions between work and "family." Rob's experiences demonstrate how the relationship between our public and our private lives can change over time. Further, the research cited above raises the issue that people proceed through life with different values about work, definitions of "family," and plans for how to enact their personal lives. Ethical issues raised by this case include questioning the role the organization *should* play in our private lives, equity versus equality among various employee groups, and employee power (or lack of power) to manage their work schedules in relation to their personal lives. These are complex and difficult issues to consider in relation to organizational ethics. They are issues that all employees face eventually—what challenges will you face? How will you respond?

Discussion Questions

1. What ethical responsibility do organizations have (or not have) to help their employees manage their work and family responsibilities effectively?

2. What ethical responsibility do organizations have (or not have) to help any employee, regardless of his or her personal relational status, to enjoy a fulfilling work and private life?

3. What ethical responsibilities do single employees have (or not have) to assist their coworkers when childcare challenges or emergencies arise?

4. How do our definitions of what is a "legitimate" family marginalize certain employees and keep them from getting support for their work and *family* needs?

5. If you believe that single or unmarried employees should be offered work-life benefits, what options should these employees be able to choose from? Do you know of any workplaces that offer work-life benefits that appear to meet the needs of *all* employees, regardless of relational or parental status? Explain.

6. Besides employers, what other components of our society (communities, government, families) should or do play a role in helping individuals to have fulfilling personal and work lives?

7. Visit the Web site www.unmarriedamerica.org and read about how this organization advocates for workplace rights for unmarried employees. How does this organization position the rights of unmarried employees as an ethical issue?

8. If you were an employee who had chosen a childfree lifestyle but was continually asked to work late to assist fellow employees with emergency childcare responsibilities or travel at the last minute, how would you approach your supervisor or coworkers to discuss your dissatisfaction with the situation?

❖ NOTES

1. This case study was developed from interviews with one current and one former employee at Hewitt Associates. While the employees' names have been changed, the situations and attitudes reflected in this case study represent their real experiences in the organization.

2. Background information about Hewitt Associates was compiled from the Hewitt Associates Web site: www.hewitt.com

❖ REFERENCES

Baylin, L., Fletcher, J. K., & Kolb, D. (1997). Unexpected connections: Considering employees' personal lives can revitalize your business. *Sloan Management Review, 38,* 11–19.

Bowles, S. (2004). Single employees need work-life balance too. Article retrieved October 17, 2004, from http://www.unmarriedamerica.org/workplace/work-life-story.htm

Burkett, E. (2000). *The baby boon: How family-friendly America cheats the childless.* New York: The Free Press.

Burn, M. (1998, April 20). Single employees: Do bosses assume that your job is your life? *The Washington Post.*

Flynn, G. (1996). Backlash: No spouse, no kids, no respect. *Personnel Journal, 75,* 59–69.

Galinsky, E., & Friedman, B. (1991). *The handbook of work and family policies.* New York: The Conference Board.

Single Friendly Workplace Campaign (2004). Article retrieved October 26, 2004, from http://www.unmarriedamerica.org

The Wal-Mart Way

Community Service or Sneaky Exploitation?

Edward C. Brewer

This case examines criticisms of Wal-Mart and the assertion that its economic impact "limits the ability of local businesses to survive." The case study also examines how the company has responded to charges that it negatively affects local businesses. It raises questions regarding the effect of large businesses on other stakeholders, including whether company goals are aligned with community goals and whether the company communicates responsibly with its publics. It also addresses the utility, or consequences, of economic development and its impact on relationships with others, among other ethical perspectives.

Wal-Mart has had a tremendous impact upon our society. Its pervasive presence has affected communities all over the United States. The first Wal-Mart store opened in 1962 in Rogers, Arkansas. By 1970, there were 38 stores with 1,500 "associates" (employees) and sales of $44.2 million. In 1990, Wal-Mart became the nation's number one retailer. In 2002, Wal-Mart had the biggest single-day sales in history: $1.43 billion on the day after Thanksgiving. Today, Wal-Mart is the world's largest retailer with 1.3 million "associates" in more than 3200 facilities and sales of $244.5 billion in the fiscal year ending January 31, 2003.[1] Because of this impact, Wal-Mart has been confronted with many ethical challenges.

One of the challenges the huge retailer has faced is to have a positive impact upon the communities it enters. Whether Wal-Mart has acted ethically may be a matter of perspective. Certainly, Wal-Mart does much for the communities in which it operates, but it has also faced criticism that its economic impact limits the ability of local businesses to survive.[2] This case study will examine some of the issues and explain how Wal-Mart has responded to them. It is up to the reader, then, to determine the ethical qualities of Wal-Mart's communication and actions. Does Wal-Mart show ethical consideration to the communities it enters? Do the communities have an ethical obligation to embrace Wal-Mart or fight Wal-Mart? Is Wal-Mart destroying jobs and communities or helping to revitalize them? Does the big-box retail model, which Wal-Mart has perfected, cause an ethical dilemma for local communities?

❖   THE WAL-MART PHILOSOPHY

Wal-Mart claims the following impact for the United States (accessed 4/1/04 from http://www.walmartstores.com):

Wal-Mart—Economic Impact*

WAL-MART STORES INC.	
WAL-MART STORES	1,636
SUPERCENTERS	1,093
NEIGHBORHOOD MARKETS	31
SAM'S CLUBS	502
DISTRIBUTION CENTERS	106
ASSOCIATES EMPLOYED IN UNITED STATES	1,043,970
COMMUNITY INVOLVEMENT	$196 million
TOTAL AMOUNT SPENT WITH U.S. SUPPLIERS	$107 billion
TOTAL FEDERAL, STATE AND LOCAL TAXES PAID	$1.2 billion
SALES TAXES COLLECTED AND REMITTED	$8.5 billion

* Total state and local taxes paid include real estate, personal property, other taxes and licenses, unemployment, use, and state income taxes. Sales taxes collected and remitted are state and local sales tax collected by Wal-Mart and remitted to government authorities.

According to their Web site (www.walmartstores.com), Wal-Mart stores are committed to our communities:

> Wal-Mart Stores, Inc. believes each Wal-Mart store, SAM'S CLUB, and distribution center has a responsibility to contribute to the well being of the local community. Our more than 3,400 locations contributed more than $150 million to support communities and local non-profit organizations. Customers raised an additional $75 million with the help of our stores and clubs.[3]

Wal-Mart also claims that their philosophy is to do good works:

> Wal-Mart's Good Works community involvement program is based on the philosophy of operating globally and giving back locally. In our experience, we can make the greatest impact on communities by supporting issues and causes that are important to our customers and associates in their own neighborhoods. We rely on our associates to know which organizations are the most important to their hometowns, and we empower them to determine how Wal-Mart Foundation dollars will be spent. Consequently, our funding initiatives are channeled directly into local communities by associates who live there.

Wal-Mart's approach to implementing this community involvement (again according to their Web site, noted above) is

> unique, combining both financial and volunteer support. We encourage our associates to be involved in their local communities and to support the programs that are making a positive difference. In addition, associates conceive and carry out creative fundraising efforts on behalf of local charitable causes, particularly Children's Miracle Network (CMN) and the 170-plus children's hospitals nationwide that receive support from CMN.

Wal-Mart does fund a number of programs to support communities and local nonprofit organizations. They claim to have given the following (http://www.walmartfoundation.org/wmstore/goodworks/scripts/index.jsp)[4]:

- More than $88 million in community grants
- More than $265 million in 15 years for Children's Miracle Network (CMN)

- More than $184 million in 19 years to United Way chapters
- $80 million in scholarships since 1979
- $1.7 million in Environmental Grants
- $3.1 million in Volunteerism Always Pays grants
- $20 million raised and contributed during the 2002 holidays

❖ COMMUNITY COMPLAINTS

Clearly Wal-Mart has participated in helping to make communities better, but there is another side to the story as well. In his book, *In Sam We Trust,* Bob Ortega (1998) suggests that Wal-Mart is devouring America. Among other issues, Representative George Miller's (D-CA) 25-page Report by the Democratic Staff of the Committee on Education and the Workforce, U.S. House of Representatives (Miller, 2004), suggests that Wal-Mart's low wages and unaffordable or unavailable health care cost taxpayers money. In recent years, the downtown areas of many towns have been suffering as communities have become increasingly suburban. According to critics, Wal-Mart often contributes to the decline of the downtown of small towns because they build stores at the outskirts of towns, drawing traffic away from the downtown areas.

Downtown Deterioration

For example, Wilmington, Ohio, (a community of about 10,000 when Wal-Mart moved in) saw the decline of their downtown as the traffic flow headed west of town, toward the shopping center that housed Wal-Mart. The K-Mart on the eastern edge of town eventually shut down because of the competition. A small craft store in downtown Wilmington (Clinton Art Craft) soon discovered that Wal-Mart was selling craft supplies to customers at a lower price than Clinton Art Craft could purchase them from their suppliers. Wal-Mart's return policy was also problematic for Clinton Art Craft. Their suppliers would not take back returned items like suppliers did for Wal-Mart. Customers would often get agitated when Clinton Art Craft wouldn't (because they couldn't afford to) have the same return policy as Wal-Mart. Other downtown establishments experienced similar problems and, as a result, they shut down. Business moved to the western edge of town, away from the downtown area, to be closer to the Wal-Mart traffic. Clinton Art Craft was able to stay in business in part because their service, with special attention to the customer, maintained a loyal customer base. However, some of those customers began going to Clinton Art Craft for advice and then heading to Wal-Mart to buy the materials they needed. Clinton Art Craft was forced to add an additional focus to their business (framing and matting) in order to survive. They did survive and thrive, but only because they were able to adapt to the environment Wal-Mart created. It was difficult for a Mom and Pop store run by a husband and wife with an occasional part-time employee to make such adaptations. Resources were limited. Clinton Art Craft survived for over 30 years (until the couple's retirement). For a small business, that is quite a feat, especially in the wake of Wal-Mart's impact on a small town.

The Nevada Small Business Association has claimed that Wal-Mart practices "predatory pricing" to destroy smaller competitors (Reed, 2000). According to Ronna Bolante (2003), "Hawaii [small business] retailers have learned how to co-exist with big boxers: Don't compete with 'em" (p. 16). The plan is to find a niche of different products and services that will not be in competition with Wal-Mart. However, "that's easier said than done, considering Wal-Mart and Sam's Club sell almost everything under the sun" (Bolante, 2003, p. 16). In a town in Colorado, the local government gives Wal-Mart credit for turning the economy around:

> In Sterling, officials point to the local Wal-Mart, which opened a decade ago and expanded to Supercenter in 1995, as a key to turning around a once moribund economy. "They draw from a large geographic area," said City Manager Jim Thomas. "I see license plates from Kansas, Nebraska, and Wyoming." (Peterson, 2002, p. 20)

But while public officials feel the town has benefited from Wal-Mart's presence, local business owners are not of the same opinion:

> To be sure, some of the benefits reaped from Sterling's Wal-Mart have come at the expense of local businesses. "When they come to town, if you're in competition with them, you're going to feel it," said Larry Hilty, proprietor of the Sterling Grocery Mart. "They just tear you up."
>
> When the Supercenter opened, Hilty's business suffered an immediate 50 percent drop in sales. "I'm surviving," he said, "but it'll never be back to what it was." (Peterson, 2002, p. 20)

Small towns all over the country have felt the impact of Wal-Mart. This is not a new phenomenon. Wal-Mart began having tremendous impact on communities in the 1980s. For example, by the late 1980s, Iowa had felt the effects of the growing retail giant. According to an article by Edward O. Welles (1993), "Iowa towns within a 20-mile radius felt Wal-Marts [sic] pull. Their retail sales declined by 17.6% after five years"(para. 13).

But it wasn't just the retail stores that suffered. The specialty stores also felt the impact. The only hope for small merchants was to find a niche. Because of Wal-Mart's size and strength with suppliers (which has grown tremendously since the late 1980s), the burden has been on the small business owner to change and adapt. Even if they had successful businesses, providing the same goods and products for as long as 50 years, small merchants have been forced to adapt to survive as Wal-Mart enters their territory.

As Wal-Mart prepared to enter Maine in the early 1990s, Ken Stone, a professor of economics at Iowa State University, traveled to the state to give them some advice:

> His advice was simple and direct: don't compete directly with Wal-Mart; specialize and carry harder-to-get and better-quality products; emphasize customer service; extend your hours; advertise more. (Welles, 1993, para. 25)

Merchants in small-town Maine had similar concerns to the Ohio and Iowa merchants—"that Wal-Mart would accelerate the drift of business out of downtown" (Welles, 1993, para. 48). In the minds of merchants, however, the impact goes beyond simply business. One Maine merchant put it this way:

> There's no argument that you can get a damn light bulb for 10 cents cheaper at Wal-Mart than you can at John Hichborns [sic] hardware store. But do people know that John Hichborn is a major contributor to Elmhurst [a local trade school for the handicapped]? He works at finding jobs for people from Elmhurst. If Hichborn goes out of business because people want a cheaper light bulb, then you lose more than just the tax revenues that business generated. (Welles, 1993, para. 69)

Wal-Mart has been the topic of discussion at many Main Street associations across the nation. "'Wal-Mart has gone a long way to reduce opportunity for downtowns to be successful as far as traditional retailers,' said Bob Wilson, director of program services for the Mississippi Main Street Association" (Gillette, 2002, p. 16). Wilson goes on to explain:

> It is a phenomenon a lot of downtowns are going through. A lot of areas have seen the short-term retail tax increases that happen when Wal-Mart comes to town, but it is not a long-term solution. Full-time jobs are replaced by part-time jobs with no benefits. And more employees come from surrounding areas so they don't really have that economic boost to the community. (Gillette, 2002, p. 16)

According to Wilson, Wal-Mart does not have loyalty to the communities it enters and has no problem abandoning its original building in town to move to a larger facility with better traffic flow at the outskirts of town, with no concern as to whether or not it remains in the same taxing district (Gillette, 2002).

Beyond the Small-Town Communities

But it is not just small towns and businesses that are affected. Wal-Mart is preparing to enter the grocery market with its Supercenters around the Chicago area:

> The Jewel and Piggly Wiggly stores serving Antioch will be the first local grocers to feel the Wal-Mart effect. Eventually, the impact will spread to all Chicago-area grocery stores, including two other major combination discount/grocery chains, Meijer Inc., and Target Corp. (Murphy, 2004, para. 6)

The impact can be brutal for business owners. "In exurban Sycamore, Brown County Market lost 40% of its sales after a Wal-Mart Supercenter opened in nearby DeKalb in the late 1990s" (Murphy, 2004, para. 8). The store's owner laments one of the issues: "'I pay my grocery clerks $13 an hour plus benefits. Wal-Mart pays $7 an hour with no benefits,' says owner Daniel Brown. 'It's hard for me to compete against that'" (Murphy, 2004, para. 9).

Recently, an article in *Fast Company* discussed the impact of Wal-Mart's low prices on its suppliers. A gallon-sized jar of Vlasic pickles sold for $2.97. What a deal! As Fishman (2003) puts it:

Therein lies the basic conundrum of doing business with the world's largest retailer. By selling a gallon of kosher dills for less than most grocers sell a quart, Wal-Mart may have provided a service for its customers. But what did it do for Vlasic? The pickle maker had spent decades convincing customers that they should pay a premium for its brand. Now Wal-Mart was practically giving them away. And the fevered buying spree that resulted distorted every aspect of Vlasic's operations, from farm field to factory to financial statement. (p. 70)

Because Wal-Mart has grown so big, it has developed the power to determine suppliers' prices. They put the pressure on suppliers to lower their prices, and because Wal-Mart has such a big market share of retail sales, the suppliers concede to the Wal-Mart way of doing things. Wal-Mart offers to deliver low prices to consumers. The enticement to small towns is to make them feel as if they have some of the same amenities as a big city. After Wal-Mart has descended on a town and local businesses (hardware stores, dime stores, clothing stores, etc.) have disappeared, Wal-Mart offers to make things even better. As Leslie "Buzz" Davis puts it,

Later the Wal-Mart front man swoops into your little town, slaps you on your back and says, "Boys, have I got something you are going to love: a Supercenter! This baby will be the size of four football fields and have everything you need to live except a birthing room and a funeral parlor. You won't ever have to shop anywhere else again. Aren't you lucky we chose your little city for all those great jobs the Supercenter will bring? And all that tax base we're just giving you free? Because you are such nice guys, I am going to throw in a large, late model used car lot at this Supercenter. This is a new business we are going into and you'll love it. Why, you'll be living just like those folks in the big city! Gee, aren't you lucky I came to town?" (Davis, 2003, para. 6)

Perhaps Davis's tone is a bit cynical, but there is an element that rings true. It all depends upon your perspective. Community members in Bristol, Tennessee, lost a battle to the retail giant on a rezoning issue. According to an online editorial entitled "Bristol Wal-Mart Controversy" (see www.sullivan-county.com/id2/wal-mart/),

As accusations of "back room deals" and community anger fly in Bristol, city officials decide to sue citizens for opposing their despotic rule. All of this boils down to locating a Wal-Mart "super center" adjacent to two subdivisions and rezoning the property for business to accommodate them. Bristol goes even beyond "good old boy" politics to new lows. Citizens never had a chance.

Economic Spin-Off

Yet, Wal-Mart has grown to be such a behemoth exactly because it has given customers what they wanted (or at least thought they wanted)—low prices and convenience. One can head to the local Wal-Mart and do virtually all of one's shopping in one huge building. It is often possible to find a reasonable substitution for those specialty items that can't be found at Wal-Mart. But if low prices are causing other local merchants to go out of business, are the conveniences that Wal-Mart provides worthwhile in the long run? There is a whole other side to this community economic impact in terms of the economic spin-off of a dollar spent at Wal-Mart versus a dollar spent at other local merchants. There have been myriad stories about low wages and minimal benefits provided to Wal-Mart "associates," not to mention the hiring of illegal aliens or the fact that China has become a major supplier for the retail giant that used to boast that it only carried products that were made in America.

Wal-Mart's average employee works a 30-hour week and earns about $11,700 a year, which is nearly $2,000 below the poverty line for a family of three (Miller, 2004; Wal-Mart Watch, 2004;). Only 38% of "associates" have company-provided health coverage—as compared to the national average of over 60% (Miller, 2004; United Food and Commercial Workers Union [UFCW] Local 227, 2004; UFCW Local 770, 2004; Wal-Mart Watch, 2004;). According to the United Food and Commercial Workers International Union Local 227, "Wal-Mart has increased the premium cost for workers by over 200% since 1993—medical care inflation only went up 50% in the same period" (UFCW Local 227, 2004). Furthermore, the UFCW indicates that "[t]he Walton family [owner of Wal-Mart] is worth about $102 billion—less than 1% of that could provide affordable health care for associates" (UFCW Local 227, 2004).

There have also been a number of class action law suits against Wal-Mart for underpaying associates by not paying them for overtime and making them work through daily scheduled 15-minute breaks. In addition, there is a suit alleging that Wal-Mart "systematically deprived illegal workers of labor-law protections during at least the last three years" (Rasansky, 2003, p. 34). There is evidence that

Wal-Mart actually destroys more jobs than it creates and lowers community standards. "Research shows that for every two jobs created by a Wal-Mart store, the community loses three" (Flagstaff Activist Network, 2004; UFCW Local 227, 2004; UFCW Local 770, 2004; Wal-Mart Watch, 2004).

Wal-Mart touts their "buy America" program, yet over 80% of the clothing sold in their stores is produced overseas (Flagstaff Activist Network, 2004; UFCW Local 227, 2004; UFCW Local 770, 2004; Wal-Mart Watch, 2004). In order to keep costs low enough to keep them in Wal-Mart stores, suppliers are often forced to move their production overseas. This outsourcing has become more widespread in part because Wal-Mart is big enough to demand the price it desires from its suppliers. A Salt Lake City paper addresses this issue:

> The millions of people flocking to the Wal-Marts, etc., in order to save $0.11 per roll of toilet paper have exactly the same motivation as Corporate America has in seeking a lower price for what it wants to buy. This is not to say that outsourcing American jobs to China or India is OK. In fact, this newspaper has for many years been on record as not supporting that notion. It is, however, to say that if outsourcing is not OK because of the devastating impact on parts of our population, then the local government cooperation with the spread of the Wal-Mart virus is not OK either. ("Outsourcing American jobs," 2004).

❖ COMMUNITY SATISFACTION

However one wants to criticize Wal-Mart, though, one would be hard pressed to find someone who has not purchased from a Wal-Mart store. The other side of the argument is that Wal-Mart does indeed help communities and give them exactly what they desire—low prices and convenience. It saves the customer time because he or she can consolidate shopping needs. Why go to four or five different stores when you can get everything you need at Wal-Mart? Often, you will be able to purchase the same brand for less money as well. Some suggest that Wal-Mart is good for consumers, business, and the economy. An article in Advertising Age ("Wal-Mart Creates Winners All 'Round," 2003) claims, "Wal-Mart functions as the consumer's advocate and purchasing agent, badgering suppliers to get the best deal." The article further argues, "Economists say low Wal-Mart prices help keep inflation in check, and its efficiencies have been pushed down the supply chain, further improving productivity." Sheila Danzey (2002) opined that the St. Thomas (New Orleans) housing development would greatly benefit from a proposed Wal-Mart in a "formerly troubled high crime-devalued neighborhood" through a proposed Tax Increment Financing (TIF) plan that would help in the rebuilding of St. Thomas.

Customer Choice

Karen De Coster and Brad Edmonds (2003) dispel some of the rumors often heard about Wal-Mart, such as coming to town and selling below cost until the competition is gone and then jacking up the prices. De Coster and Edmonds argue that if community members want to discourage the acceptance of Wal-Mart in their town, "they have scores of non-bullying options to pick from in order to try and persuade their fellow townsfolk that a new Wal-Mart is not the best option" (para. 16). The authors suggest that it is not easy to convince people to trade convenience for "the sake of undefined moral purposes" (para. 17). Certainly the growth of Wal-Mart is evidence of what the American public as a whole value:

> To be sure, if Americans didn't love Wal-Mart so much it wouldn't be sitting at the top of the 2002 Fortune 500 with $219 billion in revenues. And we do love Wal-Mart. We love it because it gives us variety and abundance. We love it because it saves us time and wrangling. And we love it because no matter where we are, it's always there when we need it. (De Coster & Edmonds, 2003, para. 22)

Business Success

Wal-Mart is big. Davis (2003) suggests that retailers of such size tend to monopolize markets:

> Wal-Mart is on its way to monopolizing the retail discount store and grocery trades. Over 1.4 million people now work for Wal-Mart. It's three times larger than General Motors. It's the largest private employer in the United States and the largest employer in over 20 states. It already has nearly 50 percent of the discount retail market. It already is the largest grocery store business in America. The

company grosses over $250 billion a year, with profits over $8 billion per year. It is the largest corporation in the world. Wal-Mart is mean and hungry for more. Why stop at $500 billion in sales? Why not try for $1 trillion in sales and have 6 million employees? (para. 8)

But isn't that the American way—to want more? In fact, accumulating more wealth is one of the things De Coster and Edmonds (2003) suggest Wal-Mart helps enable its customers to do:

Families who shop carefully at Wal-Mart can actually budget more for investing, children's college funds, or entertainment. And unlike other giant corporations, Wal-Mart stores around the country make an attempt to provide a friendly atmosphere by spending money to hire greeters, who are often people who would have difficulty finding any other job. This is a friendly, partial solution to shoplifting problems; the solution K-mart applied ("Hey, what's in that bag?") didn't work as well. (para. 19)

Edwin A. Locke (2004), dean's professor emeritus of leadership and motivation at the University of Maryland at College Park and a senior writer for the Ayn Rand Institute in Irvine, California, suggests, "Wal-Mart is one of the most impressive success stories in the history of business" (p. 32). He bemoans the fact that Wal-Mart is so often criticized for running its business effectively and attracting "hoards of customers." Locke admits that Wal-Mart has been successful in competing against other stores, but suggests it does this by "discovering new ways of using computer systems and other technology to manage its inventory and costs better and to reap the benefits of economy of scale" (p. 32). Wal-Mart, according to Locke, has earned its success:

Wal-Mart is especially popular among low-income shoppers who cannot afford the prices of the more upscale stores. It has put other stores out of business, but that is the way capitalism works. The automobile replaced the horse and buggy. Sound motion picture replaced the silents. No one has a "right" to business success or a "right" to be protected from competitors through government intervention. One only has a right to try to compete through voluntary trade. In a free economy, companies that offer the best value for the dollar win and the losers invest their money elsewhere. (p. 32)

Locke believes Wal-Mart should be admired, rather than feared, and that communities should thank Wal-Mart for being so good at giving customers what they want.

Helping Hand

Wal-Mart claims to contribute to the well-being of communities. Since June 10, 1996, when Wal-Mart began posting pictures of missing children in the lobbies of Wal-Mart facilities, 5,710 children have been featured. More than 4,365 have been recovered. Wal-Mart's customers and associates have assisted in the recovery of 107 of those children.[5] It is clear that Wal-Mart does much in the way of scholarships and philanthropy in addition to offering convenience and low prices. Wal-Mart's rhetoric centers on the three basic beliefs that Sam Walton established in 1962 (see www.walmartstores.com):

1. Respect for the Individual

2. Service to Our Customers

3. Strive for Excellence

If you are in a Wal-Mart store at the right time, you can hear raucous sounds from the back of the store as the "associates" perform the Wal-Mart cheer:

Give me a W!

Give me an A!

Give me an L!

Give me a Squiggly!

Give me an M!

Give me an A!

Give me an R!

Give me a T!

What's that spell?

Wal-Mart!

Whose Wal-Mart is it?

My Wal-Mart!

Who's number one?

The Customer! Always!

❖ A MATTER OF PERSPECTIVE

From the perspective of the Wal-Mart executives, and many patrons, it's all about the customer and the community. But often the community leaders have a different perspective. As the *Economist* ("My Wal-Mart 'tis of Thee," 1996) put it:

Like America itself, Sam Walton's monument excites strong reactions. People are wary of this superpower. They mistrust its motives, fear its cultural clout, deride its brashness and scoff at its contradictions. Yet they also marvel at its convenience and admire its success. And, as with America, the people keep coming. (para. 15)

Does Wal-Mart communicate and act in an ethical manner? You make the call.

Discussion Questions

1. Should Wal-Mart be expected to protect small businesses in the communities within which it operates?

2. What does it mean for an organization to be ethical in its communication and practices?

3. Does Wal-Mart truly harm the downtown areas of small communities, or does it just offer a challenge to change that is uncomfortable for the local merchants?

4. What kind of experience have you had with the local Wal-Mart, and do you go there often?

5. Does Wal-Mart's rhetoric communicate a different message than its actions?

6. Are Wal-Mart's persuasive tactics concerning its value to communities ethical in approach and intention?

7. What other local organizations have had positive or negative impacts on communities?

❖ NOTES

1. See a complete timeline at http://www.walmartstores.com. Click "news" and then "fact sheets—history, people, commitment."

2. See economic impact statements for all 50 states as well as the national numbers by going to http://www.walmartstores.com and searching their entire site for "economic impact" at the top of their home page.

3. You can find Wal-Mart's philosophy concerning their commitment to communities by going to their Web site at http://www.walmartstores.com and then clicking the "About Wal-Mart" button, then "Research Information," and then "Our Commitment to Communities."

4. From this site, click "What We Fund" button.

5. See Wal-Mart Good Works at http://www.walmartfoundation.org/wmstore/goodworks.html

❖ REFERENCES

Bolante, R. (2003, September). Friend or foe? How Wal-Mart will change urban Honolulu. *Hawaii Business,* 16–20.

Bristol Wal-Mart controversy. (n.d.). Retrieved February 6, 2004, from http://www.sullivan-county.co/id2/wal-mart/

Danzey, S. (2002, January 21). Why we win with Wal-Mart. *New Orleans CityBusiness,* p. 29.

Davis, L. (2003, September 1). Leslie "Buzz" Davis: *Wal-mart threatens our way of life, must be unionized.* Retrieved February 6, 2004, from www.madison.com/captimes/opinion/column/guest/55885.php

De Coster, K., & Edmonds, B. (2003, January 31). *The case for Wal-Mart.* Retrieved February 3, 2004, from http://www.mises.org/fullarticle.asp?control=1151

Fishman, C. (2003, December). The Wal-Mart you don't know: Why low prices have a high cost. *Fast Company,* 67–80.

Flagstaff Activist Network. *Wal-Mart myths and reality.* Retrieved April 1, 2004, from http://www.flagstaffactivist.org/campaigns/walmyths.html

Gillette, B. (2002, June 10–16). Small town retailers finding ways to compete with big chains. *Mississippi Business Journal,* p. 16.

Locke, E. A. (2004, February 20). Thwarting Wal-Mart is simply un-American. *The Central New York Business Journal, 18*(8), 32.

Miller, G. (D-CA), Senior Democrat. (2004, February 16). *Everyday low wages: The hidden price we all pay for Wal-Mart.* A report by the democratic staff of the Committee on Education and the Workforce, U.S. House of Representatives.

Murphy, H. L. (2004, March 15). Wal-Mart set to launch grocery invasion here. *Crain's Chicago Business 27*(11), 9. Retrieved April 1, 2004, from EBSCOhost database.

My Wal-Mart 'tis of thee. (1996, November 23). *The Economist, 341*(7993). Retrieved April 1, 2004, from EBSCOhost database.

Ortega, B. (1998). *In Sam we trust.* New York: Times Business/Random House.

Outsourcing American jobs: Wal-Marts and the quality of life. (2004, March 8–14). *The Enterprise*, 24.

Peterson, E. (2002, November). Wal-Mart's fans and foes. *ColoradoBiz*, p. 18.

Rasansky, J. (2003, December 5–11). Always lower prices? Wal-Mart could face epic battle over unpaid overtime claims. *Fort Worth Business Press*, 34.

Reed, V. (2000, January 10). Small business group decries chamber position on Wal-Mart. *Las Vegas Business Press*, 3.

United Food and Commercial Workers (UFCW) International Union Local 227. (n.d.). [Web site home page] Retrieved April 1, 2004, from http://www .ufcw227.org/organizing/walmart.htm

United Food and Commercial Workers (UFCW) International Union Local 770. (n.d.). [Web site home page] Retrieved April 1, 2004, from http://www .ufcw770.org/index.html

Wal-Mart creates winners all 'round. (2003, October 6). *Advertising Age, 74*(40), 20.

Wal-Mart Watch. *Bad neighbor fact sheet.* Retrieved April 1, 2004, from http:// www.walmartwatch.com/bad/page.cfm?subsection_id=108

Welles, E. O. (1993, July). When Wal-Mart comes to town. *Inc., 15*(7), 76–83. Retrieved February 4, 2004, from Business Source Premier database: http://www.walmartstores.com/wmstore/wmstores/HomePage.jsp

Working at Home and Playing at Work

*Using ICTs to Break Down the
Barriers Between Home and Work[1]*

Alf Steinar Sætre and Jan-Oddvar Sørnes

This case discusses the emerging role of new communication technologies, such as text messaging, email, and cell phones. It considers whether such technologies enable or constrain employees and also whether it is necessary for employees to align their job-related tasks and their social activities at work. The case also focuses on the extent of privacy rights for employees and the blurring of task and social relationships.

Historically, the separation between work and private life has been fairly clear-cut. When we were "in the office," we were working; when we went home, we were strictly on our own time. But this is changing. Many of us now have access to business-related information and communication technologies (ICTs) at home, so today it's not uncommon for high-level professionals to work each evening at their home computer. This is the story of how a young Norwegian high-tech company has tried to address just that challenge. It's a story about the use, and possible abuse, of ICTs when management tried to use ICTs to gain access to their key employees at all hours. Faced with long work hours and high pressure, some employees took full advantage of new communication technologies and brought their social life to work. This case addresses the ethical issues that arise when the boundary between work and private life becomes blurred and permeable. Before we turn to the use and abuse of ICTs in this case study, let's look briefly at the company.

❖ DOSSIER SOLUTIONS

Dossier Solutions provides large corporations with knowledge-management software. As a start-up company, they face intense competition and crushing deadlines. Dossier was started in the spring of 2000 by three students at the Norwegian University of Science and Technology (NTNU) in Trondheim, Norway. One of the co-founders is Kristian Mjøen, a 26-year-old civil engineering student in theoretical physics at NTNU. Though still an inexperienced manager, he appears both introspective and precocious. Like many entrepreneurs, he started his firm before finishing his university degree. The company chiefly employs fellow students of his—technology-oriented whizzes, all equipped with the latest and greatest information and communication technology.

Because Dossier was founded just before the end of the dotcom heyday, it enjoyed easy access to capital, allowing it to grow rapidly. But within a year the dotcom bubble burst, and Dossier got "the recent developments in the IT business straight in the face, as have most," Kristian ruefully recalls. "From 30 employees we are now down to 10." Their prospects are brightening, though. Dossier has recently won two large contracts with important clients, so its workload is actually higher than ever.

Dossier Solutions' chief product is a software tool for developing and managing human competencies in large corporations. According to Kristian, the product "has its basis in the so-called 'people-centric solution.'" Using Dossier's products, employees get tools to document and visualize their professional competencies, making it easier for them to get matched to the right position. It is quite common, of course, for large organizations to have employees keep their competency profiles up to date so that new projects can be matched with employees' special interests and skills, and vice versa. But the tool provided by Dossier facilitates this whole match-up process, and Kristian contends this "gives value-added for the company" by enhancing the company's "internal marketplaces for positions and projects."

When an organization anticipates needing certain skill-sets that it currently lacks, it will often buy training courses from external vendors, like Dossier, that allow employees to augment their personal competencies while also allowing the organization to expand its pool of human resources. Dossier specializes in this area. It offers various training modules that together form an integrated, seamless whole. One tool provides for performance-appraisal conversations between a leader and an associate. Another tool provides a systematic three-way evaluation of leaders—something known in the trade as a "360-degree evaluation." Leaders get evaluated from the perspective of those who work for them, from the perspective of their peers, and from the perspective of their own boss. These elements become part of a person's profile, Kristian says; the organization then uses this information to map competencies and make development plans for individual employees.

According to Kristian, Dossier assumes that all employees should "have a tool for continually documenting their own competencies in a life-long learning perspective and have the opportunity to actively develop their own career." Because it is clearly in their self-interest to do so, employees have a big incentive to update their information. The benefit extends beyond their current organization, since each update generates an electronic résumé that records their personal experience and skill development. So both the individual employees and the employer get a better overview of employee competencies. Dossier sees its product as a great way to integrate individual and organizational needs.

Let's now look at how this high-tech, ICT-intensive company uses its ICTs.

❖ THE UNINTENDED CONSEQUENCES OF ICT USE

Because it is a start-up company, created by students, who then began employing other students nearly their own age, everyone at Dossier has been simultaneously discovering how to become a company. The founders had no managerial experience, and the employees had virtually no work experience, yet the pressures to become quickly productive became intense. One of Dossier's survival tactics was to develop ways to expand their access to their employees' abilities. So, for example, Dossier provided each employee with a high-end cell phone, hoping thereby to put its employees constantly on call. Kristian says, "Our motivation for giving employees cell phones is that we have a crystal-clear policy: when the cell phone is on, we can call them anytime, day or night." The policy worked, but it also created a new and perhaps bigger problem: it blurred any boundary between the public and private domains. Carley (2002) argues that smart agents—agents that are computational, adaptive, and intelligent—will help break boundaries within and among organizations, but as we have seen here ICTs do not have to incorporate smart agents to enable the breaking of boundaries. In accepting the gift of the high-end cell phone, employees had also implicitly accepted a contract of availability, thus extending work life into their private life.

The agreement between the company and the employees, Kristian says, is stunningly simple, seductive, and absolute: "Yes, you can call your friends on the company cell phone, but as long as your cell phone is on, you are available to us." Dossier especially needed to increase the availability of its programmers. The cell phone arrangement gives Dossier and its employees what Kristian terms "a mutual flexibility." He illustrates: "For example, if we have problems with a program and need one of the programmers, we call the number, and if the cell phone is on—which it often is if you use the number for all your friends as well—then we reach the person." Being able to reach the person who actually wrote the particular component of a problematic code is obviously much more efficient than having a new programmer sit down and look through the massive amount of code in search of an error.

The employees of Dossier are primarily students who, being technology oriented, are "relatively active users of both the Internet and SMS[2] and ICQ[3] and that kind of chat," Kristian says. This kind of communication technology can be a great aid in doing and coordinating work, but it can also become a distraction that impedes performance. The use, and abuse, of these communication technologies "interrupts the workday for people who sit and program relatively complex code." When they are "interrupted every 15 minutes by an incoming email or SMS, it has some consequences for how effective" they are, Kristian says. In fact, he says there's an "incredible amount of hours" wasted on ICQ and SMS every week at Dossier. This concerns him for two reasons. First, when such "intrusive" and "interruptive" communication is basically social (i.e., for keeping up with friends), then the communication is unproductive, at least as far as Dossier is concerned. Second, even if such communication is job-related—which frequently it isn't at Dossier—it interrupts the flow of work and therefore further reduces productivity.

One way that Kristian addressed the problem was to intervene directly when he saw excessive interruptions occur in their open office. He recalls that there was an employee sitting right behind him. This employee was working on a task that required a little use of the keyboard, but a great deal of work with the mouse. This person was an avid user of ICQ, "and at regular intervals I heard her typing infernally—and then we are talking every 30 seconds on some days—then some movement on the mouse, and then back to the keyboard again." Kristian knew, based on what she was supposed to be doing, that her work should not include large amounts of text. By closely monitoring the sound coming from her desk, he soon realized that she could not possibly be very productive. Not only did these constant interruptions consume time and disrupt her work process, but they also led her machine to crash quite frequently when she was chatting on ICQ. Kristian finally told her, "'Now you have to cut it out.' She didn't talk to me for a few days, but she stopped doing it." Kristian realized, however, that he was not going to be able to monitor and comment on everyone's use of these ICTs.

Kristian and Dossier are now addressing this issue with a new policy. It asks people to close "email applications for periods of the day, instead of having a 'pling' every time an email comes in." He feels that getting rid of this distraction will improve the productivity at Dossier. Supporting this view is the article "Working from home" (2003) that tells the story of someone working from home and, as a result of being rid of all the small but frequent interruptions at work, increased his or her productivity dramatically. Kristian also acknowledges that "email should be the least problematic since it is asynchronous." But because everyone uses email and tends to answer messages throughout the day, it still interrupts work. As people fail to take advantage of email's asynchronicity and continuously respond, email becomes a distraction as well. Kristian states that even he will get "about 30–40 emails per day on some days." If you fall for the temptation of responding to all your emails as you receive them, "then you are down to relatively short periods of effective work." And if you also have a fair amount of SMS messages and ICQ chatting on top of this, the problem can become acute. But as we shall see in the next paragraphs, not all ICT usage at Dossier was unproductive or had substantial unintended consequences.

❖ USING EMAIL AND THE INTERNET PRODUCTIVELY

Hollingshead and Contractor (2002) discuss the importance of email, and other ICTs, as tools for organizing activities at the group level. Dossier's employees use all communication channels available to them. Email, especially, plays an important role there. Because it is both asynchronous and still fairly immediate, email helps keep the communication lines open once a client relationship has been established. One advantage of email, Kristian says, is that the Forwarding and Reply functions provide a log of the electronic conversation, so any newcomers to a task are more easily brought up to speed. Furthermore, with email "you have a tendency to think things through," he says, whereas communicating by phone will sometimes tempt you to "talk faster than you think." So when Kristian desires preciseness, he prefers to write an email; he knows he'll have to really think about what he aims to achieve with that message.

Besides using email to communicate with clients, Dossier increasingly uses email internally. For example, when someone has been working with a client to set the specifications of a particular module, these specs are no longer allowed to be transmitted orally. As Kristian admits, "We have burned ourselves many times. The message either wasn't received or was misunderstood." Whenever important information arrives from the client via email, that same email gets forwarded to everyone involved in the project "so that it is traceable afterwards," Kristian says. No longer can anyone say, "We didn't know that" or "We misunderstood."

Dossier's use of email to document product requirements came about, Kristian says, because the young firm had seen "lots of quarrels" about who was responsible for mistakes that occurred. These quarrels would often get quite heated, "with dirt-throwing and accusations of various sorts" of what had gone wrong and who was at fault. Using email for documentation helps Dossier avoid squandering precious time and goodwill on fruitless quarrels. Dossier's hard-earned experience is very much in line with McKristianney, Zack, and Doherty's (1992) assertions that lean media—such as email—is important for organizing activities of programming teams.

Dossier also relies heavily on the Internet and email to learn crucial information about potential clients, and to keep up with current terminology. As we'll see, this information helps Dossier know how best to approach a potential client. Kristian frequently needs specific financial information about potential clients. He gets this data by going to Brønnøysundsregistrene (www.brreg.no). The Brønnøysund Register Center, which consists of several different national electronic databases, is Norway's central register authority and source of information. Here Kristian can obtain financial information such as a company's turnover, profits, and corporate officers. This information proves crucial when he's preparing a strategy for approaching potential clients.

In the human-resource and knowledge-management software business, the style of presentation—*how* you say it—can be as important as the substance. When asked to what extent Dossier uses the Internet to search for information for product development, Kristian replies, "The most important contribution of the Internet to our organization is a high consciousness around—what shall I call it?—the jargon that is used within the 'competency' world." He smiles broadly, then adds that if you visit the home pages of large consulting companies, "you can adopt a terminology that is needed to communicate in the same language to a market." He maintains that a continual update is important because it is a terminology "in constant development." He even admits, "Often it is as much about finding [fancy] new terms as inventing new technology."

Besides monitoring the terms that are used by most important consultants in his industry, Kristian also monitors potential clients' Web pages to see which of the major consulting firms have consulted with them. Kristian indicates that he can pretty much tell inductively which consultants have been working for a given company: "You can often see much of what is done in a company—in particular, the large companies—by going in and just reading what is there. What is the focus? What words are they using?" The demands for understanding and adopting these terms seem to be fairly high. He likens these consultants to a school of fish, saying they "have an extremely well-developed ability to all turn in the same direction, and do that very quickly!" He regularly monitors both the Web pages of large corporations in Norway and the home pages of the consultant companies "that are supplying much of the premises for the terminology." Kristian may find new terminology on the Internet but it is confirmed in face-to-face meetings.

The founding partners of Dossier then use this information about clients—financial data, a list of officers, preferred buzz words, and so on—to formulate a strategy for how to approach that client: "We are very conscious when we approach, for example, Statoil, Telenor, or Hydro, or other large companies, that we must have a sizeable client plan." They need to know who the real decision makers are and be able to "relate to the decision structures that are already in place" so that they can attack from "a position of knowledge rather than ignorance." Kristian spells out that it is important to know "something about the currents in the company, what strategy they have, for example, in the competency area. Does the technology correspond to the approach to the problem formulated in that strategy? If it does not, then we have to re-evaluate or sell them another packaging."

In sum, Kristian and his partners use all this information to evaluate the potential client and to devise a strategy, or "angle of attack," that they deem best tailored to that particular client. The digital nature of their business—including the requirement for an electronic trail of customer communications and the use of the Internet to collect customer information—facilitated an unforeseen problem: Dossier's use of communication technologies. This had some unintended consequences, one of which was that the boundary between work life and private life all but disappeared.

❖ PUBLIC AND PRIVATE DOMAINS CONVERGING WITH ICTS

Internet-based communication, such as email and ICQ, has not been the only disruptive technology at Dossier. Text messaging via cellular phones (SMS) has also become commonplace. SMS adds yet another level of convenience because people can send messages even when they are away from their desk and on the move. Because Kristian gets the bills for the company's cell-phone use, he can easily monitor how much is spent on SMS versus on actual telephone calls. The problem, he says, is staggering: "We have employees who'll send 1,000 text messages a month on company cell phones!" Consider what all this means, he says. When sending SMS messages, you must use the phone keypad to type in letters, so "it takes time to send 1,000 text messages." And with the cost running at 60–70 øre (about 10 cents) per message, the aggregate cost of those 1,000 messages is considerable. But it doesn't stop there, Kristian says. If a person sends 1,000 SMS messages, then he or she will probably receive an equal number in return. One thousand SMS messages a month works out to roughly 35 messages a day. Figuring 2 minutes per message, all this adds up to just over an hour a day of using the cell-phone keypad. Little wonder that Kristian is concerned if work time is being squandered and if ICTs are an aid or a distraction! Andrew Sherwood, chairman of a New York–based consulting company, argues passionately that the major crime that employees commit against their employers is not theft of materials or embezzlement. "The major crime is time—the time employees waste every year" (Bové, 1987, p. 17).

A possible explanation for the "unproductive" use of ICTs at Dossier is the youth and inexperience of employees and managers alike. Even when the company had over 30 employees, their average age was about 25. While Dossier had planned to take advantage of these new ICTs, it was unprepared for the misuse that quickly appeared. "Many of these people had never been in a corporate setting before," Kristian recalls, so they "felt no responsibility to uphold some routines, no responsibility that the time spent was actually not their own." These individuals were still students, both literally and attitudinally. And some of them never managed to make the shift—or leap, if you will—from being a student to becoming an employee. As Kristian puts it, "The distinction between an 'every day' as a student and an 'every day' as an employee remained very blurred for some people." At Dossier these new communication technologies became more of a nuisance than a productive aid, Kristian says, because people tended to "move the social sphere into work, in a situation where they have clearly defined deadlines and tasks."

After working at building Dossier's business for over two years, Kristian sees the drawbacks of being constantly "wired" to communication technologies. "To be online is cool for a while," he says, "but when one has a lot to do, then technology becomes very tiring." As a result of this, "most of us try to show much greater respect for other people's time off than we did before—in spite of the cell-phone policy that we have." In other words, the policy remains in place, but they have raised the threshold for invoking it.

Given the incessant deadlines and the huge effort that goes into establishing a start-up, when someone finally gets some time off work, Dossier now shows a greater respect for employees' privacy. The employees themselves do as well. Kristian will even "turn the phone off for a whole day." And when at work they are all now trying to spend more time "offline" from ICTs in order to get more work done. The goal is to find the right balance. Although ICTs at Dossier have shown their potential for being seriously disruptive, these same technologies—especially email and the Internet—are also enormously useful and productive, when used appropriately.

Discussion Questions

1. What freedoms do individuals and organizations gain and lose with mobile technologies?

2. If you are doing good work, does a company have a right to know where you are doing it? Give reasons for your answer.

3. If you are working at home, or elsewhere, when you are not officially working, is it okay then to socialize with your friends when you are at work? Give reasons for your answer.

4. Why is it (or is it not) okay for an employer to have access to its employees when they are not at work, or is this the same as taking something that is not yours (time)?

5. If it is okay for an organization to have access to its members, is it then not okay for these members to take back some of this time and use company resources (time and ICTs) to keep up with their friends? Give reasons for your answer.

6. Let's assume that it is okay for organizations to intrude on their employees' private time, and conversely, that it is okay for employees to take some of this time back while at work. What are the potential social, ethical, legal, psychological, and organizational consequences of this kind of practice?

❖ NOTES

1. An earlier version of this chapter appeared in Browning, L. D., Sætre, A. S., Stephens, K., & Sørnes, J.-O. (2004). *Information and Communication Technologies in Action: Linking Theory and Narratives of Practice.* Copenhagen: Copenhagen Business School Press.

2. SMS is a text-messaging system used on cell phones.

3. ICQ is an Internet-based "chat" program that allows you to chat real-time with those of your friends who are online at the same time that you are.

❖ REFERENCES

Bové, R. (1987). Is all time wasted on the job a waste? *Training and Development Journal, 41*(11), 17.

Carley, K. (2002). Smart agents and organizations of the future. In L. A. Lievrouw & S. Livingstone (Eds.), *The handbook of new media* (pp. 206–220). London: Sage.

Hollingshead, A. B., & Contractor, N. S. (2002). New media and organizing at the group level. In L. A. Lievrouw & S. Livingstone (Eds.), *The handbook of new media* (pp. 221–235). London: Sage.

McKristianney, J. L., Zack, M. H., & Doherty, V. S. (1992). Complementary communication media: A comparison of electronic mail and face-to-face communication in a programming team. In N. Nohria & R. G. Eccles (Eds.), *Networks and organizations: Structure, form, and action* (pp. 262–287). Boston: Harvard Business School Press.

Working from home. (2003). *Management Services, 47,* 35.

The Bush Team's Moral Ethos

An Ethical Critique of the Iraq War

Mohammad A. Auwal

This case identifies several criteria for a "just war" and compares them to the justifications for, and practices of, the war in Iraq, raising challenging questions regarding ends vs. means. The case also explores features of war, such as just cause, right intention, and legitimate authority to evaluate the decision to invade Iraq. By addressing the alignment between formal, stated policy and actual behavior regarding Iraq, the author exposes us to both the duties and virtues related to justice and right actions. It also addresses the consequences of communication that is not aligned and its ultimate impact on government credibility.

War is a conjoint action in which we can study the sensemaking, relational and communicative dynamics of organizing.[1] Waging a war is an important strategic decision grounded in organizational sensemaking (Weick, 1995). It is the top leadership that makes strategic policy decisions. But any decision making involves making choices that have ethical implications, whether they lead to intended or unintended consequences, because "every action in which there is choice has moral character" (Anderson & Englehardt, 2001, p. 2). This means that, without a moral evaluation, the study of war as a strategic organizational action remains incomplete.

In this case study, I present a moral critique of the current Iraq war and its agency, President George W. Bush and his war cabinet colleagues (the Bush team), from a pluralistic just war perspective. The war has generated an intense controversy and isolated the United States from much of the rest of the world.[2] By tradition, moral analysis focuses on the characteristics and consequences of actions and the intentions and characters of agents (Anderson & Englehardt, 2001; Hinman, 1998). Just as the dancer cannot be separated from the dance, the morality of actions cannot be separated from that of the agent. I examine the characteristics and consequences of the Iraq war to estimate the morality of the war's agency, focusing on these questions: Was the war case morally justified? Has it been morally conducted? What ethical dilemmas did the Bush team experience in making the case for or waging the war? What do the justification and conduct of the war tell about their ethics? Before I discuss these questions, however, I define just war theory from a pluralistic ethical perspective, explaining how I apply its principles here and outlining some key points to provide a background to the war.

❖ JUST WAR THEORY AND ITS APPLICATION

Just war theory represents a body of moral and political wisdom governing justification and limits of warfare. Just war theory includes two intersecting sets of rules—one about "justice on the way to war" (*jus ad bellum*) and the other about "justice in the midst of war" (*jus in bello*) (Miller, 1996; Moseley, 2004; United States Institute of Peace [USIP], 2003). The *jus ad bellum* principles include just cause, legitimate authority, right intention, war as the last resort, reasonable hope for success, and proportionality of ends and means. The *jus in bello* principles include discrimination or immunity of noncombatants, proportionate use of force, and humane treatment of prisoners of war. These principles have been codified in many international treaties or declarations that include the Geneva Conventions of 1929 and 1949 (Bugnion, 2002). The goal of these treaties was to set out "laws" of war to make it ethically justified and "humane" for combatants and noncombatants (Gelb & Rosenthal, 2003).

Just war theory represents pluralistic ethics in that it integrates assumptions and principles implicit or expressed in various ethical theories. Its principles reflect Judeo-Christian and Islamic ethics and elements of relativism and universalism as well as consequentialism (utilitarian) and intrinsicism (Kantian). In fact, different religious and secular traditions have enriched just war theory since the antiquities (Hashimi, 2002; Kelsay & Johnson, 1991). Like international laws, just war principles are open to interpretation, but their underlying assumption is that war of aggression is wrong.

I apply just war theory as a form of ethical pluralism (Hinman, 1998) grounded in "good reasons" (Rachels, 2003). Unlike relativism and universalism,[3] ethical pluralism holds that there are multiple legitimate standards for moral assessment. A pluralistic moral evaluation rests on the principles of understanding, tolerance, standing up to "evil," and fallibility (Hinman, 1998). In pursuit of these principles, we have to understand issues in their proper contexts, recognize different ways to moral excellence, condemn egregious violations of evidently universal moral values, and approach moral evaluation with the assumption that our interpretation is correct but may be wrong. The bottom line in such moral evaluation is the use of good reasons. As James Rachels (2003) puts it, "Morality is, at the very least, the effort to guide one's conduct by reason—that is to do what there are the best reasons for doing—while giving equal weight to the interests of each individual who will be affected by what one does" (p. 14). In the court of ethics or good reasons, every person affected by an act should be treated equally.

We can see whether reasons are good or not by conducting a semiotic "commutation test." In a commutation test, we commute (substitute, transpose, add or delete) some elements in an issue to better understand its implications. In this case, for example, we can imagine swapping Iraqis with Americans, or adding that we didn't have the military superiority over Iraq, to see what the war would mean to us and what it means to the Iraqis. The commutation test is essentially a test of the golden rule of ethics according to which we should not do what we would not like others to do.

❖ KEY POINTS IN UNDERSTANDING THE WAR

Key Point 1: The U.S. complicity in the rise of Saddam Hussein

President Bush's cabinet colleagues who served in the former Republican administrations of 1981–1993 were complicit in the rise of Saddam Hussein. When Iraq, under Hussein, attacked Iran in 1980, the U.S. government tilted toward Iraq and supported it with weapons and intelligence, trading arms for oil and disregarding Hussein's human rights violations (Timmerman, 1991). When Hussein was gearing up for invading Kuwait in 1990, claiming it was part of Iraq's territory that colonial Britain took apart, the United States remained noncommittal about the dispute. Just before that invasion, on July 24, 1990, Margaret Tutweiller, a U.S. State Department spokesperson, announced, "We do not have any defense treaties with Kuwait, and there are no special defense or security commitments to Kuwait" (Boustany & Tyler, 1990, p. A17). This gave Hussein a sign of U.S. neutrality to the conflict. After the invasion, however, the United States played the moral police and led the Gulf War of 1991, evicting Iraqi forces from Kuwait. The present war is a sequel to that war.

Key Point 2: The Bush team decided to invade Iraq nine months before 9/11

Bush and his colleagues give the impression that the events of 9/11 triggered plans to invade Iraq. But actually, they decided to invade Iraq 9 months before 9/11 in their first National Security Council meeting in January 2001 (Scott, 2004). That decision met the demand that Bush team members Richard Perle, Paul Wolfowitz, Richard Armitage, Donald Rumsfeld,[4] and others made in a January 26, 1998, policy letter, representing the neoconservative group *Project for the New American Century* (Bunch, 2003; PNAC, 1998). The letter urged President Clinton to take up a strategy to remove Saddam Hussein from power. PNAC produced another policy document, "Rebuilding America's Defenses" in September 2000, which indicated their intention to take military control of the Gulf region ("Bush Planned Iraq 'Regime Change' Before Becoming President," 2002).

Key Point 3: The 9/11 tragedy provided an opportunity to invade Iraq

In a 1996 policy paper, Richard Perle, Douglas Feith, David Wurmser, and other neocons urged Israel to "focus on removing Saddam Hussein from power" as an "Israeli strategic objective."[5] According to Buchanan (2004), Perle, Feith, and Wurmser were all on Bush's foreign policy team on 9/11; on January 1, 2001, Wurmser urged the United States and Israel "to strike fatally, not merely disarm" several Arab regimes, adding, "Crises can be opportunities" (p. 45). Some Israeli leaders also asked the United States to attack Israel's enemies in the Middle East. In a speech before the House Government Reform Committee on September 11, 2002, former Israeli prime minister

Benjamin Netanyahu vigorously argued for a preemptive fatal strike on Iraq, saying that "prior approval of the international community" for such an attack was "immaterial" and that the Israelis were ready to risk the possible fallout of a preemptive strike on Iraq (Netanyahu, 2002). Since the decision to invade Iraq was already made, the 9/11 tragedy struck the Bush administration as an *opportunity* to go after Hussein. As Bob Woodward (2002) chronicles, "Wolfowitz seized the opportunity" (p. 83). At the war cabinet meeting on September 15, 2001, Wolfowitz argued for attacking Iraq instead of Afghanistan because "It was doable" (p. 83) and "easier" (p. 84). Donald Rumsfeld agreed with him since there were few "good targets" to bomb in Afghanistan, even as Colin Powell objected to the idea saying, "Nobody could look at Iraq and say it was responsible for September 11" (p. 87).

Key Point 4: Technical–legal sophistry in justifying an illegal war

The United States and United Kingdom justified the war with a lot of sophistry. The UN Security Council (UNSC) passed Resolution 1441 on November 2, 2002, warning Iraq of "serious consequences" if it failed to meet the UN demands over suspected WMD programs. UNSC members agreed to determine the nature of the serious consequences in a subsequent resolution. When the Bush and the Blair governments failed to engineer a subsequent resolution authorizing the use of force, they argued that previous UN resolutions still allowed them to invade. These included the 1990 UN Resolution 678, which authorized "all necessary means" (i.e., use of force) to evict Iraq from Kuwait, and the 1991 Resolution 687, which asked Iraq to disarm. But President Bush in his September 21, 2004, address at the UN General Assembly *retrospectively justified* the war as implementation of the "serious consequences." UN Secretary General Kofi Annan had categorically said that *the war was illegal* (BBC interview aired on Sept. 16, 2004). Earlier, he had euphemistically said the war was "not in conformity with the UN Charter" (Reynolds, 2004a).

Key Point 5: The shifting rationales for the war

In the beginning, the stated goal of the war was to restore UN credibility. But this looked absurd because the war itself violated the UN Charter and because the United States had ignored Israel's violation of some 75 UN resolutions and used its vetoes to shield Israel from more than 30 other UN resolutions. Next, the Bush administration cited Iraq's "hidden" Weapons of Mass Destruction (WMD) as the reason for the war. In the Iraq Survey Group's (ISG) interim report to Congress, David Kay, who led the group charged with finding WMD in Iraq, said, "We were all wrong" about the prewar intelligence on Iraq's WMD "and that is most disturbing" (CNN, 2004, January 28). Up to then, the ISG had found no trace of WMD in Iraq. Then, the Bush team retrospectively changed its rationale for the war into Iraq's having *programs* of WMD. Finally, Charles A. Duelfer, who led the ISG after Kay had resigned, concluded in the final 1,000-page ISG report that Iraq had unilaterally destroyed its nuclear program in 1991, chemical weapons stockpile in 1991, and biological weapons program in late 1995, and "there is no credible evidence that Iraq ever resumed producing such weapons" (BBC News, 2004). Finally, as the WMD claims proved false, Bush claimed the war was still worth it since Iraq had *intentions* to produce WMD.

Key Point 6: Iraqi Government–Al-Qaeda link

The U.S. officials (e.g., Rumsfeld and Colin Powell) claimed to have "bullet proof" intelligence linking the Iraqi government and terrorist groups like al-Qaeda. Eventually, after *The 9/11 Commission Report* (2004) had exonerated Iraq of the al-Qaeda links, Rumsfeld said, "To my knowledge, I have not seen any strong, hard evidence that links the two" (Reynolds, 2004b). This is the nth repeat of the history of U.S. intelligence failures related to various countries and groups. In the case of Iraq, however, the intelligence failure has served as a convenient U.S. excuse for the war.

Key Point 7: The oil factor

Deputy Defense Secretary Wolfowitz, a chief architect of the war, made no secret that oil was another factor behind the war. When asked at an Asian security summit in June 2003 why North Korea—with its own nuclear arms—was being treated differently from Iraq, Wolfowitz said, "Let's look at it simply. The most important difference between North Korea and Iraq is that economically, we just had no choice in Iraq. The country swims on a sea of oil" (Wright, 2003). It is worth noting that the initial code name of the invasion was "Operation Iraqi Liberation" (OIL), but later it was changed into "Operation Iraqi Freedom" (OIF) because the acronym OIL wasn't good for public relations purposes.

Key Point 8: Colonizer's logic of occupation

The British army occupied Iraq in 1917 in the name of "liberating" the Iraqis, but then, through puppet regimes, controlled that country for four decades. Similarly, the Bush administration has repeatedly claimed that the war was for the liberation of the Iraqis, and after keeping Iraq under official U.S. control for a year or so, set up an interim government. Iyad Allawi, now the interim prime minister of Iraq, led the CIA-supported Iraqi National Accord, which carried out covert bombing operations inside Iraq during the 1990s. In the run-up to the invasion of Iraq, he provided fake WMD intelligence to the British intelligence organization M16 to provoke the U.S.–British invasion of Iraq. Ahmed Chalabi, who led the U.S.-funded Iraqi National Congress, also provided fake WMD information to the *neocons* (neoconservatives) in the Bush administration. In any civilized country, including the United States, the Allawis or Chalabis would be tried for treason. But in the new colonizer's logic of occupation, they have become allies serving useful strategic purposes.

Key Point 9: The American Mongols

The way American forces behaved during and after the occupation have reminded Iraqis of the year 1258 when the Mongol-Tartar army led by Hulegu Khan raided Baghdad, burned and plundered the city, killed most of its people—including the caliph—and ended the Abbasid caliphate (Hourani, 1991). The Chalabi- and Allawi-type traitors of that day aided the Mongol invaders, who also burned down Baghdad's famous library that included rare ancient Greek classics (Ali, 2003). Soon after occupying Baghdad, the U.S. forces stood by when mobs burned and looted libraries and museums (Hanley, 2003, p. 12). During the invasion, the U.S. forces bombed almost all government buildings except the oil ministry, which they also protected from looting in the aftermath of the raid.

Key Point 10: More than 100,000 civilians killed as a result of the war

More than 100,000 civilians have died in Iraq as a direct or indirect result of the U.S.-led invasion, according to the first-ever scientific field study by a team of American researchers from Johns Hopkins University. The report was published in the October 2004 issue of *The Lancet*, a British medical journal. "Making conservative assumptions, we think that about

100,000 excess deaths or more have happened since the 2003 invasion of Iraq," the researchers stated in the report. These civilian deaths exclude those killed this year (2004) in the deadly assaults on Falluja, where the death rate has been much higher, and far exceed previous armchair estimates. "Violence accounted for most of the excess death and air strikes from coalition forces accounted for the most violent deaths," the report said. The journal's editor asserted that these figures are "shocking" but are a very conservative estimate, adding that the actual figure could be "as high as 200,000."[6] We have counted our dead but didn't tally the Iraqi dead. When asked about the Iraqi dead, General Tommy Franks told journalists, "We don't do body counts" (Steele, 2003).

❖ WAS THE CASE FOR THE WAR MORALLY JUSTIFIED?

For moral justification of a war, the war-initiating party must meet *all* of the *jus ad bellum* conditions mentioned above. Here, I briefly discuss how the Bush team has either met or not met each of these conditions.

Just Cause

A just war must have a just cause, which includes (1) self-defense or retaliation against aggression, and (2) humanitarian intervention on behalf of defenseless victims of aggression (Miller, 1996). The UN Charter (Article 51) explains self-defense in the retaliatory sense, not in the anticipatory sense. Anticipatory self-defense has been the self-serving logic of all aggressors throughout history. This is why the International Court of Justice has put strict limits on the logic of anticipatory self-defense.[7] The Bush administration's case for the war does not meet the standard of self-defense. First, Iraq did not attack the United States. Second, its logic of anticipatory self-defense or preemptive strike is contestable at best because the WMD claims were based on faulty intelligence. Third, even if the claims about Iraq's WMD were true, Iraq could not pose a threat to the United States. Iraq was under U.S. air surveillance and the Iraqi armed forces did not have the means to deliver such weapons to the U.S. targets. But the post–9/11 security concerns prompted Bush and his colleagues to speculate that Iraq could give the WMDs to terrorists to attack the United States. This speculation was legitimate but implausible for the fact that the secular regime of Hussein and the religious extremists like bin Laden were sworn enemies.

The Bush administration's war also does not count as humanitarian intervention. Three different humanitarian situations emerged in Iraq since the 1980s. The U.S. government was complicit in the creation of Iraq's pre-1991 humanitarian situation. According to newly declassified documents, in 1984, Donald H. Rumsfeld "traveled to Iraq to persuade officials there that the United States was eager to improve ties with President Saddam Hussein despite his use of chemical weapons" (Marquis & Shanker, 2003). The post-1991 war humanitarian situation—lack of foods and medicines for Iraqi people—was due to the U.S.-engineered UN sanctions, which killed more than a million Iraqis. Intervention on a third humanitarian situation—the possible attack on Kurds by the Iraqi forces—was already underway as the United States and the United Kingdom had been enforcing no-fly zones over Iraq since 1991. There wasn't any need for a further devastating intervention.

Right Intention

This means that a just war should be waged for the sake of justice and peace, not for any self-interest. As Key Point 5 suggests, the Bush team's motives behind the war were unfair (i.e., not right from an ethical perspective). The key points above (e.g., Key Points 2–8) show that sophistry—deceptive reasoning—has been used to technically justify the war, which the neocons initiated as an "Israeli strategic objective"[8] and as part of their involvement in a racket of arms and oil industries. Soon after the invasion, U.S. corporations that funded Bush's election received no-contest contracts for the rebuilding of Iraqi infrastructure and oil fields, while war boomed sales for the arms industry. As Smedley Butler (n.d.) put it, "WAR is a racket. . . . It is the only one in which the profits are reckoned in dollars and the losses in lives. . . . It is conducted for the benefit of the very few, at the expense of the very many. Out of war a few people make huge fortunes." This description aptly fits this war.

Legitimate Authority

The legitimate authority to declare just war is the sovereign power of a nation state. Bush and his colleagues had the political legitimacy for the war once the U.S. Congress had approved it. But this was ethically problematic because the fake intelligence produced by the CIA misled the Congress into approving a war that was illegal under international law. As philosopher Onora O'Neill (2002) argues, "Democracy can show us what is politically legitimate; it can't show us what is ethically justified" (p. 31). Also, having only political authority is not enough for a war to be just. Other conditions must be met.

Last Resort

The war-initiating party must exhaust all peaceful means of settling disputes before engaging in a just war. As Key Points 2 and 3 above show, the Bush team deliberately planned this war well before 9/11 and initially didn't even want a diplomatic solution to the dispute. Later, Bush and his colleagues went to the UN to obtain international approval of their plans regarding Iraq, not to listen to others, nor to accept UN mediation. The UN was already rigorously monitoring the disarmament of Iraq. During the early 1990s, UNSCOM (UN Special Commission) randomly raided weapons sites in Iraq and inspected destruction of most of its weapons. In fall 1998, when Iraq expelled UNSCOM, charging it with spying for the United States, the Clinton administration unleashed the massive "Desert Fox" bombing operation that destroyed Iraq's conventional defense facilities that had been rebuilt after the 1991 war. Since 1999, UNMOVIC (UN Monitoring, Verification and Inspection Commission) had replaced UNSCOM and was ransacking the country for hidden WMD. Yet, by early February 2003, the Bush administration had amassed troops on Iraqi borders to invade Iraq before the summer heat began. When the international community rejected their logic of a rush to war, they ignored the UN and went ahead with the invasion as they had planned.

Reasonable Chance of Success

In addition to meeting the above conditions, a just war must have a reasonable chance of assured victory. If defeat is inevitable, then wasting lives and property does not make sense. This is a problematic, though pragmatic, consequentialist notion, and it does not account for the values that prompt a nation under attack to fight back regardless of the outcome. Expediency, ignorance, or arrogance of power blinded neocon hawks in the Bush administration to the possible outcomes of the war— the Iraqi civilian and U.S. military casualties, resistance movements, suicide bombings, and the general chaos that prevails in the country today. They just thought that "it was doable" (Wolfowitz, in Woodward, 2002, p. 83), that it would be a "cake walk" (Adelman, 2002; Richard Perle, in various media reports), that the invading forces would be "greeted with sweets and flowers" (Iraqi dissident Kanan Makiya, in Benador Associates, 2003), and that the Iraqi oil sales would pay for the war since the country floats on a "sea of oil" (Wolfowitz, in Wright, 2003). Even Bush himself believed that the U.S. forces would achieve miraculous success, relying more on faith than on facts (Dowd, 2004). In short, the Bush administration did not foresee the worst outcomes of the war.

Proportionality

The principle of proportionality is common to both *jus ad bellum* and *jus in bello*. In *jus ad bellum*, it stipulates that the end and the price of the war be balanced. As suggested in Key Points 9–10 above, the Bush administration's stated aim of the war (which kept changing with the times) does not match the price of lives and property that were to be devastated in the war. More than 100,000 civilians have died as a result of the war. According to another tally, about 16,000 Iraqi civilians have been reported killed in the war ("Iraq body count," 2004). Note that this body count of the 16,000 dead is not based on a systematic study, whereas the count of 100,000 is. Other media reports say that more than 1,200 U.S. soldiers have perished and 8,000 have been maimed for life. In addition, the occupation has cost us $200 billion in the first two years alone. Destruction of the fictitious WMDs was really not worth the financial and human cost.

In sum, the Bush administration has failed to meet almost all the above *jus ad bellum* conditions and, hence, its case for the war remains morally unjustified.

❖ HAS THE WAR BEEN MORALLY CONDUCTED?

To assess this question of the war on Iraq, we have to see if the Bush administration has abided by the *jus in bello* principles of just war theory, which include noncombatant immunity, proportionality, and the humane treatment of the prisoners of war. Let us see how the Bush team has honored these principles.

Noncombatant Immunity

According to this principle, the legitimate targets are combatants, not noncombatants. "According to just war thinking," writes Jean B. Elshtain (2004), the political moralist who considers Bush's war on terrorism a just war, "it is better to risk the lives of one's own combatants than those of enemy noncombatants" (p. 65). The Islamic tradition widens the concept of noncombatant immunity to include the environment, animals, and trees except those killed for food and used as fuels, respectively (Hathout, 2002, p. 24). No doubt, American troops discriminate between combatants and noncombatants and use "precision strikes" to avoid civilian casualties. But that does not change the fact that tens of thousands of civilians have perished and Iraq's environment has been devastated as a direct or indirect result of the war.

There have been many instances in which the U.S. forces did not discriminate between combatants and noncombatants. When it comes to aiming at high-value targets, the U.S. forces on the ground have consistently ignored noncombatant immunity. Civilians have always become "collateral" casualties—unintended but highly expendable beings—whenever they came in between the American guns and the fugitive Iraqi government officials or "insurgents." Since the beginning of the war, U.S. fighters have hit many homes or buildings knowing that civilians would be killed. One such hit was a bomb intended to kill Hussein that actually destroyed a hotel and killed 14 civilians. In an attempt to kill General Ali Hasan al-Majid, the U.S. forces bombed a civilian neighborhood in Basra on April 5, 2003, killing 10 children, women and men of the Hamoodi family that had nothing to do with the Iraqi regime (Dilley, 2003; Singer, 2004). Four months later, General al-Majid was captured alive. About two months after the Hamoodi family killing, U.S. fighters wiped out a convoy of cars near the Syrian border, intending to kill the Saddam Hussein family but actually killing 80 smugglers and local civilians (Singer, 2004).

This bombing pattern has been repeated many times during the postwar fight against the Iraqi resistance. All attacks that risked killing more than 30 civilians required Pentagon approval at the highest level. During the early days of the war, Rumsfeld approved all 50 requests that reached him, allowing the massacre of 1,500 civilians (Singer, 2004, p. 51). In addition, depleted uranium used in bombs and other munitions have contaminated Iraq's environment, while our forces have cut down thousands of rare trees along the streets of Baghdad to keep snipers away (Cockburn, 2003).

In the first half of 2004, U.S. fighters have destroyed homes and buildings in Falluja on a daily basis, claiming to kill terrorists but actually killing civilians in every attack.[9] In April 2004, they turned part of the city of Falluja into rubble in a week, killing more than 600 Iraqis in an attempt to avenge the killing of four U.S. mercenaries. In November 2004, a "final" assault turned the rest of the city into ground zero, killing 52 American troops and more than 2,000 resistance fighters and civilians. According to Francis Boyle (2004), professor of International Law at the University of Chicago, the destruction of Falluja "constitutes a war crime for which Nazis were tried and executed." The 1945 Nuremberg Charter, based on which the Nazis were tried, defines war crime as "wanton destruction of cities, towns or villages" (Article 6b).

Proportionality

In *jus in bello,* this principle holds that a disproportionately greater amount of force against an enemy is morally unacceptable. For example, if country A takes a piece of country B's property by force, country B can use enough force to take just that piece of land back and no more (Moseley, 2004). It is obvious that the force the Bush team has used in this war is way out of proportion. This war resembles a fight in which elephants crush ants under their feet.

Humane Treatment of Prisoners of War

According to the Geneva Convention of 1949, "Prisoners of war must at all times be humanely treated" (Article 13) and never ill-treated or denied food, shelter, and other necessities of life. Unfortunately, the U.S. soldiers have established new precedents by videotaping their acts of torture, rape, sexual humiliation, and sadism on POWs. The Bush administration brushed aside as propaganda the reports of POW abuse when they appeared in the press in May 2003 and did not investigate the allegations until January 2004 when a U.S. military whistleblower brought the graphic torture pictures to the attention of his superiors. Subsequently, those reports came to light as a result of the Taguba report and revelations by CBS's *60 Minutes* in May 2004. The Taguba report described numerous instances of "sadistic, blatant, and wanton criminal abuses" at Abu Ghraib prison. In August 2004, an independent review panel led by former defense secretary James R. Schlesinger faulted the Pentagon's top civilian and military leadership for the abuse of POWs in Iraq. At a press conference on the report, Schlesinger said that nightly sadism by our soldiers turned the Abu Ghraib prison into an "Animal House" (CNN, 2004, September 25). As Hersh (2004) shows, a handful of people framed the policies, often based on selective information, that led to the torture of POWS. All the reported torture techniques were insinuated and approved at the highest level by Donald Rumsfeld. Instead of exploring the truth, the Pentagon officials tried to rig investigations and pressed CBS's *60 Minutes* not to broadcast the stories of abuse.

In sum, the Bush administration has failed to uphold just war principles during the course of the war, as well.

❖ THE QUESTION OF DILEMMA

A dilemma is a situation in which one is faced with two or more equally obliging choices only one of which can be accepted (McConnell, 1996). Any war is a serious undertaking as it involves potential devastation of human lives and property. But what ethical dilemmas did Bush and his colleagues experience in making the case for and waging the Iraq war?

In making the case for the Iraq war, the Bush team had a potential dilemma over a choice between (a) letting the UN inspection play out and ensure Iraqi disarmament or go to war eventually with UN backing, and (b) taking immediate unilateral military action as a matter of anticipatory self-defense. The above discussion makes it clear that this was really not a genuine dilemma. The weight of good reason favors the first choice.

For Bush and his colleagues, too, this was not a case of dilemma at all. For them, the moral course of action has been clear from the beginning. They made the decision for the war as part of their strategic objective well before 9/11 (refer to Key Points 2–7 above) and then campaigned for public consent to the war in a single-minded way. Both in words and deeds they have shown no sign of the vacillation that people experience while dealing with complicated ethical dilemmas. Similarly, in the current operations against the resistance fighters in Iraq, in which civilian lives are at stake, there is no lack of single-mindedness with the Bush team to "stay the course." The final assault to "liberate" Falluja from the resistance fighters has turned the entire city into the rubble of ground zero. The entire operation was sealed off from the media other than those embedded with our troops.

In the worldview of Bush and his war colleagues, the world is divided as polar opposites between good and evil. There are no shades of gray or other positions in between this binary division (Coe, Domke, Graham, John, & Pickard, 2004). In a joint session of Congress on September 20, 2001, President Bush said, "Every nation, in every region, now has a decision to make. Either you are with us, or you are with the terrorists." Bush and his colleagues have since reinforced this black and white distinction of the world, presenting intelligence, which was contested at its best, as a heroic rhetoric of certainty (Hartnett & Stengrim, 2004). They are so blind in their faith that they kept on justifying their actions even when their deceit and hypocrisy were exposed.[10]

With the exception of Colin Powell, none in the Bush team has admitted having any remorse for sending American troops to kill and die in a war based on fabricated or faulty intelligence. Months after the ISG interim report, when no signs of WMDs were found, Powell admitted the mistake, saying that *"the sourcing was inaccurate and wrong and in some cases, deliberately misleading. And for that, I am disappointed and I regret it" [emphasis added]* (Meet the Press transcript for May 16, 2004).

❖ THE BUSH ADMINISTRATION'S MORAL ETHOS

The Sophists observed that "the only reason for acting justly is that one cannot get away with acting unjustly" ("Ethics," 2004). Accordingly, there is a view that war is none of the business of ethics because war itself is a violation of peaceful ethical principles and once at war, especially when victory is set as the ultimate goal, nobody plays by ethical rules (Moseley, 2004). This has been the reality of most wars in history. For example, all means foul and fair were applied to ensure the defeat of Germany and Japan in World War II. This view of war ethics has guided the Bush administration in the Iraq war.

In the above analysis, we have seen that the Bush administration officials are in violation of almost all principles of just war. They did not have a just cause for the war. Their motives behind the war were anything but right. They had hidden agendas and political interests to which they later admitted. The war was illegal according to international law. Bush and his colleagues did not use the war as a last resort, nor did they weigh costs and consequences for the good they thought would come out of the war. They used excessive force against a disarmed and virtually defenseless third-world country. They have ignored noncombatant immunity and tortured prisoners of war.

Basically, the Bush administration has acted self-righteously as the judge, jury, attorney, and police all at the same time just because it could. This "logic of power" is reminiscent of a medieval "might is right" mentality or a social Darwinist philosophy that says only the powerful or the fittest should survive. In the logic of power, there are no worries about "fair" and "foul" play in war.

I find that the line from Shakespeare's *Macbeth* (Act 1, Scene 1, line 11), "Fair is foul and foul is fair" sums up the Bush administration's moral philosophy of war. The three "weird sisters" (witches) that chant these words in the opening scene have no qualms about the fairness or the foulness of what is to unfold in the gory drama. In their amoral consciousness, the foul actions may be fair and the fair actions may be foul.

❖ CONCLUSION

In the book *Predictable Surprises*, Max Bazerman and Michael Watkins (2004) argue that, like the collapse of Enron, 9/11 was not a true surprise. It was largely predictable. Predictable surprises are a common result of leadership failure or organizational recognition failure (pp. x, 161). The Clinton administration officials had enough information about the aims, organization, and methods of al-Qaeda. Yet, they did not "connect the dots" and take care of the security loopholes in our commercial airlines. The Bush administration officials too conducted business in the same mode prior to 9/11, failing to recognize even more specific intelligence about terrorist threats. Similarly, they failed to foresee many clearly predictable post-occupation surprises in Iraq, like the mass looting of the Iraqi museum treasures, the Abu Ghraib prisoner tortures, and the resistance movement.

The concept of organizational recognition failure provides insight into what happened during the course of the Iraq war and why, but it does not mitigate the violation of organizational or leadership ethics in the war. I have shown above that in the war on Iraq, the Bush administration members are in violation of almost all just war principles. For example, they did not have just cause or right intention, nor have they

waged the war as a last resort, weighing well its costs and consequences. They have used disproportionate power, ignored noncombatant immunity, and failed to prevent torture of prisoners of war. Their
moral ethos that emerged in the war is basically an ethos of power.

Discussion Questions

1. To what extent does just war theory represent an ethical pluralism?

2. If you were to redefine just war theory, how would you do it?
   What changes would you make?

3. Conduct your own application of just war theory to the Iraq
   war. What conclusions do you reach about the morality of the
   war and its agency?

4. Compare and contrast your just war analysis of the Iraq war
   with the one presented in this chapter.

5. Use the semiotic commutation test or the golden rule of ethics
   (discussed above under "Just war theory and its application") to
   analyze the ethical implications of the Iraq war. What would the
   war be like if Iraqis were the ones who invaded our country to
   "liberate" us?

6. Identify some historical leaders who used (the killing of) people
   (soldiers and civilians) as a means to political ends and compare
   and contrast their actions to those of President Bush and his
   colleagues.

7. What questions of organizational ethics does the use of people
   as means to political ends raise?

❖ NOTES

1. Karl Weick (1995) defines organizations as "sensemaking systems"
(p. 170). For Anderson and Englehardt (2001), "The term *organization* is not
synonymous with the terms *business, corporation,* or *firm*" (p. 10, italics original); instead, the organization is "a meaningful and significant set of ordered
relationships that is the ongoing product of organizing" (p. 249). Accordingly,
conjoint communicative action, the relational process of membership and the
communicative practices of organizing are three key elements of organizations
(Anderson & Englehardt, 2001).

2. The war has also triggered publication of thousands of popular books in addition to numerous media reports and commentaries. In an Amazon.com search on November 5, 2004, I found 14,006 book references to the key words "Bush Iraq War." While not all these books have the Iraq war as a central theme, the number of those that do is quite significant. I have found that of the 100 books that topped my search list at Amazon.com, 20 are supportive of the war, 25 are noncommittal about it, 40 are critical of it, and the other 6 have little to do with it. Like most popular books, a majority of some 100 scholarly articles, which I found to have discussed the war, share a criticism of the U.S. policies regarding Iraq. But virtually none of these books or journal articles on the war debate represents a contribution by scholars of organizational communication.

3. Relativism represents the view that what is right or good depends on the culture we are in, and there is no way for us to judge what is right or good for another person, group, or culture (Hinman, 1998). This means that moral values are not fixed or universal; they vary according to groups/cultures (conventional/cultural relativism), individuals (subjective relativism or ethical subjectivism), and social situations (situational ethics). In contrast, ethical absolutism holds that there is one right moral position that should be universally applied to moral evaluation in all times and places. It considers actions to be inherently moral or immoral, as we see in Kantian theories, divine rights and divine commands theories (e.g., in Judaism, Christianity, and Islam), and the modern human rights theory. According to Kantian ethics, for example, being a moral agent means being guided by universal principles—moral rules that have no exception under any circumstances. Yet, neither relativism nor universalism is geometrically applicable. True, much morality is relative to cultures and we must respect local traditions, but some moral principles must also apply to all people and in fact "there are some features common to virtually all human moralities" (Ethics, 2004). This is why philosophers and moralists like Louis Pojman (2004), R. M. MacIver (2004), and Martin Luther King, Jr. (2004) agree that tolerance of local customs must end when, for example, they represent racism, torture, genocide, and other violations of human rights like those enshrined in the United Nations Charter: The Universal Declaration of Human Rights, even though these values (rights) are relativistic in origin. Similarly, absolutistic ethics are untenable when dilemmas arise.

4. Perle recently chaired the Defense Policy Board but was forced to resign over conflict of interest; Wolfowitz is deputy defense secretary, Armitage is deputy secretary of the State Department, and Rumsfeld is defense secretary. Wolfowitz has argued since 1992 that it was a mistake to leave Saddam Hussein in power in the 1991 war (Woodward, 2002).

5. The paper text is available at http://www.freerepublic.com/focus/news/860941/posts

6. I could not access the actual report Web site, as I did not have a subscription to *The Lancet*. This abstract of the report is based on its summaries published in the *New York Times* (Rosenthal, 2004), Aljazeerah.com, and the BBC World News Web sites.

7. See Miller (2004) for a brief take on this issue, its historical precedents, and how the world court has limited its potential use.

8. For an overview of this and related issues, see Buchanan (2003, 2004), Chomsky (2003), and http://www.nowarforisrael.com/

9. The pictures of civilian and U.S. soldier casualties are blacked out in the mainstream the U.S. media. For a current portrait of the war, visit http://www.aljazeerah.info/index.htm, http://english.aljazeera.net/HomePage, or http://www.iraqbodycount.net/

10. There are literally numerous Internet resources that expose the "lies" the Bush team has told us about Iraq before and after the war (e.g., Kramer, 2003). Book-length expositions of the lies include *The Politics Of Truth* (Wilson, 2004), *The Five Biggest Lies Bush Told Us* (Scheer, Scheer, & Chaudhry, 2003), *Secrets and Lies: Operation "Iraqi Freedom" and After* (Hiro, 2004), *Worse Than Watergate: The Secret Presidency of George W. Bush* (Dean, 2004), *Weapons of Mass Deception: The Uses of Propaganda in Bush's War on Iraq* (Rampton & Stauber, 2003), and *War on Iraq: What Team Bush Doesn't Want You to Know* (Pitt & Ritter, 2002). This genre of books shows the lies, "dirty tricks," phony intelligence reports, and even staging of heroic actions (e.g., the rescue of Private Jessica Lynch) the Bush administration has used to engineer public consent for the war. They point out that the Bush team's lies are not like the "ordinary" personal lies for which President Bill Clinton was impeached by the House of Representatives (though not by the Senate). John Dean (2004), who was President Nixon's White House counsel, even argues that Bush is impeachable for his lying, cover-ups and paranoid secrecy.

❖ REFERENCES

Adelman, K. (2002, February 13). Cakewalk in Iraq. *The Washington Post*, p. A27.

Ali, T. (2003). *Bush in Babylon: The recolonization of Iraq.* London: Verso.

Anderson, J. A., & Englehardt, E. E. (2001). *The organizational self and ethical conduct: Sunlit virtue and shadow resistance.* Philadelphia: Harcourt College Publishers.

Bazerman, M. H., & Watkins, M. D. (2004). *Predictable surprises: The disasters you should have seen coming and how to prevent them.* Boston: Harvard Business School Press.

BBC News. (2004, October 6). *WMD Report: Key points.* Retrieved October 14, 2004, from http://news.bbc.co.uk/1/hi/world/middle_east/3722016.stm

Benador Associates. (2003, March 17). Transcript of Iraq Seminar with Richard Perle and Kanan Makiya. Retrieved November 29, 2004, from <http://www.benadorassociates.com/article/664>

Boustany, N., & Tyler, P. E. (1990, July 25). US pursues diplomatic solution in Persian Gulf crisis, warns Iraq. *The Washington Post*, p. A17.

Boyle, F. A. (2004, November 15). A war crime in real time: Obliterating Fallujah. *Counterpunch.* Retrieved November 28, 2004, from http://www .counterpunch.org/boyle11152004.html

Buchanan, P. J. (2003, March 24). Whose war? *The American Conservative.*

Buchanan, P. J. (2004). *Where the right went wrong: How neoconservatives subverted the Reagan revolution and hijacked the Bush presidency.* New York: St. Martin's/Thomas Dunne Books.

Bugnion, F. (2002). Just wars, wars of aggression and international humanitarian law. *International Review of the Red Cross, 847*(84), 523–546 (Originally published in French). Retrieved October 13, 2004, from http://www.icrc .org/Web/Eng/siteeng0.nsf/htmlall/5FLCT4/$File/bugnion%20ang% 20.pdf

Bunch, W. (2003, January 27). Invading Iraq not a new idea for Bush clique. 4 years before 9/11, plan was set. *Philadelphia Daily News.* Retrieved October 26, 2004, from http://foi.missouri.edu/evolvingissues/invadingiraq.html

Bush planned Iraq "regime change" before becoming President. (2002, September 15). *Sunday Herald* (Glasgow, UK), p. 1.

Butler, S. (n.d.). *War is a racket.* Retrieved October 24, 2004, from http://lexrex .com/enlightened/articles/warisaracket.htm

Chomsky, N. (2003). *Hegemony or survival: America's quest for global dominance.* New York: Metropolitan Books.

CNN. (2004, January 28). *Transcript: David Kay at Senate hearing.* Retrieved October 22, 2004, from http://www.cnn.com/2004/US/01/28/kay.transcript/

CNN. (2004, September 25). *Report: Abu Ghraib was "Animal House" at night.* Retrieved October 22, 2004, from http://www.cnn.com/2004/US/ 08/24/abughraib.report/

Cockburn, P. (2003, October 12). *US soldiers bulldoze farmers' crops.* http:// news.independent.co.uk/world/middle_east/story.jsp?story=452375

Coe, K., Domke, D., Graham, E. S., John, S. L., & Pickard, V. W. (2004). No shades of gray: The binary discourse of George W. Bush and an echoing press. *Journal of Communication, 54*(2), 234–252.

Dean, J. W. (2004). *Worse than Watergate: The secret presidency of George W. Bush.* New York: Little, Brown.

Dilley, R. (2003, April 16). Basra bombing "destroyed my family." *BBC News Online.* Retrieved October 10, 2004, from http://news.bbc.co.uk/1/hi/ world/middle_east/2952339.stm

Dowd, M. (2004, October 21). Casualties of faith. *New York Times,* p. A29.

Elshtain, J. B. (2004). *Just war against terror: The burden of American power.* New York: Basic Books.

Ethics. (n.d.). Retrieved September 16, 2004, from *Encyclopedia Britannica Online.* http://search.eb.com/eb/article?tocId=60000

Gelb, L. H., & Rosenthal, J. A. (2003, May/June). The rise of ethics in foreign policy: Reaching a values consensus. *Foreign Affairs,* pp. 2–7.

Hanley, C. J. (2003, April 16). Looters burn and ransack main libraries. *Toronto Star*, p. 12.

Hartnett, S. J., & Stengrim, L. A. (2004). "The whole operation of deception": Reconstructing President *Bush's* rhetoric of weapons of mass destruction. *Cultural Studies/Critical Methodologies*, 4(2), pp. 152–197.

Hashimi, S. H. (2002). *Islamic political ethics: Civil society, pluralism, and conflict.* Princeton, NJ: Princeton University Press

Hathout, M. (2002). *Jihad vs. terrorism.* Pasadena, CA: Dawn Books.

Hersh, S. (2004). *Chain of command: The road from 9/11 to Abu Ghraib.* New York: HarperCollins.

Hinman, L. M. (1998). *Ethics: A pluralistic approach to moral theory* (2nd ed.). Philadelphia: Harcourt Brace College Publishers.

Hiro, D. (2004). *Secrets and lies: Operation "Iraqi freedom" and after.* New York: Nation Books.

Hourani, A. (1991). *A short history of the Arab peoples.* Cambridge, MA: The Belknap Press of Harvard University Press.

Iraq body count. (2004). Retrieved October 19, 2004, from http://www.iraq bodycount.net/

Kelsay, J., & Johnson, J. T. (1991). *Just war and jihad: Historical and theoretical perspectives on war and peace in Western and Islamic traditions.* Westport, CT: Greenwood Press.

King, M. L. Jr. (2004). I have a dream. In C. Sommers & F. Sommers (Eds.), *Vice and Virtue in everyday life: Introductory readings in ethics* (pp. 198–202). Singapore: Wadsworth.

Kramer, K. (2003, March 23). *A list of Bush lies.* Retrieved October 23, 2004, from http://www.buzzflash.com/contributors/03/03/27_lies.html

MacIver, R. M. (2004). The deep beauty of the golden rule. In C. Sommers & F. Sommers (Eds.), *Vice and virtue in everyday life: Introductory readings in ethics* (pp. 194–198)). Singapore: Wadsworth.

Marquis, C., & Shanker, T. (2003, December 23). Rumsfeld made Iraq overture in '84 despite chemical raids. *New York Times*, p. A10.

McConnell, T. C. (1996). Moral residue and dilemmas. In H. E. Mason (Ed.), *Moral dilemmas and moral theory* (pp. 36–47). Oxford: Oxford University Press.

Meet the Press transcript for May 16. (2004). Retrieved November 1, 2004, from http://www.msnbc.msn.com/id/4992558/

Miller, R. (2004). *Self-defense doesn't fly.* Retrieved October 14, 2004, from http://www.robincmiller.com/afghan2.htm

Miller, R. B. (1996). *Casuistry and modern ethics: A poetics of practical reasoning.* Chicago: University of Chicago Press.

Moseley, A. (2004). Just war theory. *The Internet Encyclopedia of Philosophy.* Retrieved October 12, 2004, from <http://www.iep.utm.edu/j/justwar .htm

Netanyahu, B. (2002, September 17). US must beat Saddam to the punch; If he gets nukes before we get him, it's all over [Commentary adapted from remarks Netanyahu made to the House Government Reform Committee]. *Chicago Sun-Times*, p. 23.

The 9/11 Commission Report. (2004). Final report of the national commission on terrorist attacks upon the United States, official government edition. Retrieved October 20, 2004, from http://www.gpoaccess.gov/911/

O'Neill, O. (2002). *A question of trust: The BBC Reith lectures 2002*. Cambridge, UK: Cambridge University Press.

Pitt, W. R., & Ritter, S. (2002). *War on Iraq: What team Bush doesn't want you to know*. New York: Context Books.

Pojman, L. (2004). Who's to judge? In C. Sommers & F. Sommers (Eds.), *Vice and virtue in everyday life: Introductory readings in ethics* (pp. 179–189). Singapore: Wadsworth.

Project for the New American Century (PNAC). (1998, January 26). [letter to Clinton] Retrieved October 12, 2004, from http://www.newamerican century.org/iraqclintonletter.htm.

Rachels, J. (2003). *The elements of moral philosophy*. Boston: McGraw-Hill.

Rampton, S., & Stauber, J. (2003). *Weapons of mass deception: The uses of propaganda in Bush's war on Iraq*. New York: Jeremy P. Tarcher/Penguin.

Reynolds, P. (2004a, September 16). Choice of words matters. *BBC News Online*. Retrieved October 15, 2004, from http://news.bbc.co.uk/1/hi/world/middle_east/3661976.stm

Reynolds, P. (2004b, October 5). Rumsfeld weakens a pillar of war. *BBC News Online*. Retrieved October 28, 2004, from http://news.bbc.co.uk/1/hi/world/americas/3717024.stm

Rosenthal, E. (2004, October 29). Study puts Iraqi deaths of civilians at 100,000. *New York Times*. Retrieved November 1, 2004, from http://www.nytimes.com/2004/10/29/international/europe/29casualties.html

Scheer, C., Scheer, R., & Chaudhry, L. (2003). *The five biggest lies Bush told us*. New York: Akashic Books & Seven Stories Press.

Scott, P. D. (2004, September 1). How to fight terrorism: A reading of the 9/11 Commission report. *California Monthly, 155*(1). Retrieved October 25, 2004, from http://www.mindfully.org/Reform/2004/Fight-Terrorism-Scott 1sep04.htm

Singer, P. (2004). *The president of good & evil: The ethics of George W. Bush*. New York: Dutton.

Steele, J. (2003, May 28). Body counts. *The Guardian*. Retrieved November 1, 2004, from http://www.guardian.co.uk/usa/story/0,12271,965235, 00.html

Timmerman, K. R. (1991). *The death lobby: How the West armed Iraq*. Boston: Houghton Mifflin.

United States Institute of Peace (USIP). (2003, January). Would an invasion of Iraq be a "Just war"? *Special Report 98*.

Weick, Karl E. (1995). *Sensemaking in organizations.* Thousand Oaks, CA: Sage.

The White House. (2001, August 9). *Remarks by the president on stem cell research.* Retrieved October 25, 2004, from http://www.whitehouse.gov/news/releases/2001/08/20010809–2.html

Wilson, J. (2004). *The Politics of truth: Inside the lies that led to the war and betrayed my wife's CIA identity—A diplomat's memoir.* New York: Carroll & Graff.

Woodward, B. (2002). *Bush at war.* New York: Simon & Schuster.

Wright, G. (2003, June 4). Wolfowitz: Iraq war was about oil. *The Guardian.* Retrieved October 19, 2004, from http://www.commondreams.org/headlines03/0604–10.htm

The National College Registration Board

A Case Study in Organizational Legitimacy

Rebecca Meisenbach

This case examines the communication strategies used to build the legitimacy of a small, student-run company that sold debit cards to college students. It also explores stakeholders' responses to its strategies, as well as the company's efforts to manage the ensuing crisis. The case raises questions regarding the openness and candor of the company and the subsequent impact on its relationships with students, parents, and college administrators.

In April 1998, college administrators across the United States began fielding calls from confused parents regarding a mailing about a national campus card. Campus-specific identification cards, which serve a variety of functions from providing dorm access to dining hall money and library checkout privileges, are standard issue at most institutions of higher education. The Campus Card resembled these identification cards by promising campus purchasing privileges and discounts through a debit checking account card. However, University Student Services, Inc., and specifically its National College Registration

111

Board (NCRB) subsidiary, were drawing attention and lots of questions about their Campus Card. The company's debit card was soon labeled a scam in the press ("Fraudulent Card Company," 1998; "Scammers to Pay," 1998), and the company closed its doors after a July 8, 1998, settlement was negotiated by 36 attorneys general. On the one hand, the case appears to be one of obviously unlawful fraud, but on the other hand, the company appears to have had a legitimate core technology— a debit card designed for and aimed at meeting the needs of college students and their parents. NCRB's story is complicated and offers insight into the roles of rhetoric, responsibility, and legitimacy in determining an organization's survival. At the same time, it highlights tensions that businesses and their managers frequently face in trying to balance what *can* be done with what *should* be done. Varied and competing determinations of what should be done further complicate such cases, illustrating difficulties of successfully negotiating legitimacy and raising crucial questions about whether and how to use available means of persuasion in pursuit of organizational legitimacy. What options did NCRB have to market its product and build its reputation? What did different groups believe it was right for the company to do, and how did NCRB negotiate and position itself amidst these various expectations both before and during the controversy?

Legitimacy has been defined as "a generalized perception or assumption that the actions of an entity are desirable, proper, or appropriate within some socially constructed system of norms, values, beliefs, and definitions" (Suchman, 1995, p. 574). In other words, legitimacy addresses public acceptability of organizations. Hearit (1995) offers a more rhetorically based definition of legitimacy, describing corporate social legitimacy as "the rhetorically constructed and publicly recognized congruence between the values of a corporation and those of a larger social system in which it operates" (p. 3). Organizations rarely, if ever, "convince" physically; they rely on rhetorical persuasion to achieve their goals (Cheney & McMillan, 1990; Llewellyn, 1998). NCRB created a variety of messages in its attempts to persuade publics of its legitimacy.

There are several different rhetorical methods by which organizations may seek and build legitimacy. First, an organization may choose to adapt activities and methods of operating to conform to society's perceptions of legitimacy standards (Dowling & Pfeffer, 1975). Suchman (1995) referred to this first method as conforming to the environment. Berger (1967) developed a similar strategy in his discussion of plausibility alignment, arguing that organizations must move to align with society's needs and values in order to survive. A second legitimacy strategy involves changing and moving public perceptions to match an organization's unchanged values and positions (Dowling & Pfeffer, 1975). Changing public perceptions is more difficult than changing an organization's position and so it is less successfully and less frequently used by organizations. In the search for legitimacy, an organization may also use a third legitimacy-building strategy—using rhetoric to identify itself with other legitimate organizations (Dowling & Pfeffer, 1975). Use of these strategies is perceived typically as a route to organizational success, yet their use contributed to ethical and legal problems for NCRB and its founders.

❖ MODEST BEGINNINGS

In the fall of 1996, a group of four undergraduate students in the University of Pennsylvania's prestigious Wharton School of Business turned what started as a class management project into a real business (Sherwin, 1998b). Students Chris Cononico, John Guiljord, Matthew Levenson, and Michael Vaughn turned to parents and friends to finance their endeavor. Cononico argued that they had taken the project "way past the class" (LaPlaca, 1996).

Their organization, University Student Services, Inc. (USS), introduced a debit card, named the QuakerCard, which could be used instead of cash at local businesses around Penn's campus. USS initially negotiated contracts with 11 favorite student businesses, providing the stores with free card-reading machines in exchange for a small percentage of QuakerCard purchases going to USS and a small discount being passed on to the user. QuakerCard users chose from five different plans and deposited money into their QuakerCard accounts. These funds were kept in a trust account with a Great Neck area accounting firm, where the mother of one of the students worked (LaPlaca, 1996). The funds could be used at any time during the semester, and any unused money could be refunded at the end of each semester. Furthermore, users could call an automated online system to report lost or stolen cards, to obtain a balance, and to request printed statements (Axt, 1996).

At the time, Penn offered very limited dining options on its official school debit card over the weekends. Even school officials noted that the card would help fill this void on the weekends (LaPlaca, 1996). USS marketed the card as a safe, cashless way for students to purchase discounted food close to campus through a meal card accepted at all hours and on weekends at specific locations.

❖ EARLY PROBLEMS

The QuakerCard experienced a few difficulties when Penn officials reported receiving calls from confused families during the initial roll-out of the program. Some appeared to confuse the QuakerCard with a national student discount program called the Student Advantage Card. In addition, Penn's Dining Services and Penn Student Agencies, which operated the official school meal card program, reported fielding dozens of calls from parents and students who thought that the QuakerCard was affiliated with Penn. The generic company name of University Student Services, Inc., was cited as a potential source of the confusion. Dining Services Meal Contracts and Marketing Coordinator Adam Sherr, who handled many calls about the QuakerCard, noted, "Most people are disturbed when they find out the QuakerCard is not affiliated with Penn. We are receiving more calls everyday [sic]" (LaPlaca, 1996).

The school warned the company not to imply that the QuakerCard was officially connected to the school ("Campus Card Gives," 1998; LaPlaca, 1996). Penn's registrar's office released a statement indicating that the QuakerCard was in "no way affiliated, sponsored by, nor endorsed by Penn" (LaPlaca, 1996). The school's general counsel investigated the matter, noting that it was concerned both about the use of Penn's name and about potentially misleading impressions. However, while the school's general counsel investigated the corporation, the university did not press any charges against the company, and by the second year the QuakerCard had well over 3,000 customers using the cards (Lanman, 1997).

As further evidence of the QuakerCard's initial success, Penn began pursuing a similar feature for its student ID card in 1997, attempting to add a small debit function to its PennCard (Lanman, 1997). At the time, the QuakerCard was valid at over 30 local businesses. Even after the QuakerCard had folded, students referred to the card and its program as a positive model for the PennCard to follow in expanding its services off campus (Undergraduate Assembly, 2000–2001).

❖ GOING NATIONAL: SEEKING LEGITIMACY

In 1998, while still operating the QuakerCard, University Student Services, Inc., decided to develop its product on a national scale. On April 8, 1998, USS's newly created subsidiary, the National College Registration Board (NCRB), mailed approximately 1.8 million information packets to college-bound high school seniors and their parents. The mailing introduced a Campus Card to be used for purchasing privileges and discounts on college campuses. The mailing indicated a $25 fee requirement to open an account. NCRB was offering a debit card, a type of credit card that has become common in recent years, where charges are deducted from an existing fund. By mailing their solicitation, NCRB used a standard communication channel for setting up credit card accounts and college registration.

Students and their parents received a detailed and professional mailing. The original mailing included a high-quality brochure showing pictures of the card, describing its services, and even providing quotes from satisfied users. The information led many readers to believe that this card was a required part of attending the college of their choice. The reader is told the following:

> The Campus Card is the student identification card issued to all registered college students. It is required for many services and purchasing privileges at whichever college or university your student chooses to attend. Students should also expect to receive a second card when they arrive on campus in the fall for access to school buildings among other functions. Both cards are an essential part of a student's everyday life and should be carried at all times.

NCRB's rhetoric tried to convince publics that the Campus Card was an essential item for the college student. It was the assertion that the card is required that caused the most trouble for NCRB and the Campus Card.

NCRB also used other persuasive strategies. The original mailing directed students to the organization's home page. Corporations are increasingly expected to maintain a professional Web site (White & Raman, 2000); thus, Web sites are also a public-endorsed communication medium. NCRB's Web site (www.campuscard.org)[1] restated the information from the original mailing and provided links to the home pages of colleges and universities across the United States.

The original mailing to prospective Campus Card users included a reference to several memberships in established agencies. The National Association of College and University Business Officers (NACUBO), the National Association of College Auxiliary Services (NACUS), and the National Association of Campus Card Users (NACCU) were all listed at the bottom of the introductory letter in the original mailing as member associations. Although not well known by the average American, these three well-established organizations all have their own offices and Web sites. University Student Services, Inc., had paid membership fees for all three organizations.

The mailing also tried to tie the company closely to colleges and universities across the United States. In addition to the Web site's list of links to many of the colleges' home pages, the original mailing also included a two-page document listing colleges and universities across the nation. Students were asked to fill in the corresponding number on a Scantron sheet of the institution they would be attending as part of signing up for the Campus Card. It should be noted that the company could have asked students to write down the name of the college they would be attending without using the official-looking listing of universities. This method would have cost the organization less money, but it might not have been as efficient. The brochure also implied official ties to schools by showing a sample card called a Wolverine Card with the University of Michigan printed across the bottom. The brochure stated, "Your Campus Card ID is specific to your own school."

Finally, it appears that NCRB used symbolism to imply a connection with the well-known organization, The College Board. The College Board is an organization based in Princeton, New Jersey, that commands respect from high school students and their parents as the administering body for the Scholastic Achievement Test (SAT). The combination of NCRB's name (National College Registration Board) and its business address (Princeton, New Jersey) would almost instinctively make the targeted public associate the mailing with The College Board. The mailing envelope was even the same size as The College Board mailings of SAT test scores.

Interestingly, NCRB did not take advantage of a less contestable potential source of legitimation. There was no mention in the original mailing of the small-scale success and legitimacy of the QuakerCard at Penn. The successful product that brought University Student Services, Inc., into being was curiously omitted from the original mailing to students. The company could have used the QuakerCard as proof of the company's good intentions and track record, thus persuading the public to approve of the organization's methods and linking itself to an existing legitimate program.

Publics Respond: Challenges to Legitimacy

The confusion surrounding the rollout of the earlier QuakerCard was repeated during the rollout of the Campus Card with more serious results. Colleges and universities began receiving calls from confused and concerned parents and students about NCRB's Campus Card. As questions began to arise about the Campus Card, NCRB faced many threats to its legitimacy. Ironically, many of the challenges to the organization's legitimacy stemmed from the company's use of strategies described above that had been designed to enhance legitimacy. A wide range of publics, including students, parents, higher education administrators, and legislators, questioned whether NCRB's product really matched societal expectations, and many of the legitimate organizations to which NCRB had linked itself in the original mailing questioned and denied the implied relationships.

First and most damaging to the legitimacy of the Campus Card, publics questioned the appropriateness of the rhetoric suggesting that students were required to have a Campus Card. When consumers began calling colleges to ask about the card, it quickly became apparent that the card was neither required nor endorsed by the schools, as many argued had been suggested by the mailing. Many colleges (e.g., Carleton College, Harvard University, University of Texas) posted information on their Web sites reinforcing that the Campus Card was not required to be a student at their schools. Universities and colleges were upset about the confusion over whether the Campus Card was the official card issued by their campuses. Leo Reisberg (1998), a writer for *The Chronicle of Higher Education*, noted that most institutions of higher education immediately labeled the Campus Card a scam. Writers for *The Daily Pennsylvanian* recalled similar levels of confusion that had surrounded the implementation of the QuakerCard (Reiss, 1998; Sherwin, 1998a).

As the crisis escalated, the legitimacy of the debit feature of the Campus Card was also questioned. Media reports suggested that the company did not yet have a contract agreement with any bank to handle its debit card accounts (Sherwin, 1998b), and NCRB never explicitly responded to these challenges. NCRB's original mailing asked students to wait for further information before sending in money for the debit accounts.

The validity of the other Campus Card features was also challenged on various levels. Universities charged that the majority of the discounts offered by the Campus Card could be obtained by anyone with proof of student status. In other cases they challenged the veracity of the discount claims. For example, a statement on Harvard University's Web site noted, "The claims [NCRB makes] of discounts offered to Campus Card holders cannot be substantiated in general; the 32% textbook and school supply discount they advertise is *not* offered through the Harvard Coop, the primary textbook seller for the university" ("NCRB Campus Card," n.d.).

Attorneys general quickly joined the voices condemning the Campus Card as a scam aimed at their constituents. Maryland attorney general Joseph Curran was quoted by the *Daily Pennsylvanian* as saying, "there were serious doubts as to whether the cards themselves were even worth the paper they were printed on" (Sherwin, 1998a). New York attorney general Dennis Vacco suggested, "In reality, it was nothing more than a rip-off" (Sherwin, 1998a). Minnesota attorney general Hubert Humphrey III declared that "NRCB gets an 'F' for trying to cheat Minnesota students with its Campus Card scam" (Sherwin, 1998a).

All three of the national organizations listed at the bottom of the introductory letter, as well as The College Board in Princeton, New Jersey, publicly disassociated themselves from NCRB and USS, Inc., through press releases and statements on their Web sites. For example, NACCU published a disclaimer on its Web site saying, "This mailing and promotion was done without the knowledge of NACCU and our name was used without our permission and NACCU has no relationship with this promotion and in no way endorses the product offered" (NACCU, 1998). Many people felt that publics interpreted the inclusion of the names of these organizations as proof of endorsement or sponsorship of NCRB's Campus Card. The College Board responded to NCRB's "hidden" references to its organization by announcing that The College Board had no affiliation with NCRB and that it had not sold NCRB its mailing list (Student Search Service, 1998).

The unofficial use of college and university names and trademarks also hurt NCRB's legitimacy. Critics of the program noted that the use of school names and the presence of school links on the company's Web site implied a direct association with the colleges and universities. While the company probably included a University of Michigan logo on the sample Campus Card to increase the product's legitimacy, its inclusion eventually had the opposite effect. University of Michigan officials soon began investigating the case. A representative of the Association of Collegiate Licensing Administrators said that using the university's trademark implied that the Campus Card originated from the school (Reiss, 1998). Furthermore, some universities questioned the links to their institutional Web sites provided on NCRB's Web page. These questionable operating methods added to the case against the legitimacy of NCRB. Officials implied that a legitimate organization would not make unlicensed use of trademarks and university names. The public rejections of these implicit and explicit legitimacy claims hurt the reputation and legitimacy of the company, labeling its actions and claims of association as illegitimate.

NCRB Responds: Rebuilding Legitimacy

Thus far, this case has covered NCRB's original attempts to build legitimacy through a mass mailing and the negative public responses to these attempts. NCRB faced a legitimacy crisis as publics questioned whether the organization had the right to exist. The company's president, Matt Levenson, released a statement on April 24, 1998, that attempted to respond to these concerns, trying to realign NCRB with public values and expectations. He clarified that the Campus Card was a debit card designed for students with special discounts attached and that it was not officially affiliated with or required by any institution of higher education. Furthermore, he pledged to offer a refund to anyone who felt they had registered for the card "without fully understanding the nature of the services offered" (Levenson, 1998).

Levenson addressed the basic charges against the validity of the various features of the Campus Card. In response to confusion about whether the card was required and affiliated with particular colleges, he stated,

> The Campus Card program is offered by the National College Registration Board, which is a private organization that currently has no affiliation with or endorsement from any college, university, or other institutional or educational organization. The Campus Card has no affiliation with any school ID or charge cards issued to students by their college or university. The Campus Card is a separate debit card and discount program. It is not required, sponsored, or approved by any college, university, or educational institution or association.

The majority of the letter focused on clarifying the implied associations with various other legitimate organizations through questions and answers. Levenson clarified that although his company was a member in good standing of all three campus card organizations, these organizations did not directly support NCRB or the Campus Card program. Furthermore, Levenson wrote that the Web links to colleges and universities were included only as a helpful resource for students, and that the list of schools in the original mailing was for tracking purposes to inform NCRB of which schools the students were attending. He further asserted the card's true function as "a debit card affiliated with a national credit card organization that will allow parents and students to set aside funds specifically for the student's essential living needs." The letter did not say much about the details of the discount program, but did clarify that book discounts would be available only by purchasing textbooks on NCRB's Web site.

Levenson also used the April 24 statement to introduce concerned individuals and organizations to the existing legitimacy of the Campus Card's predecessor, the QuakerCard:

> The company currently offers Penn students the QuakerCard, a closed network debit card program that utilizes local merchants in the Penn community. The QuakerCard continues to serve the needs of the students at the University of Pennsylvania while managing millions of dollars in deposits annually.

The company had taken down its Web site at this point, but Levenson noted that a revised site would be up soon. However, the Web site never returned. His detailed letter did not stop the public pressures to shut down NCRB and the Campus Card.

❖ SHUTTING DOWN

All of these threats to NCRB's legitimacy worked quickly, stripping the company of its core technology and freezing its operations as early as May 1998. Crisis communication theory suggests that if a company acts quickly, it may be able to redefine the issue. NCRB did respond on April 24 with the open letter, 20 days after the original mailing, but by then many agencies had contacted NCRB, strongly recommending further company clarification, and the wheels were already turning in the offices of attorneys general.

Levenson's statement did little to stop the tide of ill feelings toward the company that culminated in the July 8 settlement involving Levenson, Cononico, and Vaughn. By the middle of May, QuakerCard users found their cards inactive, with the card-reading devices having been removed from area businesses (Sherwin, 1998b). The local office was closed with only a brief note on the door explaining that the company was permanently closed and that refunds would soon be mailed.

As complaints and concerns were mounting, the New Jersey attorney general's office launched a full-scale investigation. Post offices began intercepting letters from NCRB and did not deliver them. As part of an agreement to avoid formal charges on the national level, NCRB issued refunds to all the more than 6,000 students who had already sent in the $25 fee for the Campus Card. Uncashed $25 application checks to NCRB were returned. The company also faced possible charges for fraud and unapproved trademark use (Reiss, 1998). A July 8, 1998, agreement formally put University Student Services and the National College Registration Board out of business, refunded all money to Campus Card customers, and prohibited the company from doing business for three years. Attorney general offices and college campuses declared the result a victory. Maryland attorney general Joseph Curran said, "I'm happy we stopped this company before more parents and students were defrauded" (Sherwin, 1998a).

❖ DISCUSSION

Where did this young company go wrong? Did NCRB set out to run a nationwide scam? It is hard to believe that students enrolled in such a prestigious school of business would be attempting to deliberately scam the country, but recent years have revealed many examples of companies and their leaders knowingly engaging in unlawful activities. NCRB's core technology ostensibly was a debit card designed specifically for college students with discounts and a discount text-book-purchasing program. However, its claims to legitimacy and its navigation of the legitimation process met with significant resistance and rejection by its stakeholders. This case has presented the communication strategies used to build legitimacy in the original mailing, public responses to the various strategies, and NCRB's rhetoric in attempting to manage the ensuing legitimacy crisis. In investigating the case, it was surprising how many of the company's practices appear to match corporate standards of legitimate business practices.

Was there one particular strategy that crossed the line or was it the combination of so many legitimacy-seeking strategies? The case raises important questions about the ethical distinctions between *observing* the available means of persuasion in a given situation and *using* them.

This case has focused on the ethical communicative aspects of the legitimacy-seeking strategies and processes of a young organization. A legitimacy crisis is a crisis of values and actions of both organizations and publics. NCRB used rhetorical strategies during the initial announcement of the Campus Card as it tried to match its activities to society's standards and tried to link itself to several legitimate organizations. However, NCRB may have hurt itself more in the long run by suggesting practices, endorsements, and connections that it had not yet earned or developed according to public perception. After facing public disapproval, the organization made one attempt to rebuild its lost credibility, but ultimately failed and was forced to close its doors.

This case also highlights some concerns about strategically pursuing legitimacy by revealing the dangers of trying too hard to establish legitimacy too quickly. Even as organizations recognize the importance of succeeding in the marketplace and of obtaining legitimacy, they must not forget society's larger values and constraints on organizational behavior. Scholars and practitioners alike can see in this example that legitimacy cannot be pursued without consideration of whether it is right to use the legitimacy-building strategies. Organizations as well as scholars need to remain mindful of the dangers of treating legitimacy as a product that is easily sought and obtained through specific marketing strategies.

Discussion Questions

1. Where did NCRB go wrong in its promotion of its debit cards? Or did it go wrong?

2. How can NCRB's efforts be seen as attempts to build and regain legitimacy and which of these strategies would you have used in this situation?

3. What other types of legitimacy claims could NCRB have presented for public evaluation?

4. What ethical standards legitimate the actions and choices of NCRB? Which standards condemn NCRB? (Think about what standards you relied on in question #1 to determine the ethicality of NCRB's actions.)

5. Who, besides NCRB and its founders, might be held at least partly responsible and accountable for the company's actions? Why?

6. What are the implications and consequences of colleges, attorneys general, and the press rhetorically labeling the controversy "a scam"?

7. How appropriate were the punishments meted out to the founders of NCRB? Would you have resolved the situation differently? If so, how?

❖ NOTE

1. As of November 2003, this Web address was operated by a group completely unrelated to NCRB.

❖ REFERENCES

Axt, J. (1996, September 5). Wawa, LeBus say they will not yet accept QuakerCard. *The Daily Pennsylvanian*. Retrieved November 15, 2003, from http://www.dailypennsylvanian.com/vnews/display.v/ART/3adb21d498ce8?in_archive=1

Berger, P. (1967). *The sacred canopy*. Garden City, NY: Doubleday.

Campus Card gives refunds to students. (1998, September). *Direct Marketing*, pp. 14–15.

Cheney, G., & McMillan, J. J. (1990). Organizational rhetoric and the practice of criticism. *Journal of Applied Communication Research, 18*, 93–114.

Dowling, J., & Pfeffer, J. (1975). Organizational legitimacy: Social values and organizational behavior. *Pacific Sociological Review, 18*(1), 122–135.

Fraudulent card company agrees to pay students and parents. (1998, July 14). *Christian Science Monitor*, p. B3.

Hearit, K. M. (1995). Mistakes were made: Organizations, apologia, and crises of social legitimacy. *Communication Studies, 46*, 1–17.

LaPlaca, J. (1996, August 30). Students develop restaurant debit card. *The Daily Pennsylvanian*. Retrieved November 15, 2003, from http://www.dailypennsylvanian.com/vnews/display.v/ART/3adb21ddf0e9d?in_archive=1

Lanman, S. (1997, September 18). Will PennCard battle QuakerCard? *The Daily Pennsylvanian*. Retrieved November 15, 2003, from http://www.dailypennsylvanian.com/vnews/display.v/ART/3adb243155d99?in_archive=1

Levenson, M. (1998, April 24). *To all interested parties*. Retrieved October 6, 1998, from http://www.nacubo.org/website/campuscard_ltr.html

Llewellyn, J. T. (1998). Evaluating corporate claims of social responsibility: Developing a citizen checklist. *Research in Corporate Social Performance and Policy, 15,* 89–106.

NACCU. (1998). *DISCLAIMER!* Retrieved October 6, 1998, from http://www .naccu.org/NCRB/disclaimer.html

NCRB Campus Card scam targets incoming students. (n.d.). Retrieved October 6, 1998, from http://www.huid.harvard.edu/frame_bot_ncrb.html

Reisberg, L. (1998, June 26). Company that offered controversial debit card for students shuts down. *The Chronicle of Higher Education,* p. A40.

Reiss, J. (1998, May 15). QuakerCard spurs controversy. *The Daily Pennsylvanian.* Retrieved November 15, 2003, from http://www.daily pennsylvanian. com/vnews/display.v/ART/3adb27ae449c2?in_archive=1

Scammers to pay up. (1998, August). *State Government News, 41*(6), 9.

Sherwin, E. (1998a, July 16). QuakerCard operators settle with 35 state AGs. *The Summer Pennsylvanian.* Retrieved November 15, 2003, from http:// www.dailypennsylvanian.com/vnews/display.v/ART/3adb27753c3f5? in_archive=1

Sherwin, E. (1998b, September 4). QuakerCard company folds without warning, settles legal charges. *The Daily Pennsylvanian.* Retrieved November 15, 2003, from http://www.dailypennsylvanian.com/vnews/display.v/ART/ 3adb276420eb4?in_archive=1

Student Search Service (1998, May 11). *Board announces no affiliation with NCRB.* Retrieved February 12, 1999, from http://www.collegeboard.org/press/ html/980511.html

Suchman, M. (1995). Managing legitimacy: Strategic and institutional approaches. *Academy of Management Review, 20*(3), 571–610.

Undergraduate Assembly. (2000–2001). *Proposal to expand PennCard access to off-campus locations.* Retrieved November 15, 2003, from http://dolphin .Penn.edu/~ua/resources/documents/2000–2001/penncard.html

White, C., & Raman, N. (2000). The World Wide Web as a public relations medium: The use of research, planning, and evaluation in web site development. *Public Relations Review, 25,* 405–419.

The Sulzer Hip Replacement Recall Crisis

A Patient's Perspective

Keri K. Stephens, Scott C. D'Urso, and Penny Holmes

This case discusses a product recall that resulted from a manufacturing defect and the degree to which the company distributed accurate and timely information to affected patients. More specifically, the case examines the crisis communication of Sulzer Orthopedics and its efforts to negotiate the interests of various stakeholders, while limiting liability. Written from the perspective of a patient, the case raises interesting questions regarding organizational duties related to product liability. It also provides valuable insights into how organizational communication may have both short- and long-term effects on its relationship with patients and physicians, among others.

Organizations can find themselves in ethical dilemmas when unexpected problems occur. Product recalls resulting from manufacturing defects are one of those unexpected situations because companies need to decide when to announce the recall, how to distribute information, and whether they will compensate those affected adversely. One major challenge that companies face when they need to recall a product is how to remedy the situation without exposing them-selves to extensive financial liability. If they say the wrong things, the crisis can bankrupt them.

Companies that manufacture medical products have a particularly difficult dilemma during a crisis. Typically, they have many constituent groups—*stakeholders*—that they need to simultaneously please. As they communicate to diverse groups such as patients, doctors, the public, and the Food and Drug Administration, the actual words they use can matter substantially. In the case that follows, Sulzer Orthopedics, a medical device manufacturer, is faced with the dilemma of how and when to tell their various stakeholders that one of their products, an artificial hip, was contaminated during production. This is particularly sensitive because this recalled product was surgically implanted inside of people and now requires additional surgery to remove it.

Whereas many organizational ethical issues are explored from the organization's viewpoint, this case includes the voice of Tom, a patient experiencing complications after both of his hips were replaced. Here, we provide his perspective to show the severity of the recall situation, and the ramifications of poorly executed communication decisions. In Tom's efforts to seek information about the recall, he relies heavily on the Internet because Sulzer chooses to avoid direct communication with the affected victims. By accessing the Internet, Tom realizes that Sulzer is telling different stories to its various stakeholders, likely for legal reasons. The case that follows is presented in two parts: (a) a historical description of a product recall that resulted in the initial communicative response of Sulzer Orthopedics, and (b) the continued development of the case including latter communicative responses by Sulzer Orthopedics.

❖ PART 1: WE WILL TAKE CARE OF YOU

Christmas 2000

It was not a very merry Christmas for the Taylor[1] family. Tom, a for-merly physically active man in his mid-50s, was in constant pain. He was unable to ride in a car and he had to sleep upright in a lounge chair. In April of 2000, Tom had both of his hips replaced and, after rapid improvement through the first six to eight weeks of physical therapy, he hit a wall in his recovery. Despite his continual efforts to seek assistance at orthopedic and pain management centers in his city, he was making no progress. His surgeon treated him as if his problems were all in his head and offered him and his family little support. Then, on Christmas Eve, eight months after his surgery, Tom's surgeon called him at home to notify him that his hip replacements were being recalled.

Analysis of Product Failure

In October of 1999, after a manufacturing review, Sulzer began producing a new lot of artificial hips. Almost a year later, in July of 2000, complaints began to surface from surgeons who were reporting that some of their patients were having problems during rehabilitation. After these cases mounted, Sulzer began an investigation to see if there were any abnormalities that could be associated with their product. As part of this investigation, Sulzer hired North American Science Associates (NAMSA), an outside firm specializing in nonclinical fine testing services to ensure medical device safety and compliance, to test the hips in question. In mid-November, NAMSA reported back to the company that during their tests, they had discovered an oily residue present on the surface of the hip socket portion of the device. They believed that this residue could prevent the device from properly attaching to the patient's existing bone. Approximately three weeks later, Sulzer's parent company, Sulzer AG of Europe, announced through an overseas press release that they were voluntarily recalling the affected hip product, which included some 40,000 units. Three days later, they officially notified the U.S. Food and Drug Administration of the recall. On December 7, 2000, Sulzer notified all the surgeons who had performed hip replacement surgeries using their products. This notification is what the FDA currently requires. Sulzer gave the physicians copies of a suggested letter template that they could use to contact all their patients directly.

To best understand the ramifications of this recall, it is helpful to understand the complex nature of the surgery involved. The surgery involves removing a portion of the upper leg bone that includes the ball section of the hip joint. This is replaced by one portion of the artificial hip. In addition, part of the patient's hipbone is graded away in order to implant the hip shell, or socket portion. This section has a semi-porous side that comes into contact with the bone. In normal situations, the bone will grow into these pores, forming a strong bond with the implant.

Most patients who received the hip implant, like Tom, did well at the outset of the procedure; however, within a few weeks some patients began noticing problems. Sulzer describes the problems in their recall letter to surgeons (G. Sabins et al., personal communication, December 7, 2000):

> 4–6 Weeks: Patient progressing well or reporting groin or anterior pain.
>
> Up to 6 Weeks: Observe increased groin pain
>
> Patient has significant startup pain with rising from a seated position, may have buttock pain.
>
> X-Ray evaluation may show component migration
>
> 6 Weeks to 3 Months: Significant pain with weight bearing, may require cane or crutch.
>
> Patient cannot exert resistance in leg movement tests.
>
> 3 Months +: X-rays may reveal a slight separation between the implant and the bone and may show some component movement.

In short, because of the residue found on the porous portion of the hip shell, the hipbone could not properly bond. In some cases, this led to poor attachment and, in more dramatic instances, it produced complete hip failure.

Sulzer's Position

Sulzer Orthopedics, the fourth-largest supplier of orthopedic implants in the world at the time of the recall, was often seen as the premier manufacturer in this industry. As of 2002, between 150,000 and 200,000 hip replacements were being performed each year (Hip Replacement Surgery, 2002) and Sulzer was particularly well known for their hip and knee replacement devices.

The hip replacement recall can be considered a crisis for Sulzer. Fink (1986) defines an organizational crisis as a situation that can potentially escalate in intensity, fall under close government or media scrutiny, jeopardize the current positive public image of an organization, or interfere with normal business operations, including damaging the bottom line in any way. According to Pearson and Mitroff (1993), crises are composed of five dimensions: 1) high visibility, 2) immediate attention is required, 3) surprise is a common part of the crisis, 4) action is needed, and 5) control is not always possible. Sulzer's crisis fits all five of these dimensions.

In Sulzer's situation, they quickly found themselves needing to contain the damage being caused by the tragic product contamination. This phase, called *damage containment,* is common to nearly all crises (Pearson & Mitroff, 1993). The purpose of damage containment is to prevent the crisis from contaminating other parts of the organization or environment not immediately affected. During this crisis phase, organizations seek to protect their image by modifying public perception of responsibility for the crisis or to manage the public's impression of the organization in crisis (Coombs, 1999).

When the recall was made public, Sulzer began to contain the damage by initially issuing a statement to the press that they would cover all medical expenses and lost wages resulting from the defective implants. "It was our fault," said Sulzer's Steven Whitlock in February of 2001 (Roser & Park, 2001). In an open letter to surgeons published in several central Texas newspapers, Sulzer pledged openness and restitution for the patients who received defective implants. In the crisis communication literature, how an organization responds to a crisis is called a *message strategy* and Coombs (1999) has developed a comprehensive typology describing these strategies. In this phase of the crisis, Sulzer consistently used a message strategy known as *remediation,* since they accepted blame and offered to correct the damage their implants caused.

Tom's Second Surgery

Considering the previous lack of support from his surgeon, Tom had no desire to continue the relationship with the surgeon that had performed his first hip replacement surgery. He and his wife began searching the Internet to find surgeons that specialized in the removal and replacement of these defective parts. They found a surgeon in Houston and scheduled the first available appointment.

The specialist worked exclusively with joint replacements of this type and had had years of prior experience using Sulzer products. The specialist assured them that Sulzer was a solid company that would take care of its customers, so they rescheduled the second hip replacement surgery. Since Sulzer made the "Cadillac" of hip replacements, the specialist recommended that they replace the defective parts with new Sulzer parts. Tom agreed and wanted both hips replaced at once;

however, the specialist explained that a second hip replacement surgery was much more serious and he recommended doing two surgeries, to replace each hip separately. By May of 2001, both of the defective hips had been removed and replaced with new materials. The rehabilitation began for the second time.

The surgeons are in a unique position during a medical recall. Usually, they are responsible for making the selection of the medical device, such as the artificial hip, and the patient has no input. Essentially, the surgeon has the direct relationship with Sulzer. When we talk about direct and indirect relationships between communication parties, it is useful to look at *stakeholder theory* (Freeman, 1984). This theory defines a stakeholder as any group or public impacted by the organization's operation. Wolfe and Putler (2002) explain, "the purpose of stakeholder management is to facilitate our understanding of increasingly unpredictable external environments, thereby facilitating our ability to manage within these environments" (p. 64). But in addition to the managerial concerns of stakeholder theory, it can also be used to expand the ethical considerations of organizations to actively include the voice of their stakeholders (Deetz, 2001). As these definitions suggest, stakeholder theory provides a solid way to ground an understanding of health-related crisis communication.

The relationships with stakeholder groups are often quite dynamic, especially during a crisis. Botan and Soto (1998) explain that the relationship with the public stakeholder group can be defined by its longitudinal nature and the relationship complexity. Strategic communication campaigns "are characterized by their intended role in positioning an organization or group to negotiate relationships with relevant environmental forces" (p. 23). One way to think of stakeholder relationships is using a framework of coalitional relationships (Pfeffer & Salancik, 1978). In coalitional relationships, organizations respond to pressures from the environment, accede to the demands of some coalitional interests, avoid the demands of others, establish relationships with some coalitions, and avoid them with others. Shifting stakeholder relationships creates problems for organizations because the criteria and expectations may be incompatible or competing. Faced with conflicting demands, the organization must decide which groups to attend to and which to ignore (Pfeffer & Salancik, 1978). These difficult decisions contributed to the complexity of the ethical issues Sulzer faced.

❖ PART 2: SULZER AS A "NON-ENTITY" IN THE PATIENT'S MINDS

As of February 2, 2002, nearly 2,800 hundred Sulzer patients had undergone surgeries to replace the defective hips. In addition, a similar defect was found with Sulzer's knee replacement parts, and an additional 560 patients have had surgeries to replace defective knee implants. It was still unknown how many more surgeries needed to be performed.

April 2002–What Happened Since Part 1?

It is now several years since Tom's first hip replacement, and one year since the second surgeries. Tom is still not completely recovered. His wife, Mary, explains, "We have not been able to leave town for two years." She further explains that only recently can he travel in a car and when he goes to a movie he has to get up and walk around five times. Furthermore, he still cannot put on his shoes and socks without her help. He had to quit his job shortly after the problems began and every day he spends hours at the gym working on his rehabilitation. He is also out tens of thousands of dollars for medical expenses that have *not* been reimbursed by Sulzer. Now Tom's hip replacement surgeon has adopted a more neutral tone toward Sulzer and no longer suggests that Sulzer will take care of these patients.

Severity of Effects

While some patients who received the recalled implants have shown no signs of problems, there are a significant number who have. Some have experienced minor discomfort not requiring surgery, while others have had near catastrophic incidences with the defective parts. One patient has had to endure the situation twice. "I was told if I had this hip replacement, I'd be as good as new," said Rhonda Silva, one of 15 plaintiffs in a subsequent class action lawsuit filed in San Francisco (Bernstein, 2001). "It has ruined my entire life." Silva's first hip failed a few weeks after the surgery when the synthetic hip separated from the bone, leaving her leg unattached to the rest of her body structure. Her doctors recommended another replacement. However, this happened before the recall was announced. The second hip came from the same batch of flawed hips and the operation failed once again. She is currently scheduled for a third surgery with a new doctor who has been instructed not to use Sulzer equipment.

Legal Battles

Almost immediately after the recall announcements, lawsuits were filed on behalf of some of the early recipients of the recalled devices, and new surgeries were scheduled to replace the defective units. The problems for Sulzer continued. In May of 2001, they announced a second recall because a similar manufacturing problem had been discovered with the company's artificial knee implant. This recall affected nearly 1,500 individuals.

Sulzer made its first offer to settle the growing number of lawsuits related to the first recall in August of 2001. They proposed a settlement of $750 million to cover all affected parties. This offer would have given each hip replacement patient who had one hip replaced approximately $51,500, while patients with two hip replacements would receive about $97,000. Most patients rejected the offer outright.

Just over two weeks after the initial proposed settlement, the first court case involving the recalled implants ended in Corpus Christi, Texas. There, a jury awarded three women over $15 million dollars, saying that Sulzer had acted with "malice" for not informing patients and doctors sooner, and for continuing to sell the product while it was under investigation. Earlier in this case we mentioned that Sulzer waited to report the recall until after they investigated the concerns. Sulzer called the decision way out of line ("Sulzer to appeal $15.1M verdict," 2001). They believed they had communicated the problem appropriately. Within days, Judge Kathleen O'Malley, U.S. district judge in Cleveland, Ohio, ordered a halt to all court trials involving the recall until the settlement offer from Sulzer was reviewed.

A few days later, Sulzer scrapped its initial settlement offer and proposed a new one. In the revised settlement offer, Sulzer agreed to pay $1 billion dollars to settle the pending lawsuits. This would give the average patient an award of approximately $200,000, which would cover medical expenses, legal fees, and other expenses. It was Sulzer's contention that the problems associated with the recalls were not as significant as portrayed in the media. "We are trying to make sure all parties are comfortable [with the settlement]," said Harlan Loeb, a Sulzer spokesman ("Sulzer Agrees to Negotiated Settlement," 2001). Judge O'Malley set a hearing for May 14, 2002, to discuss approval or rejection of the class-action settlement offer.

Sulzer defends itself in court

Despite Sulzer's initial acceptance of blame for the recall—a remediation message strategy—the company told a different story in the courts. Documents filed by Sulzer in March of 2001 indicated that the patients and unidentified third parties are at fault for the hip failures (Roser & Park, 2001). When explaining the crisis in court, they not only failed to accept blame, but they also blamed others for the product problem. Sulzer spokesperson, M. J. Nicchio, said that the arguments presented are standard in this type of case because they give the company every means of defense in a case. However, Ron Weddington, a lawyer for one of the plaintiffs, questions this legal move by saying, "It's rare that there is such a stark contrast between what they are saying in the newspaper and what they are saying in court" (Roser & Park, 2001). Not only did they change their message strategy from one of accepting blame to blaming others, but Sulzer also refused to identify the third parties mentioned in their defense. This raised concerns for many of Sulzer's stakeholders.

During damage containment and recovery, organizations experiencing a crisis must decide how to address the concerns of multiple individuals and organizations, yet maintain their own legitimacy. Suchman (1995) describes legitimacy as "a generalized perception or assumption that the actions of an entity are desirable, or appropriate within some socially constructed systems of norms, values, beliefs, and definitions" (p. 574). Pearson and Clair (1998) state that the "failure to provide consistent information" (p. 72) exacerbates and elongates crisis situations. Massey (2001) claims that consistency during a crisis response requires that the focal organization provide the same account to all stakeholders. In Sulzer's situation, they were inconsistent in many areas. Not only did they change their strategy over time, but they also used different strategies across stakeholder groups. The problem is that with the proliferation of technology, these inconsistencies can become much more transparent.

Implications for the doctors

Throughout most of this recall, the doctors have found themselves in a precarious ethical position. They are caught between the manufacturer with a defective product, and patients with problems resulting from the device. While it appears that the majority of the patients' anger and legal actions are being directed at the manufacturer, some doctors may get caught in the fray. We can see that despite their direct stakeholder relationship with Sulzer, they also need to satisfy their patients, who barely know Sulzer.

Some surgeons now refuse to use Sulzer equipment, while others publicly blame Sulzer for the problems associated with the recall. Dr. Ira Kirschenbaum, a prominent orthopedic surgeon in New York who did not use Sulzer equipment, said that the company should have halted manufacturing and distribution immediately, "the minute somebody said we may have a problem here." Not only were the surgeons left in the dark, but Sulzer's own quality-assurance head was not informed of the problem until September of 2000 (Roser & Park, 2001).

The Affected Patients

Lawyers for the patients see problems ahead for the company. "Sulzer cost these people the first good chance," said Chad Roberts, a lawyer with the law firm of Spohrer, Wilner, Maxwell, and Matthews. "The second one's never as good. They should've done the Tylenol thing which is [say], 'Hey, we don't know why people are dropping dead after taking Tylenol, but we want you to stop buying our Tylenol'" (Park, 2001). He referred to the 1982 incident in which seven people were killed by tampered with, cyanide-laced Tylenol pills. Tylenol issued a very quick, yet financially costly recall strategy that is often considered an excellent example of how to handle a product recall crisis. This is particularly worth noting considering that Johnson & Johnson (makers of Tylenol) is one of Sulzer's competitors in the hip replacement market.

Tom's Relationship With Sulzer

Though Sulzer did begin to send out e-mail updates to hip replacement patients in early 2002, Tom and his family never received any direct, personal communication from Sulzer. These e-mails were typically a recap of what was already known about both the recall and the settlement initiative. When they learned new information, it was from the newspaper, the Internet, or their attorney. They actually know the names of the various reporters for the *Austin American-Statesman*, including Amy Schatz, who writes articles concerning the recall. The Taylors also know which Internet sites provide the most complete and credible medical information to help Tom with his recovery. Finally, despite the fact that they have never sued anyone before, the family felt compelled to hire an attorney to learn more about their options.

The Taylors expected to receive their first piece of direct communication from Sulzer on March 26, 2002, since they thought it was court mandated; but this never occurred. Mary, Tom's wife, explains that Sulzer is a "non-entity" in their minds: "They have a wonderful media blitz going, since the public thinks we are being taken care of, but that could not be further from the truth." The Taylors also explained that the settlement proposed in the federal court for the class-action lawsuit had some significant issues that were not being publicized. The $200,000 per hip settlement offer includes out-of-pocket expenses and approximately 15% covers attorney fees. Thus, there is little left to compensate for lost wages, the fact that Tom will never work again, the years of physical therapy ahead, and the pain and suffering experienced when you learn that a piece of metal in your body is making you sick. Despite the fact that he can no longer work, under the terms of the settlement, Tom does not qualify for extra compensation, provided for in extreme cases, because there is no way for him to prove that the pain he is now suffering is a direct result of the recall issue. He believes that no doctor is willing to step forward to support his claim because that risks his or her relationship with Sulzer.

On May 8, 2002, Judge O'Malley accepted the settlement offer in its final revised form. One witness testified in the final hearing that the agreement was "the best opportunity for the most people to recover the most money the soonest" (Lieff, Cabraser, Heimann, & Bernstein, 2003). The final settlement totaled $1.035 billion, which was deposited into a settlement trust on November 4, 2002. During this time, Sulzer Medica and its subsidiary, Sulzer Orthopedic, changed their corporate names to Centerpulse and Centerpulse Orthopedics, respectively. It is expected that upon verification of claims by the claims administrator of the settlement, claimants in the case will have received full compensation by the middle of 2003.

Tom and his family are unsure of what lies ahead. They were unaware that money had been placed in the trust or that they could see compensation relatively soon until the authors of this case study informed them of this in late January 2003. They feared that Sulzer would drag out the legal case as long as possible, since most of the hip replacement patients are over 65 years of age and will probably not live another 10 years. The Taylors also feared that Sulzer would simply declare bankruptcy, preventing any of the victims in this case from ever seeing compensation. They had completely lost faith in Sulzer as a company and are in a state of disbelief that they have never even received an apology, and to date, no compensation for the second surgery has been received.

Discussion Questions

1. How could Sulzer have done a better job of balancing its liability concerns with its stakeholders' need for information?

2. Given the difficulties and constraints of this balance, did Sulzer act ethically? In what ways might it have used more ethical means of communication?

3. With the tremendous impact that the Internet has had on information retrieval, what potential effects might we expect from organizations dealing with a crisis involving multiple stakeholders? How could an organization faced with this situation avoid sending conflicting messages to the various stakeholders?

4. Using this distributed set of relationships as a guide, on which stakeholders did Sulzer choose to concentrate its crisis communication efforts? What suggestions do you have to improve this process in the future?

Figure 6.1   Sulzer Stakeholders

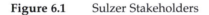

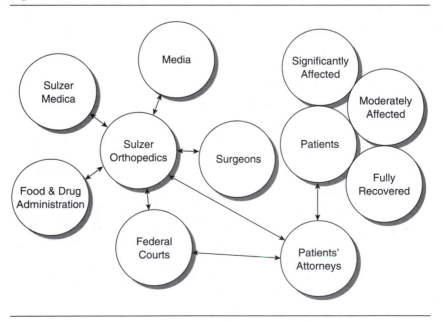

5. If you were a physician needing to contact your patients and tell them about the recall, how would you approach this task?

6. If you worked for Sulzer and were challenged to study this case and make suggestions for how future recalls should be handled, what would you recommend?

❖ NOTE

1. The Taylor family name, including the first names of Tom and Mary, are pseudonyms. This is at the request of the family that was interviewed.

❖ REFERENCES

Bernstein, S. (2001, February 14). 341 have had surgery to replace faulty hip. *Los Angeles Times.*

Botan, C. H., & Soto, F. (1998). A semiotic approach to the internal functioning of publics: Implications for strategic communication and public relations. *Public Relations Review, 24,* 21–44.

Coombs, W. T. (1999). *Ongoing crisis communication: Planning, managing, and responding.* Thousand Oaks, CA: Sage.

Deetz, S. (2001). Conceptual foundations. In F. M. Jablin & L. L. Putman (Eds.), *The new handbook of organizational communication: Advances in theory, research, and methods* (pp. 3–46). Thousand Oaks, CA: Sage.

Fink, S. (1986). *Crisis management: Planning for the inevitable.* New York: AMACOM.

Freeman, R. E. (1984). *Strategic management: A stakeholder approach.* Boston: Pitman.

Hip Replacement Surgery. (2002, March 17-24). *Copy Editor,* Editor's choice, 3.

Lieff, R. L., Cabraser, E. J., Heimann, R. M., & Bernstein, W. (2003). *Sulzer settlement and federal lawsuit update from HipImplantLaw.com.* Retrieved January 28, 2003, from http://www.hipimplantlaw.com/federal.htm

Massey, J. E. (2001). Managing organizational legitimacy: Communication strategies for organizations in crisis. *Journal of Business Communication, 38,* 153–183.

Park, A. (2001, February 4). Sulzer continued manufacturing device after problems were reported. *Austin American-Statesman.*

Pearson, C. M., & Clair, J. A. (1998). Reframing crisis management. *The Academy of Management Review, 23,* 59–77.

Pearson, C. M., & Mitroff, I. I. (1993). From crisis prone to crisis prepared: A framework for crisis management. *Academy of Management Executive, 7,* 48–59.

Pfeffer, J., & Salancik, G. R. (1978). *The external control of organizations: A resource dependence perspective.* New York: Harper & Row.

Roser, M. A. & Park, A. (2001, March 20). Sulzer backing off in court. *Austin American-Statesman.*

Suchman, M. C. (1995). Managing legitimacy: Strategic and institutional approaches. *Academy of Management Review, 20,* 571–610.

Sulzer agrees to negotiated settlement. (2001, December 1). *Austin American-Statesman.*

Sulzer to appeal $15.1M verdict (2001, August 31). *Austin Business Journal.* Retrieved from http://www.bizjournals.com/austin/stories/2001/08/27/daily47.html

Wolfe, R. A., & Putler, D. S. (2002). How tight are the ties that bind stakeholder groups? *Organization Science, 13,* 64–80.

The Circle of Truth

An Examination of Values, Truth-Telling, and Alignment at Mount Carmel Health[1]

Bethany Crandell Goodier

This case examines the alternatives to hierarchy emerging in today's organizations, which emphasize social and ethical responsibility, integrity, interconnectedness, personal development, and values-centered leadership. Specifically, this case explores the ethical dilemmas associated with organizational and cultural shifts requiring organizational members to become highly identified with the organization through self-disclosure and personal development. In addition, this case highlights the complexity of implementing a values-centered approach amidst the socio-economic pressures of the contemporary marketplace. As such, it addresses the virtues and challenges for organizations that seek to foster personal growth among employees, as well as the impact of such efforts on communication norms.

S teaming hot air choked from the vents in Leigh's[2] black Jeep Cherokee as she revved the engine and drove quickly out of the hospital parking lot. It was the middle of July in Columbus, Ohio, and the air was thick with the promise of an afternoon thunderstorm. Leigh cranked the air conditioner to high and lowered the automatic windows so she could feel the hot, sticky breeze rush through the car as she jetted toward the highway. Twisting her long blonde hair into a knot and securing it with a clip she kept on the dash, she lowered her sunglasses and merged easily into traffic. She was running late for a meeting with the senior leadership team of Mount Carmel Health System, and after her staff meeting this morning, this was one meeting she didn't want to miss.

Leigh had been with Mount Carmel since 1983, beginning in a mid-level position and quickly working her way up through the ranks to executive vice president. Her job was fast-paced, something she enjoyed most of the time, and there were always new challenges to explore. While she liked her work, she had become increasingly dissatisfied with the culture of Mount Carmel in recent years. The amplified focus on competition and resources had created a climate of fear where backbiting and lying were becoming the norm. She had seriously considered resigning six months earlier, but that all changed after she attended the Higher Ground Leadership Retreat.

The senior leadership team of Mount Carmel goes on retreat annually to strategize and plan for the coming year. While it has always been a good opportunity to get away from the office and focus on new objectives, it was rarely "fun." Much of the leadership team had begun to mistrust one another and often conflicts and turf wars erupted at these retreats. Leigh had been dreading it for months. But a few weeks prior to the retreat, Joe Calvaruso, the president and CEO of the hospital, announced that this retreat would be different. Leigh remembered how tentative, but confident, he had been as he approached the group, explaining how he had recently attended a retreat about something called "Higher Ground Leadership." "It's a lot different than what we are used to," he began, an edge of excitement in his voice. "It's a model of leadership based in values, not control. It's about inspiring people, not scaring them; about finding real connections with people, not just superficial relationships that get our needs met." He went on to explain that a values-centered approach was about putting others before oneself, people before profit and materialism, focusing on strengths instead of weaknesses, shifting from a focus on fear to love, and engaging in creative continuous improvement.[3] Leigh remembered the nervous glances around the conference room as Joe continued to explain this new philosophy. "I know it's different from what we are used to here, but I really think it's worth considering. Just keep an open mind and we'll learn more about it at the retreat next week."

Despite the confused and wary looks that day, the retreat proved to be a transformational experience for most every participant. Leigh remembered how Julie, who had since become the vice president of Higher Ground Leadership, had described the retreat as "a life-altering experience," allowing her to "rediscover" her "true self."[4] Other people talked about being less angry, less stressed, more at peace, and rejuvenated and committed to their work. The experience had really brought the senior leadership team together and they became even more committed to making Mount Carmel a better place to work.

The retreat was separated into three basic areas: learning about Higher Ground Leadership through content presentations and discussions, activities that reinforced content material, and rituals that supported and enhanced these values. For example, one day of the retreat was dedicated to learning about "Inspirational Leadership," which distinguishes between old story leaders (those who seek to control, manipulate, and exploit) and new story leaders (who focus on relationships and inspiration). Participants discussed the importance of truth-telling and promise-keeping to a new story leader and acknowledged that most people lie (usually out of fear) and that most organizations support that dishonesty (usually to remain profitable). They learned that Higher Ground Leadership demands a safe space for telling the truth with no recrimination for honesty shared in a helpful and positive way. To support this ideal, participants practiced the ritual of a wisdom circle. Grounded in Native American traditions, wisdom circles are used to renew a sense of community, generate new ideas, and offer a safe space for sharing perspectives. In a circle, one person speaks at a time without fear of repercussion or reprisal. The ritual was practiced several times at the retreat, facilitating open communication and problem solving about current issues and challenges, and building a sense of community and connection through the sharing of personal stories about joy and loss.[5] For Leigh, these circles had been one of the most meaningful aspects of the retreat.

Another important moment of the retreat came when participants were asked to reflect on and articulate their destiny, calling, and cause. Leigh recalled how challenging it had been to wrap her arms around these ideas at first—how could anyone really articulate his or her destiny?! She remembered how they were led through a series of activities and discussions that allowed them to consider their purpose in the world and their unique gifts that would allow them to achieve that destiny. From this, they were asked to create a "Cause" statement that articulated what they stood for and offered a vision for what the future should or could be. Most of the participants were still working on their personal Cause statements even months after the retreat, but they had finalized Mount Carmel's Cause statement within a month of their return: "Honoring Every Soul With Loving Service." While there had been some initial resistance to the word "loving," people came to embrace the idea and appreciate that it was actually okay to love the people with whom you work, treat one another in caring and respectful ways, and share their feelings of affection with one another both verbally and physically.

Since their return to Mount Carmel, things had really started to change. As the leaders began to practice what they learned at the retreat, the people in their departments responded exceptionally well. The climate at Mount Carmel began to shift as people began to treat one another more humanely, emphasizing the importance of respect, honesty, and interdependence rather than competition and fear. Organizational leaders were listening more and really responding to the individual needs of their employees. Leigh truly believed the culture was beginning to change. But that perception had been shattered one morning when one of her staff members approached her after their weekly meeting.

"Leigh?" the shy, young programmer asked timidly, her silver-framed glasses slipping slightly down the bridge of her nose.

"Yes, Maggie, how may I serve you today?" Leigh asked jovially. It seemed silly sometimes, but this simple phrase introduced at the retreat had really changed her relationship with her employees. Leigh stopped abruptly when she saw the look of concern and fear shining in Maggie's soft brown eyes. "Maggie, what's wrong? You look worried."

"Uh, I guess I am . . . a little. I'm not sure how to talk to you about this," she stammered quietly. "It's just . . . well . . ."

"Go on," Leigh said seriously. She put a hand on Maggie's shoulder. "Let's sit." She motioned to the large blue office chairs that had just emptied at the end of the meeting. Leigh reached behind her to close the door to the conference room before sitting down.

"Well, uh, I was talking to my friend Sally—she's a nurse in the O.R.," she began quietly, "and she . . . well . . . she's had a rough time of it lately with one of the doctors."

"Go on," Leigh encouraged. She had a hollow feeling in the pit of her stomach that was growing with each passing moment. While most of the physicians at Mount Carmel were nothing short of exceptional, she had heard some negative stories about a select few.

"Well, she called me to tell me she was going to quit," Maggie continued, tears glistening in her eyes.

"Did she say why?" Leigh prompted.

"Yeah, she said that she had had the worst day of her life and had been humiliated in front of her colleagues and patients. She said she didn't think she could show her face in the hospital ever again." Maggie was talking more quickly now, trying to get the story out as quickly as possible. "See, Dr. McGee—you know him right?" Leigh nodded, feeling the hollowness in her stomach deepen. He was one of the ones she had heard about. "Well, he got upset in the operating room—something about instruments not being exactly where he wanted them to be or something. It had been a long day and things weren't running as scheduled," Maggie continued. "He was very frustrated when the operation began and had been barking out orders to everyone, but when he asked Sally for some instrument—I don't know what it was; it wasn't something they used very often and she couldn't locate it right away—he started screaming at her. He called her incompetent and pathetic. He said that if she couldn't find what he needed right then, then she should just get out of *his* operating room and never come back." Maggie paused for a moment and swallowed hard. "After all we have been talking about lately in terms of honoring and caring for one another, it was really hard to listen to her story. Even though she eventually found what he was looking for he continued to make fun of her for the rest of the procedure. She said it was all she could do to stay in the room." Maggie slumped in her chair, her story complete. Leigh looked at her remorsefully.

"Maggie, I am so sorry that this happened to your friend. I want you to give me her phone number. I am going to call her personally to talk to her about it, but I want you to know that this is *not* the way we do things at Mount Carmel and I am going to make sure that it does not happen again." Leigh patted Maggie's shoulder and stood cautiously. Maggie looked up apologetically.

"I'm sorry Leigh. I know you have really been excited about the changes here at Mount Carmel and I know this sort of changes things . . ." her voice trailed off.

"No. Don't apologize," Leigh countered. "This doesn't change things for me, it just lets me know that we have more work to do." Resolved, Leigh gave Maggie a warm hug and thanked her for trusting her enough to share her concerns. Leigh recalled the look of hope on her young staffer's face as she left the room. "I sure hope I can make good on my promise to her," Leigh said aloud as she pulled into a space at Mount Carmel West. Quickly removing the clip and shaking out her hair, she grabbed her brown briefcase and darted through the parking lot into the administrative building.

Moments later, Leigh was sitting at a large round table with other members of the senior leadership team. She had called Joe, the president and CEO, and Julie, the vice president of Higher Ground Leadership, before she left the office to let them know that there was a situation she needed to discuss at the meeting. Because of the nature of the conflict, they all felt that a truth-telling circle, a version of the wisdom circles they had practiced at the retreat, would be appropriate. Leigh glanced down at her watch. "9:42—they must be running on hospital time," she thought. People here were notoriously late. Many joked that time in the hospital just didn't work as it did in the "real world" and most meetings and appointments generally started 15 minutes past when they were scheduled. Other members of the leadership team were busily reviewing papers, finishing up cell phone calls, or chatting noisily with those next to them.

Leigh glanced around the room marveling at how much it had changed recently. The standard medical board room had been redecorated to include family photos, fresh flowers, a small table fountain, and warm lighting. There were plans to create a new conference room resembling a living area with comfortable couches, easy chairs, and shag carpeting. A small kitchen boasting drinks, cookies, fruit, and small snacks would be connected to the room and accessible to all. Everyone agreed that the new design would facilitate interaction and create a more positive environment for decision making and discussion. It could also be used for group meditation sessions and receptions. In Higher Ground terms, they were creating a "soul space"—a place that nurtured their souls and enhanced their spirits.

"Having a space like that certainly would help make what I am about to do a little easier," Leigh thought, nervously picking a piece of lint off her pants. "It's hard to feel connected to people with this big table in the way!" Of course, the table also would offer some element of protection if what she had to say isn't well received. She glanced apprehensively about the room. Julie smiled reassuringly at Leigh, nodded and looked down at the table in front of her. Julie, a personable woman with an engaging smile, was usually fond of chatting with her peers before meetings, but today she was sitting solemnly as she prepared for the truth-telling circle. On the table in front of her sat a flat, heart-shaped purple rock polished to a high shine. Next to it, a smaller golden rock of similar luster stood ready. The rocks were instruments of the truth-telling circle. The person who held the heart-shaped rock was invited to speak, to share his or her truth with the group—whatever that might be. No one else could interrupt or speak until the rock was passed to them. The golden rock was reserved by the facilitator of the circle and only used as a gentle reminder to the speaker if he or she held the floor for more than 15 minutes. Leigh stared at the two rocks, knowing that she would soon be holding one of them as she recounted the story she had heard that morning.

The energy in the room changed noticeably as Joe, the president and CEO of Mount Carmel, entered the room. Leigh shifted quickly in her seat, readying herself for the meeting. Conversations around the room ceased, and Joe welcomed everyone to the circle.

"Good morning, everyone," he said positively. "It's nice to see all of you again." There was an edge to his voice that wasn't normally present.

"He's worried about this too," Leigh thought. They hadn't really had a truth-telling circle since the retreat. There was no telling how it would go in the "real world."

"We have a lot to do today, so let's go ahead and get started. Tom, could you start us off with that poem you sent me earlier this week?" Joe asked. Tom, a senior leader who had been with Mount Carmel for many years, shuffled through the papers in an open file on the table and began reading aloud. They had always opened their meetings this way with a poem, prayer, quotation, or simple words of inspiration. It helped to set the right tone for their meetings. Today, Tom read a poem about trust and faith.

"Poignant," Leigh thought as Tom's gentle voice trailed off.

"Normally, we would begin our meeting with a review of old business, but we've had something come up that deserves our immediate attention," Joe said strongly, his brown eyes carefully surveying the circle of leaders. "One of our members has asked for a truth-telling circle and I am going to turn the meeting over to Julie at this time to facilitate that. I am sure that I don't have to remind you how important this is and I ask for your full cooperation and participation. Please turn off your beepers and cell phones unless it is absolutely necessary that you remain accessible." People shifted noticeably in their seats as they fumbled with beepers and cell phones. Joe sat back in his chair and nodded toward Julie, who cleared her throat and began to speak.

"As you know, the truth-telling circle is an important tool on our journey to Higher Ground Leadership." She smiled as she spoke and relaxed slightly in her chair. Members of the circle nodded accordingly. "There are a few ground rules I want to remind you of before we begin." Julie reiterated the basic guidelines for a circle and held up the two rocks for everyone to see. "Please remember that when you choose to speak, you should begin with a statement of how you are feeling, not what you are thinking. In the past we have used the phrases, 'I'm mad, glad, sad, or afraid.' I think those will work well here as well." Everyone in the circle nodded. "One last thing: Remember that since everyone here will be sharing his or her truth, we should not contradict or argue directly against someone else's statement. You can address issues raised, but it should be from your perspective and not presented in a way that negates the other person's. Does everyone understand?" Julie finished, looking around the room hopefully. The circle nodded in agreement as the leaders started looking from side to side to see who had called the circle. "Since the person who has called the circle does not wish to remain anonymous, I will now pass the speaking stone to Leigh."

Leigh looked cautiously around the circle. These were her colleagues, her friends, and the people with whom she had become quite close over the last few months. She knew that they believed in Higher Ground Leadership and in the Cause, but there was a part of her that was still apprehensive. Dr. McGee had a lot of friends at the hospital and he was one of the top revenue-producing physicians in the system. This was not going to be an easy issue to resolve.

She took a deep breath and began carefully. "I'm sad," her voice cracking slightly as she spoke. "I'm sad because one of my staff members is extremely upset about how her friend, a nurse in the O.R., was treated recently by one of our surgeons." Her voice steadily grew stronger as she recounted the story in her own voice. She noticed that members of the circle shifted uncomfortably in their chairs and winced as she detailed the events that had occurred. She continued, "I'm sad because I don't think this should have ever occurred at Mount Carmel, but I think it's doubly worse given all the emphasis and publicity we have given our Cause. How is this honoring *every* soul with loving service?" Leigh continued sharing her concerns, her voice quivering at times with a mixture of sadness and anger. "I'm mad too," she admitted honestly. "I'm mad that it happened, but I'm even madder that no one, not one person in that O.R., said anything to stop him." Leigh finished forcefully, looking around the table resolutely. A number of people were looking down at their laps, while others were looking directly at her, nodding in agreement.

After a minute or two of quiet reflection, someone three seats down from Leigh took the stone from the table. He was a large man, with graying hair and pale skin. He had joined the leadership team two years ago as a physician representative. As he took the stone, he sighed heavily and his cheeks reddened slightly.

"I'm sad," he began, "I'm sad that one of my fellow doctors would treat another human being this way and that it has obviously affected a lot of people, not just this nurse, negatively." He took a deep breath and continued, "I am also afraid." The rest of the circle looked on intently. "I'm afraid because this is not a situation that is going to be easily handled. Dr. McGee has a temper—he has always had a temper and we all know this isn't the first time he has blown up in the operating room." Knowing looks were exchanged around the circle. Dr. McGee had a reputation for bad behavior. "Not that that makes it right, but if we haven't said anything to him about it before . . . well, what makes us think we can change it now?" The man searched the faces around the circle. "There are a lot of issues that need to be considered here—we want to do the right thing for our people, but we also have to consider what's best for the hospital as a whole. There are no complaints about the care he provides to our patients. He is tops in his field. He's one of our top revenue producers. If he gets mad, he could easily leave and set up shop at one of the three other hospitals in town." He looked around the circle slowly, allowing his colleagues to consider this point. "Like I said, he has a temper and it wouldn't take much to send him packing." Members of the circle looked uncertainly at one another. "I'm not saying we should condone his behavior in any way—I just think we have to be careful about how we handle it." Looking down as he finished, he placed the rock on the table and sat back in his chair. Tina, a short, energetic redhead grabbed it quickly and began to speak.

"Well, I'm glad. I'm glad that Leigh had the courage to bring this to our attention and that we have this truth-telling circle to get things out in the open." Tina smiled at Leigh and looked around the room. "I am also mad. I'm mad that someone who works for Mount Carmel would treat one of our fabulous nurses this way." Tina had worked as an RN for several years prior to joining the administrative team. "It's hard enough to find good nurses, but it's not going to be any easier with incidents like this." The leadership team had recently been discussing the nursing shortage in the country and how important it was to re-recruit and celebrate their experienced staff. "I'm also afraid. I'm afraid of what will happen to us if we make decisions about how to deal with this based on money and revenue. We have to send a message here." Her blue eyes were shining with challenge and resolve. "We have to tell everyone here that we mean it when we say we are 'honoring *every* soul with loving service' and that that means we will not tolerate behavior that degrades or dishonors another human being." Her voice was steady and firm. "If we lose Dr. McGee's business, then we lose it. I have no doubt that another doctor will quickly take his place. We can't allow him to abuse our employees just because he makes money for us. It sends the wrong message to our people and to our patients." Her voice was rising now, becoming more high-pitched and determined. "I agree that we have to be careful how we handle the situation, but we have spent a lot of time talking about our values lately, and money or revenue was *not* at the top of that list—our people were." Tina placed the rock back on the table and looked around the room. Some people nodded; others looked doubtful. Mike, a senior physician on the team, reached for the rock and quietly cleared his throat.

"I'm afraid," he began in a soft voice. "I'm afraid because this is a situation we could and should have anticipated, but didn't—and I am afraid because it is bound to happen again. And as long as it does, it will continue to erode whatever progress we have made with Higher Ground Leadership at double the pace." Mike had been a surgeon at Mount Carmel for over 25 years, and his kind, gentle nature had always yielded tremendous respect from the members of the team. "I'm also mad because I feel like with as much as we have learned about Higher Ground, we haven't been trained on how to respond to these kinds of situations in a higher ground way. We haven't been given any tools for deflating situations like these and addressing them with our fellow employees. I'm sure that people in that O.R. would have liked to speak up—but if they are like me, they had no idea what to say. And even if they knew what to say, they might not have felt that they were in a position to correct the doctor. I know this man; I have worked with him. I know that he is the type to call nurses into the room just so he can yell at them and assert his authority." He looked down at the rock in his hands regretfully. "The nurses rarely report it because they know they will have to pay for it on their next shift if he finds out. I'm mad at myself too—because I have never said anything to him or to anyone else. I always knew it was wrong, but now I feel like we have to do something about it. What, I am not sure, but something has to be done. We can't allow bullies to run this playground any longer." He placed the rock on the table again and looked up. George, a slight young administrator, picked it up.

"I'm sad," he said quickly. "I'm sad that it happened and I am wondering if the real problem is that there is really just a difference between the physicians and the rest of the people who work in the hospital. Sometimes it seems like it's hard to find common ground. More importantly, we are talking about Higher Ground and all of the changes we are trying to make and all, but really, very few physicians have been a part of that. The reason I think, as some people have mentioned, that it is hard to approach them about it, is because we aren't speaking the same language anymore and we aren't coming from the same place of experience. Maybe we needed to start a concerted effort to include the physicians in more of the retreats." Knowing looks and nods of agreement were exchanged around the circle. "I am not sure how many of them will want to go, but we should do what we can to encourage it." Leigh listened intently and wondered about this last suggestion. It had been difficult to get even a few physicians to take a week away from their practices and families for the first retreats.

The conversation continued around the circle for over an hour, with nearly every leader offering his or her thoughts on the situation. The tone remained civil, but challenging at times, with members disagreeing on how best to address the situation. Some thought that Dr. McGee was too valuable to risk losing; others thought he was a negative influence on the system and should be asked to leave. After everyone who wanted to speak had taken a turn, Joe looked around the circle expectantly. When no one took the stone he stood and thanked everyone for participating. "I appreciate all of your honesty and willingness to take part in this circle," he began casually. "This is a difficult situation—one that I think we all agree needs to be addressed in a careful and thoughtful way." He looked purposefully at each member of the team. "With your permission, I would like to meet with this young woman to hear her story directly. I would also like to meet with those of you who are most directly involved in this situation," he nodded toward individual members of the team, "to best determine our course of action. I think we have gotten a good start on ideas here, but now I'd like to have a smaller group further assess the situation and determine how to proceed. We will communicate our decision to the rest of you as soon as possible. Is that acceptable?" The rest of the group nodded in agreement. "Okay. Well then, let's close the circle, take a quick break, and get back to our scheduled business." All the members of the team stood, joined hands, and Julie read a quote about courage. As she finished, members of the circle began to hug one another and chat idly as they left the room. Joe turned to her as they were leaving and gave her a strong hug.

"Thank you for your courage," he said sincerely. "Thank you for keeping us moving toward Higher Ground." Leigh nodded hopefully. She was too overwhelmed to speak. "I love you Leigh," he said as they parted.

"I love you too," Leigh said quietly. She still wasn't entirely used to using the word "love" at work. She knew that Joe meant it; he truly did love everyone in the room, but it still shocked her to hear it out loud sometimes.

As she gathered her things, Leigh marveled at the change in her teammates. A few months ago, they would have been racing to the bathrooms and outer halls to talk about what had just occurred and bad mouth those with whose opinions they disagreed. Now, they were all hugging one another, drinking coffee together, and talking about other business. She wasn't sure how the situation would be handled, but she was confident that it would be with wisdom, as well as grace.

❖ EPILOGUE

In the weeks that followed, interested members of the senior leadership team met with those involved in the incident described above to gain a better understanding of what had occurred and to consider the perspectives of all those involved. While the details of the resolution of this case must remain confidential, it is fair to say that members of the senior leadership team agree it was vital in raising awareness about issues previously unaddressed in the adoption of Higher Ground Leadership. They began meaningful dialogues with physicians and practitioners with hospital privileges about Higher Ground and the culture of trust and care they were trying to sustain. They also focused on understanding the needs of their practitioners; acknowledging their concerns and challenges and finding ways to serve them more effectively. More physicians began attending the Higher Ground retreats and as they and other members of the hospital staff experienced Higher Ground Leadership firsthand, empathy for one another increased. While no new policies have been created, a tacit agreement exists among practitioners and employees of Mount Carmel Health to act in ways that "honor every soul." Those whose behavior contradicts these values will continue to be called to task for their actions.

Discussion Questions

1. Given what you know about the situation, Mount Carmel, and Higher Ground Leadership, how do you think this situation should be handled?

2. What long-term actions would you recommend to prevent situations like this from arising in the future?

3. Is it possible for an organization in a turbulent industry such as health care to be both pro-people and pro-profit? What challenges might they face other than those suggested in this case? How could those challenges be addressed?

4. To what degree is it appropriate to introduce self-discovery and personal transformation initiatives into the workplace? What are the implications of "required" retreats that create expectations for personal disclosure?

5. Are there some people or cultures that would find this approach difficult to handle? Why? Does this approach allow for diversity?

6. What are the ethical responsibilities of trainers or consultants who facilitate such programs? How do these differ from more traditional training programs? What level of support is needed following the retreat?

7. What do you think of the use of truth-telling circles in the workplace? What would be needed for these to work effectively? How would issues of power and hierarchy impact a truth-telling circle?

8. What are the ethical implications for leaders/managers who decide to implement new programs (e.g., Higher Ground Leadership; truth-telling circles, etc.) even when some employees may be uncomfortable with them?

9. Throughout the case, we see examples of coworkers displaying physical affection for one another and using the word "love." How would you feel about this? What challenges do you think it might create? What positive impacts do you think it could have on an organization?

10. How important is context or the environment in creating a positive work atmosphere? What impact do you think "soul space" has on productivity or effectiveness? What might your ideal "soul space" look like?

❖ NOTES

1. Special thanks to the people of Mount Carmel Health who have allowed me to adapt their stories to create this case. While the specific details of this case are fictional to protect confidentiality, it is grounded in the real experiences of my participants and was constructed using data from personal interviews and observations. Direct quotes are referenced throughout the case.

2. Most names have been changed to protect participant confidentiality.

3. For more information about Higher Ground Leadership and/or Values-Centered Leadership, see Secretan (1997, 1999, 2004).

4. Personal interview, January 29, 2001.

5. An entire evening of the Higher Ground Leadership retreat was devoted to "Sacred Storytelling," a variation of the wisdom circle that was intended to engage participants at increasingly deeper levels of compassion through the telling and hearing of one another's stories. Participants were asked to share their greatest joys and pains with the group, and the rest of the circle was asked to hold the space, people, and stories revealed as sacred.

❖ REFERENCES

Secretan, L. (1997). *Reclaiming higher ground: Building organizations that inspire excellence.* New York: McGraw-Hill.

Secretan, L. (1999). *Inspirational leadership: Destiny, calling and cause.* Waterloo, Ontario, Canada: Macmillan.

Secretan, L. (2004). *Inspire: What great leaders do.* Hoboken, NJ: Wiley.

Ethical Storm or Model Workplace?

Joann Keyton, Paula Cano, Teresa L. Clounch, Carl E. Fischer, Catherine Howard, Sarah S. Topp, and Michaella M. Zlatek

This case addresses the claims of sexual harassment made by female employees of Mitsubishi in both private and class action lawsuits, and explores those claims and the company and union responses to them. It considers how organizations that presumptively support values such as honesty, fairness, and respect react and renegotiate these values when organizational incidents reveal value lapses. It also addresses the degree to which organizations meet their ethical duty by developing and implementing sexual harassment policies, complaint procedures, and training.

Honesty, fairness, and respect are desirable ethical characteristics of any organization, and their absence is often the basis of employee complaints. These characteristics are central to the story[1] of Mitsubishi Motors Manufacturing America (MMMA), a medium-size automobile manufacturing plant in Normal, Illinois. MMMA was the site of a landmark sexual harassment case brought by the U.S. Equal Employment Opportunity Commission (EEOC) and settled for $34 million.

Beyond the monetary relief for the plaintiffs, court-imposed remedies included the development and implementation of sexual harassment policies, procedures, and training, and helped the organization evolve into a model team-based workplace.

In 1994, a total of 29 female employees filed suit claiming sexual harassment—the first public notice of ethical problems at MMMA. From 1994 until the May 23, 2001, filing of the consent decree court monitors' final report, MMMA was at the center of an ethical storm in which the values of honesty, fairness, and respect were violated. Why would male employees sexually taunt, harass, and humiliate their female colleagues who were also their neighbors? Why did MMMA managers or union leaders to whom the women brought their complaints do nothing? Why did so few women initially complain about their sexual harassment when ultimately more than 300 would be certified as claimants in the class action lawsuit brought by the EEOC? What did MMMA hope to achieve in sponsoring a protest against the EEOC? Is it possible that the procedural and policy changes that the court monitors oversaw at the plant could create a welcoming environment for women? Can a zero tolerance policy ever really be successful in eliminating sexual mistreatment at work? These questions, and the ethical dilemmas they raise, can be studied in the case of EEOC v. Mitsubishi Motor Manufacturing of America, and by exploring the cultural, political, and legal milieu in which this case is situated.

❖ SEXUAL HARASSMENT IN AMERICAN SOCIETY

The Working Women United Institute and the Alliance Against Sexual Coercion have been credited with the first use of the phrase "sexual harassment." But it was journalist Lynn Farley (1978) and law professor Catherine MacKinnon (1979) who brought sexual harassment from obscurity into the legal, organizational, and public domains by conceptualizing it as a feminist issue. Farley described sexual harassment as unsolicited and nonreciprocal behavior of men toward women in which female sex roles overshadow female work roles, and blamed capitalism and patriarchy as its foundations. MacKinnon defined sexual harassment as "the unwanted imposition of sexual requirements in the context of a relationship of unequal power" (p. 1), and argued that since workplace sexual harassment is primarily a problem for women, it should be regarded as sex discrimination, and that victims of sexual harassment should be provided the same legal protection as for other forms of discrimination. Soon after, the EEOC—the federal government's agency to protect American workers against discrimination and harassment—developed this country's definition of sexual harassment.

The Equal Employment Opportunity Commission

Created when Congress enacted Title VII of the Civil Rights Act of 1964, the EEOC began operations in July 1965. The EEOC enforces federal statutes prohibiting employment discrimination in the private, public, and federal sectors; interprets employment discrimination laws; is responsible for the federal sector employment discrimination program; provides funding and support to state and local Fair Employment Practices Agencies (FEPAs); and sponsors outreach and technical assistance programs. EEOC headquarters in Washington, DC, and its 50 nationwide offices are primarily responsible for conducting EEOC enforcement litigation under Title VII, the Equal Pay Act (EPA), the Age Discrimination in Employment Act (ADEA), and the Americans with Disabilities Act (ADA).

Adopting many of MacKinnon's positions, the EEOC published guidelines to define sexual harassment and ruled that sexual harassment would be considered an unlawful employment practice under Title VII of the 1964 Civil Rights Act. Prior to issue of the EEOC guidelines in 1980, circuit courts had not been receptive to claims of sexual harassment, viewing them as characteristic of ineffective relationships or the result of natural or romantic attraction. Thus, the EEOC's administrative guidelines defining sexual harassment became a powerful force in directing attention toward the intersection of the societal imbalance of power between men and women and male–female relationships in American workplaces.

The EEOC guidelines defined sexual harassment as the

unwelcome sexual advances, requests for sexual favors, and other verbal or physical conduct of a sexual nature when (1) submission to such conduct is made either explicitly or implicitly a term or condition of an individual's employment, (2) submission to or rejection of such conduct by an individual is used as the basis for employment decisions affecting such individual, or (3) such conduct has the purpose or effect of unreasonably interfering with an individual's work performance or creating an intimidating, hostile, or offensive work environment.

Ultimately, this statement and the subsequent judiciary findings testing or reaffirming it have proven to be a powerful cultural force in advancing victims' rights and social awareness (Wood, 1994).

Although intended to provide direction, the guidelines are admittedly vague. "To be sure, the EEOC very intentionally wrote a broad, general definition so all possible forms of sexual harassment would be covered" (Linenberger, 1983, p. 243). As a result, the definition leaves executives, managers, and individual employees with the responsibility of recognizing sexual harassment on a day-to-day basis as it occurs, as circuit courts lack agreement about the behaviors that meet the test of the EEOC guidelines (Woerner & Oswald, 1990). Despite the problems presented by a case-by-case determination of sexual harassment (McCaslin, 1994), the EEOC guideline became the basis by which individuals could allege sexually harassing treatment at work and pursue civil lawsuits against their employers. In those cases where there are many plaintiffs with comparable claims, the EEOC files a class action suit on their behalf—many of which end in some type of settlement before the case is heard at jury trial.

In addition to providing a definition of sexual harassment, the EEOC guidelines distinguish between two types of sexual harassment: quid pro quo and hostile work environment. Quid pro quo is characterized as intentional harassment in which the victim is required by the harasser to provide sexual favors to avoid threatened loss of economic opportunity. The U.S. Supreme Court upheld this characteristic, ruling that this type of unwelcome behavior is a form of illegal sex discrimination (*Meritor Savings Bank v. Vinson*, 1986). A sexually hostile work environment was characterized as that which interferes with an employee's work performance or creates an intimidating, hostile, or offensive work environment and has been upheld by the Court of Appeals for the Eleventh Circuit (*Henson v. City of Dundee*, 1982), which put the responsibility for a harassment-free workplace on the employer.

❖ ORGANIZATIONAL HISTORY OF MITSUBISHI

Mitsubishi Motor Manufacturing of America (MMMA) began its American organizational life in October 1985 when a joint venture between Chrysler and Mitsubishi Motors Corporation (MMC) created Diamond Star Motors. This agreement put Japanese executives in charge of design and construction of the plant, as well as production of the vehicles at the plant—half of which would bear the Chrysler logo.

Placing Mitsubishi in a central role in both production and management reflected U.S. automakers' deference to Japan for manufacturing small cars. In 1991, MMC purchased Chrysler's 50-percent share and took over operations in the Normal, Illinois, plant, which became a wholly owned American subsidiary of MMC. On July 1, 1995, Diamond Star Motors was renamed Mitsubishi Motor Manufacturing of America. The 2.5 million square-foot plant covering 6.36 acres can produce nearly a quarter-million vehicles each year, and has produced 10 different Mitsubishi, Chrysler, Dodge, and Eagle models for domestic use and exportation to 14 countries.

The communities of Normal and Bloomington, Illinois are home to about 100,000 people, surrounded by farmland, and situated halfway between Chicago and St. Louis along key interstates (I-39, I-54, and I-74) and rail lines. The twin-city community is a predominantly white population center situated in a productive agricultural area enhanced with insurance, manufacturing, healthcare, and educational employment opportunities. In the 1980s, Japanese companies sought out isolated, homogeneous communities in the United States for overseas expansion of its manufacturing plants. Towns like Normal jockeyed for position and granted tax abatements and other enticements to attract the huge multinational interests that brought economic growth. Although most of the 4,000 employees were hired from the twin cities area, about 70 Japanese managers were transferred to the plant, most in senior management.

MMMA became one of Normal's largest employers, employing 4,600 in 1996. Although not the largest, MMMA became the highest-paying employer, paying an average of $19 per hour with average annual salaries ranging from $35,000–$40,000 in addition to generous benefits. The town's largest employer, State Farm Insurance, and two universities offered employment opportunities but no other employer offered the salary or benefits provided by MMMA. Securing employment at the plant was perceived as a good opportunity and landing a job there was cause for celebration. Despite the economic benefits, employment at the MMMA Normal plant soon became associated with a different set of characteristics.

❖ THE UNION

The 1935 enactment of the National Labor Relations Act gave skilled and unskilled employees in the United States the right to form together as unions in order to protect the interests of the workers, and to bargain collectively on their behalf. Founded the same year, The International Union, United Automobile, Aerospace, and Agricultural Implement Workers of America (UAW) has become one of the largest and most diverse unions in North America, with 710,000 members employed in 3,200 organizations ranging from multinational corporations, small manufacturers, and state and local governments to colleges and universities, hospitals, and private nonprofit organizations. The UAW has been credited with a number of collective-bargaining breakthroughs, including employer-paid health insurance for industrial workers, cost-of-living allowances, job and income security provisions, and comprehensive training and education. According to its Web site, the UAW has had a voice in every piece of civil rights legislation, including the Civil Rights Act of 1964, the Voting Rights Act, the Americans with Disabilities Act, and legislation fighting discrimination against women.

The *local*, or United Auto Workers Local 2488, began representing workers at MMMA in 1989. Unlike UAW contracts with other auto manufacturers, Local 2488's contract with MMMA lacked an equal-application clause—a clause that would have required joint union–company investigation of sexual harassment complaints. As a result, the union contract did not contain specific provisions for handling sexual harassment claims. Although Local 2488's civil rights committee initially presented the clause to MMMA, company officials rejected it.

❖ ACCUSATIONS OF SEXUAL HARASSMENT

Although the sexual harassment suit against MMMA was not filed until 1994, female plant employees begin compiling public complaints in November 1992. A variety of sources reported that sexually harassing behavior had been part of the plant's culture as early as the late 1980s—implying that women perceived sexually inappropriate behavior directed toward them but took no formal actions. Maintaining a division of the sexes common to Japanese culture, Japanese managers acted in ways that reinforced the inequality of women and men. Although hired, female employees were told that they should not be working in factories. According to one woman, they were treated as second-class citizens from the time that they were hired.

In making their complaints, women alleged they were repeatedly told they did not "belong in the plant, they were not welcome and they

Figure 8.1   Mitsubishi Time Line

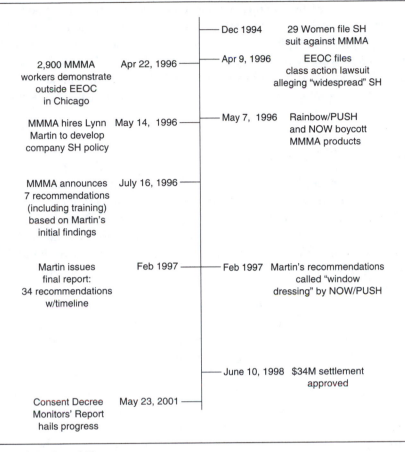

	Dec 1994	29 Women file SH suit against MMMA
2,900 MMMA workers demonstrate outside EEOC in Chicago — Apr 22, 1996	Apr 9, 1996	EEOC files class action lawsuit alleging "widespread" SH
MMMA hires Lynn Martin to develop company SH policy — May 14, 1996	May 7, 1996	Rainbow/PUSH and NOW boycott MMMA products
MMMA announces 7 recommendations (including training) based on Martin's initial findings — July 16, 1996		
Martin issues final report: 34 recommendations w/timeline — Feb 1997	Feb 1997	Martin's recommendations called "window dressing" by NOW/PUSH
	June 10, 1998	$34M settlement approved
Consent Decree Monitors' Report hails progress — May 23, 2001		

Note. SH = Sexual Harassment.

were considered second-class employees"; another reported that she was told to shut up because she was "just a woman." Women claimed men taunted them routinely, calling them "bitch," "whore," and "slut." Crude drawings depicting sexual acts and sexual graffiti were drawn on the cars being manufactured; graffiti also appeared in the bathrooms, often including the names of female employees. Models of male and female genitalia were created from scrap material and displayed publicly. Male employees were reported as exposing or fondling themselves and simulating masturbation in front of women. Large pneumatic air guns were placed between women's legs and fired. In one particularly graphic and violent example, a male employee was reported as speaking frequently of wanting to kill women by forcing a woman to perform oral sex on him and then blowing her away (shooting her with a gun) as he ejaculated. As if suffering through these types of sexually abusive behaviors were not enough, the women who made the complaints and followed through by filing a lawsuit also faced ridicule, ostracism, physical threats, disciplinary action, and retaliation after filing reports with MMMA about the harassment. Many found their workstations sabotaged.

More Women Come Forward

Twenty-nine women filed the initial private lawsuit against MMMA alleging sexual harassment, as well as sexual and racial discrimination, after receiving a right-to-sue letter from the EEOC, which had investigated the credibility of the charges brought against shop-floor workers, supervisors, and managers. This filing, one of the 14,420 filed nationwide that year with the EEOC (2004), was so severe that the federal agency launched its own 15-month investigation and uncovered additional cases. During the EEOC investigation, the original 29 complainants faced additional harassment and retaliation.

The final EEOC sexual harassment suit filed April 9, 1996, represented 350 to 400 female employees. In all, estimates suggest that 50 percent of the female employees in MMMA's plant were sexually harassed. According to one woman, a four-year employee at the plant, women at all levels were harassed. "It's not just down on the [plant] floor," she said (Grimsley, 1996, p. A9). Another female employee described widely varying conditions from one part of the plant to another. In her work area, she was exposed to sexually harassing behavior within her first two weeks of work, but initially endured the sexist treatment because it was a good job with a generous salary and benefits, and plenty of overtime. Eventually, her work environment improved when a female supervisor was transferred in and put an end to the overt sexual harassment. But still, she sought to leave her work area; she requested a transfer to a different section where the work conditions were better.

Although women have long worked in automobile manufacturing facilities, these operations, and the automotive industry in general, are dominated by men. Consider the way in which women are often positioned in the auto industry—glamorously dressed pointing to new models or as scantily clad celebrants at the finish line. Moreover, there are relatively few car salespeople that are women, and even fewer women are auto mechanics. These stereotypical views of women relative to cars, combined with the MMMA's subordination of women dictated by the cultural norms of its management, made MMMA a difficult place for many women to gain acceptance and respect.

MMMA's Response to the Allegations

MMMA's first response to the charges of sexual harassment was an unmitigated denial. Going on the offensive, MMMA mounted an aggressive campaign to discredit its accusers and to portray itself as a victim of corporate slander. In a dramatic step on April 22, 1996, just 13 days after the EEOC filed its sexual harassment suit against MMMA, 59 buses with approximately 3,000 workers were driven to Chicago to protest and picket in front of the EEOC regional headquarters in Chicago. Although initially claiming that the employees arranged the bus trip and protest, it was later revealed that MMMA provided the transportation and lunch and paid a day's wages to those who participated. Those who stayed behind? Ironically, they were mandated to attend sexual harassment training.

Despite MMMA's denial, the EEOC submitted a formal memorandum on September 15, 1997, describing, in graphic detail, specifics of the sexual harassment the female employees endured. The EEOC memorandum described the sexually harassing behavior as constituting a hostile work environment in the following ways:

1. Female employees were characterized as inferior during orientation, a time at which men were given hosted trips to sex bars.

2. Women were told they were unwelcome in the plant and treated less favorably.

3. The work environment included sexual graffiti, comments, objects, and gestures—male employees exposed themselves to female employees.

4. Pornography was on display, including images of MMMA employees and members of management engaged in sexual acts at company sex parties.

5. Women were victims of verbal and physical assaults.

The harassment was widespread, with reports indicating that 400 male employees were involved—one out of every eight employees—in the sexual harassment of between 300 and 500 women.

Within a month, MMMA had hired former U.S. labor secretary Lynn Martin to evaluate its workplace policies and procedures and to provide recommendations for future policies and practices. Martin, who had served as the secretary of labor under President George H. W. Bush, was promoted by MMMA as a noted authority on sexual harassment training. Concluding a nine-month investigation in February 1997, Martin presented a 34-point model workplace initiative with an accompanying roadmap for implementation. According to an MMMA press release, Martin developed recommendations addressing management incentives, salary structures, promotion opportunities for women and minorities, quality-of-life issues, streamlining of rules and procedures, and sexual harassment prevention and policy enforcement—including a zero tolerance task force and mandatory sexual harassment training for all MMMA employees by February 20, 1997. Upon formal release of the plan, MMMA asked Martin to remain and coordinate the implementation and monitoring phase. Both her hiring and the report she generated were generally met with great skepticism because neither focused directly on the alleged sexual harassment. Indeed, many critics characterized the report and even Martin's role as an independent consultant as window dressing and a public relations device. For her efforts, Martin earned $2.2 million.

The Union Response

The local union members did try to defend some of the women in their initial complaints, but were themselves the target of hostile gestures. Union members were warned about sexual harassment, and the EEOC's phone number was printed twice in the union newspaper. In practice, however, the union took a middle-ground position, defending itself by saying that disputes between members were hard to mediate, without knowing who was telling the truth. Without the equal application clause in the MMMA/UAW contract, the union could not file a grievance with MMMA until employees first talked with their direct supervisors. If dissatisfied, they could speak with their union coordinator, who then had to meet with MMMA officials. After that lengthy process, a grievance could then be filed.

Despite 20 women bringing complaints to the local union, union leadership refused to investigate or intervene. One woman complained to the union for years about a male coworker's disgusting behavior. She tried to file a grievance with the union against MMMA. Eventually,

MMMA fired him—but then, the union filed a formal grievance to reinstate him. Although dozens of complaints were presented to its leaders, the union filed only six sexual harassment complaints with MMMA— this compared to the hundreds of grievances filed on other issues in the same eight-year period. One woman, a union leader and ex-MMMA employee, said that the Local 2488 raised sexual harassment complaints with MMMA every week, "but the company wouldn't acknowledge that any claim had merit. Neither the company nor the union knew how to deal with sexual harassment. They didn't know the complexity of it. They probably didn't believe a lot of it" (Sharpe, 1996, para. 9).

The Public Response

Reactions from equal rights organizations to the claims of harassment at MMMA were swift and critical. In May 1996, National Organization for Women (NOW) president Patricia Ireland led a national campaign to improve working conditions at the MMMA plant, alleging "rampant" harassment. Rev. Jesse Jackson, founder and president of the National Rainbow Coalition and PUSH (People United to Save Humanity)—a multiracial, multi-issue organization working for social, racial, and economic justice—called for a boycott of Mitsubishi cars, and Jackson personally led a protest at a Mitsubishi dealership in suburban Chicago. But by January 1997 when changes at MMMA were made public, Ireland and Jackson implored their supporters to suspend boycotting and protests, announcing a breakthough in negotiations between the organizations.

The Settlements

On August 29, 1997, MMMA settled the private lawsuit out of court with 27 of the original 29 women for a reported $9.5 million. Walter Connolly, attorney for MMMA, indicated that the company was not admitting wrongdoing by settling the case. Rather, the settlement was in response to an obligation the company had to deal with the women. John Hendrickson, regional attorney with the Chicago Regional EEOC office, saw it differently. "The agreement represented an assumption of responsibility by the company for many of the employee practices" ("MMMA, accusers settle, 1997").

Then, nearly a year later, on June 10, 1998, MMMA agreed to a consent decree to settle the out-of-court lawsuit filed by the EEOC. Not only did MMMA put $34 million in a settlement fund to provide monetary relief to eligible claimants covered by the EEOC's class action, MMMA also agreed to revise its sexual harassment policy and complaint procedures, implement policies designed to promote supervisor accountability with respect to sexual harassment, and provide mandatory annual sexual harassment training to all employees as efforts to effectively support MMMA's zero tolerance policy and equality objectives. The consent decree, agreed to by all parties, also required that both MMMA and the EEOC appoint consent decree monitors who would oversee the implementation of these requirements for three years. Finally, the consent decree admonished all parties to not disclose the names of the claimants or the amounts they were awarded from the settlement fund, and required that MMMA bear all costs associated with the consent decree monitors' three-year review.

Although the consent decree's legal language indicates that the decree was not a finding on the merits of the case, nor to be used as evidence of liability, the settlement was viewed as an indication that the MMMA had discriminated against women at the plant. John Hendrickson, EEOC attorney, said, "It suggests that those charges had merit, and it also suggests that the company recognized that and is now prepared to do something about it" (Wills, 1997, para. 3). Patricia Benassi, attorney for 27 of the original 29 plaintiffs, was also optimistic: "It's a real credit to MMMA that they chose to try to resolve this. There are lots of companies out there that wouldn't try to resolve this. In fact, they drag women constantly through the mud" (Wills, 1997, para. 7).

❖ CHANGES AT MITSUBISHI MOTOR MANUFACTURING OF AMERICA

Even before the settlement of the lawsuits, MMMA began implementing corrective actions. MMMA made changes to its internal organizational structures and procedures based extensively on recommendations contained in an initial report from Lynn Martin, the independent reviewer hired to evaluate its workplace policies, procedures, and practices. MMMA's chairman and CEO, Tsuneo Ohinouye, announced these changes in a July 16, 1996, press conference.

Organizationally, two new positions were created: a Director of Opportunity Programs to strengthen equal economic opportunities for women and minorities, and a Director of Corporate and Community

Communications to be responsible for internal and external communications. Six months later, MMMA created a Manager of Diversity Operations position at its national office to interface with NOW and other advocacy groups, and promised to promote women and minorities to top management positions—a move announced in January 1997 in a NOW press release.

Procedurally, MMMA began comprehensive restructuring of its sexual harassment training and education programs. The initial training plan called for separate and thorough programs for all employees, from senior executives to the lowest-level employees, under an aggressive timeline (e.g., all managers were to have received training within 45 days of this announcement). Upon receipt of the formal report in February 1997, MMMA initiated its zero tolerance policy and the formation of a corporate Zero Tolerance Task Force charged with oversight of sexual harassment and Equal Employment Opportunity complaints as well as the authority to hold management accountable for their performance in these areas.

The Monitors' Report

But the settlement called for more than an internal consultant to recommend changes. The consent decree required that MMMA cooperate with court-appointed monitors who, over a three-year period, documented whether the company had complied with all aspects of the settlement.

According to the final report of the monitors (Galland, Tucker, & Kreiter, 2001),

MMMA has complied with its obligations under the Consent Decree and deserves credit for its efforts. There has been a significant change in "culture" on the plant floor. . . . MMMA's procedures for investigating and disciplining sexual and sex-based harassment generally work as intended. (p. 3)

The report points out that the increased role of first-line supervisors in "detecting, discouraging and disciplining violators . . . is one of MMMA's most notable achievements under the Decree" (p. 4).

As a result of changes at MMMA, the report describes serious incidents of sexual harassment as rare. A great majority of employees believe that the atmosphere has greatly improved. Although complaints are not gone, they decreased over the three year-decree period. Over the monitoring period, employees filed 140 complaints and MMMA determined that 52 violated the zero tolerance policy, leading to the termination of 8 employees, suspension of 14, and less severe discipline for the remaining 30. The monitors reviewed these cases and determined that MMMA's zero tolerance policy "is much stricter than the requirements of federal and state anti-discrimination statutes" (p. 6).

In the end, John Hendrickson ("EEOC responds," 2001), regional attorney of the EEOC's Chicago district office said, "The report of the monitors confirms that, although our litigation and the consent decree did not create a perfect world at Mitsubishi, they did make a huge and positive difference in the daily work life of many women."

Discussion Questions

1. What ethical obligations do managers and union leaders have to their employees or members?

2. Why is sexual harassment an ethical issue in the workplace?

3. After sexual harassment has occurred in a workplace, what is an appropriate organizational response? Union response? Interpersonal response? What is the role of communication in facilitating these responses?

4. Can a monetary settlement ever be a sufficient remedy for ethical misconduct in the workplace? Why or why not?

5. What is the moral imperative of the federal government for bringing class action lawsuits on behalf of harassment victims?

6. In what way do societal and organizational norms influence what is perceived as sexually inappropriate or unethical workplace behavior?

7. In what ways or to what degree do supervisors, managers, and executives have a moral responsibility to create a harassment-free workplace?

8. In what ways do organizations satisfy their ethical responsibilities by developing and implementing sexual harassment policies, complaint procedures, and training?

9. Do organizations develop sexual harassment policies, procedures, and training to protect employees? Or to reduce liability for the organization? Which of these has a stronger moral imperative?

❖ NOTE

1. This case was compiled from publicly available news stories, press releases, and legal documents.

❖ REFERENCES

Farley, L. (1978). *Sexual shakedown: The sexual harassment of women on the job.* New York: McGraw-Hill.

Galland, Jr., G. F., Tucker, J. E., & Kreiter, N. B. (2001, May 23). *Final report to the parties and the court, EEOC v. Mitsubishi Motor Manufacturing of America, Inc.* Report filed in U.S. District Court, Central District of Illinois.

Grimsley, K. D. (1996, April 10). EEOC says hundreds of women harassed at auto plant. *The Washington Post*, p. A1.

Henson v. City of Dundee, 682 F. 2d, 897 (11th Cir., 1982).

Linenberger, P. (1983). What behavior constitutes sexual harassment? *Labor Law Journal, 34,* 238–247.

MacKinnon, C. (1979). *Sexual harassment of working women.* New Haven, CT: Yale University Press.

McCaslin, L. R. (1994). Harris v. Forklift Systems, Inc.: Defining the plaintiff's burden in hostile environment sexual harassment claims. *Tulsa Law Journal, 29,* 761–779.

Meritor Savings Bank v. Vinson, 477 U.S. 57 (1986).

MMMA, accusers settle. (1997, August 29). *The* (Bloomington, IL) *Pantagraph*, p. A1.

Paetzold, L., & O'Leary-Kelly, A. M. (1993). Continuing violations and hostile environment sexual harassment: When is enough, enough? *American Business Law Journal, 31,* 365–395.

Sharpe, R. (1996, July 10). Women at Mitsubishi say union fell short on sexual harassment. *The Wall Street Journal Online.* Retrieved March 30, 2004, from http://online.wsj.com

U.S. Equal Employement Opportunity Commission. [agency home page] Retrieved March 2, 2004, from http://www.eeoc.gov

U.S. Equal Employment Opportunity Commission. (2001). *EEOC responds to final report of Mitsubishi consent decree monitors.* Chicago. Retrieved February 26, 2004, from http://www.eeoc.gov/press/5-23-01.html

U.S. Equal Employment Opportunity Commission. (2004, March 8). *Sexual harassment charges. EEOC & FEPAs combined: FY 1992 – FY 2003*. Retrieved March 17, 2004, from http://www.eeoc.gov/stats/harass.html

Wills, C. (1997, August 29). Federal case still in the works. *Associated Press.* Retrieved February 26, 2004, from http://www.ardmoreite.com/stories/082997/news/news04.html

Woerner, W. L., & Oswald, S. L. (1990, November). Sexual harassment in the workplace: A view through the eyes of the courts. *Labor Law Journal, 41,* 786–793.

Wood, J. T. (1994). Saying it makes it so: The discursive construction of sexual harassment. In S. G. Bingham (Ed.), *Conceptualizing sexual harassment as discursive practice* (pp. 17–30). Westport, CT: Praeger.

Keeping it Real

Race, Difference, and
Corporate Ethics at Coca-Cola

Patricia S. Parker

This case explores norms and practices of racial discrimination at Coca-Cola, which limited the contributions and the pay of African American employees. According to the case, the hostile work environment also created unusually high rates of stress-related illnesses, such as depression, among the employees. The case raises important issues regarding the rights of minority employees, as well as the utility of creating organization-wide differences in compensation, promotion and career advancement that, in effect, exclude the contributions of some employees.

The Coca-Cola Company, based in Atlanta, Georgia, is a Fortune 500 multinational corporation operating in nearly 200 countries. It is arguably one of the world's most recognizable brands. In November 2000, Coca-Cola agreed to pay $192.5 million to settle a racial discrimination lawsuit filed a year earlier by Linda Ingram and three other former and current African American employees. The settlement was the largest ever among an increasing number of racial discrimination lawsuits, surpassing the $176.1 million awarded in the highly publicized case against Texaco, in which an audio tape revealed high-ranking Texaco executives referring to African American employees as "black jelly beans . . . glued to the bottom of the bag" ("Excerpts from tapes in discrimination lawsuit," 1996).

The suit against Coca-Cola accused the company of constructing a corporate hierarchy in which African American workers were clustered at the bottom of the pay scale, averaging $26,000 a year less than white employees. Furthermore, workers depicted an environment so hostile that African American employees at Coca-Cola suffered from unusually high rates of stress-related illnesses, such as depression. Many African American workers reported that upon complaining about these conditions, they were denounced, spied on by management, or fired.

The terms of the Coca-Cola settlement agreement and the events leading up to it illustrate the continued significance of race in the workplace and the complex ethical dilemmas associated with race and difference in organizations. The settlement agreement mandated that the Coca-Cola Company grant unprecedented monitoring powers to an outside task force that would oversee Coca-Cola's progress toward (a) promoting equal opportunity in compensation, promotion, and career advancement for all employees regardless of race, color, gender, religion, age, national origin, or disability; and (b) promoting an environment of inclusion, respect, and freedom from retaliation. However, this mandate raises several ethical questions: What are the limits and opportunities for corporate decision makers to create and promote an environment of inclusion, respect, and fairness for all employees? Who should lead the effort? Whose voices should be heard on important related issues? To what extent and under what circumstances are differences in compensation, promotion, and career advancement justified? What criteria should be used? How are personal biases influenced by corporate values about race and difference and vice versa? How should corporate discourse about race and difference be structured? In what ways can corporate culture influence dialogues about race, difference, and organizational outcomes?

Ethical questions such as these are central to the ongoing debates in the scholarly literature and popular culture about race, difference, and workplace democracy. These questions, and the ethical issues they bring to the forefront, can be fruitfully explored in the case of *Ingram et al. v. The Coca-Cola Company*.

❖ RACE (STILL) MATTERS IN ORGANIZATIONS

The Coca-Cola case and the increasing number of racial discrimination complaints filed with the Equal Employment Opportunity Commission (EEOC)—the government agency that monitors and enforces compliance with federal nondiscrimination statutes—illustrate the continued significance of race in the workplace. Historically, issues of race and work in the United States were primarily centered on racial justice in hiring and access to jobs for African Americans as they moved from forced labor during 200 years of slavery into legally sanctioned segregation and exclusion from certain jobs during the latter part of the 19th century and into the 1950s. The passage of Title VII of the Civil Rights Act of 1964 brought new opportunities for jobs and access to management positions for African American workers. Title VII prohibited employment discrimination on the basis of race, color, religion, national origin, and sex in the private, public, and federal sectors. It also established the EEOC, which developed affirmative action policies to redress the impact of sociohistorical patterns of discrimination against disenfranchised groups, especially African Americans and women, and to end discrimination in hiring, college admissions, and awarding contracts.

However, the central struggle over racial justice has shifted from corporate hiring practices to corporate culture, bringing into focus the complex issues of differences related to race, ethnicity, migration, and immigration. According to EEOC figures reported in the *New York Times*, the number of complaints about discrimination in *hiring* has fallen 20 percent in the last decade. Yet charges of *racial harassment* in the workplace rose nearly 100% between 1990 and 2000 (Winter, 2000). The increase in claims of racial conflict in the workplace directs attention to organizations' internal practices that promote or inhibit workplace fairness.

Ironically, the apparent rise in racial conflict in the workplace occurred as organizations were placing increasing resources into managing diversity (Cox, 1991, 1993). Johnston and Packer's (1987) influential report, *Workforce 2000*, alerted organizations to the prospect of dramatic demographic changes—along dimensions such as gender, race, ethnicity, migration, and immigration—that would transform the U.S. workforce. However, despite the proliferation of managerial philosophies espousing the value of diversity and multiculturalism in organizations, there is growing consensus that past strategies and theoretical approaches have had limited effectiveness in addressing the more complex issue of *difference* in organizations (Allen, 2004; Prasad, Mills, Elmes, & Prasad, 1997). *Difference* is associated with issues of social identity that create race tensions, gender conflicts, and cultural frictions that impede the development of organizational diversity (Prasad et al., 1997). Past strategies equated diversity management with "learning to get along," which in effect tended to obscure, conceal, and deny the real human differences among people at work

(Prasad & Elmes, 1997, p. 373). Increasingly, however, organizational practitioners and researchers are searching for new approaches to facilitate the negotiation of differences and understand how organizational discourses and power relations promote or hinder the development of equal opportunity for a diverse workforce.

❖ CORPORATE CULTURE, DIFFERENCE, AND FAIRNESS

An organization's culture is a primary means for creating an environment of inclusion, respect, and fairness, and fostering ethical practices by organizational members (Arnold & Lampe, 1999). Broadly, "culture is a system of meaning that guides the construction of reality in a social community" (Cheney, Christensen, Zorn, & Ganesh, 2004, p. 76). For formal organizations, culture can foster an environment where ethical practice regarding race and difference is the norm or, conversely, promote an environment in which unethical practices signaling racial bias are accepted behaviors. Thomas and Gabarro (1999), present a framework for analyzing corporate cultures, such as the Coca Cola Company, that promote or inhibit workplace fairness for diverse employees. They studied the cultures of three Fortune 500 organizations that had successfully implemented diversity programs, focusing on the careers of 54 African American, Asian American, and Hispanic American executives and managers who had reached the top ranks of their respective companies. Although the companies differed widely in the types of cultures they created and in their approaches to fostering discourses about race and difference, they each achieved diversity as an integral part of the organization's image and philosophy.

Conversely, based on their extensive review of the literature on diversity, Thomas and Gabarro (1999) report that firms that tend to limit the advancement of racial and ethnic cultural groups fall into two categories. First are those corporations where there is a widely shared set of unchallenged biases that have the effect of setting low targets for minority advancement. As a result, the best of their minority employees leave (Thomas & Gabarro, 1999). The second type of organization is one in which there is some genuine intent to diversify the workforce; however, there is a lack of alignment between the organization's diversity strategy and its culture and values. These organizations are often pursuing diversity as a goal, but are using a strategy that consists of a patchwork of disconnected programs and compliance efforts. Minorities often

Table 9.1   Three Cultural Approaches to Organizational Diversity*

Assimilationist Cultures: Melting Pot	Pluralist Cultures: Valuing Differences	Hybrid Cultures: Leveling the Playing Field/ Intergroup Negotiations
Premise Racial differences are irrelevant. Individual attitudesi are the problem. The goal is to be color-blind.	Premise Differences matter. Race is central to identity. Being valued for who you are is critical to empowerment and contributes to performance.	Premise Biases are built into the system. The system(s) can be changed. Mobilization of minorities is good if focused on performance and advocacy.
Principal targets Individual attitudes and behavior	Principal targets Individual attitudes Relationships	Principal targets Total system Power relations Practices that unfairly advantage or disadvantage any group
Motivating rhetoric "All people are people" and deserve "fair and equal treatment." "It's not the color of your skin that matters, it's how green [the company's logo] your blood is that counts."	Motivating rhetoric "Do the right thing." "People are effective when valued for who they are." "People [and organizations] are more effective if they can engage their differences." "Our diversity effort is about empowering people."	Motivating Rhetoric "We need to change the system so that it works for all employees." "The most important thing for minorities to focus on is performance, even in the face of bias." "Minorities' efforts at self-help benefit the company because they are better able to contribute." "Working with minorities to improve the system [level the playing field] is a form of employee involvement."
Core tactics Active sponsoring of minorities Strong mandate from the top Leadership models behavior Anti-bias training Benchmarking and monitoring	Core tactics Dialogue groups (vehicles for understanding differences/confronting stereotypes) Development of networks Minority mobilization	Core Tactics Self-help/advocacy groupsJoint problem solving and negotiating Altering/changing unfair systems or practices Benchmarking and monitoring Top-down support of bottom-up initiative

make it to threshold positions in middle or upper-middle management, but are not able to advance further (Thomas & Gabarro, 1999).

The above framework can be used to analyze organizations' efforts toward creating and sustaining cultures that promote fairness and opportunity. Where does the Coca-Cola Company fit into this framework? As with any framework, actual practices do not always fit neatly into fixed categories. And it is clear from Coke's history and recent handling of a race discrimination lawsuit that sustaining and promoting a commitment to valuing diversity is a complex and ongoing process.

❖ COCA-COLA AS "THE REAL THING":
    THE MAKING OF A MEGA BRAND

The Coca-Cola Company was founded in Atlanta, Georgia, just after the Civil War. From the very beginning, even during that tumultuous time of racial conflict and reconstruction, Coke emerged as a company marketing a feel-good product intended for every race, creed, and color. Coke's creator, John Pemberton, arrived in Atlanta four years after President Lincoln's assassination, having served as a cavalryman in the Confederate Army. He embarked on a highly successful postwar career selling medicines and other products that promised relief, as one writer put it, "for anxious southern Whites and newly liberated Blacks, and people who had been in Atlanta for generations, as well as the carpetbaggers come to afflict them" (Hays, 2004). In 1886, searching for something unique to be patented, Pemberton created a syrup he called French Wine Coca and, after some refinements, mixed it with carbonated water and began selling it from a soda fountain as Coca-Cola, a "tonic," good for brain and body.

Two years later, Asa Candler, also from Atlanta, purchased the secret formula from Pemberton and began an intensive campaign to sell Coca-Cola syrup to every soda fountain he could, first in Atlanta, then across the South, and by 1895 in every state and territory in the United States. Even as some pharmacists found it easier to make their own concoctions, Candler's aggressive marketing strategies convinced drugstore owners to sell only "the real thing." In 1902, Candler reluctantly expanded the business to include bottled Coca-Cola, in addition to the soda fountain product. In doing so, he issued contracts to independent bottlers who quickly transformed the company into a national phenomenon. By 1915, no longer restricted by the Main Street hours and Sunday-best formality required of the soda fountain dispensers,

Coke was widely available in bottles to anyone in America with a nickel to spend.

Coca-Cola bottling factories sprang up across America's heartland, making its independent owners rich and propelling the Coca-Cola Company into a multinational colossus by the time of its 100th anniversary in 1986. The Coke brand was everywhere, imprinting itself upon cultures around the world, appearing in movies, paintings, sculptures, and song lyrics. Under the leadership of past presidents and CEOs, such as Don Keough and Cuban-born Roberto Goizueta, the company was labeled by Wall Street as a growth stock, beckoning a multitude of investors.

By the late1990s, under the aggressive leadership of president and then CEO Doug Ivester, the Coca-Cola Company had wrestled control of the lucrative independent bottling enterprise and was a sprawling empire employing 29,000 people worldwide. About 6,000 of them worked in the company's headquarters in Atlanta, where the executives at the top maintained tight control over decision making. As Constance L. Hays writes in her book, *The Real Thing: Truth and Power at the Coca-Cola Company,* "As global as the Coca-Cola Company was, it was still, in its heart of hearts, a southern place. It craved formality as much as it craved profits . . . it remained in many ways hierarchical and in the grip of certain old fashioned customs" (p. 198). For many of the African American employees, the old-fashioned customs translated into limited opportunity for upward mobility at the Coca-Cola Company.

❖ RACE AND CORPORATE CULTURE
    AT THE COCA COLA COMPANY

In the 1990s, during a time of aggressive growth at the Coca-Cola Company, there was growing discontent among African American employees who believed that they did not have the same kinds of successes as whites in the company. There were very few senior executives who were black, even though by the 1980s, many African Americans were being hired by the company. Talented and ambitious, they came to Coca-Cola, lasted a couple of years, and left. Some of those who stayed formed support groups and met secretly to exchange stories about their perceptions of unfair practices and racially charged incidents at Coke. As would be revealed later, some African American employees noticed that they were paid less than people they supervised, all of them white. One African American employee working in the benefits office noticed that when he organized seminars for people receiving stock options, there were almost no blacks in the standing-room-only crowds. Others shared that they were viewed inappropriately as lacking the skills and intelligence to succeed in certain areas. The general feeling among African American employees was that Coke had created an atmosphere, consciously or unconsciously, that came across as hostile to blacks and offered little opportunity for advancement.

Conversely, many white employees at Coca-Cola did not think there was racial discrimination at their company. For people who did not receive stock options, one employee observed, "everyone is treated equally bad." In a similar vein, some Coke officials would say later that employees suffered from "benign neglect" because the company had been so intent on increasing its share price. Moreover, by the 1990s, whites in Atlanta often proclaimed that there was no "race problem" in that city, and certainly not at the Coca-Cola Company. Nevertheless, African American employees at Coke believed Coke had had a problem for a long time.

One African American executive who did ascend the ranks at Coke was Carl Ware, a former Atlanta city council member. Recruited in 1974 as a corporate affairs executive, Ware became a senior vice president in the mid 1990s, with responsibility for all of Coke's business in Africa. However, aware that he was the only black senior vice president in the company's 109-year history, and privy to the growing discontent among African Americans in the company, Ware approached then–Coke president, Doug Ivester, requesting permission to convene a committee to examine the issue of race at Coca-Cola. Was Coke doing a good job hiring, promoting, and keeping African Americans like him? Although Ivester gave Ware the go-ahead to convene the committee, the company president apparently missed the opportunity to learn from its findings.

A Missed Opportunity to Listen to African American Employees

With Ivester's approval, Ware convened a committee consisting of African American employees in some of the higher-ranking management positions at Coke to discuss what it meant to be a black executive at the Coca-Cola Company. Assisted by a consultant who facilitated their conversations, the committee produced a report that Ware delivered to Ivester in December 1995. The report concluded, "There is no evidence that the company, in the absence of laws requiring affirmative action, has a commitment to achieve further diversification of its workforce. . . . The company has no clearly articulated vision of how diversification of the workforce is linked to business success." The report contained instances recounting senior black employees' experiences of feeling "humiliated, ignored, overlooked, or unacknowledged," to which employees felt compelled to use "diplomacy, resourcefulness, and the ability to depersonalize prejudicial behavior" to minimize the psychological and material effects of these experiences (Excerpts from report cited in Hays, 2004).

The report also contained several areas where courses of action could be implemented. One of the main issues was the concern that there were so few African Americans in certain levels of the business. However, there were broader concerns cited, including "the lack of tolerance by the organization toward those who are different," the suggestion that Ivester, as president and CEO, define the company's philosophy or approach to diversity and then champion the activation of this approach in the company's business plan, policies, and programs. As a follow-up to the report, Ivester scheduled a lunch meeting with Ware to discuss the committee's findings. However, subsequent to the meeting, no apparent further action was taken.

By 1997, race issues at the Coca-Cola Company had gained the attention of the U.S. Labor Department, which requires companies with sizable federal contracts to address inequities and push forward with an affirmative action plan. In its review, the Labor Department found that Coke had violated federal anti-discrimination laws and directed the company to address the problems. At issue was the highly subjective process by which employees were reviewed and promoted. The company reached an agreement with the Labor Department in 1998 to address the problems, but it did little to revamp the highly subjective review and promotion process.

❖ FORMAL CHARGES OF RACIAL DISCRIMINATION

Linda Ingram, who is African American, had been an information analyst at Coke since 1988, but she had not been a member of Ware's committee on race relations, nor was she aware of the report delivered to Ivester recommending changes in Coke's culture. However, in 1996, a year after Ware's report, Ingram experienced a series of encounters that led her to file a suit in 1999, charging racial discrimination against the Coca-Cola Company.

By most accounts, Ingram was a loyal Coke employee who enjoyed her work and liked her colleagues. However, things changed suddenly one day when she was engaged in an intense discussion with her supervisor, Elaine Arnold. Arnold, who is white, abruptly leaned close into Ingram's face and scolded her, saying, "This is why you people don't get anywhere." The only African American in her department, Ingram said she felt shock and shame, stunned by the tenor and tone of what she heard, taken aback by having "someone . . . standing in your face and you can feel their breath on your face . . . and you start to ask yourself, 'Where am I? Am I in the fifties?'"

Committed to following corporate protocol, Ingram reported the incident to human resources executives and the company's director of equal employment opportunity. After an investigation, Arnold was fired. However, this sparked tension in Ingram's department that seemed to spiral out of control. People in her department, who had liked Arnold, blamed Ingram for their boss's dismissal. She was ignored by some of her coworkers, while others openly refused to talk to her. Feeling isolated and depressed, Ingram repeatedly asked to be moved to another part of the company, but to no avail. Ingram felt unable to escape the fallout from the incident as people continued blaming her for an incident she believed had been precipitated by nothing more than the color of her skin. As time went on, she felt helpless to change her situation. She began taking more and more sick days, and by 1998, she had stopped working and obtained a long-term disability leave.

Ingram felt that worse than the incident itself was the way Coca-Cola executives handled its aftermath. The company seemed to have no mechanisms for dealing professionally with racially charged confrontations. However, rather than an act of omission, to Ingram the company's handling of the conflict in her department, where she was the only African American, seemed to be an intentional way of avoiding race issues. Ingram found that people in the company talked about doing something about her situation, but no one seemed willing to take any action. Eventually, Ingram solicited the help of a lawyer, Cyrus Mehri, the attorney in the 1994 racial discrimination lawsuit against Texaco that had ended in a $176 million settlement. After hearing her story and that of other African American Coke employees, Mehri decided to take the case. On April 22, 1999, Ingram and three other Coke employees filed a lawsuit charging that a pattern of racial discrimination existed in the company.

Coca-Cola's Response to the Racial Discrimination Lawsuit

The summer before the lawsuit was filed, Coca-Cola stock was topping $79 a share and reaching new highs on a daily basis. However, serious problems were brewing at Coke, including sluggish growth in the United States, antitrust investigations into its business practices by regulators abroad, and an incident involving Coca-Cola being suspected of making Belgian schoolchildren sick. The charges of a racial discrimination lawsuit came as these problems and more began making news headlines.

Company officials immediately advised Ivester, who had become Coke's chief executive in 1997, to resolve the lawsuit. However, Ivester refused and vowed to fight. He denied the allegations in an e-mail sent to employees and in public statements to the media. He also announced that he had formed a special Diversity Council that would report to him on matters such as those that had spawned the lawsuit, positioning himself as the channel through which needed changes would come.

However, as Ivester and other company representatives publicly denied the allegations, and as more details of the lawsuit were made public, civil rights groups, public relations experts, and consumers from around the world hounded Coke about the allegations, some accusing the firm of acting defensively and being slow to respond to the charges. The reputation of one of the world's most recognizable brands was being tarnished, not only by the allegations of racial intolerance, but also by its response to them.

An important turning point came with the announcement of the resignation of Carl Ware, the Coca-Cola Company's one and only African American senior vice president. In what seemed to be one of many desperate attempts to stem the tide of problems Coke faced on multiple continents, Ivester had made the decision to change the top management structure. Ware would no longer report to Ivester regarding his progress in the Africa division, but to his peer, a fellow senior vice president, Douglas Daft, who controlled the Asia division. Within a week, Ware decided to quit, but agreed to announce his departure as an early retirement to spend time with his family. Six months earlier, Ware had been one of the Coke representatives saying publicly that the charges of race discrimination had no merit, despite his confidential 1995 report to Ivester describing the plight of black executives at Coke.

As news of Ware's intended retirement spread, buoying the position of the plaintiffs in the racial discrimination lawsuit, Coke officials announced that Ware had graciously agreed to remain at Coke until the end of the following year as head of the Africa division. However, a negative public image was emerging of a Coca-Cola Company so intolerant that even its top black executive was leaving. More than the slow growth and the antitrust allegations, and on the heels of the Belgian schoolchildren incident, the word of the racial discrimination lawsuit was resounding around the world.

Coke Agrees to Largest Settlement Ever in Racial Discrimination Case

In December 1999, Ivester was fired as Coke's chief executive. The new CEO, Doug Daft, set about addressing some of the most obvious problems afflicting Coke. In January 2000, he persuaded Carl Ware to reconsider his retirement, announcing that Ware would become Coke's executive vice president for corporate affairs, an operations position that involved working with governments as well as Wall Street. He also made it clear that he wanted the racial discrimination lawsuit behind him, which had become even more complicated by the announcement of thousands of job cuts in which black employees were offered a better severance package if they agreed not to pursue the lawsuit.

Meanwhile, there was more public pressure for Coke to settle the racial discrimination lawsuit. In March, the trustee of the New York State Common Retirement Fund, which owns $370 million in Coke stock, encouraged the company to take steps to halt the suit's damage to Coca-Cola's reputation and stock price. In April, a caravan of current and former employees, led by the Reverend Jesse Jackson, organized a "Ride for Corporate Justice," traveling from Atlanta to Washington, D.C., and ending at Coke's shareholders meeting in Wilmington, Delaware.

By the middle of June, Coke had reached a tentative settlement of the lawsuit, with the final agreement made in November 2000. At $192 million, it was the largest sum ever awarded in a racial discrimination case. The settlement provided as many as 2,000 current and former African American salaried employees an average of $40,000 in cash, while the four plaintiffs whose names were on the lawsuit would receive $300,000 each.

❖   A NEW OPPORTUNITY TO LISTEN

In addition to the monetary award, the settlement agreement mandated that the Coca-Cola Company make sweeping changes, costing an additional $36 million, and grant unprecedented monitoring powers to an outside task force, headed by former labor secretary Alexis Herman. In the agreement, the Coca-Cola Company committed to evaluate, and where appropriate, implement specific changes to human resource programs for its non-hourly U.S.-based employees. The Statement of Principle made the objectives of the agreement clear:

> The Coca-Cola Company commits to excel among Fortune 500 Companies in *promoting and fostering equal opportunity in compensation, promotion, and career advancement for all employees in all levels and areas of business,* regardless of race, color, gender, religion, age, national origin, or disability, *and to promote and foster an environment of inclusion, respect, and freedom from retaliation.* The company recognizes that diversity is a fundamental and indispensable value and that the Company, its shareholders, and all of its employees will benefit by striving to be a premier "gold standard" company on diversity. The Company will set measurable and lawful business goals to achieve these objectives during the next four years. (excerpt from the Settlement Agreement in *Ingram et al. v. The Coca-Cola Company,* cited in Herman et al., 2003, emphasis added)

As of this writing, the task force has made two of four reports on the Coca-Cola Company's progress toward changing its culture and improving the lot for all employees at Coca-Cola. In its second report, the committee noted that the company has done well implementing, for example, diversity training for its employees and implementing an ombudsman office. However, the report suggests that the company has been slow to implement significant changes in the areas of promotion and development of diverse employees and creating a diversity strategy that is a critical element of its overall business strategy. When it comes to diversity and difference at the Coca-Cola Company, what constitutes "the real thing"?

Discussion Questions

1. What do the terms *inclusion, respect,* and *fairness* mean to you?

2. Do corporations, such as the Coca-Cola Company, have an ethical obligation to create and promote an environment of inclusion, respect, and fairness for all employees? Why or why not? If so, what are the limits of that obligation? If not, what should employees do if they feel they are being treated unfairly?

3. To what extent and under what circumstances are differences in compensation, promotion and career advancement justified? What criteria should be used?

4. Of all the challenges faced by the Coca-Cola Company, why do you think the racial discrimination lawsuit received such strong public reaction?

5. What role should the public play in monitoring the activities of corporations such as Coca-Cola? Explain.

6. How should corporate discourse about race and difference be structured? How are personal biases influenced by corporate values about race and difference and vice versa? Explain.

7. In what ways can corporate culture influence dialogues about race, difference, and organizational outcomes? Explain.

8. In which category does the Coca-Cola Company fit in Thomas and Gabarro's (1999) framework? Explain.

9. In what ways do other organizational communication theories, such as organizational learning, leadership, and change, apply in this case?

❖ REFERENCES

Allen, B.A. (2004). *Difference matters: Communicating social identity.* Long Grove, IL: Waveland.

Arnold, V., & Lampe, J. C. (1999, Summer). Understanding the factors underlying ethical organizations: Enabling continuous ethical improvement. *Journal of Applied Business Research, 15,* 1–20.

Cheney, G., Christensen, L., Zorn, T., & Ganesh, S. (2004). *Organizational communication in an age of globalization: Issues, reflections, practices.* Prospect Heights, IL: Waveland Press.

Cox, T. (1991). The multicultural organization. *Academy of Management Executive, 5,* 34–37.

Cox, T. (1993). *Cultural diversity in organizations.* San Francisco: Berrett-Koehler.

Excerpts from tapes in discrimination lawsuit. (1996, November 4). *New York Times,* p. D4.

Hays, C. L. (2004). *The real thing: Truth and power at The Coca-Cola Company.* New York: Random House.

Herman, A., Burns, M., Casellas, G., Cooke, Jr., E., Knowles, M., Lee, B., et al. (2003, December 1). *United States District Court Northern District of Georgia, Ingram et al., Plaintifs, v. The Coca-Cola Company, Defendant, Case No. 1–98-CV-679 (RWS): Second annual report of the task force*, p. 17. Retrieved October 16, 2004, from http://www2.coca-cola.com/ourcompany/taskforce_report.html

Ingram et al. v. The Coca-Cola Company, Case No. 1–98-CV-3679 (RWS). June 7, 2001.

Johnston, W. B., & Packer, A. H. (1987). *Workforce 2000: Work and workers for the 21st century.* Hudson Institute, Indianapolis, IN.

Prasad, P., & Elmes, M., (1997). From showcase to shadow: Understanding the dilemmas of managing workplace diversity. In P. Prasad, A. J. Elmes, & A. Prasad (Eds.), *Managing the organizational melting pot: Dilemmas of workplace diversity* (pp. 3–30). Thousand Oaks, CA: Sage.

Prasad, P., Mills, A. J, Elmes, M., & Prasad, A. (Eds.). (1997). *Managing the organizational melting pot: Dilemmas of workplace diversity.* Thousand Oaks, CA: Sage.

Thomas, D., & Gabarro, J. J. (1999). *Breaking through: The making of minority executives in corporate America.* Boston: Harvard Business School Press.

Thomas, R. R. (1992). Managing diversity: A conceptual framework. In S. E. Jackson (Ed.), *Diversity in the workplace: Human resource initiatives* (pp. 306–318). New York: Guilford.

Quinn, M. (2000, July 29). Ga. Power learns from Coca-Cola; bias suit cases similar: Utility's response shows lessons gleaned from soft drink giant's actions. *Atlanta Journal-Constitution,* p. F1.

Unger, H. (1999, April 24). Discrimination lawsuit: Coca-Cola accused of company wide patterns. *Atlanta Journal-Constitution,* p. H1.

Winter, G. (2000, November 17). Coca-Cola settles racial bias case. *New York Times.* Retrieved October 16, 2004, from www.nytimes.com

Is Agriculture Spinning Out of Control?

A Case Study of Buckeye Egg Farm: Environmental Communication, News Frames, and Social Protest

Jeanette Wenig Drake

This case discusses the emergence of factory farms and their impact on public health, property values, and the quality of life for neighbors in surrounding communities. Focusing specifically on news coverage of Buckeye Egg Farm, the case asks what groups should participate in the decision making regarding not only the location of factory farms, but also the legislation that regulates them. It considers what, if any, obligations such farms have to broader communities and how their relationships with neighbors and legislators should be managed.

In August 1997, a beetle infestation of farmhouses in central Ohio swiftly mounted to the intensity of an Alfred Hitchcock film. That is how J. P. Miller of *The Wall Street Journal* described it. A nearby factory farm had imported beetles to help combat "fly populations of biblical proportions" by eating fly larvae in the mountains of chicken manure. Armies of beetles invaded up to 20 nearby homes when the manure was spread on fields. "One resident went upstairs and discovered 'the floor was just black with them.' She swept them away again and again, and each time hundreds more materialized." This factory farm wreaked so much havoc, people across the country would come to know it by name—Buckeye Egg Farm.

Although they have been banned in some European countries and significantly restricted in others, factory farms have mushroomed in the United States over the last decade. Most Americans are unfamiliar with this relatively new phenomenon, also known as *confined animal feeding operations* (CAFOs), or megafarms, that jam hundreds of thousands of animals in close confinement. Unlike traditional family farms, factory farms are usually owned, managed, and operated by different entities. Using vertical integration, they create monopolistic conditions with the same corporation often controlling all aspects of production. The industrialized practices produce unprecedented high volume and profit with little regard for public health and the environment.

During a tumultuous eight-year history, Buckeye Egg Farm accrued more than $1 million in fines for egregious violations, including infestations, fish kills, and selling old eggs. Ohio was cited as having the worst environmental record with factory farms, a designation brought about by this single operation, which, at its peak, had more than 14 million hens producing 2.6 billion, or 4% of the nation's eggs. Ultimately, the intensity of citizen protest, media coverage, and the company's continual wrongdoing effected some changes in regulations and a state order to shut down. However, the facilities never closed; they merely changed ownership.

Studies have shown that CAFOs have a negative impact on public health, property values, and the quality of life for neighbors, along with detrimental long-term effects on communities and the environment. In the United States, these facilities produce 2.7 trillion pounds of animal waste each year that often leaks into rivers—killing fish and contaminating drinking water and beaches. A single operation produces as much waste as a large metropolitan area. CAFOs pollute the air and water and spread disease due to the unprecedented high concentrations of animals.

Proponents say industrialization is the only way to keep food prices down and to feed the world's growing population. Opponents favor sustainable agriculture. Factory farms precipitate myriad ethical questions, including those about animal treatment, environment, public health, and powerful government–industry alliances. Just as difficult as the physical realities of factory farms are the challenges of the socially constructed realities that are played out in the media, where the way an issue is *framed* or presented is as important as the issue itself.

❖ THE CASE STUDY

In March 1995, a local newspaper announced that Anton Pohlmann, a poultry farmer from Germany, intended to build a large egg-laying plant in a small, rural Ohio community. Over the next five years, the company (originally called AgriGeneral and later renamed Buckeye Egg Farm) would expand to the size of 90 "barns," each the length of two football fields. When neighbors learned that the operation would put millions of chickens at several plants within a seven-mile radius in their community, they organized to form Concerned Citizens of Central Ohio. Throughout, citizens faced many obstacles, including the operation's strategic plan to cross three county lines—Marion, Hardin, and Wyandot. For residents, this meant difficulty in communicating and organizing because there were multiple governing bodies, media, and publics involved. Although activism was foreign to these residents, up to 400 citizens gathered in protest.

At the time, no regulations in Ohio governed CAFOs, even though problems from factory farms had transpired for years in other states. To set up one of the country's largest egg-laying operations, Pohlmann needed only to obtain a permit from the Ohio Environmental Protection Agency (OEPA) upon showing a satisfactory waste-management plan. The OEPA ignored the owner's criminal record and his environmental degradation in Croton, Ohio, where he'd had a facility since the 1980s. Regulations specific to CAFOs were not instituted in Ohio until 2002— after all the Buckeye Egg facilities were up and running. Until then, the state played a jurisdictional game of hot potato with CAFOs that set up roadblocks for citizens and paved the way for permits.

From 1995 to 2004, proponents and opponents employed various frames to make their case because how an issue is framed plays a key role in whether it will be perceived as a problem. To frame is to "select some aspects of a perceived reality and make them salient in a communicating text in such a way so as to promote a particular problem definition, causal interpretation, moral evaluation, and/or treatment recommendation" (Entman, 1993, p. 52). In other words, how something is portrayed will determine if there is a problem, what it is, who is to blame, and how it should be remedied.

As an issue plays out in the media, *master frames* or major themes will develop and evolve. News coverage is replete with frames, and, though framing is not always intentional, framing is not neutral. The influence of any given frame rests, in large part, with the power of the framing agent or the extent of that agent's resources such as money and access to information, the political process, and the media. Since the most effective power prevents conflict from arising in the first place (Reese, 2003), the agricultural industry is highly motivated to keep factory farms out of the news.

An asymmetrical relationship in this debate may be seen by comparing finances. The Ohio Department of Agriculture (ODA) in 2003 had a budget of $52.5 million, with some $335,000 being earmarked for communication. Its communication budget nearly tripled during the eight-year controversy. By contrast, Concerned Citizens raised and spent less than $25,000 during the same time period.

Though opponents were successful in making headlines and raising awareness, they were less able to influence content or policy. Ultimately, government and industry agents were most successful at framing the issue to create the perception that all sides were appeased. During the debate, four master frames evolved in the news as a result of unfolding events or influence from various parties: (a) progress is good, (b) regulation is necessary, (c) Buckeye is a bad egg, and (d) the ODA will take care of everything.

❖ PHASE I—PROGRESS IS GOOD

For the first four years, while Buckeye Egg was seeking and obtaining permits, the governor and ODA stayed out of the debate, which made it difficult for the issue to gain legitimacy. News coverage focused on the fight between the residents and company but did not delve into the issues behind the controversy. Reporting followed a *progress frame* by highlighting economic benefits. Through an over-reliance on official sources, coverage granted assumed legitimacy to the CAFO while it questioned the legitimacy of the protestors by using quotation marks around the group's name, for example, or when a reporter used the qualifier, *so-called*, in regard to statements from citizens.

While the company awaited its first permit, citizens contacted officials and protested at the State House and public forums. In February, 1996, the newspaper reported Pohlmann had been charged in

Germany with animal cruelty and other crimes. So the timing was conspicuous when, in March, the OEPA granted Pohlmann a permit to build the first facility. One news article reported the permit was granted and that the facility would be "safe," while an adjacent story reported that the "the public's knowledge of the chicken and egg business is a little scrambled." Both claims would be disproved by subsequent events but only after it was too late. Both articles used government and industry sources, who lent automatic legitimacy to factory farms. Just three months later, Pohlmann was convicted in Germany and banned from raising chickens there.

❖ PHASE II—PROPER REGULATION IS NECESSARY

Shortly after the first facility was constructed, neighbors began suffering from fly and beetle infestations, as well as a horrible stench, as a result of the massive amounts of untreated waste. It was so bad, families couldn't go outside or even sit down to eat inside without a fly-swatter. In an ongoing saga, the company accrued one fine after another from state and federal agencies for mismanagement, waste run-off, and spills that polluted waterways and killed fish. Citizens began to take legal action. The organization came under attack from the EPA, the Occupational Safety and Health Administration, labor unions, immigration services, the Sierra Club, a national religious group, family farmers, local and national media, and others, but the governor remained silent. A coalition of 10,000 citizens asked the state to place a moratorium on factory farms until the new form of agriculture could be studied and public health assured. The request was ignored.

To overcome opposition while the remaining facilities went through the permit process, the organization used lawsuits, cash incentives to local governing bodies, public relations ploys, and denial. In 1997, the company bought a township trustee vote in their favor, hired a new CEO, changed its name from the now much-maligned AgriGeneral to Buckeye Egg Farm, and staged an open house for the media. Sending mixed messages, the company threatened to sue neighbors for complaining about the conditions, yet news reports captured the company's spokesman promising to be a "good neighbor" while at the same time denying responsibility, saying, "they're not our flies."

News coverage focused on isolated events or *episodic framing* rather than *thematic framing*, which would provide context and in-depth coverage. Given the magnitude and frequency of violations, news coverage of Buckeye Egg fueled the master frame: Proper regulation is necessary—a theme that still allowed the company to expand.

March of 1998 marked a turning point when a local health official declared the perennial fly infestations a "clear threat" to health. The company promptly slapped him with a lawsuit. Nevertheless, his decree, along with approaching elections, forced Governor George Voinovich and state officials to call for increased oversight. Although opponents and proponents disagreed on the legitimacy of CAFOs, they agreed that regulations were needed. Concerned Citizens gained instant credibility. Still, while state officials were talking the talk, the OEPA continued to issue permits. It was four years before regulations were instituted—only after Buckeye's entire operation was up and running.

❖ PHASE III—BUCKEYE IS A BAD EGG

By 1999, the issue had gotten out of control—everyone except the organization agreed that there was a problem and that the factory farm was the cause. Mounting pressure from federal agencies motivated state officials to take action. With Voinovich now safely elected to a seat in the U.S. Senate, newly elected governor Bob Taft was forced to speak out on the issue. The coalescence of opinions resulted in a master frame with more resonance than any other throughout the debate. Newspaper editors said it plainly: Buckeye is a bad egg. This master frame, fueled by state and industry officials, diverted attention away from the larger issue of factory farms.

Yet, this period was full of contradictions. As it expanded, the company continued to cause more of the same problems. Buckeye Egg was fined the largest amount in the state's history and the newspaper called for the governor to shut it down, but the OEPA continued to grant the final permits for the additional planned facilities amidst a convenient catch-22 of jurisdictional ambiguities.

The state and industry were eager to calm public opinion; they also were motivated to get the entire operation up and running since it would set precedence. Once all the facilities had received permits, the state's activity level intensified. It took control of the issue by turning Buckeye Egg into a scapegoat, dominating media coverage, and establishing industry-friendly regulations pushed through by Senator Larry Mumper, a member of the Farm Bureau, which is a staunch supporter of CAFOs. It appeared as if the state were rectifying the problem, but new legislation merely took oversight away from the OEPA and gave it to the ODA—in essence, allowing the industry to regulate itself.

❖ PHASE IV—ODA WILL TAKE CARE OF EVERYTHING

Under fire from all sides now, Pohlmann changed top management five times in as many years. Throughout, Buckeye Egg continued to pledge to be a good neighbor but continued to violate health and environmental regulations. In 2001, Mercy for Animals broke in and documented inhumane conditions at two Ohio factory farms; one was Buckeye Egg. Their videotape, available at www.eggcruelty.com, reveals chickens with their heads trapped between the cages, unable to reach food or water; dead chickens decaying next to live hens; and sick, featherless birds with large ulcers. Public exposure of factory farm conditions was the last thing the industry wanted, so following the break-in, the legislature enacted strict laws against trespassing on agricultural property. The result was one more roadblock for citizens and the media who act as watch dogs.

After being fined hundreds of thousands of dollars and sued millions, Pohlmann threatened bankruptcy. The governor, attorney general, and other state officials now dominated the news coverage, which helped them to maintain control over the issue. Finally, in a grandiose gesture after repeated attempts at correction and compliance failed, the state threatened to send Pohlmann to jail. Citizens were quiet as they watched the heroics and waited for resolution, but neither bankruptcy nor jail time ever came to fruition. By November 2001, the state attorney general called for the shutdown of the CAFO. In August 2002, the ODA (whose mission is to "promote agriculture") took over from the OEPA the permitting and regulating functions of megafarms. In July 2003, ODA also ordered Buckeye Egg to close. By this time, Pohlmann had left the country.

The process of closing the facilities began but never materialized. By February 2004, the ODA had promptly issued permits to a new owner for the same old facilities. The state was able to frame Buckeye Egg Farm as the problem so it could get rid of "the problem" that was tarnishing the industry but still keep the facilities. CAFOs are creating similar problems across the country. The number of factory farms in Ohio has tripled and continues to grow since the ODA has streamlined the permit process. Each new CAFO causes heated protests where they locate, but the ODA has successfully contained them as local issues.

❖   THE STATE OF AGRICULTURE

This is not a case of one bad egg; factory farms remain largely unchecked across the country, and problems have become a part of doing business. CAFOs dominate the beef, dairy, pork, poultry, and egg-laying industries with just 3% of U.S. farms producing more than 60% of America's agricultural goods. Industry experts continue to tout efficiency, even though increased efficiencies do not account for *externalities*, or costs of production, such as environmental costs, borne by someone other than the producer. In other words, when industry officials claim that industrialized practices are more cost-efficient, they fail to factor in related costs such as those resulting from air and water pollution. Although the company pays for internal costs, such as animals, machinery, facilities, and labor, it does not pay for the external costs of pollution. What is the price of a major fish kill? What are the costs in medical bills sustained by neighbors in increased asthma and other diseases? What is the price of a child who dies of E. coli?

While farming has become further removed from the daily lives of most citizens, the food-agro industry has grown to be the second-most profitable industry in the country—second only to pharmaceuticals (Magdoff, Foster, & Buttel, 2000). At the same time, reporting of agricultural issues has significantly decreased in quantity and quality (Pawlick, 2001). This means decreased citizen participation and increased politicization. The Bush administration has actually reduced federal regulations on CAFOs, exempting them from air pollution standards. A lack of federal regulation has precipitated state-to-state competition to attract agribusiness, and, as a result, the industry has targeted environmentally lax states, such as Ohio, that allow factory farms to operate unhindered.

❖   PUBLIC HEALTH AND THE ENVIRONMENT

One of the most dangerous practices of factory farming is the storage and use of liquefied animal waste (Global Resource Action Center for the Environment, 2005). The massive quantities of manure generated by CAFOs are stored in holes dug in the earth (referred to as "lagoons") and then spread onto cropland. These manure pits often leak or overflow, releasing toxic bacteria and excess nutrients into groundwater. Decomposing manure emits hazardous gases that degrade air quality. Spreading waste on the ground leads to odor problems and water pollution when more manure is applied than the surrounding land can absorb. The U.S. Department of Agriculture (USDA) estimates that animals in the U.S. meat industry produced 1.4 billion tons of waste in 1997—130 times the nation's volume of human waste and five tons of animal waste for every U.S. citizen.

In 1995, 25 million gallons of manure spilled from an eight-acre "lagoon" into North Carolina's New River, killing 10 million fish and closing 364,000 acres of coastal wetlands to shell fishing. Manure at cattle feedlots can produce substantial amounts of methane and nitrous oxide, both greenhouse gases that add to global warming.

According to a 1997 Iowa State University study (Thu et al., 1997), exposure to airborne factory farm emissions can lead to tension, depression, reduced vigor, fatigue, confusion, nausea, dizziness, weakness, fainting, headaches, plugged ears, runny nose, scratchy throat, and burning eyes. The American Public Health Association in 2004 asked for a moratorium on factory farms, but no such stopgap has been considered.

❖ ETHICAL RESPONSIBILITIES TO FARM ANIMALS?

Atrocities at factory farms have been well documented but remain hidden from public view. In the egg-laying business, a *sexer* picks out male chicks at birth and drops the live chicks into a grinder, where they are processed for cattle feed (Coats, 1989). The female chick gets her beak trimmed with a heated blade so she won't peck her cagemates. She lives with millions of other hens in a windowless facility, where light, water, feed, heat, and ventilation are computer controlled. Massive manure piles accumulate beneath the bank of cages, causing strong ammonia vapors to fill the barn. When the bird is about four months old, she begins to lay eggs, nearly one a day. After about a year and a half, the hen is starved an average of 10 days to induce molting, which means she loses her feathers. This is done to increase her productivity. At about age two, she is so physically depleted that her bones often break when she is removed from her cage for disposal. About 30 percent of hens arrive at the slaughterhouse with freshly broken bones.

At the end, she is gassed to death and buried, or slaughtered and processed into food.

The Humane Society decries such animal factories. A 1999 survey found that 44% of consumers would pay 5% more for food labeled humanely raised. Only after activists are able to bring conditions to the national spotlight have small changes come about. McDonald's announced in 2002 it would not buy eggs from producers who give hens less than 72 square inches of cage space each or use starvation to induce molting. Nor would they buy eggs from producers who overuse antibiotics, a practice which has negative effects on human disease prevention. After employees at a Pilgrim's Pride slaughterhouse were shown in a 2004 videotape throwing live chickens against concrete walls and stomping on them, KFC threatened to stop purchasing from this supplier. The United Egg Producers adopted guidelines that will increase each bird's living space to about the area covered by a Kleenex. Critics say this isn't enough.

❖   ENVIRONMENTAL INJUSTICE?

Since nonmetropolitan areas do not have zoning that separates industrial from residential properties, these factory facilities are built next door to people who have lived in a community for generations. As a result, many residents end up leaving their homes. Others stay and suffer the consequences, which the industry says is "just the way it is."

Just as reality is socially constructed, so, too, is risk. Goshorn and Gandy (1995) have argued that "the determination of acceptable levels of risk is explicitly political" (p. 136). This was evident when Ohio's Governor Voinovich characterized citizens as NIMBYs (a disparaging term that stands for Not In My Back Yard). His successor, Governor Taft, inaccurately portrayed protestors as city folk unaccustomed to country life. Both tactics were part of a larger framing strategy to de-legitimize protestors and characterize the industrialized practices as normal. Goshorn and Gandy challenged, "Why do we regard some uncertainties as constituting risk, yet see other classes of harms, to which different classes of persons have different chances of being exposed, as descriptions of 'the way it is,' however unjust that status may appear to be?" (p. 138).

It is no accident that factory farms are located in the nether regions of a county—far from the government center. The same logic that argues fewer people will be impacted fails to account for the injustice to those citizens that are. For example, when the risk was relegated to residents on the outskirts of Marion County, little was done. However, officials jumped to action when manure from the factory farm threatened to cross Marion City limits and when run-off from fields threatened Columbus's drinking water. Similarly, little was done regarding North Carolina's hog farm problems until two events touched more people and, specifically, people in power. In 1997, after a proposal surfaced for a factory farm near golf courses in a powerful legislator's home district, the legislator pushed through a moratorium on new facilities. Then, only after Hurricane Floyd swirled hog waste into waters throughout the eastern part of the state did pressure mount to solve the problems that had been plaguing other parts of the state for years.

❖ CIRCUMVENTING DEMOCRATIC PARTICIPATION

Understandably, a state will promote the growth of agriculture within its borders, which is why federal standards are needed. A good student of capitalism might argue that the free market will provide necessary checks and balances; however, Mattera (2004) argued that "policies on issues such as food safety and fair market competition have been shaped to serve the interests of the giant corporations that now dominate food production, processing, and distribution" (p. 4). He contended that the USDA has promoted factory farms "with little or no regard to their public health consequences" (p. 6).

Indeed, during the Buckeye Egg debate, citizen participation was curtailed through government-industry manipulation of bureaucratic, legislative, and media processes. Although the state held public hearings, it did not listen to the public. The OEPA staunchly rebutted criticism and defended the legitimacy of factory farms. The governor refused to involve himself in the issue until forced by elections. Backroom talks were going on long before the public was apprised of the coming factory farm.

Buckeye Egg fired employees, and they sued, threatened, and paid off critics. For example, the company paid $100,000 to win a township trustee vote in favor of its facilities. Industry-sponsored research denied culpability for fly infestations on the part of Buckeye Egg, but that research was later disproved. Large settlements for class action suits quelled opposition but did not solve the problem.

Proposed legislation attempted to turn citizens who complained into criminals. When Mercy for Animals (2001) videotaped the conditions inside two Ohio factory farms, the state legislature promptly passed new legislation to penalize and prevent future attempts of "vandalism or violence on farms" by the citizenry. As more and more neighbors of factory farms began using the courts as the only recourse left them, the state legislature went to work on a bill to limit punitive measures against corporations. When the Buckeye Egg problem grew too big, citizens were appeased through a pseudo shutdown. Citizens were left impotent when a new owner took control within five months.

Government-industry agents attempted to curtail the media as well. The Farm Bureau did not like what the *Dayton Daily News* printed about CAFOs, so its public relations employee visited the editor and "picked a fight." At the height of the controversy, *The Columbus Dispatch* dropped the agriculture beat altogether. After eight years of substantial coverage of Buckeye Egg, the local newspaper, *The Marion Star,* suddenly experienced a remarkable drop in coverage in 2003 after being called to the carpet by the state for being too critical. These incidents represent a *web of impediments* (Drake, 2004), or activities of political actors to obstruct nonconforming actors.

❖ CONCLUSION

One of the most heated environmental debates of the new millennium is over the ancient vocation of farming. Even the word "farming" is contentious since industrialized practices of the 21st century more closely resemble factories with tens of thousands of animals "produced" in factory-like settings.

Cable and Benson (1993) showed that "if collective democratic pressures for environmental reform in a community are successful, the state resolves the legitimacy crisis by enforcing environmental standards only in that particular case" (p. 473), such as Buckeye Egg. Even if a grassroots group is successful, that success does not extend beyond that specific locale. Without a nationwide coalition, it is improbable that significant structural change that would adequately protect the environment can occur.

Opposition to factory farms is taking place at the local and national levels. Political rhetoric, along with dramatic and simplistic reporting, has polarized the extremely complicated issue. Rural Americans have been caught up in a losing battle with an industry that searches for regions where local control is weak, creating pockets of environmental injustice in poor communities with little political clout. Others who are concerned with humane treatment for animals, the environment, and public health, continue to wage their own, usually separate, campaigns against CAFOs.

Since public opinion is shaped by the power to name and frame an issue, industry agents seek to control the debate by spending millions not to inform or engage the public, but to exert influence. When done ethically, this is known as public relations. However, when it includes deceit, discrimination, circumvention of democratic processes, or disregard for the public interest, it is spin. Clearly, Buckeye Egg Farm violated legal and ethical boundaries; however, much larger ethical questions face the agricultural industry.

Discussion Questions

1. What positive or negative social impact will the move toward industrialized agriculture have on our culture?

2. What, if any, ethical responsibilities do we have to farm animals?

3. What should be done to protect our air and water? Can we rely on business to protect them or is regulation the only way to ensure safety? Can we rely on the state and industry to practice responsible stewardship? Who should pay the cost of externalities?

4. Should citizens have the right to decide whether factory farms move in next to them or into the community? Do CAFOs precipitate environmental injustice by locating in poorer communities? If a CAFO moves in, should residents be compensated for losses to property values, quality of life, or other factors? Should new technologies be allowed to operate until proven harmful, or should they have the burden to prove they are not harmful before they operate?

5. What ethical responsibilities regarding food production do corporations have? The agricultural industry? Government? Individuals?

6. Is the traditional American farm worth preserving or are CAFOs inevitable? What social costs are involved in the loss of the family farm?

❖ REFERENCES

Cable, S., & Benson, M. (1993). Acting locally: Environmental injustice and the emergence of grass-roots environmental organizations. *Social Problems, 40*, 464–477.

Coats, C. D. (1989). *Old MacDonald's factory farm: The myth of the traditional farm and the shocking truth about animal suffering in today's agribusiness.* New York: Continuum.

Drake, J. W. (2004). *Would a farm by any other frame smell as sweet? News frames, factory farms, and social* protest. Doctoral dissertation, Bowling Green State University, OH. (UMI publication number 3159603)

Entman, R. M. (1993). Framing: Toward clarification of a fractured paradigm. *Journal of Communication, 43*(4), 51–58.

Global Resource Action Center for the Environment (GRACE) Factory Farm Project. (n.d.). Facts and data. Retrieved July 4, 2005, from http://www .factoryfarm.org/

Goshorn, K., & Gandy, O. H., Jr. (1995). Race, risk and responsibility: Editorial constraint in the framing of inequality. *Journal of Communication, 45*(2), 133–151.

Magdoff, F., Foster, J. B., & Buttel, F. H. (Eds.). (2000). *Hungry for profit: The agribusiness threat to farmers, food, and the environment.* New York: Monthly Review Press.

Mattera, P. (2004, July 23). *USDA Inc: How agribusiness has hijacked regulatory policy at the U.S. Department of Agriculture.* (Available from Corporate Research Project of Good Jobs First, 1311 L Street, NW, 4th floor, Washington, DC, 20005)

Mercy for Animals. (2001, August 8). *Silent suffering* [Videotape]. (Available from Mercy for Animals, P.O. Box 363, Urbana, OH 43216)

Miller, J. P. (1997, November 3). That crunchy stuff in your cereal bowl may not be granola: Beetles invade an Ohio town when chicken farm's plan for fly control goes awry. *The Wall Street Journal,* pp. A1, A13.

Pawlick, T. F. (2001). *The invisible farm: The worldwide decline of farm news and agricultural journalism training.* Chicago: Burnham.

Reese, S. D. (2003). Prologue—Framing public life: A bridging model for media research. In S. D. Reese, O. H. Gandy, Jr., & A. E. Grant (Eds.), *Framing public life: Perspectives on media and our understanding of the social world* (pp. 7–31). Mahwah, NJ: Erlbaum.

Thu, K., Donham, K., Ziegenhorn, R., Reynolds, S., Thorne, P. S., Subramanian, P., et al. (1997). A control study of the physical and mental health of residents living near a large-scale swine operation. *Journal of Agricultural Safety and Health, 3*(1), 13–26.

"Moral" Leadership in the Catholic Church

Loss of Credibility and Organizational Support Amidst Charges of Sexual Abuse

Elise J. Dallimore

This case traces the chronology of the Catholic Church's sexual abuse scandal, displaying the degree to which the church was candid with the general public and its parishioners regarding the extent of abuse. The case addresses the consequences of a lack of transparency of, and accountability for, conduct and decision making within the church. It suggests that church leaders behaved inconsistently in relation to the church's core values and failed to respond to key stakeholders, thus negating its obligation to promote personal and organizational healing.

"This is a moral condemnation, as harsh as can be—the church has not abided by its own moral teachings in this case, and whether it was malfeasance or simply a lack of attention to detail, the result was the same, which is that people have been deeply hurt," asserted chairman of the theology department at Georgetown University, Chester Gillis (Paulson, 2003, July 24).

On January 6, 2002, Boston headlines read, "Church allowed abuse by priest for years: Aware of Geoghan record, archdiocese still shuttles him from parish to parish." Initial reports suggested that since the mid-1990s, more than 130 people had come forward with "horrific childhood tales" about how priest John J. Geoghan "allegedly fondled or raped them during a three-decade spree through a half-dozen Greater Boston parishes" (Carroll, Pfeiffer, Rezendes, & Robinson, 2002).

❖ INTRODUCTION

Even with the shocking details of this case, one might hardly have imagined that it would fuel an investigation and public furor lasting for years and result in an ongoing public relations and financial crisis for the Catholic Church in Boston. These initial reports fueled allegations and investigations of sexual abuse by Catholic priests around the world,[1] creating a crisis of faith among many church members and public disbelief and outrage. In Boston alone, these charges led to a settlement of nearly $85 million with approximately 540 abuse victims and contributed to Church plans to close a number of parochial schools and smaller parishes in the Greater Boston area. In addition, the Boston archdiocese, looking for ways to help pay settlement costs, put up for sale one of "its most symbolic and coveted properties" (Ranalli, 2003), the cardinal's residence and nearly 28 acres of land in the highly exclusive Commonwealth Avenue area. Surprisingly, more than two years after the allegations of abuse against priests first became widely publicized, the Boston archdiocese revealed that 7 percent of its priests had been accused of abusing minors between 1950 and 2003, which raised even greater public concern over both the scope and costs of the scandal (Paulson, 2004, February 27).

While allegations of sexual abuse should raise concern for any organization, the ethical implications for religious or nonprofit organizations both attract and deserve special attention. Much of the discussion of organizational ethics has taken place in relation to business organizations. However, nonprofits and, more specifically, religious institutions may be subject to more intense ethical scrutiny because of their morally-focused missions and the humanitarian nature of many of their professed goals. Religious institutions often cover operating expenses and provide services through the tithes of members and through donations solicited from individuals and groups (including corporations) who identify with the espoused organizational values and mission. Not surprisingly, perhaps, ethical concerns arise when religious organizations (or other nonprofits) do not adhere to what some expect should be a higher moral standard.

This case examines issues of organizational ethics in the Catholic Church by presenting a chronological account of key events in what the news media came to call "The Moral Crisis in the Church." It further seeks to demonstrate the impact ethical problems can have on stakeholder support with a stakeholder defined as "any person or group that has an interest, right, claim, or ownership in an organization" (Coombs, 1999). In addition, it identifies possible outcomes associated with behaviors that violate expressed values of an organization. More specifically, this account raises questions about (a) behavior by church leaders that is inconsistent with the church's core values, including their stated position on appropriate moral conduct such as sexual behavior and honesty; (b) the impact of a leadership structure that appears to operate from a different legal and moral standard than it advocates for its members; and (c) how a failure to respond to key stakeholders can lead to demands for change in leadership and the need for organizational healing.

❖   EVIDENCE OF SEXUAL MISCONDUCT
      IN THE CATHOLIC CHURCH

On January 6, 2002, the *Boston Globe* revealed allegations of sexual abuse against the Boston archdiocese and the actions of accused priest John J. Geoghan. In this initial story, reporters obtained a July 2001 disclosure that Cardinal Bernard F. Law knew about Geoghan's problems in 1984 (Law's first year in Boston) but still approved his transfer to another local parish. The cardinal's attorney defended his action saying, "the archdiocese had medical assurances the Geoghan reassignment was 'appropriate and safe.'" In contrast, one of Law's bishops at the time thought the reassignment was so risky that he sent a letter to the cardinal in protest. Reporters found that, in 1984, the archdiocese already had "substantial evidence of Geoghan's predatory sexual habits," including a statement by Geoghan himself who in 1980 claimed that "his repeated abuse of seven boys in one extended family" was not a "serious problem" (Carroll et al., 2002). When asked to comment on the allegations, one former priest spoke out against the church and suggested, "In Geoghan's case, the church defied its own most basic values of protecting the young and fostering celibacy" and contended that he had long believed that the church had been "too slow to deal with priests who molest children" (Carroll et al., 2002).

Action Inconsistent With Organizational Mission and Goals

On January 27, 2002, with growing evidence that the church knew of the alleged abuse by Geoghan, reports suggested that Cardinal Bernard Law's failure to deal with "mounting criminal activity by a pedophile priest has shaken the pillars of Boston's large Catholic community" (Paulson & Mooney, 2002). Further, both Catholic laity and theologians raised concerns over the potential impact of the scandal on both the moral authority of the church and on the church's $300 million fundraising campaign (designed to support the philanthropic efforts central to the church's mission). As one priest and theology professor suggested, "When you're talking about the church's missions to bring peace and justice, the first thing that comes up is, 'when will the church get its own act together.' . . . It raises issues of credibility" (Paulson & Mooney, 2002).

Further, the leadership of the Catholic Church in Boston spoke out against legislation—drafted after the Geoghan case received national attention—that would make clergy "mandatory reporters" (i.e., requiring clergy to report allegations of abuse). Opposition to the legislation by Catholic leaders stemmed from concern that if adopted, the legislation would jeopardize the confidentiality of conversations between clergy and parishioners. The state's religious denominations had differing attitudes "toward confidentiality of conversations" between congregants and clergy; however, as the director of Jane Doe Inc., a state coalition against sexual assault and domestic violence, articulated, "We fully understand that it can be difficult to balance the confidentiality of communications with the protection of children, but it is possible. . . . We've been doing it for years" (Paulson & Tangney, 2002, February 27).

Organizational Leadership Questioned

The breadth of this questioning is evidenced through a range of voices including church members, the media, and the general public, each speaking against church leadership. The following demonstrated the diminished level of support for organizational leadership as reflected through letters to the editor, editorials, and survey data.

On January 11, 2002, writing a letter to the editor, Adelaide Zabriskie wrestled with the church's inherent contradictory behavior after a Catholic education in which she was taught that to question church authority is a sin. She stated, "We still don't really believe that we could demand that Cardinal Law resign. Well it might be a sin to suggest that notes go into next Sunday's collection: 'Not another dollar until we have Law's resignation.' It might mean we will not go to heaven if we stand up, incensed, at what has (is being?) done to our children. Maybe we won't go to heaven if we don't stand up this time" (Zabriskie, 2002).

On January 16, 2002, columnist Derrick Jackson asserted that if Cardinal Law were running a corporation, "he would be fired," and questioned Law's claim that he was "profoundly sorry" about the alleged abuse by Geoghan. He further questioned why Law, having known for 17 years that Geoghan had been repeatedly accused of sexual abuse and already having paid $10 million to settle 50 other law-suits over the last four years, only now admitted that his "judgments regarding Geoghan were 'tragically incorrect.'" Jackson also questioned why the cardinal only now declared a "zero tolerance" policy regarding the sexual abuse of children by priests and instructed the public to be "more alert" to the dangers of such abuse (Jackson, 2002).

On February 8, 2002, an archdiocese-wide survey revealed that most local Catholics believed Cardinal Law had "done a poor job of dealing with clergy sexual abuse," with nearly half wanting him to resign. One respondent was quoted as saying, "He is standing before us as a teacher and a guide, and yet he knew this stuff and didn't do something to stop it right away. . . . He knew it might hurt other people. Maybe he was under a lot of pressure, but I can't give him a lot of credibility" (Paulson, 2002, February 8). The damage done to Law's reputation by the scandal was evident in a poll that found the cardinal was viewed unfavorably by 51% of Catholics in the Boston archdiocese compared to only 16% viewing Pope John Paul II unfavorably and only 4% viewing their local parish priest unfavorably (Paulson, 2002, February 8).

Traditionally, Cardinal Law offers a benediction at Boston College's graduation ceremony. However, on April 11, 2002, fearing that the sexual abuse scandal could "cast a pall over graduation cere-monies," a growing number of faculty and students at the prestigious, Boston-based Catholic university asked that college administration "bar" Cardinal Law's attendance and participation at the year's graduation (Healy & Russell, 2002).

Lay Group Lobbies for Change as Public Criticism Grows

Reports suggested that the alleged abuse was more widespread than initially thought. Subsequently, public criticism of the church and its leadership grew as the news media uncovered a history of sexual abuse allegations against priests in the Boston-area church. Further, reporters with access to church records discovered that during the nearly two decades of Law's leadership, "he and three managers whose duties included handling allegations of sexual abuse by priests knew of many abuse cases and failed to act with urgency" (Paulson, 2003, July 24). There was no recorded effort by church leadership to notify law enforcement of the allegations. Instead, records revealed a pattern of covering up abuse allegations by providing financial settlements to victims in exchange for their silence. This pattern ultimately allowed pedophile priests to continue patterns of abuse for years as they were reassigned to different parishes (after being accused of sexual misconduct in one area) (Robinson & Rezendes, 2003). Moreover, leadership failed, in many cases, to notify supervising pastors or parishioners and did not restrict or supervise priests' future contact with children.

On May 1, 2002, reports suggested that Voice of the Faithful, formed three months earlier "as a listening session for parishioners upset over clergy sexual abuse," had grown and in several weeks had drawn about 4,200 supporters from 36 states and 19 countries (Paulson, 2002, May 1). The all-volunteer group sought nonprofit status in order to raise money for Catholic causes independent of the cardinal. It was preparing to hire a full-time staff and working to establish chapters around the country. The president of the group, Dr. James E. Muller, who shared a Nobel Prize for his work to prevent nuclear war between the superpowers, stated, "my nightmare scenario is that the church successfully papers over the clergy sexual abuse problem and leaves intact an abusive power structure" (Paulson, 2002, May 1). After weeks of negotiation, the group adopted "Keep the Faith, Change the Church" as their slogan and had a mission statement calling for lay involvement in the "governance and guidance" of the church.

Attempts were made to exert financial pressure on the church as Voice of the Faithful advised Catholics to refrain from contributing funds to the church through tithes. They encouraged donations through their organization to make certain that money would be spent on charitable causes rather than for abuse settlements. Eighty-nine percent of members surveyed said they did not intend to contribute to the Cardinal's Appeal, an annual fundraiser for the archdiocese's operating budget (Paulson, 2002, May 1). In spite of the growing financial crisis felt by the Boston-area church and funding cuts to Catholic Charities (i.e., the social services arm of the church), Cardinal Law instructed Catholic Charities not to accept money raised by Voice of the Faithful. Law further "cracks down" on other efforts by laypeople to organize, claiming that efforts for a proposed association of parish pastoral councils (a group considered to be more moderate and "more traditional and deferential than members of reform groups") would be "superfluous and potentially divisive" (Paulson, 2002, April 27).

Attorney General Finds Evidence of Cover-Up

On December 12, 2002, an investigation of the Boston archdiocese by Massachusetts attorney general Thomas Reilly revealed evidence of a cover-up. The state subsequently considered prosecution of the church under a "doctrine of liability" historically used to charge companies who fail to stop wrongdoing by employees. Reilly commented, "This [abuse] could have been stopped long ago but it wasn't. . . . There was a cover up, an elaborate scheme to keep it away from law enforcement, to keep it quiet" (Kurkjian, 2002). Cardinal Law and five bishops who worked with him received subpoenas to testify before a state grand jury that was then looking into possible criminal violations by those church officials who supervised the priests accused of sexually abusing children (Robinson & Sennott, 2002).

❖ CHANGE IN LEADERSHIP ACHIEVED

On December 13, 2003, almost a year after the scandal broke, with opposition growing and himself subpoenaed to appear before a state grand jury, Cardinal Law submitted his resignation to Pope John Paul II. His resignation was "welcomed by laypeople and priests," who had been "clamoring for his departure." Law, a bishop for nearly 20 years and "the highest American church official ever to lose his job as a result of scandal," offered an apology stating, "To all those who have suffered from my shortcomings and mistakes, I both apologize to them and beg forgiveness" (Paulson, 2002, December 13). Boston University management professor James Post, the president of Voice of the Faithful at the time, responded by stating, "This is a terrible day in terms of the history of the church, because these events have brought the church to its knees in some ways, and the departure of Cardinal Law is a symbol of that." However, he called the day both "sad and hopeful" (Paulson, 2002, December 13).

Lay Group Gains Support as Interim Leadership Refuses Input

Reports on May 12, 2003, estimated that Voice of the Faithful had grown to a membership of more than 300,000. While banned from meeting in all or part of seven dioceses nationwide, including Boston, this lay group continued to fight for reform in the church. Cardinal Lennon, interim administrator at the Boston archdiocese, continued to refuse to accept money raised by the organization. The group continued to gain support according to a poll showing that 61% of Boston-area Catholics held a favorable view of the group. As one local Catholic, though not a member of the group, noted, "I'm just glad somebody's taking some action. . . . They want more say in what the church's policies are, and I think that's a good idea." This poll revealed that Lennon had "clearly failed to persuade the public of the wisdom of declining the group's money" and that even among "the minority of Catholics who opposed Law's resignation," a 72% majority believed the archdiocese should take the lay group's money (Paulson, 2003, May 12).

New Leadership Called

On July 2, 2003, headlines read, "O'Malley arrives with a plea and a promise." Bishop Sean Patrick O'Malley, with a history of taking over troubled archdioceses (Paulson, 2003, July 2), was appointed as the new archbishop of Boston. Recognizing "this very difficult time" in archdiocese history, O'Malley introduced himself to the "wounded archdiocese" by offering an apology for the harm caused by sexual abuse, pleading for priests to come together, and pledging to settle the lawsuits pending against the church. O'Malley told the crowd that "people's lives are more important than money" and acknowledged that "The entire church feels the pain of this scandal, and longs for some relief for the families and communities that have been shaken by these sad events, and by the mishandling of these situations on the part of church officials" (Robinson & Rezendes, 2003).

❖ FINAL REPORT ISSUED

On July 24, 2003, Attorney General Reilly suggested that "the clergy sexual abuse scandal in the Archdiocese of Boston was 'the greatest tragedy to befall children—ever' in Massachusetts." Results of a 16-month investigation showed that over six decades, 237 priests and

13 other church employees were accused of molesting at least 789 minors; however, Reilly suggested that the actual number of victims is likely much higher, probably exceeding 1,000. He concluded that "though he wished it were otherwise, he could find no criminal statute under which he could prosecute church leaders," including Cardinal Law (Robinson & Rezendes, 2003, July 24).

Tentative Settlement Reached

On September 10, 2003, the Boston archdiocese reached a tentative $85 million settlement agreement with lawyers representing more than 500 alleged victims of sexual abuse. Payments were expected to range from $80,000 to $300,000 with the exact amounts set through binding arbitration. Besides the money, the settlement called for the archdiocese to "include victims of sexual abuse on the boards and panels it has established to monitor abuse, to offer victims . . . 'spiritual direction and spiritual counseling services,' and to keep information about counseling and treatment it offers to victims confidential" (Cullen & Kurkjian, 2003).

❖ CULMINATING DEVELOPMENTS

On August 24, 2003, headlines read, "Former priest Geoghan is slain: Cleric at the center of sex abuse crisis strangled in prison" (Paulson, Farragher, Mishra, Smith, Tench, & Stearns, 2003). Geoghan was murdered in prison by a fellow inmate, Joseph L. Druce, a neo-Nazi and convicted killer, in a maximum-security correctional facility.

On September 20, 2003, as Druce left the courtroom after pleading not guilty to murder charges stemming from the slaying of "defrocked" priest John Geoghan, "Druce prompted raucous cheers from other prisoners when he shouted, 'Let's keep the kids safe. Hold pedophiles accountable for their actions'" (Murphy, 2003). Public response to Geoghan's murder was mixed. Some felt he had gotten off too easily, never having really "paid" for his crimes. However, others believed that even a convicted pedophile priest like Geoghan deserved protection while in prison.

Adding to the dilemma, Geoghan was to be "technically" deemed innocent of the abuse charges for which he had been convicted because of a Massachusetts' law requiring convictions be "vacated" if the defendant dies while his or her appeal is pending (Cavallaro, 2003). Many of Geoghan's victims were outraged and felt victimized again by the legal system, believing that because his conviction for abuse would no longer legally stand, he would not be held responsible for his actions even in death. They argued that his conviction had been a symbol that the legal system was finally holding him accountable for his actions but said the decision to "invalidate that conviction was an insult" (Burge, 2003). Regardless of the controversy surrounding Geoghan's death, however, both the broader allegations of sexual abuse by Catholic priests and the subsequent "cover-up" by organizational leadership raise a range of ethical issues for secular and nonsecular organizations alike.

More specifically, this case identifies challenges that organizations face when actions by key members, including organizational leaders, violate fundamental values of an organization. This case included actions violating church policy on appropriate sexual conduct and standards of honesty, as well as the broader organizational mission to positively influence the moral development of Catholic youth. It highlights not only the impact of illegal actions such as sexual abuse on organizational credibility, but also how the handling of crisis events by organizational leadership can impact the support of key stakeholders during a crisis. Further, this case raises concerns over how perceived mismanagement of a crisis may lead to demands for organizational change, which may range from the single act of replacing an organizational leader to ongoing efforts to change an organizational culture as stakeholders insist on greater involvement in organizational decision making. The ethical issues raised by this case are profound, some of which are highlighted in the following questions.

Discussion Questions

1. How is organizational credibility impacted when core organizational values are violated? How should an organization with moral standards that exceed current legal standards respond when confronted with accusations of both moral and legal wrongdoing?[2] What should organizations do when confronted by charges that organizational leaders or members have engaged in misconduct or illegal activity?[3]

2. Are there circumstances under which organizational leaders can violate core values and still maintain credibility in their

leadership role(s)? Should standards of behavior be different for organizational leaders than for its members? If so, should the standard be higher for leaders in your opinion? Why or why not?

3. How can a change in leadership help to restore organizational credibility?

4. What is the responsibility of organizational leaders to their stakeholders when core organizational values are violated (e.g., honesty, the protection of the vulnerable, etc.)? What responsibility do leaders have to accept assistance (financial or otherwise) during a crisis from what might be considered a "splinter" (stakeholder) group? What if the support of these groups allows the organization to fulfill its organizational mission in ways that might otherwise not be possible? How does this become an ethical issue if the support allows the organization to fulfill its organizational mission?[4]

5. How should the violation of key values be addressed with stakeholders? In this case, how should organizational leaders have addressed key stakeholder groups? How might a failure to embrace stakeholder groups create an exponential set of problems for embattled organizational leaders?[5]

6. What responsibility do organizations have to respond to stakeholder demands for organizational change, including change in leadership? How might this be different for ecclesiastical versus political leaders?[6]

7. How might responsibility to stakeholders change when institutions justify their policies/practices on theological, philosophical, or moral grounds (e.g., a statement suggesting that the church will not accept divorce or gay marriage because of revelation received by the pope from God)?

8. What does this case suggest about how organizations ought to address crisis events?

9. To what degree does confidentiality as an organizational value shape organizations' possible responses to a crisis? Are there organizations for which confidentiality should be a justifiable reason for failing to disclose illegal activity? What about a failure to disclose behavior, which while legal, might be of moral question? Could the church's concern over false claims of abuse provide a rationalization for their decisions in this case?

❖ NOTES

1. Some of the locations where sexual abuse claims have been made (or class actions suits filed by victims) include New Hampshire, Connecticut, Minnesota, Florida, Arizona, California, Kentucky, Ireland, Canada, Australia, South Africa, Hong Kong, Poland, etc. (e.g., Paulson, 2004, February 28; Pogatchnik, 2004; Stapleton, 2004; Whitmore & Sennott, 2002).

2. The Catholic Church has policies that govern both marital relationships and sexual behavior. For example, the church discourages divorce, prohibits divorced individuals from remarrying in the Catholic Church without the annulment of a former marriage, and may sanction parishioners (e.g., restrict full church participation including their right to take communion) if they choose to marry someone who is divorced. Church policy also discourages the use of birth control, does not condone sex before marriage, condemns homosexual relations, and strongly opposes same-sex marriages. Divorce and the use of birth control are legal, while sexual abuse is not. Further, in this case, the accusations of sexual abuse are against priests who have been entrusted to promote the moral and spiritual development of Catholic youth, thus raising the irony that pervades this case.

3. Up until early 2002, 29 states had laws requiring that clergy report any allegations of sexual abuse of minors to the appropriate authorities (e.g., the police, social service agencies). Although Massachusetts was not one of these 29 states when the alleged abuse took place, such a law was passed on February 27, 2002 (Paulson & Tangney, 2002).

4. At the time, Catholic Charities had lost a significant amount of funding for its programs, including many social service programs for low-income and immigrant populations. Funding losses were a result of the growing financial crisis in the church that many speculated was, in large part, a result of church members' decisions to withhold tithes and donations to demonstrate their dissatisfaction with the church's handling of the sexual abuse crisis.

5. By May of 2003, Voice of the Faith had gained broad popularity among area Catholics as had support for greater lay involvement in church governance. Further, results of a poll taken at the time indicated that not only did 88 percent of area Catholics agree with Cardinal's earlier decision to resign, but 57 percent believed he should face criminal prosecution for his handling of cases of sexual abuse by priests (Paulson, 2003, May 12).

6. Think about the White House sex scandal involving Monica Lewinsky and then-president Bill Clinton.

❖ REFERENCES

Burge, K. (2003, September 27). Geoghan ruling sparks anger: Alleged victims protest erasure of conviction. *Boston Globe*, p. B1.

Carroll, M., Pfeiffer, S., Rezendes, M., & Robinson, W. V. (2002, January 6). Church allowed abuse by priest for years: Aware of Geoghan record, archdiocese still shuttles him from parish to parish. *Boston Globe*, pp. A1, A14–15.

Cavallaro, R. (2003, August 29). Why, legally, Geoghan is now "innocent." *Boston Globe*, p. A19.

Coombs, W. T. (1999). *Ongoing crisis communication: Planning, managing, and responding*. Thousand Oaks, CA: Sage.

Cullen, K., & Kurkjian, S. (2003, September 10). Church in an $85 m accord: Tentative record pact with 552 over abuse. *Boston Globe*, pp. A1, A14–17.

Healy, P., & Russell, J. (2002, April 11). Some at BC say Law unwelcome at graduation: Many at BC hope Law skips graduation. *Boston Globe*, pp. A1, A29.

Jackson, E. R. (2002, January 16). Cardinal Law should resign. *Boston Globe*, p. A13.

Kurkjian, S. (2002, December 13). Reilly says he has evidence of cover up by archdiocese: Crisis in the church. *Boston Globe*, pp. A1, A58.

Murphy, S. P. (2003, September 20). "Keep the kids safe," Druce shouts in court: Pleads not guilty in Geoghan killing. *Boston Globe*, pp. A1, A26.

Paulson, M. (2002, February 8). Most Catholics in poll fault Law's performance: Poll of areas Catholics reveals Law's image tarnished. *Boston Globe*, p. A1; sect. B.

Paulson, M. (2002, April 27). Law seeks to curb organizing by laity. *Boston Globe*, pp. A1, A6.

Paulson, M. (2002, May 1). Catholics drawn to splinter group in Wellesley. *Boston Globe*, pp. A1, A14–15.

Paulson, M. (2002, December 13). Cardinal Law resigns: Pope names administrator for archdiocese. *Boston Globe*, p. A1.

Paulson, M. (2003, May 12). Most in poll would prosecute Law: Area Catholics back settlements. *Boston Globe*, pp. A1, A6.

Paulson, M. (2003, July 2). O'Malley offers plea, pledge: Bishop urges healing, vows a settlement. *Boston Globe*, pp. A1, A27.

Paulson, M. (2003, July 24). A long crisis in church returns to the forefront: Reilly lambastes "acceptance of abuse." *Boston Globe*, pp. A1, A18.

Paulson, M. (2004, February 27). Diocese gives abuse data: Report finds 162 Boston priests accused since '50. *Boston Globe*, pp. A1, A14–15.

Paulson, M. (2004, February 28). Church hierarchy faulted by lay panel on abuse: 700 priests removed by bishops in 2 years. *Boston Globe*, pp. A1, A14.

Paulson, M., Farragher, T., Mishra, R., Smith, S., Tench, M., & Stearns, J. (2003, August 24). Former priest Geoghan is slain: Cleric at the center of sex abuse crisis strangled in prison. *Boston Globe*, pp. A1, B6.

Paulson, M., & Mooney, B. C. (2002, January 27). Catholic community shaken: Scandal shakes Catholic laity, theologians. *Boston Globe*, pp. A1, A25.

Paulson, M., & Tangney, C. (2002, February 27). House closes loophole on clergy abuse. *Boston Globe*, pp. A1, B6.

Pogatchnik, S. (2004, January 31). Ireland, church hit in report on abuse. *Boston Globe*, p. A9.

Ranalli, R. (2003, December 4). Diocese to sell residence: Brighton parcel to help finance settlement. *Boston Globe*, pp. A1, A29.

Robinson, W. V., & Rezendes, M. (2003, July 24). Abuse scandal far deeper than disclosed, report says: Victims of clergy may exceed 1,000, Reilly estimates. *Boston Globe*, pp. A1, A16–19.

Robinson, W. V., & Sennott, C. M. (2002, December 12). Grand jury is said to call Law: Subpoenas for clerics in probe of abuse. *Boston Globe*, pp. A1, A39.

Stapleton, E. R. (2004, January 31). Class-action suit set to proceed against Kentucky diocese. *Boston Globe*, p. A6.

Whitmore, B., & Sennott, C. M. (2002, December 14). Around the world, clerical abuse takes toll. *Boston Globe*, p. A19.

Zabriskie, A. (2002, January 11). Wages of sin. *Boston Globe*, p. A14.

Whose Ethics?
Whose Leadership?

Revenue Sports and University Integrity

John Llewellyn

This case examines scandals and fraud in several university athletic departments, including the University of Georgia, St. Bonaventure, and the University of Colorado. It explores the ethical tension in college athletics to pursue success while fostering integrity. It also addresses important issues regarding the responsibilities of coaches, athletic directors, and university presidents to assure compliance with NCAA regulations, as well as the transparency by which decisions are made about student athletes.

Issues of ethics and leadership can be found in all sectors of our society: corporations, not-for-profit agencies, educational institutions, and religious organizations. When people operate collectively in pursuit of a common goal, there will inevitably be questions about the propriety of means and ends. Universities confront such questions about revenue-producing sports. These questions reveal the challenge to ethical leadership in pursuing success while fostering integrity.

As of this writing, both the University of Florida and the University of Notre Dame have fired football coaches with winning records. The Florida firing was not for misbehavior but for compiling a 20–13 record through three seasons, with four games remaining. The Notre Dame firing was for a 21–15 record in three years at the storied football power. All agreed that this coach epitomized integrity in his coaching methods; the athletic director said, in announcing the firing, that the team's academics had "never been stronger." Two years remained on this coach's contract. His predecessor had a 21–16 record in his first three years and completed his five-year contract. Notre Dame's rush to fire Tyrone Willingham, one of a handful of African American head football coaches in Division I programs, may have been motivated by the desire to snag the "hot" coach at Utah, Urban Meyer (11–0 at that point), a former assistant with the Fighting Irish. The ultimate irony is that Meyer, confronted with both offers, chose to take the job at Florida.

The final straw in the Florida firing was a single loss: a 38–31 defeat to "lowly" Mississippi State. No infractions were charged, just a .606 winning percentage. The coach stayed on for the remainder of the season; the university moved on by hiring Meyer. Earlier replacement rumors had centered on Steve Spurrier, the former Florida coach who had left the school three years earlier for the National Football League. This interest had bloomed despite the fact that Spurrier had left Florida during recruiting season by phoning the athletic director from his beach house. All of these problems were outweighed by the belief that he could produce "winners." After weeks of speculation and attempts to arrange an interview between Spurrier and the university president, the coach took himself out of the running.

Another recent news item on the subject of universities, leadership, and ethics is the charge from a former star running back, Maurice Clarett, that coaches helped arrange for Ohio State University boosters to provide him with cars and cash during his brief career there. Clarett led the Buckeyes to a national football championship in his freshman year. Ohio State denies the charges. The school and its former star trade barbs via the media and the reputations of both parties deteriorate.

This case study examines leadership and ethics through several high-profile collegiate athletic scandals. The purpose, however, is not to assign blame. In the aggregate, these instances present a case study of the challenge of ethical leadership at the highest level of universities. The deeper question here is the ethical responsibility of top administrators to manage athletics that are essential to the university's identity in ways that enhance and preserve that identity. The environment for coaches, athletic directors, and university presidents is filled with multiple objectives: fielding winning teams, educating and graduating athletes, dealing with misbehavior of student athletes, placating alumni and other donors, and satisfying the rules of the National Collegiate Athletic Association (NCAA). Ethics can provide a means of guidance while negotiating these competing interests.

If the contradictions among these competing interests are so widely recognized, why do they persist? Why have competent administrators not resolved these issues on their campuses? These questions concern the ethical dimensions of leadership and the countervailing forces within the academy. Among the countervailing forces are important issues: the athletic/academic tension; the exorbitant salaries paid to revenue-sport coaches; and the thinly veiled demand that a new coach turn around the fortunes of the team very quickly. The bedrock ethical challenge here will be the claim by boosters that other schools in the conference are using questionable, if not underhanded, tactics so to be competitive, we must keep pace. This charge and the accompanying reasoning can be found in social arenas from the neighborhood ("all the other parents say it's okay") to the world stage with the proliferation of chemical and nuclear weapons.

While any number of cases could be cited, this case will focus on three instances and the ethical choices made by administrators in solving or exacerbating the problems. The three schools are the University of Georgia, St. Bonaventure University, and the University of Colorado. This volume is an examination of organizational ethics "on the hoof." The concern for ethics is not an abstract exercise. An organization's legitimacy can live and die with the public's response to its behavior. The classic cases are the enduring public respect (and commercial success) that has followed Johnson & Johnson since its handling of the tainting of Tylenol capsules that resulted in seven deaths in 1982. The downside is exemplified by negative feelings toward oil giant EXXON for the Valdez oil spill in Prince William Sound, Alaska, in 1989. More recently, the energy trader Enron has virtually ceased to be, following the unmasking of its ethical myopia. Questions of organizational ethics are at the heart of many of the stories the news media report every day.

The topic for this case study has its impetus from a late October Saturday afternoon. I'm at our kitchen sink loading the dishwasher. To keep myself amused, I am listening to the under-counter radio as it recaps the college football scores. Then I hear it: a tribute from a nearby university to its "scholar athletes!" Not "student athletes," mind you; that familiar phrase can represent a stretch given the hours revenue-sport athletes are asked to put in on football or basketball. But this institutional advertisement was in praise of the "scholar athletes" on the school's football team. The ad did not allude to one such player, or even a handful; it meant everyone on the team. Professor Murray Sperber, of Indiana University, has studied college athletics and taught athletes for 30 years. He observes, "I've encountered very few dumb jocks. I think that's a media myth. But I've met many, many young men and women who are physically and mentally exhausted from working this tremendously hard job. And as a result, academically under-achieved" (quoted in Buchholtz, 2000).

The phrase "student athlete" suggests that, at some point, players' eligibility will end and they graduate into the wider world. A very small percentage may go on to professional sports for a brief career. Universities are fairly questioned about the level of preparation they provide beyond the basketball court. It is amazing to realize that 16 of the teams in the 65-team field of the NCAA men's basketball tournament had graduation rates of 25% or less. Four of those teams had not graduated a single player within six years of eligibility. In all, 44% of men's college basketball players earn degrees; 1.3 percent of senior players will be drafted by the National Basketball Association. William C. Friday, chairman of the Knight Commission on Intercollegiate Athletics, describes the problem: "When you see poor graduation rates, recruiting violations and instances of academic fraud, any thoughtful sports fan can see that we've created an entertainment industry and, in the process, it has eroded the integrity of the university." Countervailing pressure comes from those with an appetite for glory and the $750,000 that each round of the NCAA men's basketball tournament brings the participating schools.

The late Charles Redding of Purdue University is regarded as the father of the field of organizational communication. He did much of the early research that conceptualized the field, and the several generations of graduate students he trained are among the pillars of the discipline. Redding saw the inevitable and necessary linkage between the study of organizational communication and the study of ethics. He examined the topic in a 1992 lecture at the Center for the Study of Ethics in Society; his concern with the issue was demonstrated in the subtitle of his lecture: "When will we wake up?" Redding gives a call to arms: "I charge that . . . we have remained oblivious to an area that has enormous potential for serious research: namely, the *ethical dimension* of organizational communication" (Redding, 1992, emphasis in the original). He goes on to observe that most problems of organizations are either patently ethical or have ethical issues embedded in them. He identifies six categories of unethical communication that deserve scholarly attention: coercive (intimidating, threatening); destructive (aggressive, abusive); deceptive (dishonest, lying); intrusive (surveillance); secretive (not responding); and manipulative-exploitative (hiding intentions, patronizing). Most of these communication behaviors can be found somewhere in the actions of the three schools examined here.

❖ BLUNDERS IN BULLDOG BASKETBALL

The circumstances at the University of Georgia document just how ethical problems can chain out. They also suggest just how minimal levels of oversight can be. In 2003, the men's basketball coach, Jim Harrick, was forced to resign and his son, Jim Harrick, Jr., was fired. Harrick senior had been fired as basketball coach at UCLA one year after winning a national championship and left a position at Rhode Island under a cloud on his way to coach at the University of Georgia. At Georgia, Harrick junior was accused by a former player of giving money to a player, doing schoolwork for players, and giving three players A's in a sham class he taught. All 31 students in the class, Coaching Principles and Strategies of Basketball, including 10 athletes, received A's. Here is a sampling from the 20-question final exam ("Sports News," 2004):

1. How many goals are on a basketball court?
   a. 1   b. 2   c. 3   d. 4

2. How many players are allowed to play at one time on any one team in a regulation game?
   a. 2   b. 3   c. 4   d. 5

3. In what league to (sic) the Georgia Bulldogs compete?
   a. ACC   b. Big Ten   c. SEC   d. Pac 10

4. What is the name of the coliseum where the Georgia Bulldogs play?
   a. Cameron Indoor Arena   b. Stegeman Coliseum
   c. Carrier Dome   d. Pauley Pavilion

5. How many halves are in a college basketball game?
   a. 1   b. 2   c. 3   d. 4

Leaders at the University of Georgia removed those who had misbehaved. But these violations were not discovered by university officials—not the compliance officer, not the athletic director, not the university president. A former player blew the whistle on these practices. The player making those accusations had been accused of a campus rape and was later kicked off the team for rules violations. The former player's revelation of coaching improprieties was in retaliation for the dismissal. The rape charge was eventually dropped. Without this whistleblower, would the University of Georgia ever have discovered these problems? Who would be motivated to probe for such problems?

This instance was not without warning signs. Before the crisis, Harrick senior had attempted to recruit a player to Georgia who'd been discharged from another college team for threatening a former student with a samurai sword and served four months in jail for an alleged attempt at shooting a college coach. The president of the university declined to admit the student, who had already moved to Athens.

For all the history that suggested that Harrick would bring trouble to the basketball program, there was also evidence that he would bring wins. His lifetime record is 470–235. Georgia was 57–32 under Harrick and 19–8 in the 2002–2003 season before the university pulled out of the conference and NCAA tournaments in the wake of the scandal. He was on the brink of giving Georgia its first-ever string of three straight NCAA tournament appearances when the scandal broke. Shortly after his son was fired, Harrick resigned and retired before the university's investigation came to a head.

❖ ST. BONAVENTURE'S END RUN AROUND THE RULES

The perfect illustration of the profound harms that follow ethical lapses is seen in the 2003 fate of St. Bonaventure University in New York State, a school founded by Franciscan friars to promote justice and the search for truth. Top leadership was central to the fate that befell St. Bonaventure. The university president and the basketball coach conspired to avoid standard university admissions procedures, and ignored compliance officials by bringing in a recruit who was ineligible because he had only a welding certificate from a junior college. Junior college transfers must have academic credentials, not just vocational or technical credits. The NCAA certifies the eligibility of all incoming freshman athletes, but each school is responsible for certifying the eligibility of its own junior college transfers.

When the scandal broke, the president, the coach, and the player were all dismissed. The school's good name and noble mission were called into question. The team was disqualified for using an ineligible player. The situation is placed in perspective by a faculty member at another Franciscan college: "There is a tendency for sports to exploit, and at the college level, we have to be very careful, because we're exploiting young people. This win-at-all-costs mentality really doesn't work with the Franciscan philosophy" (Auer & Harrington, 2003).

Why did the president jeopardize his school and his career? The school from which the student came was scrupulously clear about his situation. St. Bonaventure originally said there would be no problem in granting him admission, only to later ask the junior college registrar to write a letter saying that the welding certificate was equivalent to an associate's degree. She declined to do so and wrote to reiterate that the student had only a technical certificate. In the face of this clear standard, St. Bonaventure's president and coach contravened the NCAA rule in hopes that no one would notice. This practice in support of athletic glory was routine. When compliance officials denied admission to a recruit who did not meet NCAA requirements, the coach or his assistant (the president's son!) would go directly to the president for approval. This pathway skirted both the compliance official and the athletic director.

The president, a former Benedictine monk, was the school's first lay president. In the wake of the scandal, alumni called for a friar to once again lead the school. The president's motives may be reflected in the fact that he sat at mid-court at all home games and screamed at officials and behaved like a crazed fan. His ethical shortcomings in athletic decision making were foreshadowed by actions in other areas. Earlier, he had allowed the wrongful termination of two faculty members and had laid off 43 others, leading to a national censure of the university. An observer noted, "Everyone talks about the Franciscan values at that place, and he has basically gone and thrown them out the window. Well, when the hammer of justice finally comes down, it's going to come from Thor himself."

❖ COLORADO BUFFALOES FACE A STAMPEDE

In the 2003 football season, the Golden Buffaloes amassed a 5–7 record and fans were looking forward to better results in the future. However, January 28, 2004, was not a good day for the University of Colorado (CU). On that date, Mary Keenan, Boulder County district attorney, testified in a federal civil trial that the university's athletic department used sex and alcohol to lure football recruits. Gender-discrimination suits were brought by three female CU students against the University of Colorado and claimed that the school's failure to discipline the athletes had created a discriminatory climate. The three women said they had been raped by football players.

On its face, this story sounds like one more example of the necessity for organizational-crisis management. Indeed, that is true; Colorado had a real crisis on its hands and it would get worse before it got better. But there is a larger lesson in the Colorado story, a lesson very useful for students of organizational ethics. That lesson deals with the foundational conditions that gave rise to—some would say, expressed themselves in—this crisis. To offer an analogy: when there is a big fire with explosions, some people are eager to know, "Where did the spark come from?" while others ask, "Why were all these volatile materials stored so close together?" The spark surely began the fire but the climate in which that spark fell is the element that really made the fire one of disastrous proportions. Crisis managers are adept at telling leaders how to fight the flames. The deeper, more systematic, and more ethically interesting questions are these: How did this volatile environment build up in the first place? Did leadership fail to anticipate or guard against these conditions in its role as "institutional fire marshal"? Beyond those questions lies another: How can we make sure there is no next time?

Background Facts

A number of women came forward to assert that they had been raped by University of Colorado football players and that the university had taken no action. In all, nine women raised charges regarding assaults between 1997 and 2002. Three of these assaults were alleged to have taken place in connection with a 2001 football recruiting party. Those charges led to the wider claim that the University of Colorado engaged in unethical, and probably illegal, football recruiting practices involving sex and alcohol. As the public scrutiny continued to build, various members of the CU hierarchy made statements that inflamed public sentiment: football coach Gary Barnett observed that a former female player, a place-kicker, was "not only a girl, she was terrible" after the player, who had transferred, reported that she'd been raped by a CU teammate. In response to his comments, university president Elizabeth Hoffman suspended Barnett.

Nested Systems

Scholars of systems theory emphasize that all elements of an organization are interconnected. You can learn a lot by understanding the linkages within the organization and the linkages that connect it to the wider world. The Colorado scandal is, at its heart, about unethical recruiting practices. Critics say that the school was using sex and alcohol to entice promising athletes. As the issue moved beyond the university's control—into federal court and the national news media—the university's troubles began. As long as the issues were "in house," the university's definition of the situation prevailed. Once the questions moved into legal, political, and media arenas, however, the university's reputation, and that of its leadership, was destined for harsh scrutiny.

Systems theory holds that every organization has to bring in forms of energy from the outside environment in order to survive. If colleges do not bring in students, they close. If coaches of revenue sports— football and men's basketball, usually—do not bring in very talented athletes who will compile winning records and fill stadiums and arenas, those coaches will be gone, regardless of their graduation rate. But winning alone does not insure that the coach or university president will survive; if his or her behavior reaches the public arena and does not pass ethical muster, the coach or president becomes a liability in the wider, off-campus world. The institution will protect itself and jettison the individual. Whether the removal of one person can reform the ethics of a social system is doubtful. At the very least, a high-profile firing serves as a "symbolic execution" that allows the institution to claim a fresh start.

Timeline (per the Associated Press)

December 1997
High school student reports sexual assault by two football recruits at a party; no charges due to no corroboration; recruits do not enroll.

February 1998
Keenan and other officials meet with university lawyers and the chancellor; she says officials put "on notice" about sex and alcohol in recruiting; athletic director claims different memory of the meeting.

January 1999
Gary Barnett named football coach.

December 7, 2001
Off-campus party involving football recruits; three women claimed they were raped as a result; they file gender-discrimination suits against the University of Colorado.

April 2002
Prosecutors decide against rape charges.

May 3, 2002
Prosecutors file felony charges against four football players for allegedly supplying alcohol to minors at the party; their scholarships are revoked.

October 27, 2003
Keenan statements are released; they suggest that sexual assault charges were not filed because there may have been "third-party consent" for sex with at least one of the women.

January 28, 2004
Keenan's deposition is released; she accuses U of Colorado athletic department of using sex and alcohol for recruiting.

January 29, 2004
Athletic officials deny the allegations; governor demands an accounting.

February 2, 2004
President Hoffman names a commission appointed by the regents to look into the charges.

February 6, 2004
Keenan says investigators will reexamine the rape allegations at the party; police say athletic department may be tied to an escort service incident.

February 10, 2004
Adult-entertainment firm claims football players hired strippers for recruiting parties.

February 17, 2004
Former female kicker tells national magazine she was raped by football teammate.

February 18, 2004
Barnett placed on leave by President Hoffman due to disparaging comments about former kicker.

February 25, 2004

Former university president hired as liaison between administration and athletics.

February 27, 2004

Governor appoints attorney general as special prosecutor to investigate the scandal.

March 4, 2004

University tightens football recruiting rules.

March 11, 2004

NCAA tells Congressional committee that recruiting standards are under review.

May 6, 2004

Colorado faculty call for overhaul of athletics.

May 18, 2004

Regents' panel releases report, confirms use of drugs and alcohol to lure recruits, says no university officials condoned it.

November 22, 2004

Athletic Director Richard Tharp is forced to resign.

March 7, 2005

President Elizabeth Hoffman resigns, effective June 30.

In the final analysis, after a firestorm of controversy, the regents did little with the report their own commission prepared. The Golden Buffaloes finished 8–5 in the 2004 season (4–5 in conference); recruiting season will be coming up soon. Hoffman and Tharp are gone; Barnett remains as head football coach.

❖ CONCLUSION

University leaders face ethical challenges in managing successful athletic programs and maintaining the institution's integrity. The issues appear to be perennial because the tensions are perennial. In the cases of Georgia, St. Bonaventure, and Colorado, we see failures and some successes in promoting ethical behavior on the part of the organization. In a greater or lesser way, you have probably seen these tensions at work on your campus as well.

Discussion Questions

1. What clear examples of ethical lapses do you find in these cases?

2. Does a university president need a different perspective on the institution from that of an athletic director or coach? If so, why? How would one be established?

3. What is the best action taken for the preservation of the institution's reputation in the cases recounted here?

4. How can ethical standards be maintained in an environment where there is a strong sense that other competitors are bending, if not breaking, the rules?

5. Do you know students who cheer for the team on Saturday and roll their eyes as student athletes struggle with issues in the classroom Monday through Friday? What do you make of this ethical stance?

6. What are a coach's ethical responsibilities? Is winning all that matters? If coaches should not break rules, may they bend them? How far?

❖ REFERENCES

Auer, H., & Harrington, M. (2003, March 9). What went wrong at St. Bonaventure? *The Buffalo News,* p. A1.

Buchholz, B. (2000, November 12). Headed for a loss?: Book says students hurt as schools stress sports. *Austin American-Statesman,* p. J1.

Redding, W. C. (1992, February 25). *Ethics and the study of organizational communication: When will we wake up?* Lecture at the Center for the Study of Ethics in Society, Western Michigan University, Kalamazoo.

Sports News. (2004, March 3). *The Associated Press State & Local Wire, BC Cycle.*

Tricking Your Customers Without Cheating Them

Minimal Details as an Information Strategy[1]

Alf Steinar Sætre and Keri K. Stephens

This case involves an increasingly common practice in global businesses that serve customers in multiple locations: presenting a company and its employees as if they are local, when in fact they are not. The example of InterStock, a small brokerage firm that serves clients in several European countries, raises important questions regarding impression management, misrepresentation, unclear jurisdictions, and the deception of customers. The case asks whether the operations of a global business need to be transparent to customers and what, if any, effect such deceptions may have on customer relations.

InterStock is a small Norwegian Internet brokerage firm that uses information and communication technologies to make it *look like* a local company in Denmark, Sweden, and Germany. While operating in these foreign European markets, it has managed to outperform far larger, more established competitors. It accomplished this task with minimal resources and from its home base in Oslo, Norway. InterStock provides online stock trading (Web based) for its clients, as well as stock trading on the newer cell phone models. InterStock is a small organization that must manage both industry and cultural diversity.

The ethical issues facing InterStock are controversial, and involve issues of misrepresentation of the firm, unclear jurisdictions, and the deception of customers. It is a matter of trust. Would you trust your savings to a brokerage firm in Colombia if you lived in the United States and wanted to trade American stocks? Or a broker in Italy if you lived in England and wanted to trade British stocks? Generally Americans trust American brokerage firms over foreign brokerage firms, and Germans place a greater confidence in German brokerage firms than they do in, say, a Spanish firm, especially when dealing with German stocks. InterStock is very aware of this, and does not go out of their way to advertise their foreignness to their international customers.

If you examine InterStock's business strategy, you might view their efforts as those that deceive customers and misrepresent the firm. But you also might see an organization that is cleverly adjusting to the increasingly global nature of business. After all, if you can consolidate your operations into one place and use technology to help you serve a vast marketplace, then costs can be lowered. Instead of "outsourcing" or spreading their operations across the different financial markets in Europe, InterStock operates in these markets from their home base, in Norway.

Doing business in Europe has some interesting challenges. First, the individual countries are located fairly close to one another, yet crossing the border usually means that the language, laws, and sometimes currency change. This is quite different from the United States, where English is the sole language for business communication, and currency and most business laws remain consistent between the individual states. In the United States, "Wall Street" serves as the centralized place for investment in stocks. But in Europe, many of the individual countries have their own stock exchanges with unique laws. InterStock is trying to build a business in this investment and exchange industry in Europe.

❖   WORKING ACROSS DIFFERENT BUSINESS
       CULTURES AND NATIONAL REGULATIONS

Rune Karlsen is a blond, 33-year-old smiling Norwegian, whose brain works so fast that he speaks like a machine gun. Rune is in charge of all

InterStock's international activity as they enter new markets. This job involves recruiting employees and making whatever system adaptations prove necessary with each new market. For example, Rune recently completed a deal with an American broker that allows InterStock to make purchases on the New York Stock Exchange for their Norwegian and Danish customers. He is currently working on securing InterStock membership on the Frankfurt Stock Exchange—a requirement to enter the German market. This requires completing membership applications at the Frankfurt exchange, then organizing the financial settlements of their German customers' stock trades with a large bank that will handle both cash and credit settlements. Trading in Germany is different than in Norway because German laws require that banks, not brokerage firms, handle stock transactions. To meet this requirement and to support their organizational goal of showing a local presence in all their operations outside of Norway, InterStock is partnering with a German bank.

Each stock market has its own rules of engagement, making life more difficult for people like Rune. The Frankfurt Stock Exchange, though, wins his applause for posting its idiosyncrasies and protocols right on its own Web site: "They [The Frankfurt Stock Exchange] have all you need for documentation—application forms and the whole nine yards." Since it's all plainly there on the Web site, a prospective customer need only sign on as a user, download the information needed, fill out the application on paper, sign it, and send it in by snail mail—the only time paper is involved. Once the application is approved, the communication returns to the electronic mode—in this case, email.

Besides its automated application process, the Frankfurt Exchange offers—again via the Internet—training courses on various topics, such as trading in the German market. These courses are also available in a traditional classroom setting, but they cost more there, so the Frankfurt Exchange clearly employs market incentives to drive users toward technology. In fact, Rune says, "The only thing that is not via the Net is the concrete agreements that I get in my lap, and there are only a few of these, because most of the agreements are on the Net as well." Rune sees the German model as an exemplar of how to use the Internet to streamline a standardized but rigorous process. The Frankfurt Exchange's extensive use of the Internet facilitates the process of becoming a member for foreign brokerage firms.

Because countries differ in how money, stocks, and shares flow, Rune's job is to set the specifications for each system and to define the account routines for how trading will occur in each particular market. To speed up this process, he works from a generic platform that he helped create for InterStock when it was entering the Danish market; it enables him to move quickly into a different language and establish InterStock in yet another country. For each market, he also creates a Web home page. Because he uses the material previously created (now a boilerplate), he needs to develop only about 20% fresh content. As he says with a grin, "There is no reason to reinvent the wheel." For example, he identifies a group of 12 German Net brokers and then maps out a plan for how InterStock should approach the German market. This is based on the generic structure that most of the existing Internet brokers are using. When the Web site concept is complete, his work is sent on to InterStock's systems-development group.

That group numbers 22 employees, most of whom live in Oslo, Norway, and specialize in setting up the servers and the associated technology. Rune regularly uses Microsoft programs—PowerPoint, Word, Excel—since he knows that standardization is important. Once he specifies how the page needs to look, he lists his work on what is called the "Task Execution System," which displays the project he's working on and automatically invites help from others in finishing it. He says, "You put in desired tasks that you want solved, and then everybody [at InterStock] has access to it—both on the technical and the non-technical side." The Task Execution System allows those responsible on the development side to distribute tasks to be completed.

Of course, when something is unclear, which often happens when programmers tackle content in a foreign language and have little grasp of stock trading, follow-up is needed. The translation issues for InterStock's German application, for example, require a fair amount of interaction. His staff, Rune says, will not quite get what it says, so the project will require some close monitoring by individuals well versed in German. "The problem is that a system developer does not necessarily have an intuitive understanding of how, for example, a stock transaction takes place at the Frankfurt Exchange. You have to explain this in relatively explicit detail." So while the Frankfurt Exchange is very good when it comes to design, it has a bit more difficulty explaining "both what is happening and what it says."

There are other ways for InterStock's systems-development personnel to work around the language obstacles arising when aligning their technology for the German market. Since none of the other Norwegians in Rune's Oslo office speak German, they are currently hiring more German-speaking technicians in Norway to work on the project. Fortunately, the Frankfurt Exchange is also offered in the English language, which is a lifesaver for some of InterStock's technicians. There are, in fact, people who work in the Frankfurt Exchange support group in Germany yet speak no German at all! This focus on English is "of course related to the fact that the Frankfurt exchange has many non-German customers and brokers," Rune explains. "Almost one-third of the brokers are not located in Frankfurt."

But the German market and the Frankfurt Exchange are not the only foreign market or stock exchange that InterStock deals with. Access to the U.S. stock exchanges introduces new challenges since financial settlements are handled much differently in the United States than in Europe. InterStock's goal with an American partner was to establish "one-stop shopping." But that was not easy for two reasons. First, the U.S. firms that make desirable partners are large organizations with whom it is difficult to establish a working relationship from a distance. Second, InterStock is not likely to generate much business by the standards of American brokerage firms. As Rune notes, again with a smile, InterStock's one-day high trading record "corresponded to about 8 seconds on the NASDAQ." But InterStock did manage to make a workable pricing agreement with a large U.S. broker. It was no small triumph, Rune says, since "we are a small actor in the U.S., and on a good day we have only about 60 to 70 trades in the American market, so of course you don't get max attention from the big brokers. That much is self-evident." But because InterStock now offers all their Scandinavian clients the opportunity to buy on NASDAQ and NYSE, this agreement with a large foreign broker in the United States perfectly fits their clients' needs.

Once the relationship between InterStock and the various international stock exchanges was established, the ICTs (Information and Communication Technologies) currently in use all came into play. Rune says that communication "takes place in part by phone; otherwise we communicate through Internet solutions. We have a few applications that allow us to go in and check account status and transactions." In addition to consulting the daily status reports from their partners, Rune can directly monitor the current activity level that their customers generate with those partners.

From their effort at global business, InterStock has learned that "cultural differences are much larger than they appear on the surface." Just as customers in Canada and the United States can seem virtually interchangeable yet actually show subtle differences that prove decidedly important, so it is, Rune says, with Norway and its neighbor Denmark: "Even though it seems to us a very genial and likable country and that they are like us, still they are fundamentally different in some areas—in particular, in business etiquette. That is, how you build relations, how you maintain these, how you make agreements."

For all the cultural differences, Rune says, "there are also greater industry differences—that is, a given industry will have a common codex and culture, and it's stronger than geography, in this context." In other words, ironically there may be greater differences between a broker and a regulatory agency in one country than there are between two brokers from different countries. Even though industry differences are greater than national differences, InterStock has concluded that national differences, although at times subtle, cannot be ignored. Rune thinks that most Norwegians imagine doing business with Danes is easy because "we are so similar." Not so, he says. In Norway, "it is normal procedure that we communicate via email and that's it. But, for example . . . in Denmark . . . [you] cannot continue in a process until you have met them personally." In his mind, it is crucial to be aware of such differences.

❖ PROJECTING A LOCAL PRESENCE

InterStock's efforts to operate outside Norway's boundaries are more developed in Denmark than in Germany. In Denmark, InterStock has "been up and running" for a while, and they are a member of the Copenhagen Exchange. In Germany, they partner with a Danish stockowners' association (DSA). Rune says, "We have collaboratively rolled out campaigns with very low prices for members of DSA, and we have marketed ourselves in their magazine and on their pages, and then we have run joint marketing campaigns in large newspapers. Those are our primary collaborative partners in Denmark."

In Germany, not only does InterStock use German banks for credit and settlement statements, but it also has a relationship with several large stock clubs and stock owners' associations. "German stock clubs have membership of about 20,000–25,000," Rune says. "We will make some cooperative agreements there, both to gain credibility for ourselves and to gain access to customers." Having local partners helps to keep the cost of market entry down, and it also gives them both greater credibility and a broader market impact. Most important, however, is that it fits hand-in-glove with their ambition of projecting a local presence.

In the case of Denmark, the projection of a local presence has been enhanced by hiring a Dane to be responsible for much of InterStock's efforts there. After Rune handled the application and certification, InterStock was "very lucky and managed to recruit a trading manager—the trading manager from our largest competitor in Denmark—and he brought a mountain of networks and competencies with him." Turning the Danish operations over to a Dane suited Rune because his next task was to focus on the U.S. market.

Rune knows that being close to InterStock's different markets is important. "In my case," he says, "I am a great deal in Germany in order to gain a certain closeness to the market." InterStock learned this lesson early from watching the failure of an American Internet broker that entered the Scandinavian market and tried to control everything remotely. InterStock has a different approach: "We establish a branch office, we have an address, the Germans are calling German phone numbers, the Danes are calling Danish phone numbers. They send mail to local addresses. So, for the customer, we are perceived as local."

With his 1959 book, *The Presentation of Self in Everyday Life,* Erving Goffman created the foundations of what has been know as impression management. Impression management refers to the process by which people or organizations try to influence the image that others have of them (Rosenfeld, Booth-Kewley, Edwards, & Alderton, 1994). Presenting themselves—and thus being perceived—as local is an impression that InterStock has carefully cultivated. In fact, if you visit InterStock's home pages in the different countries, you will not easily find any information about their "true" location, except on their German home pages. On these, you will find this information under the link "Impressum." This is a legal requirement for all companies in Germany, whereas there is no such minimum requirement in the other countries where InterStock operates.

In an interview on the German Web site www.brokertest.de, Rune does not hide where InterStock is located, but instead he emphasizes that their German customers are mainly heavy day traders that have an affinity for reliable high-tech solutions that give them the most flexibility at competitive prices. When confronted with examples of other "foreign" broker firms going bankrupt and withdrawing from the German market and asked about the risks of using InterStock, he calmly explains about the low fixed costs of their business model.

In their business model, all personnel are located in Norway. As opposed to their technical staff, all their customer service people always "speak the native language." He continues, "You can say that we are compensating for the lack of closeness as much as we can by using these methods." Behind the scenes, all the mail is automatically forwarded to Oslo. Meanwhile, all the mail from InterStock to its Danish and, eventually, German customers is mailed with Danish and German stamps and postmarks, though it originates in Oslo.

Speaking with someone who not only speaks your language fluently, but is indeed from the same country, facilitates initial trust formation. According to McKnight, Cummings, and Chervany (1998), there are two types of trust relevant to new relationships: knowledge-based trust and initial trust formation. Knowledge-based trust comes from experience in a relationship, whereas initial trust formation is based on the impressions we get of someone when we are in the initial stages of a relationship. One major part of communicating, or projecting, a local presence involves having people who not only speak the language, but are natives, to represent the company. InterStock knows this. So, all calls that are made to local numbers in Denmark and Germany are answered by Danish and German customer-service representatives, respectively—and they are all sitting physically in Oslo!

InterStock is well aware, too, that there are ethical issues at play when communicating a local presence. Rune says that the careful observer can find the company's true location, though to the casual observer the company appears Danish or German. In this way, InterStock is perceived to be more present in their local markets than they actually are.

Although advantageous in many ways, not being physically present in a market has other costs associated with it, Rune says, "You can say that what you lose, then, is the more informal relationship-building that is not planned but that often happens by coincidence." Meeting someone new in an unplanned fashion can often be valuable, but it is hard to estimate this value, Rune concedes: "How important is that? Difficult to say, really." When your people are located in a different country, the informal relationships cannot happen as easily.

❖ DISTANCE AND MEDIA USAGE

As the physical distance is increased, electronic communication media becomes increasingly important, even in the world of the already digitalized Internet stock brokers. But the closeness to the market that rich face-to-face communication affords cannot be over-looked. The minus with InterStock's innovative approach is that "you don't have the closeness to the market that you would want during an internationalization process," Rune says. "The core in all internationalization is that you should be close to the market." InterStock's Danish head of operation understands this all too well himself, "because he cannot have these small informal meetings that you can have if you are, for example, sitting in Copenhagen," says Rune. With InterStock's approach, they "have to plan to a much greater extent, and the cost—well, you don't know what a meeting will bring and therefore it is difficult to budget it, because you don't buy airfare for USD 1,000 just to have coffee for an hour with a journalist." But Rune feels that "you can still build a relation toward a local market by traveling a great deal. In my case I am a great deal in Germany in order to gain a certain closeness to the market." Getting that closeness, though, might just take a little longer when you must travel to meet that objective.

In business, it is common practice that the smaller firm will visit the larger firm, not vice versa, but with InterStock's U.S. deal-making, the opposite occurred. Rather than little InterStock going to the United States for acceptance, representatives of the U.S. brokerage firm traveled to Oslo—to "check out" the applicant. Rune explains, "They actually want to see who they have as clients. They know very well what they are selling, and they want to know who we are. They wanted to get an impression both of the person they were talking to and also the organization." Rather than viewing face-to-face meetings as some soft, interpersonal preference by the Americans, Rune sees them as entirely sensible—and a reflection of American business practice:

> The Americans display a very rational behavior. They shall build relations, and they shall only be built where they can obtain the maximum amount of information—when you have the personal contact. So it is actually a rational affair. If you think about it, it is the right way to do things.

By traveling to Oslo, the U.S. brokerage firm not only met with the people they would have met if InterStock had traveled to the United States, they also got to see InterStock's facilities and its operations.

Rune reports that Norwegians see themselves as cooler and more factual in their interactions, so they think they have less of a need than Americans for such a face-to-face encounter. "This is also a cultural issue," he says. "In Norway, it is much stricter—we communicate via email and that's it. In Norway, we stick to the issues and manage to exchange information via the Internet, mail, or telephone." But in its effort to become a global company, InterStock discovered that Germany and Denmark, much like the United States, preferred face-to-face communication as part of the engagement process. Rune says, "In Denmark they have a very fixed opinion that you cannot continue a process until you have met them personally. In terms of being stringent, then, Denmark is strongest when it comes to personal relations. Then [comes] the U.S., and then Germany."

❖ ORGANIZATIONAL LEARNING
AND EMERGENT STRATEGY

InterStock, like most dotcoms, had great expansion plans around the year 2000 "that we fortunately were not able to realize." Rather than executing these plans, Rune says, InterStock "focused on consolidation in Norway, trimmed the organization, prepared a completely different strategy in connection with market entry, and still wanted to enter new markets, but wanted a totally different cost profile." Its original plan was to set up actual offices with a new group of people, which would incur a cost profile with a great deal of fixed costs, but they quickly halted these plans. One of their competitors, who was not that agile, "entered with a huge staff of 60 people in Frankfurt alone, and managed to acquire a small number of clients," Rune recalls. "In the time they were there they burned several millions and pulled back out."

InterStock opted for a different strategy in the face of a declining economy and a bursting dotcom bubble. Now they focused on costs. InterStock's basis for entering Denmark was that everything was run out of Oslo. Rune claims that this led them to "have an extremely low marginal cost when we enter a new market—we only need a couple of hundred trades in order to break even, actually." This strategy is radically different from the dotcom economic model of pouring in resources to capture market share rapidly. Rune says that InterStock's current strategy "enables us to enter new markets with a very low exposure, test out the systems, and quietly and carefully grow." This more careful approach has afforded InterStock continued growth in an economy in decline after the dotcom bubble.

The Internet brokerage business is facing not only a declining economy but intense competition within its own industry. Rune says proudly, "We are the price leader—well, actually not quite as well as we thought. We do have a competitor that offers free trading." [2] When asked how InterStock is still managing to beat a rival that is making stock trades for free, Rune confesses,

> That surprised us as well. But it has to do with different things. We have very good systems, to begin with. They also have that, in a way. But our customer service is extremely good. The follow-up of customers is very quick if it is through email. Or if they pick up the phone, they get a very competent and sympathetic person at the other end.

InterStock might have the best technical solutions and outstanding customer service, but Rune suspects that their success against this competitor might also be explained by some customers' fear of being duped:

> We are wondering if free is suspect—that it might be perceived as more honest to have a discount, or a favorable price, because then the customer feels that, OK, then it is less. You very often get negative associations when it comes to a free offer. It gives a negative feeling: *What is wrong with this?* Right?

The result is that InterStock has "beaten the heck out of them in market share."

When probed further on their strategy for market entry, Rune admits that it was not as premeditated as it may seem. Actually, he says, "we toyed with the idea [of having no brokerage fee] as well. Then they came before us and we couldn't very well do the same, so we set the price at a low level, but still not free." Now that they're outperforming their non-charging competitor, they're in the ironic position of having been "saved by our competitor, because we were considering the same strategy!" This again shows how InterStock pragmatically adapts to both changing environmental conditions and competitive situations. At InterStock they are extremely quick and flexible learners.

InterStock is using a clever combination of ICTs to shape their market entry strategy so as to project a local presence—in today's terms, a "virtual presence"—instead of physically building one. Using ICTs instead of bricks and mortar has also significantly reduced their cost of operations, while allowing them to exploit the commonalities between their different markets. Knowing that trading slows in a declining (bear) market and that their revenues depend on trading volume, InterStock has adopted a more cautious and cost-effective approach, which has helped make it a survivor where its Goliath competitors have stumbled. In the process, they have disguised their physical location to appear local in a variety of European countries.

Discussion Questions

1. What are the ethical and legal implications of presenting yourself as Danish to your Danish customers and German to your German customers, with hopes of getting more business? Is it deception, or just good business sense?

2. What are the pros and cons of using technology to communicate with customers?

3. If most traders—day traders (those who do not hold stocks overnight) in particular—care more about price, reliability, and quality of service than the nationality of their provider, then is it really an ethical violation to represent yourself as a "local"?

4. By now you have made up your mind as to the extent to which you believe that InterStock is behaving ethically or unethically when they portray themselves as native to each market. Now go visit the national pages of large companies such as Exxon ("Esso" in Europe), Coca-Cola, Pepsi, Ford, and Microsoft. To what extent do they misrepresent themselves and pretend to be local? Does this in any way alter your opinion of InterStock?

5. Dell Computers is one of the most successful companies in the computer market. Dell has exploited the Internet and computer age fully. Customers order from their national Web site and computers are manufactured and shipped across national borders. When you call a local number for customer support, chances are that the representative you speak with is in another country. Why do you think it is so important for a company to be perceived as being local?

6. Let's assume that the InterStock business model is unethical. What risks do they take using this strategy as opposed to using one of full disclosure?

7. What role does culture play in business interactions? How important is it for a businessperson to be familiar with local idiosyncrancies?

8. Considering the trend to outsource customer service to countries where labor costs are low, how do the ethics of this practice relate to the current case?

❖ NOTES

1. An earlier version of this chapter appeared in *Information and Communication Technologies in Action: Linking Theory and Narratives of Practice* (2004) by L. D. Browning, A. S. Sætre, K. Stephens, and J-O Sørnes, published by Copenhagen Business School Press.

2. In other words, their competitor does not charge a brokerage fee.

❖ REFERENCES

Goffman, E. (1959). *The presentation of self in everyday life*. New York: Doubleday.

McKnight, D. H., Cummings, L. L., & Chervany, N. L. (1998). Initial trust formation in new organizational relationships. *Academy of Management Review, 23*(3), 473–490.

Rosenfeld, P., Booth-Kewley, S., Edwards, J. E., & Alderton, D. L. (1994). Upward impression management: Goals, influence strategies, and consequences. *American Behavioral Scientist, 37*, 672–682.

Corporate Ethics in the Pharmaceutical Industry

The Lipobay/Baycol Case of Bayer

Nicola Berg and Martin K. Welge

This case examines the potential conflict between medicine and economics in the pharmaceutical industry. More specifically, it explores the decision by Bayer to take Lipobay/Baycol, a cholesterol medicine, off the market because of undesirable effects on patients. However, the fact that Bayer first informed its shareholders of the recall before physicians and pharmacists raises questions regarding its long-term relationship with those groups, as well as consumers of its medicines. The case also examines the challenges of transparency in drug development and delivery in a highly competitive industry in which errors can be costly both in terms of human health and in terms of company profits.

❖ ETHICAL DILEMMAS OF PHARMACEUTICAL COMPANIES

Pharmaceutical companies are faced with substantial ethical dilemmas. On the one hand, patients hope to be cured of diseases, to get well after taking safe drugs, or even to extend their lives when they are seriously sick. Research and development in the pharmaceutical industry, on the other hand, is very costly[1] and it often takes many years after clinical research until a drug finds its way to the pharmacy. This means that, for pharmaceutical companies and their shareholders, people who buy drugs are not only patients who need medical help but also customers who are needed to provide profits.

Because of this conflict between medicine and economics, the pharmaceutical industry is one of the most regulated industries. Regulatory authorities such as the Federal Institute for Medication and Medical Products (BfArM) in Germany or the Food and Drug Administration (FDA) in the United States set high standards for research, development, and the approval of new drugs or their prescription by physicians.[2] While the regulation of drugs is an issue of national institutions, the pharmaceutical industry is entirely global. In the last several years, a strong consolidation process took place in the industry with only a handful of global players left who are able to spend large amounts of money needed to develop new drugs for illnesses such as cancer, HIV/AIDS, or heart disease.

The case of Lipobay/Baycol demonstrates how global competition and shareholder orientation may force a company to neglect warnings of scientists and to misinterpret reports of doctors, pharmacists, and patients. In the following case study, a general portrait of Bayer AG is first given. Second, the effects of Lipobay/Baycol and reports of undesirable side effects of the preparation are explained. Finally, the case proceeds with a discussion of the public reactions on the recall and concludes with future directions for research.

❖ PORTRAIT OF BAYER AG

On August 1, 1863, the merchant Friedrich Bayer and the master dyer Johann Friedrich Weskott founded the dye company "Friedr. Bayer et Comp." in Wuppertal-Barmen (Germany). In 1884, the chemist Carl Duisberg joined the company, under whose management the Bayer chemists were to make numerous important developments. The most important of these was the synthetization of the agent acetylsalicylic acid into a chemically pure and stable form by Dr. Felix Hoffmann in 1897. The registration of aspirin, the medication that was based on this agent, followed in 1899. In 1925, the former dye works Friedr. Bayer & Co., which had in the meantime been established in Leverkusen (Germany), was incorporated into the company I.G. Farbenindustrie AG. After World War II, the company I.G. Farben was seized by order of the Allied army and it was later demerged. In 1951, the "Farbenfabriken Bayer AG" refounded and changed its corporate form to "Bayer AG" in 1972. By 2003, Bayer was represented on all five continents with around 350 companies and 116,900 employees. The core business activities are in Europe, North America, and the Far East. The group headquarters is in Leverkusen, where the global group activities are steered and coordinated.

Bayer is different from other European companies that are active in the chemicals field such as Aventis or Novartis, in that, contrary to these, it has a high degree of diversification. By contrast, the other companies have recently concentrated on just a few lines of business. The Bayer group currently has 15 lines of business, which are to be found in the four business units of health, agriculture, polymers, and chemicals.

The drug Lipobay has become very important within the health care business. Among the four drugs that were responsible for a turnover amounting to 0.5 billion Euro annually in the pharmaceuticals business, Lipobay has provided the third-highest turnover after the drugs Ciprobay and Adalat. With a growth of 205 percent in 1999 and 82 percent in 2000, it achieved the highest growth rates in the industry (Table 14.1).

The annual sales potential for 2000 was estimated at 2.5 billion Euro. According to estimates, six million people took Lipobay regularly during that year, 0.5 to 1 million of these in Germany and 700,000 in the United States (Bayer, 2001b, p. 4; 2001d).

Table 14.1   Bayer Products in the Health Care Business Unit, Which Generates the Highest Sales in Millions Euro

Products in the Health Care Business Unit	1999	2000	2001
Ciprobay	1,519	1,785	1,964
Adalat	1,021	1,155	975
Lipobay	345	636	—
Aspirin	580	632	723
Kogenate	377	491	250[1]
Glucometer Elite	354	472	492

Source: Bayer, 1999, 2000, 2001

[1] The turnover of Kogenate declined 49 % in 2001 compared to the previous year. Therefore, in 2001 it was only the ninth strongest product in the health care business unit (Bayer 2001, p. 9).

❖ THE EFFECTS OF LIPOBAY

The drug Lipobay was prescribed to patients with a raised cholesterol level, which can result from diabetes or an unhealthy diet, or it can be congenital. An increased blood cholesterol level is deemed to be a main risk factor for cardiac infarctions, apoplexies, and circulatory disturbances.

The cholesterol-reducing agent, which is included in the Lipobay medication, prevents the creation of a lipoprotein that has negative effects on humans and supports the formation of a lipoprotein that has positive effects on humans because it transports superfluous fat from the cells to the liver. In this way, it is possible to reduce the blood cholesterol rate. However, patients who are administered the medication can potentially suffer from a destruction of the muscle tissue. The simultaneous taking of medication containing another cholesterol-reducing agent results in a reinforcement of these side effects of Lipobay. In a small number of cases, this disintegration of the muscle tissue can be life-threatening or even fatal should the muscle disintegration block the renal tubules. This results in an impairment of the renal function, at the least, or renal failure at the worst (Abdata Pharma-Daten-Service, 2001).

❖ REPORTS ON UNDESIRABLE
   SIDE EFFECTS OF THE PREPARATION

In Germany, the medical practitioners, dispensing chemists, other members of the medical profession, and the patients themselves are obliged to report medication-related side effects. The pharmaceutical industry is obliged to report side effects and interactions with other medications, in addition to any cases of medication misuse. On the basis of contractual agreements, the Medication Commission passes all reports it receives on to the authorities. Only the pharmaceutical companies are legally obliged to submit spontaneous reports to the authorities. In addition to submitting the reports, suspicious cases must also be scientifically assessed by medication experts. Should serious side effects be determined, the reporting and assessment must be made available to BfArM and the Paul Ehrlich Institute within a period of 15 days so that these organizations are able to take action aimed at avoiding risks. This period is not only valid for suspicious cases that occur in Germany, but also with regard to suspicion reports submitted from foreign countries (BfArM, 2002; Medication Act, Sect. 15, para. 1).[3]

Not only must pharmaceutical companies make these spontaneous reports, they must also submit regular reports to the approving authorities after the medication has been approved. Medication experts are to submit reports to the BfArM every six months during the two-year period following the approval, annually during the subsequent three years, and thereafter at five-year intervals (Medication Act, Sect. 15, para. 1). Should the reports or other information received indicate any possible medication risks, action is taken on the basis of a determined phased plan (BfArM, 2002): In Phase I, the pharmaceutical companies concerned are initially requested to provide information on the suspected medication risk. They are then assessed through a national and international exchange. Phase II is activated should the suspected health risk be substantiated during the exchange of information or as a result of other information received. The pharmaceutical companies concerned are requested to provide a statement on detailed aspects or they must take action to be ordered in an official ruling in the case of acute risks. These can even include the suspension or revocation of the approval and the recalling of the medication.

The BfARM received a total of eight periodic reports in the period after the cholesterol-reducing agent that was used in Lipobay was approved in 1997. Although the first four reports included information on a few cases of undesirable medication effects on the muscular apparatus, there was no reason to believe that these occurred more often when taking this cholesterol-reducing agent than when taking other medication from the same group of substances. The summarized periodic report 5/6 (BfArM, 2001b) included intimations that the destruction of the muscle tissue would occur more often if the cholesterol-reducing agent is taken in combination with another lipid reducer from the fibrate group. Although the problem of these undesirable side effects manifesting themselves as a result of a co-medication with two lipid reducers initially only appeared to exist in the United States, Bayer was induced to also amend the product information in the European Union (EU) accordingly (BfArM, 2001b, p. 7).

After considering the reports concerning undesirable side effects received from both Germany and abroad and assessing the periodic reports from Bayer, the BfArM saw no reason to revoke the approval of Lipobay. Together with the first approving country—Great Britain—and all other EU member states, the BfArM deemed it necessary and sufficient to restrict the approval status of Lipobay in order to guarantee the medication's safety.

After receiving new information, this approval amendment process—which commenced at the beginning of 2001—was upgraded to an "urgent safety restriction" in June of the same year. This was initiated on June 19, 2001, the aim being the inclusion of the joint application of the cholesterol-reducing agents as a contra-indication in the production information. Article 1 of Directive 541/95/EC (European Union, 1995) formed the legal basis for this. Upon conclusion of the "urgent safety restriction proceedings" on June 26, 2001, a standardized European approval amendment was concluded, which resulted in the sending of what is referred to as a "red hand letter" (BfArM, 2001b, p. 7).[4]

All reports pertaining to (mainly serious) undesirable side effects that the BfArM received from Bayer as individual case reports were officially assessed and documented. Parallel to this, additional steps were taken with regard to a detailed benefits-risk assessment and an exchange of information with other agencies both in Germany and abroad in addition to the assessing of periodic reports. By August 10, 2001, a total of 234 reports had been submitted in Germany concerning the undesirable side effects of the cholesterol-reducing agent. In the majority of the cases, these side effects affected the muscular and skeletal system, the liver, the alimentary tract, and the skin. Ninety-one of the 234 reports concerned suspicion of an acute destruction of the skeleton musculature. Nine of these 91 reports document a combination treatment with another cholesterol-reducing agent. The combination treatment with this lipid reducer is of no great importance in Germany and is relatively seldom applied (BfArM, 2001b, p. 5). From the 91 cases since 1998 in which there was a suspected destruction of the skeleton musculature, 84 were not fatal. In 67 cases, it was possible to either heal the muscle damage or the patient's state of health improved. In 16 reports, the progress of the undesirable side effects is unknown.[5]

The first mortality cases in connection with Lipobay were reported in 1998. Of the 91 cases suspected of the destruction of the skeleton musculature, seven ended in death. The BfArM believed that it was possible that three of these seven cases could be connected with Lipobay. In four other cases, no direct connection could be determined (BfArM, 2001b).

At the end of 2001, a total of 1114 reports of suspected destruction of the skeleton musculature had been made worldwide. From these, 52 deaths were connected with taking Lipobay. The United States, where the medication was sold under the name "Baycol" after being approved by the American health authority, the Food and Drug Administration (FDA), was more adversely affected than Europe. Here, approximately 1.5% of the patients treated with the cholesterol-reducing agent of Lipobay were also administered another cholesterol-reducing agent. From the 31 deaths reported by the FDA, 12 (38.7%) of these resulted from the combination therapy, according to their information. The relatively high number of deaths in the United States can also be attributed to the fact that the medication was administered there with a higher maximum daily dosage than in Europe (Bayer, 2001d).

❖ RECALLING THE MEDICATION FROM THE MARKET AND ITS COMMERCIAL EFFECTS ON BAYER AG

After a telephone conference with the American medication authority— the Food and Drug Administration (FDA)—Bayer decided on August 8, 2001, to take Lipobay off the market (Albrecht, 2001, p. 25). The decision surprised not only the BfArM, but also the medical practitioners, pharmacists, and patients who depended on the medication. On August 8 and 9, 2001, the medical practitioners and pharmacists in Germany were informed in writing of this decision in what is referred to as a "Red Hand Letter," the content of which was agreed upon by local health authorities. A total of 130,000 letters were sent, information for patients was placed on the Internet, and a patient hotline was set up (Bayer, 2001b, p. 5).

In mid-August 2001, Bayer postponed the planned listing on the stock exchanges in the United States after the first actions were taken there and in France for damages (Wirtschaftswoche, 2001a; 2001c). On August 23, Bayer also took Lipobay off the Japanese market, the last country in which the medication was still available.[6] On September 4, 2001, the Cologne Department of Public Prosecutions initiated investigations against Bayer employees on the grounds of the suspicion of a contravention of the Medication Act (Wirtschaftswoche, 2001b). However, on September 13, 2001, the BfArM retracted its accusation that Bayer had retained information pertaining to the safety of Lipobay (Bayer, 2001c). The BfArM determined that Bayer had passed all of the relevant information on to the responsible European approval authority, the Medicines Control Agency (MCA) in London. In turn, the MCA passed the information that Lipobay was not to be taken together with another cholesterol-reducing agent on to the BfArM in Bonn.

Figure 14.1   Development of the Quoted Share Price of Bayer Shares in
August 2001 (Final Daily Quotation Xetra)

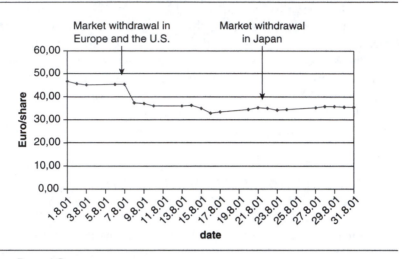

Source: Bayer AG

The BfArM merely criticized that the information had not been passed
to the BfArM at the same time as to the MCA. This meant that it was
possible to settle the argument concerning the exchange of information
on the side effects of Lipobay. For this reason, Bayer was not heard in
court (Bayer, 2001a).

In comparison, the commercial effects of the recalling of the
medication were considerable. After the announcement was made on
August 8, 2001, that Lipobay was to be taken off the market, Bayer's
shares lost 17 percent of their value, and a further loss of 6 percent was
suffered just one day later. By August 10, 2001, the shares had suffered
a loss of 20 percent. As a result, the company value had been reduced
by approximately 6 billion Euro (Figure 14.1).

❖ PUBLIC REACTIONS

Immediately after Bayer announced the recall of Lipobay, the Federal
Minister of Health, Mrs. Ulla Schmidt, requested a full report from the
BfArM with information on the situation. The BfArM report stated that
it agreed with the other EU member states that continuous, reasonable,
and sufficient risk-reducing measures were to be adopted.

Therefore, during the period up to the removal of the drug from the
market, there was no reason for the BfArM to take action over and

above that taken, since they were not in possession of information which would have necessitated further action. However, the situation changed when the BfArM received a requested study from Bayer on August 10, 2001. Bayer had been in possession of this study since June 15, 2001. It is stipulated in Sect. 29, para. 1 of the Medication Act that the responsible superior authority is to be informed by pharmaceutical companies of each case of a known suspicion of serious side effects or a serious interaction with other medication in addition to new knowledge that is not included in the approval documents. The Federal Ministry of Health (BfArM, 2001a) stated that this was the case. Therefore, Bayer was obliged to pass the latest information on to the BfArM.

In addition, when taking a medication off the market, the responsible supervisory authorities (i.e., the BfArM and the Federal Supervisory Office for Stock Exchange Trading) were to have been informed at around the same time. This would certainly have done justice to both the obligation to notify stipulated in the Medication Act and the ad-hoc publicity obligation stipulated in Sect. 15 of the Securities Trading Act.

The fact was that Bayer informed its shareholders first and the medical practitioners and pharmacists second. The reasons given for this decision were that companies are obliged to make all notifications to the shareholders that might be relevant to the market price in what is referred to as an ad-hoc notification. Bayer believed that medical practitioners and pharmacists were not to be informed in advance since this would be considered "insider information" (Bayer, 2001a, p. 5).

This is also the reason why Bayer argued that the accusation (often made by the media) that they had an unacceptable information policy was not valid. Accordingly, in a letter to the Federal Minister of Health, Mrs. Ulla Schmidt, the company refuted the claim that it had provided the authorities with insufficient information in connection with the withdrawal of Lipobay. Bayer argued that studies had been commissioned with regard to the active cholesterol-reducing agent aimed at the further evaluation of the benefit–risk ratio and that the initial results were only received in February 2001. This information was passed on to the MCA in London and the BfArM in the form of a Periodic Safety Update Report (Bayer, 2001b, p. 6). The BfArM received this information on April 28, 2001.

In accordance with European law, the authority in the reference member state is responsible for approval changes and, therefore, for prescribing information. This authority also has a coordinating function.

The reference member state in the case of Lipobay is Great Britain and the responsible authority is the Medicines Control Agency (MCA) in London. The results report with regard to this data was completed on June 15, 2001, and immediately sent to the MCA, where it was assessed.

On the basis of the aforementioned result report, Bayer suggested an accelerated process for the immediate amendment of the prescribing information and also implemented this in cooperation with the MCA. All of the national authorities, including the BfArM, were included in this process. Bayer notified the British health authority (the MCA) of the imminent withdrawal of Lipobay on August 7, 2001, the evening before this took place.

❖ FUTURE DIRECTIONS

While it has been possible to generally remove the accusations made by the BfArM, the commercial effects for Bayer are still incalculable. As of this writing, hundreds of lawsuits for damages have been filed against Bayer, with their chances of success varying. Suits have been filed, for example, against Bayer in the United States in connection with Baycol. Bayer believes that the suits are also unfounded there. The company assumes that, although the known death cases occurred at the same time as Baycol was taken, no causal connection could be proven. It is also the case that the package circular and the information for medical practitioners include sufficient information pertaining to the risks resulting from the dosage being too high. For this reason, Bayer assumes that the company "[has] at times acted fully responsibly and in the interest of the patients' health and safety. This is why Bayer is able to wait for the action; there is no reason to form reserves" (Bayer, 2001a, p. 11).

The two attorneys, Michael Witti and Kenneth B. Moll, are still attempting to include German and other non-American plaintiffs in an American class action lawsuit to be brought before American courts of law against Bayer AG and its subsidiaries (Kenneth B. Moll & Associates, 2002). The choice to file a lawsuit in the United States is due to the much higher compensation payments that are customary.[7] Bayer believes that the attempt to select a foreign jurisdictional venue is impermissible because, under German law, disputes between German nationals and a German company are only to be brought before a German court of law (Bayer, 2002a). However, should the action be admitted, Bayer will have to face claims for compensation and injury, which could come to millions.[8]

Discussion Questions

1. Describe the socio-political issue that is at the center of the case.

2. Outline the life cycle that this issue covers.

3. Which socio-political stakeholders are involved in this case? Describe their aims, power, and risks.

4. Which instruments of public affairs management did Bayer use in dealing with these socio-political stakeholders? How would you have reacted if you were a board member in this case?

5. Describe the cross-cultural aspects of public affairs management that characterize this case.

❖ NOTES

1. But research shows also that pharmaceutical companies spend a lot of money on advertising and the development of copycat drugs. In addition, the U.S. government pays a large share of the costs for research and development.

2. Although it is widely discussed, there is disagreement about whether the standards of the regulatory agencies are high enough.

3. However, these reports only have a restricted probative strength. A causal connection between the taking of a medication and a side effect can often only be proven with difficulty, an example being, if no information is provided, it would be uncertain whether the patient also took other medication. In addition, it is difficult to differentiate between a fatality resulting from an existing, prior, or accompanying illness and one which is a direct result of the side effect of the preparation taken. In addition, many of the patients treated with other medications that include substances from the same group that are in Lipobay are older and suffer from serious accompanying illnesses, especially cardiovascular diseases with a high morbidity and mortality rate (Bayer, 2001d).

4. Section 27 of the Codex of the Federation of Researching Medication Manufacturers (VFA) stipulates that when sending information on newly recognized serious side effects, the recall of faulty batches or other information, which is to be directly sent to a medical practitioner or pharmacist with the aim of excluding a risk to patients as far as possible, the members obligate themselves to apply the symbol of a red hand with the wording "Important Medication Information" to letters and envelopes. In especially urgent cases, it might be necessary to make these reports orally, by fax or by means of public announcements through the press—radio and television, for example. Other types of scientific information, advertisements, or mailings are never to be sent

in these envelopes nor by express mail, recorded delivery, telegram, or fax. They are also not to be labeled "Important Information" (VFA, 2002).

5. In the source cited, no reference was made to the remaining case.

6. Japan was initially excluded from the global withdrawal of the medication as another cholesterol-reducing agent that was often prescribed with Lipobay was not at that time available on the Japanese market. However, the recall was also effected here after the Japanese health authorities provided the notification that this active agent was also to be approved there in the near future (Bayer, 2001b, p. 6).

7. Up to now, 7,400 lawsuits have been filed against Bayer. Since November 2002, this number has increased by 1,700 (Reuters, January 15, 2003), although more than 160 of these are collective lawsuits (Bayer 2002b; for lawsuits from different countries, c.f. Coordination Gegen Bayer Gefahren, 2002).

8. Since January 2003, Bayer has reached a compromise with 400 plaintiffs (AFP news agency, January 15, 2003) and paid US$200,000 per case (Handelsblatt, 2002, p. 13).

❖ REFERENCES

Abdata Pharma-Daten-Service. (2001). *Pharmazeutische Stoffliste.* Eschborn, Germany: Author.

Albrecht, H. (2001, August 16). Mittel, die daneben wirken. Die Senkung des Cholesterinspiegels kann tödlich enden. Ein vermeidbares Risiko? *Die Zeit, 46*(34), p. 25.

Bayer. (1999). *Geschäftsbericht 1999.* Leverkusen, Germany: Author.

Bayer. (2000). *Geschäftsbericht 2000.* Leverkusen, Germany: Author.

Bayer. (2001a). *Geschäftsbericht 2001.* Leverkusen, Germany: Author.

Bayer. (2001b). *Aktionsärsbrief 2001. Sonderausgabe zum Vermarktungsstopp von Lipobay/Baycol.* Leverkusen, Germany: Author.

Bayer. (2001c). *Kompetenz und Verantwortung.* Retrieved October 5, 2001, from http://bayer.de

Bayer. (2001d). *Sustainable Development Report 2001.* Leverkusen, Germany: Author.

Bayer. (2001e). Arzneimittel-Institut nimmt Vorwurf gegen Bayer zurück. Retrieved October 5, 2001, from http://www.lipobay.bayer.de

Bayer (2002a, January 13): *Internationale Sammelklage: Bayer rechnet mit Zurückweisung durch US-Gerichte* [Press release].

Bayer (2002b, November 13). *Information by e-mail from the Bayer AG concerning lawsuits.* Leverkusen, Germany.

Bundesinstitut für Arzneimittel und Medizinprodukte (BfArM). (2001a, September 5). *Press release.*

Bundesinstitut für Arzneimittel und Medizinprodukte. (2001b, August 16). *Bericht an das Bundesministerium für Gesundheit über die Zulassung von*

Cerivastatin-haltigen Arzneimitteln (Lipobay, Zenas, Vazqol) und die nachfol-gende Sicherheitsüberwachung. [Final version]. Bonn, Germany: Author.

Bundesinstitut für Arzneimittel und Medizinprodukte. (2002). *Informationen und Hinwiese zur Zulasssung.* Bonn, Germany: Author. Retreived from http://www.bfarm.de

Coordination Gegen Bayer Gefahren (2001): *SWB 02/2002 — Ticker.* Retrieved November 6, 2002, from http://www.cgbnetwork.org

European Union (1995): *Commission Regulation (EC) No 541/95 of 10 March 1995 concerning the examination of variations to the terms of a marketing authorization granted by a competent authority of a Member State.* Retrieved November 6, 2002, from http://europa.eu.int/eur-lex/lex/Notice.do?list=307071:cs, 307881:cs,307880:cs&val= 307880:cs& lang=de

Handelsblatt. (2002). *US-Anwälte sprechen von 104 Vergleichen zu je 200.000 $. Bayer einigt sich mit ersten Lipobay-Klägern.* (Nr. 181, 19.09.2002, p. 13) http://online.wdr.de/online/wirtschaft/bayer/stichwort_lipobay.html

Kenneth B. Moll & Associates, Ltd. (2002). *Beschwerdeschrift der Sammelklage an das Bezirksgericht der Vereinigten Staaten für den nördlichen Bezirk von Illinois östliche Kammer.* Retrieved February 20, 2002, from http://www.kbmoll. com

Medication Act (Gesetz über den Verkehr mit Arzneimitteln). Version of December 11, 1998 (BGBl. I 1998, p. 3586; 1999, p. 1666; 2000, pp. 1002, 1040, 1045; 2001, p. 2702).

Securities Trading Act (Wertpapierhandelsgesetz) of 26 July 1994 (BGBl. I, p. 1749), in the version of the announcement of September 17, 1998 (BGBl. I, p. 2709).

Verband Forschender Arzneimittelhersteller (VFA) (Federation of Researching Medication Manufacturers). (2002). *Kodex der Mitglieder des VFA.* Berlin: Author.

Wirtschaftswoche. (2001a). *Lipobay: Risiken und Nebenwirkungen.* Retrieved November 29, 2001, from http://wiwo.de

Wirtschaftswoche. (2001b). *Bayer: Die Staatsanwaltschaft ermittelt.* Retrieved September 4, 2001, from http://www.wiwo.de

Wirtschaftswoche. (2001c). *Bayer: Lipobay-Klage in Frankreich.* Retrieved September 17, 2001, from http://www.wiwo.de

Should We Stop Using the Letter C?

*Three Key Players Respond to the
February 1, 2003, Columbia Shuttle Events*

Michelle T. Violanti

This case reflects back on the communication and decision-making
processes prior to the Shuttle Columbia launch, based on lessons that
should have been learned from the Challenger disaster. It also explores
the responses of President Bush, NASA, and the media to the explosion
of Columbia, which occurred during re-entry. The case considers the
extent to which NASA has been accountable for its mistakes and the
degree to which it has compromised its ethical obligations in favor of
time- and money-driven decisions.

Some friends and I were sitting in a college dorm room on January
28, 1986, watching the space shuttle Challenger take off. At that
time, a shuttle launch was still considered newsworthy enough to be
carried by all of the broadcast networks in the United States. John was
commenting on how he could not wait until the day when he would be
one of the mission specialists on a space shuttle. His life plans and the
lives of many others changed dramatically that day as Challenger

caught fire and exploded in front of a national audience. No longer did John desire to be that mission specialist; many wondered about the virtue of sending a teacher into space to her death. An entire country mourned the loss of these brave astronauts, and after the dust settled, we were left with an endless list of questions. For example, what caused the explosion, who was responsible for the accident, and was space exploration really worth the loss of seven lives? Over time, these questions were answered and we continued the space program.

Fast forward to January of 2003 and the launch of the space shuttle Columbia occurs with little fanfare or news coverage. The astronauts go into space, transmit back progress reports, and complete their mission. Upon re-entry on February 1, 2003, the shuttle and Mission Control in Houston lost contact. Pieces of this shuttle broke off and fell to Earth in a small town called Nacogdoches, Texas. At this point, the story became newsworthy and the broadcast networks began covering the story. This time I was at a professional meeting and one of the women with us knew Commander Husband. Again, a nation mourned and asked the same questions they had asked 17 years earlier. The only difference this time was that we added a question about whether terrorism prompted the events surrounding Columbia's return to Earth.

This case study sets out to provide background information necessary to understand the NASA space program generally and the space shuttle program specifically, a series of turning points that call into question the decision-making abilities of those directly and indirectly involved in the space program, and how three key players (President George W. Bush, NASA, and the media) responded to the events of February 1, 2003. Each of these three players faced different ethical dilemmas, some of which they may not have realized at the time. For example, President Bush needed to respond in a way that would respect the families of those who lost loved ones, as well as respect a program he supported by continuing to provide financial support in his budget. Similarly, NASA had to respond in a way that respects the families of those who lost loved ones, illustrates they have learned from their past mistakes with the Challenger incident, and emphasizes the importance of continuing space exploration. Finally, the media had some of the most difficult dimensions to balance because they want people to choose their media outlet over others—to what extent do you sensationalize the situation and to what extent do you honor the privacy of those who have lost loved ones (i.e., where does the newsworthiness of a story end and the entertainment or tragedy of the situation take over the story?). While there are no clear-cut right or wrong answers in this situation, the material presented about Columbia provides a framework for exploring the importance of organizational culture, impression management, and language choices.

❖ BACKGROUND

At the outset, we need to examine NASA's culture and communication practices that led up to the Challenger and Columbia incidents. First, NASA never had a single unified culture, but rather it has always been composed of multiple, often competing, cultures (McCurdy, 1993). Tompkins (2004) presents a full history of the space program from which I lift the aspects that are most critical to this case. First, NASA was created in 1958 when President Eisenhower merged multiple groups to compete with the former Soviet Union for advances in space exploration and satellite-monitoring systems. Each group had its own location, brought its own culture to NASA, and they never truly became a united organization. This was coupled with a focus on research, hands-on experience, exceptional people, in-house technical capability, acceptance of risk and failure, open communication, and identification with NASA as an organization in the early days.

As time passed, the way NASA did business also changed. By the early 1980s, the number of people working at NASA was less than half of what it was in the 1960s. Similarly, management had gone from being composed primarily of technical people who had worked their way up through the ranks to being composed primarily of "a burgeoning layer of bureaucrats who never wielded a monkey wrench and could only manage by means of orders, memos, rules, and regulations" (Jensen, 1996, p. 363). When the Rogers Commission (1986) report on the Challenger accident was released, it determined the technical cause was a failure of the O-ring pressure seal, and the human failures behind the technical one included the following:

The decision to launch the *Challenger* was flawed. Those who made that decision were unaware of the recent history of problems concerning the O-rings and the joint and were unaware of the initial written recommendation of the contractor advising against the launch at temperatures below 53 degrees Fahrenheit and the continuing opposition to the engineers at Thiokol after their management reversed its position. They did not have a clear understanding of Rockwell's concern that it was not safe to launch because of ice on the pad. If the decision makers had known all of the facts, it is highly unlikely that they would have decided to launch 51-L on January 28, 1986. (p. 82)

The Rogers Commission report essentially indicated that it was a lack of communication between the various units because the contractors were required to prove that it was unsafe to launch rather than proving it was safe to launch. The lack of interdepartmental communication led to the technical problems associated with Challenger. Clearly, this was a change within the culture from the open communication on which NASA had prided itself in the 1960s. What is interesting is that in the Columbia report, the writers go so far as to define culture as "the assumptions that employees make as they carry out their work. It is a powerful force that can persist through reorganizations and the change of key personnel. It can be a positive or negative force" (Columbia Accident Investigation Board [CAIB], 2003, p. 97).

After Challenger exploded, it took $12 billion and 32 months to begin launching shuttles again (CAIB, 2003). In addition to the amount of time and money involved in restarting the shuttle program, NASA appointed new directors at each of the three space centers in an effort to reform the culture that did not put safety first. External criticism and attempts to make changes following Challenger were met with resistance to the point of being counterproductive. In addition to the trench that the NASA employees dug, federal support sought "valuable scientific and symbolic payoffs for the nation without a need for increased budgets" leading to the 1990s slogan of "better, faster, cheaper" (CAIB, 2003, pp. 103, 106). To deal with this flattened budget, NASA chose to become more efficient rather than to eliminate any of its programs. Based upon the recommendations of a Functional Workforce Review, NASA eliminated 5,900 jobs because it was believed that this would not compromise safety. These cuts continued into the 1990s when NASA cut another 25% of its workforce and utilized a hiring freeze to prevent new, young blood from entering the organization or penetrating the status quo culture (CAIB, 2003). Essentially, NASA became the first government agency to be privatized (i.e., private, non-governmental organizations become responsible for handling many of the jobs associated with running a space program).

The other burning question during the 1990s was when to replace the shuttle. How many missions was it really equipped to handle?

How often could parts be replaced without compromising the vessel's integrity? After Challenger, the initial date for replacement was 2002 and by the Columbia launch, the date for replacement had moved to 2020 (CAIB, 2003, p. 111). Nothing remained consistent about the policy of when to replace the shuttle and more importantly, it had little to do with safety and much to do with money. Because no one was sure exactly when the shuttles would be replaced, upgrade investments were often deferred or ignored because it is impossible to hit a moving target. Someone might decide to scrap an entire vessel into which they had just invested large amounts of money.

As early as 1999, people within the NASA family were voicing concern about continued launching of the space shuttles. NASA administrator Daniel Goldin indicated we faced a "Space Launch Crisis" because the shuttle upgrade budget for the upcoming year was inadequate to create significant safety improvements (CAIB, 2003, p. 114). This, coupled with the number of "close calls" in 1999, prompted the creation of a Shuttle Independent Assessment Team whose findings included the following:

> Over the course of the Shuttle Program . . . processes, procedures, and training have continuously been improved and implemented to make the system safer. . . . this critical feature is being eroded. . . . [We] must rigorously guard against the tendency to accept risk solely because of prior successes. . . . [We feel] strongly that NASA Safety and Mission Assurance should be restored to its previous role of an independent oversight body, and not simply be a "safety auditor." . . . [and] Communication of problems and concerns upward . . . from the "floor" also appeared to leave room for improvement. (CAIB, 2003, p. 114)

Similar complaints were lodged by former members of NASA's Aerospace Safety Advisory Panel who since 1998 had claimed that "space shuttle budget and personnel cutbacks were excessive and were eroding safety margins. They said they were 'particularly ignored' by NASA when they urged costly upgrades of hardware and space center infrastructure" (Pianin, 2003, October 4, p. A10). To them, it appeared NASA found it easier to eliminate people raising concerns than to address budget issues. In 2001, Sean O'Keefe became the NASA administrator, replacing Goldin.

In early 2003, NASA began readying Columbia for its final voyage. During the Flight Readiness Review, the issue of foam shedding was raised and "characterized as an 'acceptable risk' rather than a . . . 'safety-of-flight' issue. Space Shuttle Program management accepted this rationale" and signed off on the shuttle's readiness for launch (CAIB, 2003, p. 126). With all of the paperwork signed, sealed, and delivered, Columbia launched on January 16, 2003. Foam separated and struck the left wing 81.9 seconds after liftoff. During the days that followed, NASA held many meetings to make critical decisions about that incident. Linda Ham, who was in charge of the next launch, spent most of her days attempting to determine what impact this would have on the next launch of Atlantis rather than inquiring about how this would affect the current mission. In an email dated January 22, Ham asked Ron Dittemore to have the person who came up with the faulty rationale for an acceptable risk for Columbia to start working on the foam-shedding issue and presumably come up with a better rationale for Atlantis, very soon (CAIB, 2003). Clearly, people were thinking ahead to a schedule they had created rather than thinking about the present and what impact it would have on this vessel and crew.

In hindsight, holding the shuttle launch to address these safety concerns would have made perfect sense, but most organizations do not live in the ideal world and must make practicality decisions on a regular basis. NASA was no different. They were attempting to meet a deadline for upgrading the International Space Station by February 19, 2004 (CAIB, 2003). To meet this date, they would have to launch a total of 10 flights in less than 16 months. If any of these flights were delayed, it would delay their work on the space station and that would further undermine their credibility with and funding from the federal government. In many ways, this launch became part of NASA's survival technique: If we can just prove to them that we can right the International Space Station ship, then we can ask for the money necessary to upgrade the current space shuttle program.

During the course of Columbia's mission, NASA missed at least eight opportunities to address the foam-shedding incident that occurred during takeoff (CAIB, 2003, p. 167). On day 4 of the mission, Rodney Rocha asked if the crew had been instructed to inspect the damage and received no response. On day 6 of the mission, Mission Control failed to ask for video of the External Tank separation, which could have indicated the extent of damage, to be downloaded. Also on day 6 of the mission, NASA and the National Imagery and Mapping Agency personnel discussed a possible request for imagery but no action was taken. On day 7 of the mission, Wayne Hale phoned the Department of

Defense to begin identifying imaging assets (the possible visual pictures of the foam-shedding incident or damage) but was stopped by Linda Ham's orders. On the same day, Mike Card, a manager from Safety and Mission Assurance, discussed imagery with two separate people, but no action was taken. On day 8 of the mission, Barbara Conte requested imagery and after it went through three more levels, the request was denied. Finally, on day 14 of the mission, Mike Card again discussed the imaging request and was told it should only be gathered on a "not-to-interfere" basis (no imagery was forthcoming). On Day 16 of the mission, Columbia attempted to re-enter Earth's orbit and land at 9:16 A.M. Eastern Time at Kennedy Space Center in Florida.

❖ RESPONSES TO COLUMBIA

At approximately noon on February 1, 2003, the White House lowered its flag to half staff to honor the fallen astronauts. At this point, the country came to know there was no reason to continue to hold out hope. Later that afternoon, President Bush did what President Reagan had done 17 years earlier—he spoke on television about the events surrounding Columbia ("They Had a High and Noble Purpose," 2003, p. 4).

> My fellow Americans, this day has brought terrible news and great sadness to our country. At 9 A.M. this morning, Mission Control in Houston lost contact with our space shuttle Columbia. A short time later, debris was seen falling from the skies above Texas. The Columbia is lost; there are no survivors. . . . These men and women assumed great risk in the service to all humanity. . . . The cause in which they died will continue. Mankind is led into the darkness beyond our world by the inspiration of discovery and the longing to understand. Our journey into space will go on.

To make it clear and unambiguous that he would put money where his mouth was, President Bush proposed a 3 percent increase in NASA's budget for fiscal year 2004 (Pianin, 2003, February 4). That would translate into a $15.5 billion proposed budget for 2004 with the possibility of additional funding for safety initiatives.

While the response from the White House in both the Challenger and Columbia shuttle situations was almost identical—we mourn the loss, send our heartfelt sympathy out to the family and friends, and vow additional support for the program's continuation—NASA had clearly learned a few communication lessons in the time between incidents. Very early in the crisis process, NASA chose Sean O'Keefe to be its speaker on all matters related to Columbia. In his early remarks, he referred to the incident as a "mishap" (Shales, 2003)—a term that means an unfortunate accident, bad luck, or misfortune. Clearly, NASA chose a word that indicated no organizational or individual responsibility—it was outside of everyone's control. Their message was reinforced when NASA created the Mishap Interagency Investigation Board (Tompkins, 2004). On Sunday February 2, Mr. Ron Dittemore, NASA's shuttle program manager, held his first official news conference, at which he cautioned people that they were only 30 hours into the investigation and said, "I am confident that whatever I tell you today will be fluid and will change from day to day for a while" (Broder, 2003, p. 1).

As the week progressed, attention turned to the "significant problems" associated with the left side of the craft where heat-shielding tiles had been damaged during liftoff (Broder, 2003, p. 1). It was at this point that NASA made it clear that nothing could have been done to prevent this "accident of epic proportion" (Broder, p. 1). Five options were presented for rescuing the astronauts: a shuttle rescue, escape to the space station, repair the heat insulation tiles, Russian spacecraft to the rescue, and change re-entry to minimize heat. NASA had a response for why each would not have worked: Atlantis was not on the launch pad yet, and it would take three weeks before it could launch once it got there; the shuttle did not have enough fuel to fly to the space station; the tiles are individually shaped and there is no way to carry 28,000 of them on each mission, not to mention that there was no mechanism available to repair the tiles; the Russian spacecraft could only bring back one person if it were able to get there in time; and the current re-entry plans were already minimizing heat as much as possible (Ritter, 2003). The question that remained unasked and answered at this point in the process was why the shuttle mission was not aborted after takeoff. Even if one of these solutions might have worked, NASA would have had to have viewed the debris created during launch as significant enough to warrant altering the mission.

As we turn our attention to the media, we see a variety of presentations of the events surrounding Columbia's return to Earth. When the broadcast network coverage began that morning, they started with verbal commentary speculating about what type of an explosion had occurred over Texas less than an hour earlier in the morning. As time passed and they were able to get images, they showed the visual footage that existed of the debris and interviewed a variety of people (e.g., John Glenn, family and friends of the astronauts). About four hours into the process, ABC-TV's Peter Jennings remarked, "This is what we do on television—we sit around and talk about it," even when there is nothing new to say (Roeper, 2003, p. 11). As they are prone to do, the 24-hour cable news networks each adopted a title for the event—CNN called it "Columbia: The Shuttle Tragedy" and Fox News called it "Tragedy in the Sky." Interestingly, both organizations chose to name it a tragedy—a disastrous event, a calamity.

Print news sources typically lag behind television news sources because of their daily publication schedule. This gave newspapers and magazines more time to craft their portrayal of the events. Interestingly, each of the largest newspaper sources chose to frame the events in more negative terms than the television outlets or NASA. For example, the *New York Times* referred to it as "Loss of the Shuttle" (e.g., Broder, 2003) and *The Washington Post* referred to it as a "disaster" (e.g., Shales, 2003). On Sunday, each of the broadcast networks' morning news programs included people talking about Columbia and the role of the space program. Following the morning news shows, the broadcast networks carried their regularly scheduled sporting events and left the daytime television coverage to the all-news channels. At this point, CNN and Fox News had to make a programming decision: Should they continue to cover the story and carry interviews that had little or no visual interest or should they switch to something with more visual impact. They opted to stay with the Columbia story and use a split screen or voiceover to be able to show shots of the debris, the Challenger memorial, and a Columbia patch on the ground presuming it was worn by someone on the flight (Shales, 2003). By Monday the third, television coverage focused primarily on the investigation and was relegated to the news programming slots that already existed (e.g., Lou Dobbs on CNN and *Dateline* on NBC).

After a week, media coverage of the events surrounding Columbia's return to Earth dissipated until questions were raised about the investigation in May and the report was released in August of 2003. In May, the five civilian members of the investigative board were temporarily hired by NASA at salaries of $134,000 per year each (Pianin, 2003, May 12). Similarly, congressional lawmakers raised concerns about the number of interviews that were classified as "privileged" and not open to access by those outside the investigative team.

Team members claimed this was the only way they could get top officials and engineers directly involved with Columbia to talk to them (Pianin, 2003, May 12). Coupled with the board being created by NASA at the outset, these events called into question the investigative team's impartiality. Less than eight months after Columbia's unsuccessful re-entry, the investigative report was completed and released to the public on August 27. Reaction to the report opened old wounds (some of which went back 17 years to Challenger). If there were doubts about the neutrality of those creating the report, they were quickly squelched when the investigative report revealed NASA's culpability in the events of February 1. Lt. Col. Michael Anderson's family had the following to say when they found out that the report suggested a NASA culture where safety is compromised in favor of budgets and time schedules (Sweeney, 2003):

> When it was an accident, you could accept it and get over it. . . . We were so proud of NASA. . . . We've got to do more prayers for the leaders of our country. . . . To think that safety was compromised takes you back to thinking they would still be here. You don't want to go down that road. We take comfort this was something he dreamed of doing. (p. 8)

Within Congress, the reaction was very similar. John McCain of Arizona commented that the report "must serve as a wake-up call to NASA and to the nation that we have for too long put off hard choices, and forced the space program to limp along without adequate guidance or funding. Most importantly, we will have to figure out where we want the space program to go and what we expect to get out of it" (Pianin, 2003, September 4, p. A2). Ernest Hollings of South Dakota also criticized the report and the team that chose not to assign individual responsibility, saying, "I'm not trying to embarrass anybody . . . but I'm trying to break past this 'culture' finding and fix responsibility" (Pianin, 2003, September 4, p. A2).

In the final Columbia Accident report, the Board concluded the following (CAIB, 2003):

> The organizational causes of this accident are rooted in the Space Shuttle Program's history and culture, including the original compromises that were required to gain approval for the Shuttle Program, subsequent years of resource constraints, fluctuating

priorities, schedule pressures, mischaracterizations of the Shuttle as operational rather than developmental, and lack of an agreed national vision. Cultural traits and organizational practices detrimental to safety and reliability were allowed to develop, including: reliance on past success as a substitute for sound engineering practices (such as testing to understand why systems were not performing in accordance with requirements/specifications); organizational barriers which prevented effective communication of critical safety information and stifled professional differences of opinion; lack of integrated management across program elements; and the evolution of an informal chain of command and decision-making processes that operated outside the organization's rules. (p. 177)

The original thought was that it would take NASA until September, 2004, to launch Atlantis. In July of 2005, NASA launched Discovery and the shuttle encountered similar foam tile issues with a much more positive outcome. Once again, the shuttle program is in a holding pattern.

Discussion Questions

1. To what extent does the way President Bush responded to Columbia contribute to the culture that has been so much of NASA's problem over the last 20 years?

2. What difference does it make if news media portray the story as a tragedy, disaster, crash, accident, or loss?

3. What role should the media play in reporting on national incidents such as Challenger and Columbia?

4. If you were hired as a communication consultant for NASA to recreate the public's image of NASA from an organization that is more concerned with its own invincibility and time/schedules over safety, what recommendations would you make to them? How would you go about generating these recommendations?

5. What could be done internally to promote a more unified culture within NASA?

6. To what extent is it possible to change a culture that has spent the last 25–30 years compromising its ethics in favor of a time- and money-driven operation?

❖ REFERENCES

Broder, J. M. (2003, February 3). Loss of the shuttle: The overview. *New York Times*, p. 1.

Columbia Accident Investigation Board. (2003, August). *Columbia accident investigation report*, Vol. I. Arlington, VA: Author. Available: http://caib.nasa.gov/news/report/pdf/vol1/full/caib_report_volume1.pdf

Jensen, C. (1996). *No downlink: A dramatic narrative about the* Challenger *accident and our time*. New York: Farrar, Straus, Giroux.

McCurdy, H. E. (1993). *Inside NASA: High technology and organizational change in the U.S. space program*. Baltimore: Johns Hopkins University Press.

Pianin, E. (2003, February 4). Bush proposes increase to NASA's FY '04 budget. *The Washington Post*, p. A13.

Pianin, E. (2003, May 12). Shuttle panel neutrality a concern: Payroll, secrecy lead to questions about ties to NASA. *The Washington Post*, p. A8.

Pianin, E. (2003, September 4). Congress scrutinizing manned spaceflight: Fix for long-term problems sought. *The Washington Post*, p. A2.

Pianin, E. (2003, October 4). NASA panel's ex-members fault shuttle funding. *The Washington Post*, p. A10.

Ritter, J. (2003, February 5). No matter what, fate of shuttle was sealed. *Chicago Sun-Times*, p. 3.

Roeper, R. (2003, February 4). If only we'd all shut up when we've little to say. *Chicago Sun-Times*, p. 11.

Rogers Commission (1986, June 6). *Report of the Presidential Commission on the space shuttle Challenger Accident*. Available: http://www.challenger.org/about/assets/nasa_report.pdf

Shales, T. (2003, February 3). A compelling story, numbingly repeated. *The Washington Post*, p. C1.

Sweeney, A. (2003, August 27). NASA's failings make tragedy worse for astronaut's family. *Chicago Sun-Times*, p. 8.

They had a high and noble purpose in life (2003, February 2). *Chicago Sun-Times*, p. 4.

Tompkins, P. K. (2004). *Apollo, Challenger, Columbia: The decline of the space program*. Los Angeles: Roxbury.

Blaming the Dead

*The Ethics of Accident
Investigation in Wildland Firefighting*

Jennifer Thackaberry

This case discusses the ethical judgments made by an official accident investigation team when it blamed wildland firefighters for their own deaths in the Storm King Mountain fire. It shows how insider-investigators struggled with dilemmas of timing, scope, objectivity, and accountability in assigning responsibility for the deaths. Ultimately the case shows how the team resolved these dilemmas in ways that shamed firefighters among members of their own community for failing at virtue and presented them to the public as disloyal employees who had failed in their duties, thus provoking a backlash in the firefighting community.

Forty-nine people were fighting a fire on Storm King Mountain near Glenwood Springs, Colorado, on July 6, 1994, when a cold front entered the area and generated an unexpected "wave of flame" (Maclean, 1999) that sent them scrambling for their lives. While most of the firefighters escaped, 14 did not. When the smoke cleared, the bodies of three Smoke Jumpers and nine Hot Shots were discovered within 100 yards of the top of Hell's Gate Ridge. After two days of searching, the bodies of two missing Helitacks were discovered in a rock chute half a mile away.

The tragedy occurred on Bureau of Land Management (BLM) property, but the majority of the fallen were United States Forest Service (hereinafter, the Forest Service) firefighters who had been sent there on an "interagency" assignment. The heads of the BLM and the Forest Service convened an accident investigation team to investigate the deaths. The South Canyon Accident Investigation Team (SCAIT)[1] issued their report 45 days later. Without naming any names, the report concluded that the deaths occurred because "The can-do attitude of supervisors and firefighters led to a compromising of eight out of the 10 Standard Fire Orders and a lack of recognition of 12 of the 18 Watchout Situations" (U.S. Department of the Interior [USDI] BLM & USDA Forest Service, 1994, p. 36).

The national press reported that the firefighters had died because they had broken safety rules (e.g., Davis, 1994; Kenworthy, 1994). But the findings also conveyed a sense of *moral* indignation that might not be expected in an otherwise straightforward analysis of the facts. Specifically, the report chided firefighters for an overly aggressive "can-do attitude" that had caused them to break those rules. Relatives and other stakeholders in the wildland firefighting community cited errors made by dispatch and supply offices that had compounded the disaster, and complained that the accident investigation team had conveniently—and unfairly—blamed the victims for their own deaths.

❖ DILEMMAS OF ACCIDENT INVESTIGATION

The Storm King Mountain story offers an opportunity to explore ethical dilemmas that arise when organizations investigate their own accidents and present their findings to the public. Clearly, it would be ideal for all accident investigations to be conducted by "independent" parties, like the National Transportation Safety Board (NTSB) for the airline industry, the 9/11 Commission for the September 11 terrorist attacks, or the *Columbia* Accident Investigation Board for the explosion of NASA's shuttle (Tompkins & Tompkins, 2004). Independent investigators can presumably maintain impartiality as they sift through evidence, conduct and interpret interviews, draw conclusions from data, and present their findings to the public.

But some occupations are so specialized that the best people available to investigate accidents are other organizational insiders.

Whenever federal wildland firefighters are "entrapped," or overrun by the very fire they are trying to put out, their agencies are required to investigate. According to fire historian Stephen Pyne (2001), this practice dates back to the early 20th century, when Congress required investigations before death benefits could be paid to relatives of fallen firefighters. Investigation teams are often assembled with federal employees who are actively involved in fire work. They are considered independent insofar as they were not involved in the actual fire they are investigating and have no other direct conflict of interest.

An examination of the SCAIT illuminates four ethical dilemmas that "insiders" face when investigating and reporting about their own organizations: dilemmas of timing, scope, objectivity, and accountability. Dilemmas of *timing* deal with how quickly an accident investigation will be completed and a report issued to the public. These are necessarily coupled with dilemmas of *scope*, which relate to how far an investigation will probe into the specific accident and beyond to the inner workings of the organization. Next, dilemmas of *objectivity* arise concerning the standards that will be used to make claims and present evidence. Finally, insiders experience dilemmas of *accountability* when the time comes to assign blame to specific individuals, to the organization, or to a combination of the two. While all accident investigators may wrestle with dilemmas of timing and scope, for insider-investigators, dilemmas of objectivity and accountability are particularly salient.

This case explores the specific dilemmas of timing, scope, objectivity, and accountability faced by the SCAIT in their examination of the firefighter deaths on Storm King Mountain. In order to understand their particular choices, as well as stakeholders' reactions to them, it is also necessary to understand the "military metaphor" for wildland firefighting that helped to give rise to the specific rules that were invoked in the investigation: The 10 Standard Fire Orders and the 18 Watchout Situations.

The Military Metaphor for Wildland Firefighting

The Forest Service was chartered under the U.S. Department of Agriculture at the turn of the 20th century to preserve national forests for the sake of conservation, but also to generate renewable crops for the sake of economic growth (Bullis & Tompkins, 1989). After the "Big Blowup" of 1910 burned three million acres in the West and killed 78 firefighters (Pyne, 2001), the Forest Service "declared war" on wildfire, and the agency's military metaphor for firefighting was born (Pyne, 1994).

U.S. involvement in World War II further reinforced the agency's mission to suppress the "enemy"—fire—as it inherited surplus war equipment and hired returning soldiers (Pyne, Andrews, & Laven, 1996).

For its first few decades, the militaristic approach to firefighting worked well for the fledgling agency. Then, in the 1930s the Forest Service began to see an increase in the numbers of firefighters who were being killed in "burnovers." After a particularly devastating fire in 1956, the Forest Service chief assembled a special task force to review the worst tragedy fires from the previous three decades and to make recommendations that would help to save lives. In their review, they discovered that sometimes even well-trained firefighters "just did not pay adequate attention to the good fire fighting practices that seem like small details but could become *the* critical item in an emergency" (USDA Forest Service, 1957, p. 8).

Consistent with the root metaphor for wildland firefighting, the task force turned to the military for inspiration, noting that military organizations seemed adept at "training men to remember certain fundamental instructions" called "General Orders" that helped them to react appropriately in emergencies (USDA Forest Service, 1957, p. 8). The task force reasoned that a similar set of General Orders for firefighting might help firefighters to remember what they know during an emergency and to react effectively. The chief agreed with their recommendation, and in 1957 issued 10 "Standard Fire Fighting Orders" to all agency firefighters, ordering them to memorize them immediately (McArdle, 1957).

The Fire Orders were still in effect in 1994, the year of the Storm King Mountain fire. However, the original list had been revised over the years to form the "10 Standard Fire Orders" shown in Table 16.1.

Soon after the Fire Orders were created, a second list was developed. The "Situations That Shout 'Watch Out!'" were descriptions of potentially dangerous conditions where firefighters need to exercise greater caution, such as building a fireline downhill or arriving in unfamiliar territory after dark (National Interagency Fire Center [NIFC], 2005). Over the years these were expanded and revised to become the "18 Watchout Situations" shown in Table 16.2.

Although the Fire Orders were revised yet again in 2002 (NIFC, 2005), both lists continue to be part of required training for all federal wildland firefighters.

With the military roots of wildland firefighting and the "10/18" as a backdrop, the remainder of the case draws upon archival data such

Table 16.1   The 10 Standard Fire Orders (ca. 1994)

---

1. Fight fire aggressively but provide for safety first.

2. Initiate all action based on current and expected fire behavior.

3. Recognize current weather conditions and obtain forecasts.

4. Ensure that instructions are given and understood.

5. Obtain current information on fire status.

6. Remain in communication with crew members, your supervisor, and adjoinng forces.

7. Determine safety zones and escape routes.

8. Establish lookouts in potentially hazardous situations.

9. Retain control at all times.

10. Stay alert, keep calm, think clearly, and act decisively.

Source: From the *Report of the South Canyon Fire Accident Investigation Team*, USDI BLM/ USDA Forest Service, 1994, p. 36. The initial letters spell the mnemonic "Fire Orders." The Fire Orders were later revised in 2002 (NIFC, 2005).

as news accounts, research articles, books, and documentaries about the fire to detail the four dilemmas of timing, scope, objectivity, and accountability faced by the SCAIT when they investigated the 14 deaths on Storm King Mountain. However, the case also shows how instead of closing the book on the accident, the choices made by the team provoked a backlash from relatives and other members of the wildland firefighting community, prompting the agencies to take a closer look at safety, including the role of the Fire Orders in accident investigation.

Dilemmas of Timing

Experts recommend that when accidents happen, organizations should deliver timely messages to the public (Coombs, 1999). When investigating one's own organization, however, to produce a report too quickly risks taking shortcuts, relying on incomplete information, rushing to judgment, or even creating the appearance of doing so. On the other hand, making the public wait too long for "the final answer" can raise questions about the organization's honesty and even its competence for conducting the investigation in the first place. Moreover,

Table 16.2   The 18 Watchout Situations

1. Fire not scouted and sized up.
2. In country not seen in daylight.
3. Safety zones and escape routes not identified.
4. Unfamiliar with weather and local factors influencing fire behavior.
5. Uninformed on strategy, tactics, and hazards.
6. Instructions and assignments not clear.
7. No communication link with crew members/supervisors.
8. Constructing line without safe anchor point.
9. Building fireline downhill with fire below.
10. Attempting frontal assault on fire.
11. Unburned fuel between you and the fire.
12. Cannot see main fire, not in contact with anyone who can.
13. On a hillside where rolling material can ignite fuel below.
14. Weather is getting hotter and drier.
15. Wind increases and/or changes direction.
16. Getting frequent spot fires across line.
17. Terrain and fuels make escape to safety zones difficult.
18. Taking a nap near the fire line.

Source: From *10 Standard Fire Orders and 18 Situation,* National Interagency Fire Center, 2005. These Watchout Situations were in effect in 1994 and are still in effect today.

a delay potentially invites others to introduce explanations that solidify public opinion before the organization has a chance to tell its side of the story. Ethical *dilemmas of timing* thus give rise to questions like the following: How soon can we release our report and still have it be accurate and believable? How late can we release it and still be perceived as responsive, and for our findings to be taken seriously?

The first eight members of the South Canyon Accident Investigation Team (SCAIT) convened in Glenwood Springs, Colorado, on July 7, 1994, the day after the fatalities. Arizona BLM director Les Rosenkrance and Forest Service deputy chief Mark Reimers led the investigation jointly (USDI BLM & USDA Forest Service, 1994). Two researchers who had arrived from the Forest Service research lab in Missoula to collect data, Dick Mangan and Ted Putnam, were also invited to join the team.

One of the first tasks of the 10-person team was to decide upon a time frame for the investigation. The team was subject to conflicting federal policies. One dictated that a report had to be issued within 30 days, while another said a report had to be issued within 45 days. Some members of the investigation team lobbied for a deadline longer than 45 days to complete the task, due to the multiple fatalities and the complexity of the accident. After the team compromised on the 45-day deadline, according to Rosenkrance, they "intended without fail" to meet it (Maclean, 1999, p. 214). In addition to this time pressure, members of the team were still responsible for their regular duties during an otherwise extreme fire season. The pressures to complete the investigation before the deadline, coupled with these competing demands, necessarily affected the *scope* of the investigation, or what the team could reasonably accomplish within the 45-day window.

Dilemmas of Scope

When trying to determine the cause of a fatal accident, investigators must consider what factors to include in the investigation and what to leave out. In the case of wildland firefighting, obvious environmental factors include weather, terrain, and "fuels" like trees and shrubs in the area. But factors involving people run the gamut from individual actions to organizational policies: from individual firefighter qualifications to how crews from different agencies were assigned during a busy fire season; from the performance of equipment at a given moment to how resources were allocated throughout the whole region; from isolated tactical decisions to broader organizational policies. Therefore, questions arising from ethical *dilemmas of scope* include the following: What factors should we investigate? What should we leave out? Where should we punctuate the time line of events? How far up the managerial chain of command should we trace decisions? Should we evaluate the effects of organizational policies?

The team received some guidance about scope from a National Wildfire Coordinating Group (NWCG) memo that recommended that they look at things like weather, fuels, involved personnel, and so forth. (USDI BLM & USDA Forest Service, 1994, p. A12). Team member Dick Mangan was also in the process of developing a set of protocols based on his experiences as an investigator, which he later published (Mangan, 1995). However, the team still needed to decide where to punctuate the time line of events. Ultimately, the decision was made to freeze the time line of the report at the moment of the firefighters' deaths, and to limit the scope of prior events to the days immediately preceding the accident. In one interview, Rosenkrance characterized the scope of the report in this way: "the fire started, the employees were killed, a little bit of what led to the disaster, and that was the end of our report" (Maclean, 1999, p. 214). He explained that due to time pressure, "we didn't try to go into things like, 'why was the budget cut, why was the head count reduced,' those kinds of things" (p. 214). Instead, the team left those items for an "Interagency Management Review Team" (IMRT) who would review the report and make organizational recommendations (USDI BLM & USDA Forest Service, 1995).

Later, some lamented that this decision suppressed an opportunity to learn from a botched rescue operation that unnecessarily prolonged the search for the two Helitacks (Maclean, 1999). In addition, Ted Putnam feared that any items that were excluded from the official report and left for the IMRT would never actually get fixed. He explained in a later account that as a young supervisor on the Battlement Creek Fire in 1976, he had been asked to withhold information about another firefighter's actions the day before a fatal accident occurred. He claims that in exchange for his silence, he was promised that a follow-up review board would ensure that the person would be relieved from fire duties. However, he heard during a SCAIT meeting that the firefighter had gone back on the fireline in a supervisory role. This left him feeling betrayed, and mistrustful of such promises (Putnam, 2001a).

Dilemmas of Objectivity

Emerging policies had provided the team with some guidance for dilemmas of timing and scope, but had merely dictated the maximum time they could work and the minimal factors they were required to look at. Once they set the boundaries of scope, the team still needed to decide how to evaluate all the data they collected, including the standards they would use for evidence. On these two points, the investigation team came face to face with *dilemmas of objectivity*.

For findings to be taken seriously by outsiders, an internal fact-finding mission must convey the impression that *if* independent experts were actually available, they would arrive at similar conclusions.

Therefore, they must decide upon the standards they will use, and must make those clear in their report. But even when insiders attempt to use objective standards, they may nevertheless find it difficult to "bracket" their personal experiences during an investigation.

In wildland firefighting, dilemmas of objectivity can arise from personal experience with firefighting, personal experience with danger, and personal and work relationships with people involved in the accident. Investigators may make assumptions about how *they* might have acted under similar circumstances, and they may use those assumptions in evaluating their peers. Moreover, personal feelings of loyalty, grief, or even anger toward the living and the dead may affect their judgment, for better or for worse. Even when they try to set these feeling aside, they may discover their colleagues accusing them of such biases anyway.

Dilemmas of objectivity can also arise from professional commitments such as technical expertise, loyalty to one's organization, and even identification with the broader profession. In wildland firefighting, the dilemmas of objectivity are compounded by the fact that the team composition itself can make it difficult to agree upon such standards for evidence in the first place. Teams are often assembled with experts in fire behavior, incident command, aviation, equipment, weather forecasting, and other specialties. In addition, all of the agencies involved in the accident, such as the BLM, the Forest Service, and the National Weather Service, are typically represented. While this composition might help to expand what will be examined, and on whose behalf, expertise is not necessarily additive. Different experts will disagree on evidence needed for claims, as well as the standards to be used for such evidence. Furthermore, representation does not necessarily lead to cooperation. Even though they are all in the business of wildland firefighting, members may feel compelled to represent their own agencies in the best light. Thus, when organizational members investigate their own accidents, ethical dilemmas of objectivity include the following questions: To what extent should our own personal experiences and emotions be brought to bear on the investigation? Which professional and organizational standards should we bring to bear on employee decisions and actions?

When disputes arose on the SCAIT, members accused each other of biases stemming from these personal and professional sources. In his own investigation of the fire years later, former journalist John Maclean (1999) discovered that "the conflict over who should shoulder the most blame, fire managers or firefighters, eventually split the investigation team and was never resolved" (p. 215). Maclean, whose father had written a bestselling book about an earlier fire (i.e., Maclean, 1993), had received a green light from the chief of the Forest Service to conduct his own investigation; agency people were told to cooperate with him. He reexamined much of the same evidence, and re-interviewed many of the same people. He also interviewed members of the accident investigation team. SCAIT member Dick Mangan later discussed the dispute in a documentary:

> As we went on through, John, it seemed like all the blame was being put on the firefighters for things that went wrong. And there was no accountability for the BLM district at Grand Junction for the things that they failed to do. We knew the firefighters there made some mistakes. There's no doubt about that. They died. They'll never make those mistakes again. The people at the Grand Junction District and the Coordination Center made mistakes [and] are still there to make the same mistakes over and over again. [They will continue to] put other firefighters at risk unless they get held accountable.[2] (in Wolfinger & Bacon, 2002)

While this statement anticipates dilemmas of accountability by discussing where blame should be directed, dilemmas of objectivity are nevertheless evident in this and other accounts offered about the dispute. Mangan, for one, had become suspicious that teammate Roy Johnson, a former fire management officer for that very BLM district, "was taking the district's side in every dispute" (Maclean, 1999, p. 224). Johnson later denied the accusation, explaining that "There were people who wanted to hug you, but you're part of the investigative team. You want to heal with them, but the healing process hasn't started for you" (p. 224).

Similarly, Ted Putnam claimed that the sections of the report controlled by the BLM representatives were "whitewashing" evidence that could have focused more attention on their offices' failure to properly staff the fire and to fill necessary resources for the firefighters (Kelleher, 2001). Rosenkrance, in contrast, felt that Mangan and Putnam were "too close to" the fallen firefighters: "They got so defensive of the people who died that they could not say that those people were at fault in any way" (Maclean, 1999, p. 234). Dick Mangan had once been the administrative head for the Prineville Hot Shots, many of whom had perished in the fire. And, in addition to the broken promises he experienced on the Battlement Creek fire, Ted Putman had also been a Smoke Jumper. However, Putnam later explained that he had been ready to show that some of the firefighters may have slowed down the rest of the group during the escape attempt (therefore implicitly blaming the firefighters), but he claims that he was never allowed to present the evidence to the team (Kelleher, 2001; Putnam, 2001a).

As the deadline approached, Mangan and Putnam lobbied for the report to direct greater attention to the actions of the BLM district and regional offices. After the BLM's failure to brief the firefighters about an important weather warning was raised from a "contributory" to "direct" cause of the tragedy, Mangan was satisfied (Maclean, 1999, p. 232). Putnam, however, asked for another meeting but was denied. Seeing that his changes had not been incorporated in the final revision, he requested that his signature be dropped from the report. In a letter to the chief, he explained: "My responsibility was to answer the question, *why did they die?* Because key evidence is still unavailable—coroner's evidence and critical witness statements—my technical report remains incomplete and this question unanswered" (Maclean, 1999, p. 233).

The report went to press anyway. The ranking Forest Service member on the team, Mark Reimers, later cited Putnam's professional commitments as the reason for going forward without him: "I realized Ted Putnam was a researcher and probably could not in good conscience sign the report, and would go on doing research on this, perhaps for years. I told [Rosenkrance and Thomas] it was unlikely he was going to sign, and we shouldn't worry about it" (Maclean, 1999, p. 233). Indeed, both Putnam and Mangan helped to coauthor a follow-up study that reanalyzed the fire's behavior (Butler et al., 1999). Years later, reflecting back on his participation, Putnam surmised that "what seemed like strong human factor causal links to accidents and fatalities to me were seen as weak links to managers with mostly fire and forestry backgrounds" (Miller, 2004, p. 5).

Despite their discrepancies, these accounts reveal that personal experiences and professional loyalties can lead to dilemmas of objectivity. However, they also show that insider investigators do not always resolve those dilemmas in self-serving ways. Often their convictions can fuel passions that demand that the investigation be conducted with the proper scope, that the findings be accurate, and that the potential impact on the community be anticipated. Unfortunately, these accounts also reveal that when team members don't see eye to eye, failing other explanations, they can attribute each other's obstinacy to personal and professional blinders.

Dilemmas of Accountability

Finally, after data are collected and analyzed, and the deadline is looming for a report to be issued, the time comes to assign blame to specific individuals, to the organization, or to a combination of the two. It is at this point that insider-investigators experience *dilemmas of accountability.*

Whenever employees die in organizational accidents, it is necessary to examine how the organization might have failed to ensure their safety. However, criticizing the organization too much can potentially tarnish its image, and (ironically) undermine its credibility for investigating its own accidents in the first place. But failing to criticize the organization *enough,* and failing to suggest avenues for improvement, can be perceived as myopic, self-protective, or worse yet, as a "whitewash."

In addition to examining the organization's role in safety failures, it is also necessary to evaluate how specific individuals contributed to the accident. However, focusing too much on the culpability of individuals who died risks being perceived as insensitive. It can aggravate the pain of surviving family members, friends, and coworkers, who might have been expecting an apology or an admission of guilt from the organization. Furthermore, pointing the finger at survivors potentially threatens their careers, including the careers of the leaders who commissioned the investigation in the first place.

There are also dilemmas of accountability that lie at the intersection between the individual and the organization. If safety procedures exist, it is a good idea to examine whether they were properly communicated to employees (organizational responsibility). But it is also necessary to determine whether employees actually followed them (individual responsibility). Failing to do the latter sets a poor example for other employees, who may conclude that there are no consequences for disregarding the rules. But scrutinizing rule compliance too closely can result in crackdowns that punish other employees for their colleagues' mistakes. On the other hand, the very existence of safety procedures tends to foster the assumption that just because rules exist, they are therefore effective and are being taught properly. When their efficacy is not tested, employees may be blamed in error. Concerns about how an accident investigation may affect organizational morale further complicate dilemmas of objectivity.

Thus, in investigating their own accidents, organizational members face ethical dilemmas of accountability such as these: Should the organization be blamed for its poor (or poorly enforced) policies? Or, should specific individuals be blamed for failing to follow the rules? How does blame affect remembrance of individuals who died, or the continued employability of those who survived? What will be the impact of our findings on employees and organizational functioning going forward? What messages will our findings convey to surviving and future firefighters? Should our findings attempt to send a message to correct unacceptable behavior?

Moral Judgments

The Fire Orders and Watchout Situations, described above, were included in the scope of factors considered by the SCAIT. After the details of the fire were gathered, they were sifted through the 28 items, and the quantities of broken rules were tallied (total came to 8 Fire Orders and 12 Watchout Situations). As mentioned in the introduction, after the report was released, national headlines emphasized the number of rules that had been broken. But the actual *wording* of the findings conveyed a much stronger sentiment than might have been expected from an otherwise straightforward analysis of the facts.

Blaming the 14 deaths on the "can-do attitude of supervisors and firefighters" that "led to a compromising of eight out of the 10 Standard Fire Orders and a lack of recognition of 12 of the 18 Watchout Situations" (USDI BLM & USDA Forest Service, 1994, p. 36) went beyond simply evaluating firefighters' job performance. Specifically, these findings levied two different *moral* judgments against the firefighters: a failure of virtue and a failure of duty.

First, by evaluating firefighter "attitudes" (and by chiding them for their "can-do attitude" in particular), the official investigation criticized the firefighters for failing to live up to an implicit *virtue ethic* to check their aggression in light of the dangers of firefighting. Second, by measuring firefighters' actions and decisions against the Fire Orders and Watchout Situations (and by finding them guilty of violating 20 of the 28 items), the official investigation criticized firefighters for failing to live up to an explicit "duty ethic" to follow stated principles under all circumstances. As a result, the firefighters were not only shamed among members of their own community for failing at *virtue*, but they were also presented to the public as disloyal employees who had failed in their duties.

❖ PUBLIC RESPONSE

For family members and friends of the fallen firefighters, public airing of these otherwise "internal" matters compounded feelings of grief, and in some cases sparked new feelings of anger. Father of fallen firefighter Jon Kelso, for example, reacted emotionally to a headline that appeared in his local paper that emphasized the "can-do attitude": "I personally felt like they were saying that my child wasn't intelligent enough to save his own life. And that really bothered me, personally" (in Wolfinger & Bacon, 2002). Mother of fallen Hot Shot Kathy Walsleben Beck claimed that she "wasn't even angry at anybody until they released that investigative report" (Kowalski, 1994b, p. A16). Likewise, father of fallen Smoke-Jumper-in-charge Don Mackey challenged that "if my son . . . didn't have a can-do attitude he never would have taken the assignment in the first place" ("Dead firefighter's dad," 1994, p. 10A).

When Maclean interviewed Rosenkrance about the report's emphasis on the "can-do attitude," the team leader explained the rationale as follows:

> Had they had safety zones identified? Sure they did. They [were] too far away. Had they identified someone to be lookouts? Yeah, they had lookouts but they weren't in the right places, nor were they doing the right kinds of things. You know, they did a lot of *things*. They just didn't do them very *well*. They had made comments like they thought they could get down there and *hook* that fire before it could get away. And that's where the "can do" attitude kind of came in that we put in our report: "They really *thought* they could *do* that!" (in Wolfinger & Bacon, 2002)

Rosenkrance's comments about safety zones and lookouts refer to specific Fire Orders (numbers 7 and 8 in Table 16.1). But the statement, "They really *thought* they could *do* that!" conveys a sense of moral indignation over the possibility that the firefighters not only failed to check their aggression, but also that they didn't seem to *know* that they should have done so. He maintained that while the BLM offices made mistakes, it was the incident commander's decision to build the fireline downhill "that got them committed" (Maclean, 1999, p. 226). (Mangan, on the other hand, maintained that if the firefighters had gotten the critical weather forecast from the BLM, as other firefighters in the area had, they would have been off the mountain and out of harm's way.)

Other family members of the fallen firefighters, like the sister of Hot Shot Tami Bickett, reframed the "can-do attitude" as a badge of honor: "I'm proud of my sister and people like Don Mackey. If mistakes were made, it was because they were trying to do the right thing" ("Dead firefighter's dad," 1994, p. 10A). Not all family members were grief-stricken, angry, or defiant, however. Father of fallen Hot Shot Bonnie Holtby, a former firefighter himself, explained that he and his daughter had accepted that "fire is a risky business. And even though you've taught everything you can to somebody, and even though they've got all this knowledge in their head, things still can go wrong" (in Wolfinger & Bacon, 2002).

Management Accountability

Reactions presented thus far suggest that stakeholders felt that the investigators focused the spotlight too much on the individual firefighters, and not enough on broader organizational issues. Indeed, some stakeholders began to question why decisions made by managers in the days and weeks before the tragedy had not been singled out in the report. For example, mother of fallen Smoke Jumper Don Mackey said that "people sat back in air-conditioned offices and sent those kids to their deaths" (in Wendel, 1995, p. 1A). Later, she and her husband explained to John Maclean that after they had read the report, they had wondered the following:

Bob: Why are they blaming the firefighters? When the firefighting *command*—

Nadine:—who put them on the fire—

Bob:—and are making the big bucks . . . screwed around for three days without putting anybody on the fire. No resources, no men, no equipment, nothing. And then when it all goes to hell, you send in the grunts, and let them try to take care of their mistakes [pounds the table]. Cost 'em 14 people. (in Wolfinger & Bacon, 2002)

Here Mackey was complaining that focusing too much on the actions of the firefighters drew attention away from earlier management decisions that may have created a fire that would have been difficult for any firefighters to survive. Indeed, a later investigation by the Occupational Safety and Health Administration (OSHA) found that safety rules had indeed been broken, but that *management* was to blame for failing to enforce its own rules, including the Fire Orders and Watchout Situations. The director of the investigation explained that OSHA was "putting the responsibility higher than the people on the mountain" because "there was a lack of management oversight and a lack of management commitment to safety in that fire" (in Angwin & Kowalski, 1995, p. A1). OSHA criticized managers for failing to maintain a clear chain of command and criticized field offices for failing to give the firefighters resources they needed, including the critical weather update. Some family members viewed the OSHA report as a vindication of the Storm King Mountain firefighters (Chronis & Kowalski, 1995).

❖ CONCLUSION

When insiders investigate accidents in their own organizations, they may experience all four dilemmas of timing, scope, objectivity, and accountability. The experience of the SCAIT shows that how they decide to deal with these dilemmas is not always easy, popular, or—in the case of working with a team—unanimous. The official report of the fire on Storm King Mountain had intended to close the book on the incident, but analyses continue to be written about it (including this one) (e.g., Butler et al., 1999; Larson, 2003; Putnam, 1995a, 1995b; Thackaberry, 2003; Weick, 1995). For some, a "cloud" continues to hang over the investigation and the individuals connected to it (Downhill, 2005, p. 27). In other respects, the fire and its aftermath have directed more attention to the importance of safety, particularly the use of the Fire Orders in accident investigations.

Questioning the Fire Orders

Whereas the official report had suggested that the Storm King Mountain firefighters had broken the rules as a group, some firefighters complained that they had unsuccessfully tried to question "direct orders" from supervisors that actually *contradicted* the Fire Orders. However, the details about those disagreements never made it into the official report (Kowalski, 1994a; cf. Maclean, 1999). Yet, firefighters expressed that they felt caught in a double bind because they also worried that speaking up or leaving the fireline would result in formal or informal retaliation (Withen, 1994). Still others have maintained that effective firefighting sometimes requires "breaking" Fire Orders (Rhoads, 1994).

As a result of these concerns, members of the wildland firefighting community started to question whether the Fire Orders worked as they were supposed to work, whether they could actually be followed, and whether there might be a better way to manage safety. Ted Putnam (2001b) later critiqued them from a cognitive perspective, arguing that in their current form, the Fire Orders were "humanly impossible" to follow while still actually fighting the fire (p. 3). He recommended that they be prioritized, reworded, and reinforced better on the job. A comprehensive study of the culture of wildland firefighting proposed other recommendations for the Fire Orders, such as clarifying which should never be broken "unless you have a darn good reason not to" follow them, and which should remain simply "guidelines" (Tri-Data, 1998; cf. Thackaberry, 2004). The Fire Orders themselves were conservatively reordered in 2002, with "Fight fire aggressively, *having provided for* safety first" placed at the bottom instead of the top (NIFC, 2005, emphasis added). Accident investigations continue to invoke the Fire Orders, although in different ways. Looking again to the military for inspiration, the Forest Service is currently exploring "doctrine" that might help the agency to reframe the Fire Orders as principles, not rules, that can help firefighters to "achieve the commander's intent" (Hollenshead, Smith, Carroll, & Keller, 2005).

Finally, some question whether wildland firefighting accidents should continue to be investigated by insiders. As Pyne explains, even if the Forest Service conducts its investigations with the "utmost integrity," it is still subject to criticism because "right from the beginning the agency has been allowed to act as its own jury and judge [on] itself" (as quoted in Kelleher, 2001, p. A1). This case has provided a window into some of the ethical dilemmas faced by such insider-investigators, showing how the choices they make about dilemmas of timing, scope, objectivity, and accountability can affect not only what they discover about an accident but also the community at large.

❖ GLOSSARY

BLM (Bureau of Land Management): federal land management agency in the U.S. Department of the Interior
Burnover: a specific cause of death where firefighters are entrapped and killed by the very fire they are trying to control

Fireline: trench dug by wildland firefighters to stop a wildland fire from spreading

Helitacks: elite firefighters who rappel from helicopters to control fires in remote areas

Hot Shots: elite ground-troop firefighters typically sent to control larger or more dangerous wildland fires

OSHA (Occupational Health and Safety Administration): federal agency in the U.S. Department of Labor that sets and enforces workplace safety laws

Smoke Jumpers: elite firefighters who parachute from airplanes to control fires in remote areas

United States Forest Service: national forest agency in the U.S. Department of Agriculture

Wildland fire: fire that burns on designated state or federal wildlands; used instead of "wildfire" to emphasize fire location rather than controllability

Wildland firefighters: firefighters who control forest fires typically by removing fuels from their path; distinguished from "urban firefighters" who attack fires directly in structures

Discussion Questions

1. Why do you think the public demands a quick assignment of blame after an organizational accident? Is this a uniquely American cultural ideal?

2. Do you think that federal agencies like the BLM or the Forest Service should continue to investigate their own wildland firefighting accidents? Why or why not?

3. Should the Fire Orders and Watchout Situations continue to be used in accident investigations? In what ways? What are the advantages and disadvantages of doing so?

4. What is the proper role of government agencies like OSHA in ensuring the safety of federal employees who work in dangerous occupations? All employees who work in dangerous occupations?

5. In what ways does an official investigation answer important questions about an accident but also raise new ones?

6. How might the wildland fire community's continued use of the "military metaphor" (i.e., wildland fire "fighting") be affected by
   a. Contemporary attitudes toward the environment?
   b. Current U.S. military involvement in war overseas?
   c. Renewed admiration for urban firefighters after the September 11 attacks?

7. Thinking about another high-profile accident you are familiar with, how did investigators (insiders or otherwise) cope with the dilemmas of timing, scope, objectivity, and accountability? What were the results?

❖ NOTES

1. In the confusion of a busy fire season, the original location for the fire was erroneously recorded as "South Canyon," and the name stuck. Thus, the joint BLM/Forest Service investigators were called the "South Canyon Fire Accident Investigation Team" (SCAIT) (USDI BLM & USDA Forest Service, 1994). However, the fire and resulting deaths actually took place on "Storm King Mountain" near Glenwood Springs, Colorado.

2. Later, a BLM employee was reassigned, the head of the state BLM office took early retirement, and one of the branches was closed.

❖ REFERENCES

Angwin, J., & Kowalski, R. (1995, Feb 9). Feds blamed in deaths. *Denver Post*, p. A-1.

Bullis, C. A., & Tompkins, P. K. (1989). The forest ranger revisited: A study of control practices and identification. *Communication Monographs, 56*, 287–306.

Butler, B., Bartlette, R. A., Bradshaw, L. S., Cohen, J. D., Andrews, P. L., Putnam, T., & Mangan, R. J. (1999). *Fire behavior associated with the 1994 South Canyon Fire on Storm King Mountain, Colorado.* Missoula, MT: U.S. Department of Agriculture Forest Service.

Chronis, P. G., & Kowalski, R. (1995, Feb 12). Storm King Fire report sparks relatives' anger. *Denver Post*, p. C-4.

Coombs, W. T. (1999). *Ongoing crisis communication.* Thousand Oaks, CA: Sage.

Davis, R. (1994, Aug 23). Probe: Safety corners cut in firefighter deaths. *USA Today*, p. 8A.

Dead firefighter's dad assails report. (1994, Aug 23). *Denver Rocky Mountain News*, p. 10A.

Downhill, S. (2005, Feb). Born of tragedy: The human factors movement rises out of South Canyon. *Wildland Firefighter, 26–29.*

Hollenshead, E. D., Smith, M., Carroll, F. O., & Keller, P. (2005). *Fire suppression: Foundational doctrine.* Custer, SD: U.S. Department of Agriculture Forest Service.

Kelleher, S. (2001, Sep 2). Fire experts fault Forest Service's own probes. *Seattle Times,* p. A1.

Kenworthy, T. (1994, Aug 23). Report says errors led to Colorado fire deaths. *Washington Post,* p. A10.

Kowalski, R. (1994a, Sep 11). Dissent preceded fire tragedy. *Denver Post,* p. A-1.

Kowalski, R. (1994b, December 18). Parents might sue for fatal Storm King blaze. *Denver Post,* p. A16.

Larson, G. S. (2003). A "worldview" of disaster: Organizational sensemaking in a wildland firefighting tragedy. *American Communication Journal, 6.* Retrieved July 12, 2005, from http://www.acjournal.org

Maclean, J. N. (1999). *Fire on the mountain: The true story of the South Canyon Fire.* New York: William Morrow.

Maclean, N. (1993). *Young men and fire.* Chicago: University of Chicago Press.

Mangan, R. J. (1995). *Investigating wildland fire entrapments.* Missoula MT: U.S. Department of Agriculture Forest Service, Missoula Technology and Development Program.

McArdle, R. E. (1957, Oct). Standard firefighting orders. *Fire Control Notes, 18,* 151.

Miller, B. (2004, Dec. 7). *Leaders we would like to meet: Ted Putnam.* Retrieved June 20, 2005, from http://www.fireleadership.gov

National Interagency Fire Center. (2005). *10 standard fire orders and 18 situations that shout watch out.* Retrieved July 12, 2005, from http://www.nifc.gov

Putnam, T. (Ed.). (1995a). *Findings from the Wildland Firefighters Human Factors Workshop.* Missoula MT: U.S. Department of Agriculture Forest Service, Missoula Technology and Development Program.

Putnam, T. (1995b). *The collapse of decision making and organizational structure on Storm King Mountain.* Missoula MT: U.S. Department of Agriculture Forest Service, Missoula Technology and Development Program.

Putnam, T. (2001a). *Fire safety: Up in smoke?* Retrieved July 12, 2005, from http://www.myfirecommunity.net

Putnam, T. (2001b). The ten standard fire orders: Can anyone follow them? In B. W. Butler & D. Mangan (Eds.), *Proceedings of the 2001 International Wildfire Safety Summit (Missoula, Montana, November 6–8, 2001).* Montana City, MT: International Association of Wildland Fire.

Pyne, S. J. (1994, Aug 8). Flame and fortune: Why fighting fire is different from fighting wars. *New Republic,* pp. 19–20.

Pyne, S. J. (2001). *Year of the fires: The story of the Great Fires of 1910.* New York: Penguin Books.

Pyne, S. J., Andrews, P. L., & Laven, R. D. (1996). *Introduction to wildland fire.* New York: John Wiley.

Rhoads, Q. (1994, Aug 26). Effective fire-fighting calls for bending rules some-times. *The Missoulian.*

Thackaberry, J. A. (2003). *Management, drop your tools: Ritual and resistance to "safety" legacies of tragedy fires of the U.S. Forest Service.* Paper presented at the annual meeting of the International Communication Association, San Diego, CA.

Thackaberry, J. A. (2004). Discursive opening and closing in organizational self-study: Culture as trap and tool in wildland firefighting safety. *Management Communication Quarterly, 17,* 319–359.

Tompkins, P. K., & Tompkins, E. V. (2004). *Apollo, Challenger, and Columbia: The decline of the space program.* New York: Roxbury.

Tri-Data Corporation. (1998). *Wildland firefighter safety awareness study: Phase III–Key findings for changing the wildland firefighting culture.* Arlington, VA: Author.

USDA Forest Service. (1957). *Report of task force to recommend action to reduce the chances of men [sic] being killed by burning while fight[ing] fire.* Retrieved July 12, 2005, from http://www.fs.fed.us

U.S. Department of the Interior Bureau of Land Management, & USDA Forest Service. (1994). *Report of the South Canyon Fire accident investigation team.* Glenwood Springs, CO: Authors.

U.S. Department of the Interior Bureau of Land Management, & USDA Forest Service. (1995, June 26). *Final report of the interagency management review team: South Canyon Fire on Storm King Mountain, Colorado.* Denver: Authors.

Weick, K. E. (1995). South Canyon revisited: Lessons from high reliability orga-nizations. In T. Putnam (Ed.), *Findings from the Wildland Firefighters Human Factors Workshop.* Missoula, MT: U.S. Department of Agriculture Forest Service, Missoula Technology and Development Program.

Wendel, T. (1995, Jun 14). Did 14 firefighters have to die? *USA Today,* p. 1A.

Withen, P. (1994, Sept/Oct). Fire culture. *Inner Voice,* 12–13.

Wolfinger, L. Q. (Writer, Director, and Producer), & Bacon, T. (Co-Producer). (2002). *Fire on the mountain.* New York: Lone Wolf Pictures for the History Channel.

Why Companies Tell Lies in Business

A Japanese Case in the Food Industry

Toru Kiyomiya, Kaori Matake, and Masaki Matsunaga

This case examines an example of milk poisoning and beef mislabeling within the Japanese food industry. It explores the unwillingness of the Snow Brand Group to provide accurate information to consumers regarding its responsibility for both problems and their potential health effects. Based on an understanding of the company's cultural practices, Japanese cultural norms, and market forces, the authors question whether the company met its duty to adequately inform the public.

In the last decade, we have observed various types of business scandals or corporate misdeeds which, increasingly, have become a major managerial issue. For example, as Enron and WorldCom have been criticized for their unethical actions in the United States, Japanese industries have also struggled with similar business scandals recently. As Figure 17.1 shows, the news media have also been paying more attention to ethical problems that have appeared in industrial, medical, and public organizations in Japan.

Figure 17.1   Number of Newspaper Articles About Business Scandals

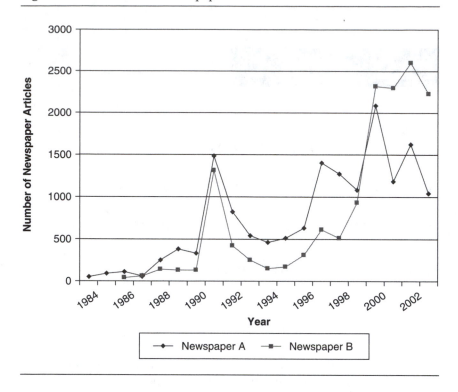

While public concern about injustice and unethical practices in business has increased, many business scandals have become increasingly public and, therefore, open to scrutiny. One of the most serious recent business scandals is the case of Snow Brand Group in the Japanese food industry. It had both an economic and social impact on the entire industry in Japan. The case involved two incidents; the first was a massive milk poisoning that occurred in 2000 and the second was a beef mislabeling scam in 2002. These high-profile business scandals appeared within two years of each other and involved organizations within the same Snow Brand Group—Snow Brand Milk Products (SBMP) and Snow Brand Foods (SBF), respectively.

We identify a variety of ethical dilemmas and unethical practices arising from these two incidents. In the food poisoning case by SBMP, the most significant ethical dilemma was the company's decision concerning whether to throw away the contaminated milk or to utilize it for producing powdered milk. The milk contained high levels of bacteria, but it still met legal standards. The company struggled to choose among the competing factors of hygiene control, group interests, and economic efficiency.

Another type of dilemma was the timing of the company's disclosures regarding the contaminated milk; the plant managers and top executives had to decide whether to remain silent for a while or tell the truth immediately. For example, a plant manager was asked by city health officials to disclose customer complaints about food poisoning, but he attempted to keep silent. Ultimately, important information about the contaminated milk was not accurately communicated, nor was information about a contaminated valve.

In contrast, SBF's beef mislabeling case raises a series of different ethical issues. The company's ethical dilemma was whether to face the hardship caused by the effects of bovine spongiform encephalopathy (BSE) or to engage in a riskier decision, namely mislabeling foreign beef to abuse the buy-back system and illegally obtain subsidies. This case, then, considers whether the company abused the buy-back system that the Japanese government offered to save beef-related industries from the impact of the outbreak of BSE.

From an outsider's point of view, these decisions may not seem particularly difficult. For example, if you ask someone to choose between hygiene control and economic efficiency, most people would choose hygiene. After all, the health of the company's customers would be at risk. However, the organizational members in SBMP took the alternative choice.

In order to better understand the case, however, we need to consider why and how the company and its employees engaged in specific behaviors. In particular, we should take into account the contextual factors that affected their decision making. For example, employees within companies are seldom aware of their own decisional premises in the workplace. As a result, we should pay attention to commonsense knowledge and values shared by the organizational members that affect their decisions to act ethically or unethically.

In this case study, three contexts of the workplace (organizational, Japanese cultural, and socio-economic contexts) may be relevant for understanding the ethical dilemmas at these companies of the Snow Brand Group. First, the organizational context refers to the unique organizational culture shared by employees, which includes their sense-making practices. In this case, it is worth considering whether the concept of "organizational identity" (Papa, Auwal, & Arvind,

1997; Tompkins & Cheney, 1983, 1985) affected their decision making in the ethical dilemmas noted above. Employees may be more likely to accept the organization's premises and make decisions consistent with organizational objectives when employees identify with the organization.

Second, the cultural context may also be important in order to understand the process of ethical decision making, since employees are not always aware of their own underlying cultural premises. According to Furuta (1996), for example, the Japanese possess a strong cultural tendency to follow the norms of the community to which they belong (i.e., *uchi*). In an *uchi* community, the members strive to assimilate into the group. The primary goal in such a group is to maintain and enhance the harmony within the group, even at the cost of individuals' freedom to act or the rules of out-groups (e.g., laws). The more involved people are in an uchi community and the more they internalize the community's values and norms, the narrower their perspectives are likely to be (Furuta, 1996).

Third, ethics and decision making may be understood in terms of the socio-cultural context. Modern society relies on capitalistic systems, which are characterized by market determinism and strong competition. Polanyi (1977) states that the market system violently distorts one's view of humans and society. In this case, assumptions about "free markets" may have affected employee and company decision making—such as a choice between hygiene control and efficiency, or a choice between compliance and abuse in the buy-back system.

In addition to exploring business decisions in terms of these three contexts, it is also important to consider a "communication perspective" (Deetz, 1994) to ethical dilemmas. On the basis of intersubjective approaches and social constructionist traditions, communication should be recognized as a dynamic process by which realities are constructed. From this perspective, unethical business practices may be understood as communicative forms of organizational deception, which we define as collaborative practices that conceal and distort information important to various publics. In that regard, this case focuses on the generative process by which organizational members might choose to conceal or distort information.

In the following sections, we first provide a brief introduction of the companies and describe the two incidents. Then, we explore relevant communication concepts, introduce significant issues raised by the case, and offer points of discussion.

❖ ORGANIZATIONS: SNOW BRAND MILK
PRODUCTS AND SNOW BRAND FOODS

The two organizational incidents at Snow Brand are independent and different in nature. However, the organizations are closely related as parent company and subsidiary. Snow Brand Milk Products (SBMP), the parent company, was responsible for a mass food poisoning (the first incident), while Snow Brand Foods (SBF), a subsidiary company, was responsible for a beef mislabeling scandal (the second incident).

Begun in 1925, SBMP has grown to have 6,900 employees, 32 plants, and 29 branch offices, as of 2003. It provides Japanese consumers with a variety of dairy products, such as milk, butter, various spreads, cheese, ice cream, and frozen foods, among others. Established in 1950, SBF had 1,100 employees in 2002 and three meat-processing plants in Japan. Ham, sausage, and other processed foods make up 86 percent of its revenues.

The Snow Brand Group was universally recognized as the top firm in the dairy and food industry in Japan and, as a result, was highly respected by consumers. However, the business scandals suddenly created a credibility problem for the company.

❖ FIRST INCIDENT: FOOD POISONING

Widespread food poisoning caused by SBMP products, from which 31,721 victims were alleged to have suffered, came to light on June 27, 2000. It was one of the most striking business scandals in the history of Japanese industry. The truth of the case became known to the public and revealed the ethical challenges faced by employees and managers in the organization. Table 17.1 briefly represents the chronological summary of the first case.

On June 27, consumers complained of suffering from symptoms of food poisoning such as diarrhea, stomach pain, and vomiting after drinking Snow Brand low-fat milk products made by the Osaka plant. By July 1, more than 1,500 people complained of illness in Osaka and seven other prefectures in western Japan. Officials at a medical laboratory detected a gene linked to the toxin present in yellow staphylococcus in leftover milk that the victims had drunk. SBMP stopped low-fat milk production at the Osaka plant and started to recall the affected milk on June 29. Osaka city health officials and SBMP had

Table 17.1   Chronological Summary of Massive Food Poisoning

Date	Incident
March 31, 2000	Electric power failure occurred during the production process of nonfat dry milk at the Hokkaido Plant, used as ingredient on April 1.
April 9	Unused portion of nonfat dry milk described above is reutilized at Hokkaido on April 10.
June 27	The Osaka City Authority confirmed food poisoning caused by the low-fat milk produced at the Osaka Plant.
June 28	General meeting of the Snow Brand's stockholders was held in Sapporo, Hokkaido.
June 29	The SBMP initiated the recall of nonfat dry milk products.
July 2	The Osaka City Authority detected staphylococcus aureus at the Osaka Plant.
July 14	The admission of HACCP (Hazardous Analysis and Critical Control Point) of the Osaka Plant was repealed by the Ministry of Welfare.
July 28	The head of the SBMP, Ishikawa, resigned his position.
Aug. 2	A declaration vouching for the safety of all the plants of the company, except for Osaka, was issued by the Ministry.
Aug. 18	The Osaka City Authority detected the toxin from skimmed milk produced at the Hokkaido plant.
Aug. 29	The SBMP confessed to the falsification of the manufacturing date of skimmed milk.

acknowledged the poisoning outbreak by 10 P.M. on June 27, but failed to reach a decision on a recall until two days later after the initial calls about food poisoning ("Snow low-fat milk makes 1,500 sick," 2000).

On July 1, the SBMP president announced that the staphylococcus aureus bacteria was found in a valve that carries low-fat milk leftover in the production process to a spare tank, which was believed to have caused the food poisoning. "We do not know where the staphylococcus aureus originated from. Maybe the cleaning [of the production line] was insufficient. I would have to say it was an oversight on our part," the SBMP president told reporters ("Milk production line found contaminated," 2000).

People thus came to believe that the bacteria found in the valve at the Osaka plant caused the massive food poisoning. On August 18, however, the Osaka local government announced that the food poisoning was not caused by the bacteria found at the Osaka plant, but rather by a toxin in the powdered milk produced at the Hokkaido plant two months prior to the incident. In fact, Enterotoxin A, produced by the bacteria staphylococcus aureus, was detected in the powdered skim milk used for production in Osaka. The powdered milk was produced April 10 and delivered to the Osaka plant on June 20 for making low-fat milk and other dairy products ("Police to probe Snow plant toxin," 2000).

Unfortunately, a variety of questionable actions led to the widespread milk poisoning. An ineffectual communication process and unethical decisions are evident in all three situations: at the Hokkaido plant, the Osaka plant, and the company headquarters.

The Hokkaido Plant

The critical decision at the Hokkaido plant was made by the plant manager to approve the use of problematic powdered milk and to keep silent about the facts related to the food poisoning. The initial incident occurred on March 31: a huge icicle broke the roof of the plant and led to a power failure in the plant. While the employees were engaged in repairs on the roof,[1] they forgot that the electricity to the milk chambers had been shut off. As a result, the raw milk was left in the storage tank for several hours without the cooling systems and became warm enough to allow the growth of staphylococcus aureus bacteria. On April 1, company officials found a concentration of 11,000 bacteria per gram in the powdered milk,[2] a 10-times higher level than the company standard, but still within the legal food safety limit. According to Fujiwara (2002) and Hokkaido Shinbunsha (2002), the workers, nevertheless, made a decision not to throw the problematic milk away. These workers confessed that they did not dump the contaminated milk because they were afraid of financial losses to the company and, as a result, they sought to protect themselves as well as the company. Likewise, the plant manager approved the use of the contaminated milk, (Fujiwara, 2002; Hokkaido Shinbunsha 2002). Thus, the employees and managers faced an ethical dilemma. They could follow the safety rules and dump the problematic milk, or protect themselves from financial responsibility for economic losses and use the problematic milk.

Another dilemma was inherent in the decision to conceal the information; they did not report problems to the executives before or after the food poisoning. The facts about the contaminated powdered milk did not appear either within the company or in the media for more than four months. It is clear, then, that the employees and managers at the Hokkaido plant had another ethical dilemma: they could either be honest and forthcoming with the facts related to the food poisoning or they could conceal the facts within the plant to protect their group interests.

The Osaka Plant

The ethical problems in the second situation, at the Osaka plant, concerned the poor hygiene control and the concealment of initial complaints from the consumers. It was revealed that the valve for milk manufacturing had not been regularly washed as the corporate manual directed. Apparently, some workers were not even aware of the contents of the manual. Continuing poor hygiene control with the tacit approval of workers and managers implied that the safety of consumers was being completely neglected. In fact, the manager had not posted any notices about unsanitary working habits or hygiene environment and had failed to accurately communicate the degree of contamination in the valve. Initially, he had announced that a small part of the inside valve was contaminated, but later it was revealed that nearly every part of the valve was contaminated.

Furthermore, when Osaka city health officials demanded the disclosure of information regarding the customer complaints about the food poisoning, the head plant manager rejected this request. When another manager submitted customer complaints to the health officials on June 28 without the head manager's approval, he received a severe reprimand from the plant manager.

The Headquarters

Top executives faced an ethical dilemma at the company headquarters related to crisis communication after the massive food poisoning appeared. On June 28, a general meeting of stockholders was held in Sapporo, the capital city of Hokkaido, with the top executives of SBMP spending time in bars that evening. The executives knew that the food poisoning might be related to the products from the Osaka plant, but they did not take any proactive actions. They just observed the situation and did not go to the Osaka plant. Despite several calls from customers warning of poisoning, their pride as a top brand delayed them from recalling their products and making a public announcement. In the end, the recall decision was made two days after the initial telephone calls. In addition, the corporate leaders may have asked their employees to engage in unethical practices, which was evidently consistent with communication practices and organizational norms at SBMP.[3]

❖ SECOND INCIDENT: BEEF MISLABELING SCAM

Another important incident occurred one year later in the now-defunct Snow Brand Food Company (SBF). According to news reports ("Snow Brand beef scam," 2002), SBF abused the Japanese government's beef buy-back program, which sought to help an industry hit hard by BSE (more popularly known as mad cow disease). A critical decline occurred in the sales volume of beef in late 2001 because BSE had been identified in a couple of Japanese cows in September of that year. The Japanese government decided to introduce a buy-back program in October to incinerate about 12,600 tons of beef from Japanese cows butchered before nationwide cattle testing for mad cow disease was begun on October 18 ("Snow Brand beef scam," 2002). Apparently abusing this system, SBF disguised about 30 tons of imported (Australian) beef as domestic (i.e., Japanese) meat. Consequently, the company received approximately 195 million yen (approximately 1.8 million U.S. dollars) in subsidies under the buy-back program. Their decision to mislabel beef in order to receive buy-back money came to light because of whistle-blowing by the company's business partner. Eventually, the president and three officials from SBF formally apologized for their company's misdeed in a press conference on January 23, 2002 (see Table 17.2 for a chronological summary of the case).

SBF's beef mislabeling involved the decisions of more than 10 people and various types of ethical dilemmas may be evident in their decision making. First, it appears that the three SBF officials[4] conspired to abuse the government's buy-back program. The BSE impact was so serious in the beef-related market that many large product retailers could not overcome a large decline of beef sales and, as a result, they faced bankruptcy. These officials of SBF faced the dilemma of either holding the "dead stock" of Australian beef and swallowing the economic damage, or making the best of the government's buy-back

Table 17.2　Chronological Summary of Snow Brand Food's Beef Mislabeling

Date	Incident
Feb. 1995	The Hanshin-Awaji earthquake hit the Kansai region of Japan.
Fall 2001	A large daily product retailer, Mycal, went bankrupt.
Sept. 2001	First BSE-infected cows were identified in Japan. (Beef sales volume sharply declined in Japan.)
Oct. 2001	The Japanese government's beef buy-back program was introduced. Nationwide cattle testing for BSE began in Japan.
Oct.–Nov., 2001	SBF officials at Kansai Meat Center ordered the repackaging of Australian beef to pass as domestic (i.e., Japanese) beef.
Oct. 29, 2001	The head of SBF Kansai Meat Center asked Nishinomiya Refrigerating (NR) to cooperate with their beef mislabeling.
	Yoichi Mizutani, the president of NR, received the feedback from his subordinates about the SBF's mislabeling of beef. After confirming the facts with the head of Kansai Meat Center, Mizutani revealed the fraud and disclosed it to the media. (Meat industry cut their business with NR).
Jan. 22, 2002	The media reported on SBF's beef mislabeling scam.
Jan. 23, 2002	SBF officials apologized for wrongdoings.

scheme and obtaining buy-back money. They chose to use the program inappropriately by ordering employees to repack foreign beef and mislabel it.

Second, the SBF employees who relabeled the beef faced their own ethical dilemmas. When the boss ordered them to repack the foreign beef into boxes with domestic labels, the employees might have noticed the company's misdeed. In this situation, employees from the Meat Center did not refuse to comply with the request of their boss. From the workers' point of view, they may have felt they were just following orders and had no choice but to mislabel the beef. While it is easy to blame them for not blowing the whistle at that time, we need to understand the organizational structure and the dynamics of the case, and take into consideration the factors related to the workers' decision making.

In addition, several related parties outside SBF also faced ethical decisions. For the mislabeling to succeed, the deception could not be limited only to the corporate boundaries of SBF and, as a result, the deception expanded to other organizations. For example, one of the SBF officials asked another Snow Brand group company (Hokuriku Snow Brand Ham) to prepare false labels and the president of Hokuriku Snow Brand Ham chose to cooperate. Immediately after the mislabeling was revealed, he attempted to hide his role but he later admitted that he had participated in it. Ultimately, then, the president of Hokuriku had to consider whether or not to reveal his colleague's fraud.

Furthermore, the mislabeling deception was expanded to another business partner of SBF, who played the last, yet perhaps the most important, role in the case: whistle-blowing. The mislabeled beef had been stored at a warehouse company, Nishinomiya Refrigerating Co. (NR), before the beef was subjected to the buy-back scheme. The employees of SBF repacked the beef at the warehouse and asked warehouse employees to falsify the inventory certificate to submit to an industry group for government reimbursement (Matsubara, 2004). Such an assumption of compliance by the warehouse employees was largely dependent upon the strong business relationship between SBF and NR. In 1995, when the Hanshin-Awaji earthquake hit NR, the employees of SBF helped the warehouse company recover. One of the SBF employees who helped NR after the earthquake devastation was the official who ordered the warehouse workers to falsify the certificates. By telling them, in effect, "it's going to be okay because no one tells the truth," he encouraged the warehouse employees to keep silent. He may have assumed that his assistance during the earthquake made it easier for him to gain NR's cooperation. However, Mr. Yoichi Mizutani, the president of NR, made a courageous decision and informed newspapers of the wrongdoings by SBF. According to Hokkaido Shinbunsha (2002), Mizutani could not agree to SBF's request, because only the company would benefit; the farmers and beef producers themselves faced a financial crisis because of the BSE problem. He also took offense at SBF's attempts to involve his employees in the cover-up.

While the SBF's deception came to light because of Mizutani's whistle-blowing, he paid a heavy price. After the SBF case developed into a major scandal, the entire meat industry responded to his action by cutting their business ties with his firm (Matsubara, 2004). Unfortunately, Mizutani's ethical decision caused an economic hardship for his company.[5] The dilemma that Mr. Mizutani faced left him only two choices: either to collaborate in the deception and maintain a business relationship with SBF (and others in the industry as well) or to disclose the truth even though doing so might have severe repercussions for himself and his business.

❖ COMPARISON BETWEEN THE TWO INCIDENTS

The business scandals in this case study appeared within two years of each other and they also involved the same Snow Brand Group. However, the two cases were in many ways unique and different from each other. In the food poisoning case, SBMP's misjudgments in ethical dilemmas are typically characterized as "defensive." Because they were strongly concerned with internal affairs within the company, the organizational members involved in this case failed to solve dilemmas appropriately. For example, one of the important reasons why the manager failed to dispose of the contaminated milk was his fear of losing his status, power, and face in the organization. Therefore, employees tried to avoid their responsibilities and thus protect themselves and the company.

In contrast, SBF's misjudgments in the beef mislabeling case were somewhat different. The SBF officials struggled with a serious decline in the beef market, so they felt compelled to take action. They decided to choose the risky action of mislabeling foreign beef to illegally obtain the subsidies. The motivation for this deception was economic, rather than self-protection. Thus, it seemed like an *offensive* move, rather than a defensive one, amid the market disruption in the mislabeling case.

Although the nature of ethical dilemmas might be different in each incident, a similarity can be found in their organizational cultures. For example, in both organizations, concealing and distorting information seemed to be usual or taken-for-granted behavior. The cultures of each organization, as described below, encouraged employees to distort or conceal information. Also, because many employees were aware of the deception, peer pressure from coworkers encouraged them to participate—or, at the least, to avoid blowing the whistle against the company. In this sense, organizational deception was underpinned by collaboration within the group, and misjudgments in ethical dilemmas were related to group interests. The organizational members who were involved in the unethical practices were motivated (or compelled) to deceive consumers for the sake of group interests, not individual gain.[6] One focal point of understanding their decision making should therefore be the influence of the work group rather than the personal characteristics or background of the employees themselves.

❖ IMPLICATIONS

Organizational Context: Organizational Identity

When we think of the unique organizational context that produced the Snow Brand scandals, it appears that conformity with group interests or corporate objectives was underlying both cases. For example, in the case of the food poisoning, managers and workers in the Hokkaido plant conformed to organizational norms to stifle their opinions regarding the use of contaminated powdered milk. In the case of the beef mislabeling scam, the workers at the Meat Center did not disagree, and assisted in mislabeling. These examples indicate that workers were encouraged to defer individuals' decision making in favor of the group interest. In other words, the Snow Brand workers were unconsciously persuaded into wrongdoing.

The concept of organizational identification in the context of group decision making is useful to understanding these examples. Identification is central to understanding the ongoing process of decision making because "an organization can communicate decisional premises with relative ease to an individual who seeks to identify with the organization" (Tompkins & Cheney, 1983, p. 127). In the two cases, both SBMP and SBF were traditional organizations that emphasized organizational identity and strong group harmony. The workers who were involved in the scandals may have assumed that wrongdoing was justifiable if it met group objectives. This implies that group identity distorted ethical decision making and lowered resistance to engaging in misconduct.

Organizational identification is related to *groupthink*, "a mode of thinking people engage in when they are deeply involved in a cohesive in-group, when members' striving for unanimity override their motivation to realistically appraise alternative courses of action" (Janis, 1982, p. 9). Groupthink often results in a deterioration of reality testing and moral judgment, and the cases of food poisoning and mislabeling reflect the effects of such groupthink. It is typical that SBMP officials had considerably optimistic attitudes toward customers' warnings about food poisoning and overlooked the seriousness of the situation in the early stages of the crisis. In the other case, it is possible that the workers and managers at Osaka Meat Center optimistically believed that the mislabeling would never become public.

Japanese Cultural Context: In-Group–Oriented/Uchi Perspectives

People usually think that their own culture is a priori, and they are not aware that cultural background affects decision making. It is necessary to consider how Japanese culture influences organizational deception in these cases. The Japanese style of communication is unique in its strong concern for in-group matters but less interest in out-group matters. Similarly, Furuta (1996) maintains that the Japanese typically focus on following the norms of the community to which they belong (*uchi*). An *uchi* society, Furuta (1996) contends, encourages its members to assimilate and become just the same as other members. As a result, the respective community develops unique norms that are shared only within the boundary of the community; its members come to take it for granted that their community is homogenous, and clearly linked to the harmony so highly valued within the society. Furthermore, the more people assimilate into their uchi society, the more they become xenophobic and tend to ignore outsiders. People are afraid that they may be exiled from their *uchi* community.

Turning back to the Snow Brand scandals, the uchi perspective may be relevant. Perhaps the company had a highly developed uchi community and its members were primarily concerned with carrying out what was good for the company or their groups, even though the company norms might run counter to the social/moral standard. According to one survey (Makino et al., 2000), about 60% of responses indicate that organizational deception and concealment is caused by in-group–oriented perspectives. A director of SBMP, for example, repeatedly mentioned that many people in the company had uchi perspectives that affected the food poisoning scandal. Within an uchi community, in addition, workers are discouraged to blow the whistle. If they do, those inside informers could be retaliated against as betrayers. A victim of such sanctions by uchi society is the president of Nishinomiya Refrigerating, the whistle-blower in the mislabeling of beef, whose company subsequently went out of business. Both SBMP and SBF maintained uchi society in order that no one would blow the whistle. Along with organizational identity, uchi society enhances self-protection in case of failure. Failure can lead to exile of a person to outside the group; therefore, one who has found a fault attempts to protect oneself.

Socio-Economic Context: Capitalistic Knowledge

Capitalism is considered a socio-economic context that always impacts human relationships and communication. According to Polanyi

(1977), "the economy did now consist of markets, and the market did envelope society" (p. 9). This means that the market has become a primary determinant in society and has often disturbed human and social relationships. The organizational deception is one of the structural and communication problems under such a market society, and it supports Polanyi's presumption: the market system violently distorts one's view of human life and society and these distorted views provide the main obstacles to human communication (Polanyi, 1977). Namely, the market has power in present society, and it affects not only economic activities but also human interactions in general. For example, in the food poisoning case, the president of SBMP admitted that economic achievement came first and safety came second in the organizational culture of SBMP, even though safety must be the primary concern in the food industry. By the same token, the mislabeling of beef was aimed at achieving an economic goal and ignoring corporate social responsibilities even though everyone in the company understood this was wrong. As long as market society distorts human relationships and ways of thinking, the organizational members will sacrifice themselves for corporate survival and market competition.

A socio-economic context, therefore, influences our knowledge formation and, as a result, our common-sense knowledge and sense making are biased toward the principles of capitalism. People are rarely aware that their knowledge and interpretation (sense making) reflect capitalistic values. Our frame of reference on what is good and what is bad heavily relies on such capitalistic knowledge of common sense. This is conceptualized as *ideology*, which is defined as "taken for granted assumptions about reality that influence perceptions of situation and events" (Deetz & Kersten, 1983, p. 162). So, ideology structures our thoughts and controls our interpretations of reality (Eisenberg & Goodall, 2001).

In the case of organizational deception, knowledge and power are central. On the one hand, for instance, mislabeling was directed by one of the SBF officials and the workers followed his orders. This is an authoritative style of organizational deception. On the other hand, when we interpret many situations involving groupthink, such as excessive optimism about safety in the food poisoning case, this is regarded as a tacit or unobtrusive style of organizational deception that uses commonsense knowledge. Thus, organizational deception was not only conducted by direct orders from bosses, but commonsense knowledge was also unconsciously used to conduct wrongdoing and deception. A capitalistic sense of prioritization and market-oriented communication became the employees' ideology, which mutually influenced the organizational climate of the Snow Brand Group.

When business scandals have appeared in the United States, Japan, and elsewhere, we tend to think that such problems as organizational deception might be universal across nations. Individual cases will all be different, but we can also see, from the above two cases, the importance of "cultures" in understanding the dynamics of organizational structure and communication. We believe, therefore, that this case is beneficial for not only American readers but also international readers. The issues of business scandals have gained the attention of the public, and it is important to discuss these issues from a communication perspective and consider the embedded contexts. The cases of the Snow Brand Group illuminate a variety of issues that are useful for both students and practitioners to understand the generative process of business scandals. In the future, more effective solutions, along with business ethics and risk management, will be embodied by taking account of communication perspectives.

Authors' Note: We would like to thank Mr. Yoshio Okada, a director of the Compliance Department, Snow Brand Milk Production Co., who was willing to provide us with an in-depth interview. We would also like to thank Mr. Susumu Saito, a graduate of Seinan Gakuin University, who helped to collect information about the cases. We also appreciate Dr. Duane L. Olson, Seinan Gakuin University, who reviewed our manuscript and gave us constructive comments and suggestions for English expressions. The preparation of this chapter was supported, in part, by MEXT (Ministry of Education, Culture, Science, Sports, and Technology), research grant number KAKENHI 15530360.

Discussion Questions

1. Identify the facts of organizational deception in this case. In particular, what various ethical dilemmas are present?

2. Interpret and describe the organizational cultures of SBMP and SBF that were related to unethical judgments. Are there important similarities or differences in the cultures of the organizations? If so, how did the organizational cultures affect the decisions made within them?

3. What made the employees distort or conceal information? By contrast, what made the managers distort or conceal information?

4. Imagine that you have been working at the Snow Brand Group for five years. Do you think that you would feel an "uchi" community in the Japanese workplace? What affect would it have on your decision making?

5. What are the similarities and differences between ethical dilemmas of the Snow Brand cases and those of a recent business scandal in the United States or other countries?

6. With your fellow students, share a recent ethical dilemma and describe its context. Which of the three contexts (organizational, cultural, and socio-economic) that can be identified in the ethical dilemma is most significant?

❖ NOTES

1. Hokkaido is a northern area of Japan and it is quite cold during the winter. Therefore, it was necessary to fix the factory roof as soon as possible.

2. It is usual that companies in the dairy industry check the level of bacteria but do not check existence of toxin. Therefore, at this stage, the company could not detect Enterotoxin A.

3. As a result of this scandal, the amount of sales at SBMP decreased by about 77%. Guilty verdicts were found for three of the accused, and the trials in the civil court are in progress at this writing.

4. The former head of the Meat Sales and Procurement section conspired in the scam with a former senior official in the same section and a former head of the Kansai Meat Center.

5. Unlike in the United States or United Kingdom, the Japanese legal system has not been established well enough to protect whistle-blowers and encourage them to reveal the truth (Matsubara, 2004).

6. It might be interesting to compare the Snow Brand case with the Enron case, which was caused by the desire for individual monetary gain.

❖ REFERENCES

Deetz, S. A. (1994). Future of the discipline. In S. A. Deetz (Ed.), *Communication Yearbook 17* (pp. 565–600). Thousand Oaks, CA: Sage.

Deetz, S. A., & Kersten, A. (1983). Critical models of interpretive research. In L. L. Putnam & M. E. Pacanowsky (Eds.), *Communication and organizations: An interpretive approach* (pp. 147–171). Beverly Hills, CA: Sage.

Eisenberg, E. M., & Goodall, J. (2001). *Organizational communication: Balancing creativity and constraints.* New York: St. Martin's Press.

Fujiwara, K. (2002). *Yukizirushino rakuzitsu* (The setting sun of Snow Brand). Tokyo: Ryokuhu.

Furuta, G. (Ed.). (1996). *Ibunka Komyunikaeshyon* (Intercultural communication), 2nd ed. Tokyo: Yuuhikaku.

Hokkaido Shinbunsha (2002). *Kensho Yukijirushi Houkai* (Viewing collapse of Snow Brand). Tokyo: Kodansha.

Janis, I. (1982). *Groupthink: Psychological studies of policy decisions and fiascos.* Boston: Houghton Mifflin.

Makino, H., Shiota, H., Takayanagi, M., Hiromatsu, T., Sakai, K., Kaneda, S., et al. (2000, October 2). Kaishagakowareru (Breakdown of firms). *Nikkei Business.*

Matsubara, H. (2004, February 14). Whistle-blower law in the pipeline: Bill stops short of real protection against company retaliation. *The Japan Times.*

Milk production line found contaminated. (2000, July 2). *The Japan Times.*

Papa, M. J., Auwal, M. A., & Arvind, S. (1997). Organizing for social change within concertive control systems: Member identification, empowerment, and the masking of discipline. *Communication Monographs, 64*(3), 219–249.

Polanyi, K. (1977). *The livelihood of man.* New York: Academic Press.

Police to probe Snow plant toxin. (2000, August 20). *The Japan Times.*

Snow Brand beef scam was systematic, police say. (2002, February 4). *The Japan Times.*

Snow Brand Foods execs face probe. (2002, May 2). *The Japan Times.*

Snow low-fat milk makes over 1,500 sick in Kansai. (2000, July 1). *The Japan Times.*

Tompkins, P. K., & Cheney, G. (1983). Account analysis of organizations: Decision making and identification. In L. L. Putnam & M. E. Pacanowsky (Eds.), *Communication and organizations: An interpretive approach* (pp. 123–147). Beverly Hills, CA: Sage.

Tompkins, P. K., & Cheney, G. (1985). Communication and unobtrusive control in contemporary organizations. In R. D. McPhee & P. K. Tompkins (Eds.), *Organizational communication: Traditional themes and new directions* (pp. 179–210). Beverly Hills, CA: Sage.

"Call 'Em Like We See 'Em"

Responding to Unfair and Unethical Charges

Joy L. Hart, Stuart L. Esrock, and Greg B. Leichty

This case discusses the efforts of a nonprofit organization, Kentucky ACTION, to courageously confront one of the state's largest industries—tobacco. The organization sought to increase the state's excise tax on cigarettes and other tobacco products through lobbying and public media information. The case also explores the actions of anti-tax representatives who attacked the credibility, motives, and intelligence of the organization's members. In response to the attacks on their integrity, members of Kentucky ACTION faced difficult decisions regarding whether it was more appropriate to respond in a confrontational manner or to adopt a "high road" approach. Members had to consider whether they would compromise their organization's own ethics in pursuit of a greater good—public health.

As Mike Curtis took his seat at the meeting, he couldn't help but think how tired he was of being cast as a liar, an idiot, and a jerk. He knew that the group as a whole needed to figure out how to handle such charges. Perhaps today's strategy-planning session was the time to do that.

The rest of the members of Kentucky ACTION (The Alliance to Control Tobacco In Our Neighborhoods) joined Mike at the table and the meeting[1] began. They'd held neighborhood meetings and press conferences, participated in several televised programs, sent numerous press releases to various media, mounted a large e-mail campaign, designed and executed an extensive telephone campaign, and lobbied the state legislature. Despite their successes in getting their main issue on the public and legislative agenda, they hadn't succeeded in reaching their primary goal—increasing the state's excise tax on cigarettes and other tobacco products.

Within tobacco-control circles, Kentucky ACTION was regarded as well informed and it had received positive national attention. In the state, ACTION was considered the key group lobbying for the increase in the excise tax and several other tobacco-related matters. They had assembled a broad-based coalition of more than 250 community, religious, and health groups in support of the tax proposal. They had consulted with health experts and researchers who emphasized that a cigarette excise tax increase would lower youth smoking. They had conferred with economists who guaranteed that the proposal would raise significant new revenues for the state with only a negligible effect on farmers.

But, along the way, ACTION had aroused stiff resistance and met rough tactics. Attacks on the credibility, motives, and intelligence of organization members by farm organizations, smokers, and the anti-tax movement were unrelenting. In several editorials and letters to newspapers across the state, Kentucky ACTION members had been labeled liars and conspirators with a hidden agenda. A series of four 1-hour programs that discussed the excise tax on statewide public television yielded additional condemnations. ACTION representatives were accused of fabricating evidence as well as being stupid, uninformed, disingenuous, heartless, and even unpatriotic. For example, excise tax opponents[2] claimed the following:

"There is no proof that raising the excise tax on tobacco will make anybody stop smoking, will substantially reduce the smoking rate. And they have no statistics! You won't hear statistics!"

"Children don't get lung cancer and lung cancer only kills 2% of the people who die in the world. Two percent! It's not one of the top five killer diseases."

"I think the health groups sometimes don't stop and really reflect on what it's going to do to our state, what it's going to do to retailers, what it's going to do to farmers."

"You can make numbers say whatever you want."

"If they want to change people's lifestyle, they should stick to education and not worry about taxing us all to death."

"I have been whooped on as a farmer and tobacco smoker. I've done been stomped, kicked, and whooped all over the place. And I want all of you folks to share in the pain, all right? If you are going to whoop up on me, then you go after these [pro-tax] women that are doing this false advertising [in support of the tax on the program] for their hair color and makeup!"

Given the deep cultural roots of tobacco in Kentucky and the deep emotions tied to the subject, the use of such hardball tactics was not surprising. The ACTION leadership felt they needed to find some way to answer. But just how could the organization best respond to what it considered to be unfair and unethical charges? What ethical parameters did organization members need to consider as they made their decision? What could the organization do to defend its credibility against such assaults and still not give up what its leaders felt was the moral high ground on this issue? After all, their mission was saving thousands of Kentucky youth from a life-long and life-threatening addiction to nicotine.

❖ HISTORICAL AND CULTURAL CONTEXT

Tobacco has long been a cash crop in Kentucky, and, until relatively recently, proceeds from its sales have supported many family farms. There are still over 40,000 farms raising tobacco in Kentucky (President's Commission on Improving Economic Opportunity, 2001), and only one other state exceeds Kentucky's tobacco production (University of Kentucky College of Agriculture, 2002).

But it is not just the economic impact that has garnered tobacco a nearly mythological status in Kentucky. A number of cultural practices have shaped views of tobacco in the state (Berry, 2002)—families and neighbors getting together to help each other with tobacco planting, cutting, and stripping; big noontime meals as family, friends, and paid tobacco laborers gathered together; community celebrations at harvest time; and the swapping of stories during breaks and in the tobacco-stripping rooms. Even as public attention was drawn to the dangers of smoking, many Kentuckians continued to cling to their existing practices and beliefs (Licari & Meier, 2000)—disputing the ills of smoking and asserting their rights to behave as they pleased.

This history and these views likely play a role in the fact that Kentucky has one of the highest smoking rates in the nation (Centers for Disease Control [CDC], 2002). In addition, citizens of the state have considerably high rates of smoking-related illnesses—cancer, emphysema, and heart disease. For example, Kentucky tops the national statistics in the per-capita death rate for lung cancer (CDC, 2002). Each year, the state spends over a billion dollars of taxpayers' money to provide treatment for these illnesses (Lindblom, 2002).

Without change, the future is bleak for Kentucky. Current statistics, assessing existing smoking rates, suggest the state's problems with tobacco and disease will be around for at least another generation. Kentucky youth are more likely to smoke than those in most other states. For example, Kentucky's middle and high school smoking rates are among the highest in the nation (Hahn, Plymale, & Rayens, 2001); thus, the state's addiction to tobacco is expected to remain substantially high for many years to come.

❖ RECENT OCCURRENCES

For the last several years, public health groups have worked to increase the Kentucky cigarette excise tax, as a means to reduce the state's high rates of consumption. Research has shown that increasing the excise tax is the single-most effective tool that can be implemented to reduce youth smoking; a 10% hike in the price of cigarettes typically results in a 7% decline in consumption (Tauras, O'Malley, & Johnston, 2001).

But there are other potential economic reasons to raise the cigarette tax as well. The Kentucky excise tax is 3 cents a pack, the second lowest in the nation (the national average for cigarette excise taxes is 73 cents) and has remained unchanged for 30-plus years (Lindblom, 2003). An excise tax increase would add needed revenue to help offset a mounting budget crisis. Furthermore, by decreasing smoking rates, the extraordinary financial burden that Kentucky taxpayers must bear each year to help pay for treating tobacco-related illnesses would be reduced over time.

Still, in a state like Kentucky with a long history of tobacco production and consumption, it is not surprising that public health organizations and their pro-tax efforts have met stiff resistance. This resistance has emerged from several quarters including anti-tax constituencies as well as groups representing farmers, retailers, and smokers. Many farmers believe that the tax will reduce sales of a crop on which they rely. Some convenience retailers believe the tax will reduce cigarette sales, which make up a significant portion of their revenues—especially in areas that border states with higher excise taxes. Most smokers oppose the tax because they believe it unfairly singles them out for using a legal product.

Despite garnering increased citizen and legislative support, mounting health costs linked to smoking-related illnesses, and severe statewide budget problems, ACTION has not yet secured its desired excise tax reforms. However, it has succeeded in securing attention to its proposals and in placing this issue on the public agenda. In a period of three years, the cigarette excise tax issue moved from being a source of public ridicule by some citizens and lawmakers to front-page news. Lawmakers introduced tax-increase proposals during state legislative sessions in 2002—which initially was thought impossible—2003, and 2004.

As public attention and debate have increased, so has the visibility of stakeholders in the various camps. From these differing viewpoints, information is evaluated differently—in the media coverage, rivals marshal different evidence to support their positions.

❖ CURRENT STRATEGY DILEMMAS

As organizations like Kentucky ACTION vie for public acceptance of their positions, they present and interpret information as well as respond to opponents' claims. This information includes polling data; scientific studies; statewide statistics; and the opinions of an array of health, government, and other key leaders. In this case, information becomes a key tool for campaign organizers to employ to sway public and legislative opinion.

If ACTION is to reach its goals, it is crucial for the group to use and frame information to maintain its credibility and to deflect charges that it is manipulative, deceptive, and conspiratorial. The strategy session noted at the beginning of this case was designed to address just such issues.

To begin the meeting, ACTION executive director Carol Davis asked those at the table to review the following sections of dialogue from recent televised programs where proponents and opponents "debated" the excise tax:

Tom Miller—smokers' rights advocate: "It's a tax scam to say that we're saving lives by increasing taxes. That's not true. . . . I've heard figures that we're going to save 10,000 lives a year. These are all made-up statistics. They are, in fact, well-intended lies to convince us that we ought to tax ourselves. We are taxing the poorest people. We are going to put out of business a lot of your average convenience stores. . . . People will be smuggling cigarettes. . . . It's ridiculous to think that it is going to stop people from smoking."

Julie Brewer—ACTION coalition member: "Those aren't numbers that we come up with. Those are numbers that the Centers for Disease Control come up with. Every year in this state 8,000 people die of smoking-related diseases. It's not just lung cancer. It's heart disease. It's other forms of cancer. It's emphysema. We're talking about the most preventable cause of death in this nation and certainly in this commonwealth."

Tom Miller: "The people who are talking about the health concerns really want to prohibit tobacco. They know that they can't do that con-stitutionally. . . . The Kentucky Supreme Court says you can have a right to smoke—a constitutional right. So, what they want to do is use the coercive power of government and tax people's behavior to the point that it will discourage them. . . . They want to keep raising taxes until they convince people that it is too expensive to smoke. Now, why don't they do the brave thing and come right on out and say we want to make smoking illegal? Why don't they do that? They know that they can't get away with it. So, this is sort of the camel's nose under the tent—44 cents is the camel's nose; 75 cents is the first hump; pretty soon they're going to keep doing this until they legislate tobacco out of existence. That's their ultimate goal. . . . There is no evidence that rais-ing the tax, and that's what we're talking about, raising the excise tax on a pack of cigarettes is not going to stop anybody from smoking."

Mike Curtis—ACTION coalition member: "The reality is that most people are going to continue to smoke when the excise tax or the price of ciga-rettes goes up. But we know . . . that 44 cents tax means a 10% reduction in youth smoking. I don't know what rock you crawled out from under, and I don't mean that in a mean way. But . . . this is archaic thinking."

During the Kentucky ACTION strategy session, Executive Director Davis said, "They say that we are liars and scam artists who make up statistics and violate people's rights. Do we need to fight these charges or can we ignore them? Should we suggest that these people crawled out from under rocks or make other claims about them? Or is it best to fight back with facts and figures?"

Curtis, who had clearly been frustrated with the charges from opponents during the televised program, responded, "Well, I don't know. I'm just tired of getting called bad names and having our motives attacked. We know that we're on the side of good—looking out for public health and kids. Maybe it's time we called them names, too—and questioned their motives, which are pretty bad, I think."

Brewer, who had been less confrontational with tax opponents on the program, suddenly warmed to this idea. "You're right on target. We really can't let them get away with this anymore. For too long now, we've taken it and been nice. I say 'turn the other cheek no more'— we're just letting them promote incorrect assertions. Let's play hardball. They're the liars and the distorters—and let's call 'em like we see 'em."

But Davis urged caution, perhaps because she was most responsible for negotiating possible support from other interest groups and lawmakers. "I don't think that's the best path. The data and the facts are on our side. The public will see this eventually. Firing back with name calling only moves us to their level and away from the real issues that we want to promote. If we get really nasty too, it could also inhibit our ability to persuade other groups and lawmakers to support us."

Curtis, however, still fuming from the exchange that he had had with the smokers' rights representative, said, "I say no more talking out of both sides of their mouths. On the one hand, they claim that the tax increase won't work toward getting anyone to quit smoking. Then, on the other, they turn around and argue that raising the tax will hurt farmers and convenience store retailers because everyone is going to quit. That's stupid—they can't have it both ways. Let's point out how ridiculous this disparity is and make them look silly."

Davis believed that sticking to the core of the campaign was the most prudent strategy because it would keep Kentucky ACTION "on message" and proactive. "The best way to triumph here is to stick with our key points—focus on health care costs, stress damage and dangers to people, talk about protecting kids. I don't see what we gain by trying to duke it out over this or that study or a particular poll. What carries the heaviest weight for our side is the sheer volume of evidence we have supporting our camp."

However, some of the arguments against the tax and claims about ACTION members puzzled the group. "What do we do about these people who are arguing that smoking is not dangerous? Do we even acknowledge these people at all, or ridicule them?" wondered Brewer. "I was stunned that someone, in the face of all of the evidence, would claim that lung cancer does not kill many people or that there is no link between smoking and heart disease! That's just plain stupid!"

Curtis argued for an aggressive stance. "I say let's go after them. When a wacko goes on television and says that Kentucky's high lung cancer rate is caused by radon gas from limestone deposits rather than our ridiculous smoking rates, we've got to call them out on the carpet to damage their credibility."

Joey Stephens, ACTION's communication director, suggested a different strategy. "Let's steer clear of attacking them as individuals and the name calling. But let's call their questionable strategies out—for example, when they try to get the public off track, let's call it what it is—it's a red herring when they distract from the issue."

Amy Mueller had been sitting back and taking in the discussion. She had worked on tobacco-control issues in Kentucky for a decade and was also now consulting with public health groups that were pushing excise tax increases in other states. Mueller advised that the group had to pick and choose its battles. "Look, the vast majority of the public knows the truth about smoking and they are not going to buy into totally ridiculous claims. We are way, way past that now. The more important issue is when your opposition charges you with being unethical for bending statistics to make the case for what you want, a higher tax, at the expense of farmers and retailers. That is a big, big problem."

Davis emphatically argued, "But we are not making up facts or statistics. We are telling the truth. And we are not out to 'get' farmers or retailers. Studies show a 75-cent hike in the tax will have a negligible impact on farmers in the state because Kentucky tobacco is sold on a global market, and it will also not devastate retailers, despite what our opponents' claim. They are making us out to be the villain when all we want to do is save lives, protect our kids from the dangers of smoking, and improve the health of Kentucky."

Brewer agreed, but further urged the group to get more aggressive against its opponents, particularly on the economic aspects of the excise tax issue. "It's not just the health aspect of the excise tax; many people in this state are simply ignoring the important economic benefits of raising the issue. We need to proactively argue that this tax increase will raise more than $300 million per year for the state at a time when our budget is running a deficit in excess of $500 million. We also need to let the public know that every year the state is spending in excess of $1 billion treating smoking-related illnesses. It's time for smokers to pay their fair share of these huge medical costs!"

"Then tell the truth," said Mueller. "Get the facts to the public and let them decide whether or not the tax should be raised. Let's see if the truth can generate enough public interest so that increased support and citizen calls to lawmakers spur the legislature to finally do something!"

But Curtis chimed in, "Some people may know the truth, but others can't see it for the smokescreen that these yahoos create. It's time—past time—for us to obliterate their smokescreen! Let's take them out with their own tactics! I'm tired of being a doormat."

❖ CONCLUSION

Will these arguments prevail in Kentucky? At this writing, the cigarette excise tax still has not been raised.[3] ACTION is still being charged with trying to hurt farmers, retailers, and smokers. Anti-tax representatives continue to criticize ACTION and its members for a hidden agenda of misusing tax increases to change behavior. And, some people in the state still stubbornly cling to the notion that smoking is just not that big a problem in the first place. Although ACTION has a clear view of the obstacles it faces, it has key decisions to make in addressing these challenges. Meanwhile, the state budget deficit mounts, while even more alarmingly, many Kentucky citizens become new smokers daily, more get sick from tobacco-related addiction and rely on taxpayer monies for their care, and more residents die each day from smoking than in any other state in the nation.

Discussion Questions

1. When one's opponents make unethical assertions, what is the best way to respond? What are some appropriate ways to respond? For example, can the gloves come off (i.e., what's fair for one is fair for all)? Are some organizations held to higher or different ethical standards?

2. Does an organization put its agenda at risk if it adopts a "high road" approach? Is the "high road" approach only feasible when

you perceive that you already have the advantage in the interaction? Is it better to be confrontational and uncivil if that is what it takes to get the truth out?

3. To what, if any, extent can you compromise your organization's (and your own) ethics in the pursuit of the greater good (i.e., accomplishing an objective that your organization believes will benefit many people)?

4. In a campaign that advocates an issue, is it inevitable that statistics or other facts will be distorted in support of that cause? What limits should organizations observe in framing and interpreting information?

5. How can an organization assertively promote a position and yet maintain an ethical and civil orientation toward opponents?

6. Do "nice" opponents deserve or warrant different treatment than "less nice" ones? To what extent should the behavior of opponents set or shape an organization's responses?

7. Describe other types of situations in which similar ethical issues are likely to occur. Would your recommendations for handling the claims remain the same across situations or change? Why or why not?

❖ NOTES

1. The strategy session detailed in this article is a composite representation of discussions that took place in Kentucky ACTION's ongoing meetings to devise tactics to advance a cigarette excise tax in the state. The names of the participants have been changed. The quotations in the strategy meeting were created to represent aspects of the ongoing discussions.

2. Quotations are verbatim from televised programs broadcast on the Kentucky Educational Television network on February 25, 2002; January 20 and July 21, 2003; and January 12, 2004.

3. The Web site www.kyaction.org contains additional information about the campaign to increase the excise tax and other tobacco-control issues in Kentucky.

❖ REFERENCES

Berry, W. (2002). *The art of the commonplace: Agrarian essays of Wendell Berry.* Washington, DC: Counterpoint.

Centers for Disease Control (CDC). (2002). *State tobacco control highlights.* Retrieved May 15, 2002, from http://www.cdc.gov/tobacco/statehi/statehi_2002.htm

Hahn, E. J., Plymale, M. A., & Rayens, M. K. (2001, March). *Kentucky youth tobacco survey.* Frankfort: Kentucky Cabinet for Health Services.

Licari, M. J., & Meier, K. (2000). Regulation and signaling: When a tax is not just a tax. *Journal of Politics, 62,* 875–885.

Lindblom, E. (2002, April 20). *Key state-specific tobacco-related data and rankings.* Washington, DC: Campaign for Tobacco-Free Kids. Retrieved April 22, 2002, from http://www.tobaccofreekids.com/research/factsheets/index.php?CategoryID=2

Lindblom, E. (2003, July 24). *State cigarette excise tax rates and rankings.* Washington, DC: Campaign for Tobacco-Free Kids. Retrieved November 10, 2003, from http://www.tobaccofreekids.org/research/factsheets/index.php?CategoryID=18

President's Commission on Improving Economic Opportunity in Communities Dependent on Tobacco Production While Protecting Public Health. (2001, May 14). *Tobacco at a crossroads: A call for action.* Washington, DC: United States Department of Agriculture. Retrieved October 25, 2002, from http://www.fsa.usda.gov/tobcom/index.htm

Tauras, J. A., O'Malley, P. M., & Johnston, L. D. (2001). *Effects of price and access laws on teenage smoking initiation: A national longitudinal analysis.* Retrieved January 31, 2004, from http://tobaccofreekids.org/reports/prices/

University of Kentucky College of Agriculture. (2002). *Agripedia.* Retrieved May 17, 2002, from http://www.ca.uky.edu/agripedia/agmania/tobacco

Nothing Fishy Going on Here

The Ethics of Openness, Culture, and Strategies

Jan-Oddvar Sørnes and Larry Davis Browning

This case examines the courageous communication of the chief informa-tion officer at Polar Seafood, the second-largest fish-farming company in the world. Faced with public concerns over the quality of fish products because of algae attacks, ocean pollution, and other problems, the com-pany has developed a series of communication strategies to maintain openness and accessibility about company performance, product safety, ecological practices, personnel issues, and acquisitions. In addition, to strengthen relationships, internally and externally, the chief information officer follows two basic communication rules: 1) gentle repetition; and 2) using clear language that everyone will understand.

In an ideal world, if you were to order some Norwegian salmon in an elegant Parisian restaurant and wanted assurance of its quality, the chef could produce for you its full pedigree—its age, provenance, nutritional value, when and where it was processed, and so forth. Polar Seafood, the second-largest fish-farming company in the world, aims to make this ideal an everyday reality. And it's experiencing consider-able outside pressure to do so. Not only do its customers—restaurants, smoke houses, specialty stores—want this information, but so do regulatory agencies. Why? Mounting health concerns. Just as the beef industry has been periodically crippled by mad cow disease, the fish-farming industry has felt the effects of its own epidemics, caused by everything from algae attacks to ocean pollution (Black, 2000, 2001, Burros, 2003; McCarthy, 2002; Pillay, 2003). So it's essential that, when an epidemic occurs, Polar Seafood and authorities can quickly determine its scope and trace the problem to its specific origin. This is known in the trade as "traceability,"[1] and new information and communication technology now makes this possible. Much of this responsibility falls squarely on the shoulders of Polar Seafood's chief information officer (CIO). At Polar Seafood, headquartered just above the Arctic Circle in a small coastal fishing community in northern Norway, Anne Eilertsen is the CIO. Anne is an engaging and charismatic woman in her late 30s, and from her modest Arctic office, lacking even a direct view of the ocean, she handles her company's internal and external information. The ethical dimensions of her tasks are complex.

In short, Anne has three critical responsibilities. First, she is responsible for acquiring fresh information on her company—information on such matters as company performance, product safety, ecological practices, personnel issues, and acquisitions. Second, she is expected to style all that information in such a way that people's impressions of the company are positive. Third, she must ensure that the information that is disseminated does not violate insider-trading laws. These are daunting responsibilities, to be sure, and because her company operates multinationally, with operations in markets as far-flung as Chile, the United States, and Indonesia, she faces the challenge of "speaking to" highly disparate audiences. But she also has disparate audiences right within her own company, an amalgam of dozens of formerly independent small companies. Actually, more and more CIOs are facing a situation similar to Anne's. Today's marketplace has become so global that a company like Polar Seafood will find many of its customers based in other countries, often with widely different cultures and, thus, widely different customs. Added to this mix of responsibilities is the belief that, in the future, organizations will be responsible for a dual transparency—what is communicated to the public about how organizational processes are managed will need to closely match what is communicated within the organization. And making these two kinds of communication exactly the same, with the many ethical dimensions involved, is difficult to do (Redding, 1993).

So how does someone in, say, Norway acquire the global sophistication needed to deal with these overwhelming responsibilities, and how does this sophistication show itself in the work that a person like

Anne does? We will attempt to shed light on these fundamental questions and the many ethical dimensions associated with them.

So, let's look at some challenges specific to Anne at Polar Seafood:

1. Create openness about ecological practices affecting its products.

2. Build a company culture, across national borders, based on strong leadership and ethical standards.

3. Establish internal and external communication strategies, especially paying attention to insider-trading laws.

❖ OPENNESS ABOUT ECOLOGICAL PRACTICES

Norway has a rich history of fish farming, and its roots can be traced back to the 1960s. As the nation's wild salmon stocks drastically decreased due to overfishing, acid rain in rivers and lakes, and over-damming, cultivators had to come up with new ways to provide fresh Atlantic salmon to European restaurateurs.

A mainstay in Polar Seafood's information strategy is to make information about the company and its practices as widely available and open as possible. Since its key customers are professional buyers who themselves monitor the production process and make purchasing decisions based on whether there are problems in any of the stages involved, that openness is a requirement that Polar Seafood has little choice but to meet. And it drops down to their subsidiary companies, too—the ones that actually market brand names in Europe and the United States. In fact, these companies specialize in good communication with their customers. At Polar Seafood, the information given to professional buyers focuses on "information about the [safe] raw materials and how the food is produced," Anne says. "And the sales part is done by those who are really good at it." Since these products depend on a clean environment, many things can go wrong with production. As one safeguard, Polar Seafood has an active question-and-answer program on its corporate Web site. Anne says, "There are many questions from customers, consumers, and journalists which concern the environment, feeding regimen, and Sellafield [UK nuclear power plant]." Questions about these topics are posted as FAQs on the Web site.

One reason for Polar Seafood's focus on ecology and ethics is that the surrounding environment for the production of food is "unbelievably important, and new issues come up constantly," Anne explains, citing problems like "Mad Cow Disease, dioxins, and emissions of radioactivity from Sellafield." Given the ecological problems faced in production, Anne says that it's essential for Polar Seafood to maintain a good environment: "We have to keep it clean. Otherwise, it is not economical." Anne ties ecology to good business practices. (See Paul Hawken's *The Ecology of Commerce* [1994] for a classic text on business and the environment.)

For this CIO, the way to face the problems of producing safe products is to provide leadership in the ecological area. "We deliver a product that *we* know is safe and that our customers know is safe," she says. "We have been leading the pack—we employed the first environmental consultant [in this industry] in Norway and started with an environmental approval of all the facilities." One issue Polar Seafood has had to face was not of its own making. Because of mad cow disease in the late 1990s, concern for food safety automatically drifted into other industries and left the company no choice but to actively get out in front of any problems.

Another important audience for its communication is environmental groups. Groups such as the National Audubon Society, Environmental Defence, Greenpeace, Green Youth, and the Sierra Club recommend boycotting farmed salmon because of what they claim to be the industry's poor environmental record and the threats to native fish and the ecosystems that depend on them. However, these environmental groups recognize that the fish-farming industry is destined to grow, so their efforts have recently been focused on moving the industry to more sustainable and ethically sound practices. As a result, some fish-farming companies are now experimenting with a closed contained system, which will reduce the problems of escaped fish and disease transfer to wild stock (Barcott, 2001).

Anne says, "Now the pressure has come from the outside concerning environmental security. The environmental organizations have become much more active. But we feel that we have been in the lead." She sees much work in the future, "but we have been aware that the demands were coming and we have tried to stay ahead."

Not only has information about Polar Seafood's ecological practices been disseminated to the public through press releases and online news, but Anne has also made sure to insert it in the materials going out to company employees. One of her goals is to have everyone in the company, no matter what his or her location or task, understand and talk about problems in the same way. She says, "Wherever people have questions, either in Norway, the United States, or Chile, we give the same answer throughout the company, so that one customer talking with two salespeople doesn't get two different answers to the same question." This shows Polar Seafood's desire to establish a common frame of reference about the ecological challenges it's facing, in order to offer professional customer relations management (CRM).

❖ CREATING A MULTINATIONAL CORPORATE CULTURE AT POLAR SEAFOOD

Anne talks in detail about Polar Seafood's corporate communication project. This initiative, called the "Leadership Training Project," began with a series of three-day seminars that resulted in a set of ethical rules for the company. "It was drafted," she says, "to show how management should work with employees, and how colleagues at the same level should work with each other—what one is allowed to do or not do, and how one behaves." The seminar's purpose was to develop a clear position on what the company stands for. Anne calls these position statements "the foundational pillars." They address the company's values, ethics, goals, and strategies, and are intended to be actualized in a variety of communication practices, including "how one interacts with the other." She sees these practices as leading to concrete behavior:

> We have ethical rules for what we are allowed to do internally and externally. It is important to make sure that this information is out in the open, understood by all, and that everyone agrees that a common frame of reference is important.

She is also clear about how to improve employees' understanding of what is expected of them in relation to these values. Expectations, she says, must be emphasized through supervisory training of employees until they become common practice: "It must be repeated and repeated until it sticks."

The corporate communication policy also contains an "information policy for the whole company," she says, "and it lays out a change in the structure of how we are going to work internally with information." This strategy includes the important authoritative element that specifies "who is allowed to say what, including who has the responsibility for making the information accessible." The program also includes the charge to build up an information library, to update information bases constantly, "so that it's easier for the rest of the organization to get correct information." The goal is to develop a policy in enough detail that whenever employees have questions and are wondering about something, "they will know who to contact and who is responsible."

Anne's confidence in this policy results from her work on the ethical rules that the company has completed and handed out to all employees. Her interview shows that not only does she buy into the policy but, because of her role in the company, she sees herself as a promoter and a spokesperson for it. "My goal is to build the culture," she says. While free to talk about the need for a common understanding and for knowing the same technical information in the same way, Anne stops short of seeing the need for everyone to think entirely alike. She leaves the door ajar for appreciating cultural differences:

> In such a large company as this we don't demand that everyone think alike, but they should have a similar basic attitude, at least. A Chilean will never think like a Norwegian, because the backgrounds are so different, but we wish for the understanding about the company to be the same.

Anne acknowledges that the company's culture comprises people from different parts of the world, and their differences require consideration when interacting. "One of the challenges is that you try to do it on the *premises* of the nation in which you will spread information," she says, citing their Chilean operation as an example. There had been a great deal of sick leave there, she recalls, and Polar Seafood researched the issue. It discovered poor health conditions among their Chilean employees. Because of the national health care program in Norway, this would have never been an issue at home, but such a program did not exist in Chile, so it fell to the corporation to provide health care to employees' families. "The workers had toothaches or their kids had toothaches, so they had to stay at home," Anne says. "So we set up a dentist's office that was open for employees and their families, and they got drastic reductions in sick leave." She understands that to empathize with, and understand, one's audience increases the likelihood of success with them. Despite having cross-cultural training as part of her formal education in economics, or through her IT (information technology) background, she is very careful when dealing with other cultures. "I am open-minded and I read a lot," she says. "I would rather get to know them before I do too much . . . myself—before I go in and put expectations on them. I want to know what they stand for." (For further readings on organizational and national culture, see Schein, 1985, and Hofstede, 1980, 1991.)

A recurring theme of Anne's story is the adaptation and planning required for Polar Seafood's multicultural and multiethnic work-force to operate effectively. She is concerned about cultural differences, across national boundaries, revealing what she considers ethnocentric-ity—how manners, customs, and communication practices in Norway are a mismatch with, or often misunderstood by, people from other countries. Here is how she describes one part of the problem:

> The challenge for Norwegians is . . . the way we are, the way we talk to each other, and the lack of politeness that we have among ourselves. It is not understood as being rude here [in Norway]. But immediately when we get to England, Belgium, or the USA we are understood as being very rude, because we haven't learned to stop and say, "Hi, good morning! How are you?" We'll just say "hi" as we pass by and then it's right to the matter.

What works fine as a conversational custom among Norwegians themselves is viewed very differently by foreign nationals within the Polar Seafood operation.

This brusqueness will often seem especially offensive, Anne says, when a Norwegian needs to ask for help or ask someone to complete a task. To themselves, Norwegians will just sound direct, not rude. When one Norwegian makes a request of another, "We just say that we want this or that done and it is considered totally fine"—including that the task be done by a particular time. This is very different, Anne says, from the extended preliminary rituals that people in other cultures use when making a request of someone. For example, they'll first check on the "possibility" of another person's fulfilling a request; then the other per-son will respond with some statement about his or her availability to comply; and then—and only then—the actual request will be made. Anne calls this cultural knowledge "social intelligence," and she sees the need for it as one of her company's challenges. She says, "You *must* know to consider the cultural differences—you *must* be aware of them." Anne believes that such awareness must be taught not only by corpo-rate training but also by having the company's main communicators both follow and promote a "communication consciousness." She further explains that "Because the development of the company has happened so quickly, and we have become so large over such a short period of time, we haven't really gotten that 'we' feeling in all parts of the company. It is still 'us' and 'them.'" She sees people from the different cultural regions, even within Norway, as being distinct and different, but thinks that the different regions "should consider themselves part of the same 'we,' not 'us' and 'them.'" Her belief in this "we-ness" comes, again, from understanding the nature of the company in the same way:

> So part of the goal is for everyone to know what Polar Seafood stands for, which involves the environmental aspect, which involves the personal aspect, which attitudes we have internally in the business—all the way from the top to the bottom. My goal is to get us to become a large family and to know collectively *what* we work for.

❖   INTERNAL AND EXTERNAL COMMUNICATION STRATEGIES

One of Anne's main tasks is preparing information material that is used throughout Polar Seafood. She is responsible for all content on the company Web site—especially how information is used technically within the business. Part of her satisfaction with doing this job is how easy email makes it for her to communicate worldwide. "We are such a large company, and you have time differences," she says, "so it's very nice to send an email and know that in six hours they can read it in Chile and there will be an answer waiting for me the next morning." One reason for focusing on the home page as a source of information is so she can send out press statements via the Internet. She sees the Polar Seafood Web site as one of the most affordable ways for outsiders to get information. If people want to read a press statement, they merely go on the Web site to receive a link via email, and when they click on it they come directly to the news page.

She also uses Intrafish's Web site—both the English and Norwegian edition—to check if there is something happening in the market that is of interest to employees. Intrafish is a Norwegian-based company providing news for and about actors in the industry in general, in addition to technical, editorial, and design services for actors such as Polar Seafood. Polar Seafood has outsourced these tasks to Intrafish, for whom she essentially provides a clipping service, selecting items in which Polar Seafood is mentioned by name or that refer to the lowest market price for their products. One edition of the company's Web site is a technical source that covers the Norwegian seafood production industry and provides much of the information she needs. There are also several analytic publications for which Polar Seafood has subscriptions, including weekly and monthly financial newspapers that provide relevant information.

Anne is also responsible for the company's Internet newsletter. To generate items for it, she makes a round of phone calls each Friday morning so the paper can be sent out by 2:00 P.M. that same day. She has a dependable network of contributors that she either calls or emails for items and then takes two or three hours to structure what she receives into a newsletter. Approximately one third of the material is taken as is, with Anne contributing only the copyediting that is needed to go to press. The remainder she writes herself. The target audience for the newsletter is employees in Norway and Denmark as well as Chile and the United States.

This newsletter goes out to the entire company, including the 3,000 workers at the production facilities who don't have an Internet connection on the job. For these people, who make up two thirds of the company, newsletters are sent out in PDF format via email to the department offices. The managers receive this email, and then print it out so that all employees will have their own copy. Because there is no time for employees to read the newsletter during work hours, the newsletter is handed out to them as they leave work so they can read it either right then or when they get home. Getting the newsletter out to all employees is critical, as this is thought to reinforce the ethical "pillars" of the company.

One of Anne's responsibilities is keeping up with all that's going on in the company. She maintains a lot of contact with people within the company, and she also goes through the various newspapers and checks Internet news sources two or three times a week to see if something relevant has happened. It's very important for her to be up-to-date on things in the event that a journalist should call, so she will know what answer to give and whom to refer them to. She uses the Internet actively to monitor what is going on with other forces in the industry: "I use these trade pages—you have environmental organizations' pages where they publish reports and make assertions. I regularly check them to see what might affect the industry. I also use special-interest organizations."

Anne's role as a corporate communicator makes her conscious of a key rule of impression management (Goffman, 1959, 1967): keep a step ahead of your audience by anticipating what they might ask about and have an answer prepared for it. Her work habits show how she does this, because the first thing she does at work is to learn what is going on: "It is the first thing I do in the morning—to use 20 minutes on the Internet to check if something has happened since I was last in." She makes a point of being connected to the company's informal network:

> When I have heard a rumor about something that has happened, then I can pursue that further. Or if I'm sitting working with something, I get needed background material from people within the company. Or if I get questions from people in the organization who need things which I'm not sure about, then I search.

One of her most critical roles requiring a strategy involves protecting confidential information at Polar Seafood. Another newsletter, called *Polar Magazine*, primarily targeting the media and the general public, is also Anne's responsibility. Beyond the logistics of putting the newsletter together, she pays particular attention to ethical conduct and the boundary issues involved in releasing information about the company to employees or to external audiences. For example, on news items concerning the stock market, "anything that might be stock sensitive" is limited, she explains, in that she cannot say anything about the economics of a topic "unless it is already known." To ensure that this important rule is followed, when an issue of *Polar Magazine* is finished, she sends it out "to four people who read through it to have an extra check in relationship to stock sensitivity." The most certain way to ensure that inside information is not given out is to list information only after it is known on the Oslo Stock Exchange. She also has to be aware of traders who have inside knowledge but who have signed a silence agreement and who can't buy stocks until results are made public. The downside of this carefulness is that the newsletter does not contain as much interesting and specific information as it would if stock market information weren't an issue. But it is a trade-off she makes for the newsletter. Anne has dealt with this issue so frequently that it doesn't cause her much worry. She uses a commonsense rule of thumb as her guide to selecting or rejecting content for the paper: "If this can be used to raise or lower the rate, you drop it."

❖ COMMUNICATING WITH PEOPLE TO DEMONSTRATE THEIR VALUE

Another of Anne's communication strategies is to maintain close contact with Polar Seafood employees so as to nurture them as sources of information. She regularly gets queries from outside the firm. If possible, she'll use information from the Norwegian version of their home page to answer them, but she'll also turn to employees when necessary. Once she gets an answer to the question and sends it out, she'll follow up with a phone call to ensure that things are understood. Occasionally, she gets a question that requires maybe a week to answer. If the question and the asker are important enough, she'll ensure that a Polar Seafood person is "sent on location to answer them." But Anne also likes to meet people face-to-face routinely. As she says, "I go and 'fish' a little—I go to ask what they are working with lately, and what moves them." She also understands the principle of information reciprocity— that to get information, you have to give it—and when people come to her office, she makes it a point to "greet them to get a feeling of what's happening." Her sensitivity to communicating with people within the organization extends to her consciousness of how people from the field perceive how those from headquarters might act superior to them and she tells of carefully avoiding this trap. She says, "When they come here, they will feel welcome." She makes sure

> that they don't come to the main office where there are just a few important people sitting and working. We are of equal value— equal value in the job we do—so I think that is very important. It is also great to know people, to have a little chat with them—hand-shake, match a face with a name. Then it is much easier later to call and say "Hi! How are you" when I need help.

And the final point of Anne's seeking information from employees is her humility about what she knows and her continuing need to learn the details of the company. "The little I know has come with time," she says. "I always ask when there is something I don't understand. I have learned along the way because I ask."

❖ SUMMARY

Anne's grand goal and approach to communicating, both internally and externally, with focus on the many ethical dimensions involved, follows two basic rules: (1) gentle repetition and (2) using clear language that everyone will understand. Anne uses repetition in her messages because she is not certain that employees will have remembered her last internal newsletter: "To be sure they do, I go ahead and repeat it—maybe not so thoroughly, but I repeat it and refer to the fact that we have dealt with it in an earlier edition." Achieving simplicity is not always easy because much of what she communicates about must be addressed in specific, technical terms. But she keeps in mind that many of the Polar Seafood employees are in hands-on working jobs and that simple, clear information is required. To identify with them, she has even worked as a technician. She says, "It is clearly a challenge. But what I see as a starting point is that the majority of the technicians and skilled workers are also those with the least knowledge of the company." She resists the desire to play to the favor of those like herself, and instead keeps her message focused on those who need to understand it.

Anne's role as a communicator crosses several boundaries including legal, ethical, technical, educational, and national borders. She works hard to employ a careful communication style that acknowledges her own culture's practices as well as adapts to the needs of different circumstances.

Discussion Questions

1. Why is it so important for Polar Seafood to be open about their ecological practices?

2. What are the implications of using the Web to make quality information public?

3. What are the implications of using colleagues as sources for internal and external information?

4. What are the advantages and disadvantages of being a CIO in a multinational corporation?

5. What are critical factors for success when trying to build a "new" corporate culture, spanning national borders?

6. What's the value of having more information about products easily available to consumers?

7. What are the differences between individual impression management and impression management for an international corporation?

8. In addition to the principles mentioned in this case, such as not listing information before it has been made public on the stock market, what criteria would you add for making information public?

9. What are the implications of making information available to all employees via different ICTs (information and communication technologies)?

❖ NOTE

1. The fish-farming industry is confronting growing demands from regulatory authorities—both national and the European Union—for detailed information on the nature and origin of farmed fish products. To meet this demand, Polar Seafood has begun implementing a traceability system—a record-keeping procedure that shows the path of a particular batch of fish, from fish eggs to the dinner plate, through all the intermediate steps in the value chain. It's imperative that relevant information be collected at every stage so as to generate a traceable path of the history and the quality of the process, not just the end fish product. Traceability of all the steps in the value chain of such products has become not only a legal necessity but a commercial and ethical one as well.

❖ REFERENCES

Barcott, B. (2001, November/December). Aquaculture's troubled harvest. *Mother Jones*, pp. 1–19.

Black, K. D. (2000). Sustainability of aquaculture. In K. D. Black (Ed.), *Environmental impacts of aquaculture* (pp. 199–212). Sheffield, UK: Sheffield Academic Press.

Black, K.D. (Ed.). (2001). *Environmental impacts of aquaculture*. Sheffield, UK: Sheffield Academic Press.

Burros, M. (2003, May 28). Issues of purity and pollution leave farmed salmon looking less rosy. *New York Times*, p. F1.

Goffman, E. (1959). *The presentation of self in everyday life*. New York: Doubleday.

Goffman, E. (1967). *Interaction ritual: Essays on face-to-face behavior*. Chicago: Aldine.

Hawken, P. (1994). *The ecology of commerce: A declaration of sustainability.* New York: Harper Business.

Hofstede, G. (1980). *Culture's consequences: International differences in work-related values.* Newbury Park, CA: Sage.

Hofstede, G. (1991). *Culture and organizations: Software of the mind.* London: McGraw-Hill.

McCarthy, T. (2002, November 25). *Is fish farming safe?* [Online] http://saup .fisheries.ubc.ca/Media/Time_25_Nov_2002.pdf

Pillay, T. V. R. (2003). *Aquaculture and the environment.* New York: Blackwell.

Redding, C. (1993, November). *Lecture presented as recipient of the Wayne Danielson Award for Distinguished Contributions to Communication Scholarship.* College of Communication, the University of Texas at Austin.

Schein, E. H. (1985). *Organizational culture and leadership.* San Francisco: Jossey-Bass.

Showdown at University Baptist Church

Brian K. Richardson, Heather
M. Osterman, and Lori A. Byers

This case examines the actions of members of a Baptist church in Austin, Texas, which had posted information on its Web site regarding the ordination of a gay deacon and a church ministry targeted to gay men and lesbians. Based on this information, the Baptist General Convention of Texas voted to disassociate from the church. As a result, the church's congregation was faced with the difficult decision of whether to continue its public support of the gay deacon and other gay members, at the risk of losing members and critical financial resources. The case further explores church leaders' crisis communication efforts to mitigate divisiveness within the church and to explain their position to others outside the church. It also explores how church leaders sought to balance their duties to church doctrine, to the Baptist General Convention, and to parishioners.

Particularly in the past 10 years, religious organizations in the United States have been involved in "culture wars" (Stout, 2003), debating and disagreeing on various controversial social issues such as the ordination of women to leadership positions, same-sex unions, and abortion. Perhaps no single denomination has been as vocal as the

Southern Baptists, the largest protestant denomination in the United States. For example, in 1997, the Southern Baptist Convention, an annual meeting featuring delegates from Southern Baptist churches across the nation, voted to boycott Disney and its subsidiaries due to what Southern Baptists perceived as Disney's promotion of homosexuality. Specifically, Southern Baptists protested Disney's extending health benefits to the same-sex partners of Disney employees and the Disney theme parks' annual "Gay Day."

Perhaps motivated by the Southern Baptist Convention's boycott of Disney, in 1998 the Baptist General Convention of Texas (BGCT) voted to disassociate with University Baptist Church (UBC) in Austin, Texas, after UBC posted information on their Web site concerning both the ordination of a gay deacon and a church ministry targeted to gay men and lesbians. This case study will outline the events leading up to the ousting of UBC from the Baptist General Convention of Texas.

❖ TROUBLE IN TEXAS

On Friday morning, January 30, 1998, Larry Bethune returned home after dropping off his daughter at school and going for a walk with his wife.[1] Bethune, who was in his 13th year as pastor of University Baptist Church in Austin, Texas, had much on his mind in recent days, and the walk was a nice, albeit temporary distraction. The distraction, however, did not last long. On Bethune's answering machine was a message that had been saved at 9:10 A.M. from Charles Davenport, chairman of the Administrative Committee of the Executive Board of the Baptist General Convention of Texas (BGCT). From the message, Bethune learned about a meeting to be held February 24, at which the BGCT executive committee would vote to decide whether monetary funds would continue being accepted from UBC. Furthermore, the executive committee would decide whether the church should remove the BGCT name from any of its literature.

On the same day, Bethune received an email version of a letter from Davenport detailing the situation. The letter included the following excerpts:

> The BGCT currently faces a situation in which a particular church, UBC of Austin, has continued to take actions that indicates that the church supports a practice that Baptists in Texas consider to be in

conflict with scriptural guidelines. Information published by the church clearly indicates approval of homosexual practice. . . .

Under the concept of autonomy of the local church, the church is, of course, free to take such a posture. The Convention is also free to determine that a church has adopted moral positions related to racism, sexuality, honesty, violence, or other moral concerns which are unscriptural and therefore unacceptable. We view the church's support of homosexual practice to be such an issue.

We recommend that the BGCT not receive funds from UBC in Austin or from any other church which openly endorses moral views in conflict with biblical teaching. We request that UBC discontinue the publication of any materials that indicate that they affiliate with the BGCT.

Bethune promptly telephoned Davenport for further information. According to Bethune, Davenport was apologetic and assured Bethune that the situation was entirely political and did not reflect the BGCT's true feelings about UBC, but those of a fundamentalist faction.

Still, the news was anything but good. Bethune knew that disassociation from the BGCT posed several concerns for University Baptist Church. First, BGCT acts as a collection point for Texas Baptist churches' state missionary and charity funds. Without such an organization, churches like UBC would be forced to send monetary funds to national organizations and/or focus strictly on local issues. Such a move could hinder the church's ability to be seen as a legitimate voice on statewide issues. Furthermore, a similar issue three years prior caused a significant rift between the church and its student ministry. Church leaders would be concerned that the present issue could cause further divisiveness between factions of the church. With but 200 members supporting the financially challenged church, UBC could hardly afford to lose a significant number of members over any issue. Finally, publicity from this issue could exacerbate fears within the congregation of being labeled a "gay church."

Bethune knew that the weeks ahead would be trying. UBC's congregation could decide to continue its public support of the gay deacon and other gay members, at the risk of losing members and critical financial resources. Conversely, the congregation could move to replace the pastor and the gay deacon and (potentially) ensure its long-term survival and legitimacy within the Baptist community. Interpretation of the Christian bible added one final layer to the dilemma. As supporters and opponents of the church's current stance built their cases, both suggested that their arguments were built upon scriptural teachings. As Bethune prepared to address the congregation, the uncertainty of the situation weighed upon him. "How will the situation be resolved," he wondered. "Will the church survive? Will *I* survive?"

The January weather in Texas is highly unpredictable. Thunderstorms, lightning flashes, and strong winds can quickly interrupt a beautiful, sunny day. Indeed, Texans are fond of saying, "If you are tired of the Texas weather, just wait a minute. It will change." For Larry Bethune and University Baptist Church, storm clouds were gathering on the horizon.

❖ BACKGROUND INFORMATION

UBC is a self-labeled progressive, autonomous Baptist church, located in Austin, Texas, across the street from the University of Texas student center. In existence since 1908, the church had about 200 active members in 1998, most of whom were Caucasian, middle class, and educated. Age of members was quite diverse as the membership included many college students, as well as young families, single individuals, and octogenarians. The church has consistently described itself as recognizing each person's right to think freely, and claims it provides an open environment for both spiritual and intellectual fulfillment. It affirms that all people are loved and embraced by God.

UBC has a history of progressive, some might say liberal, action and thinking. For example, UBC was one of the first churches in Texas to integrate when it began accepting African American members in the 1940s. In the 1950s, it added a woman to its ministerial staff, and in the 1970s voted to ordain women as deacons. Finally, in the 1990s it ordained a gay deacon. Church members view UBC as an urban church with a mission of progressive, proactive attitudes and behaviors.

❖ BAPTIST CHURCHES AND ALLIANCES

Baptist churches are generally autonomous, self-governing entities. However, they do maintain voluntary affiliations with local, state, and national Baptist alliances. Associating with an alliance may include being a voting member of an association, being involved in decision making, or simply sending money to contribute to the organization's "mission" funds. Churches may also send representatives, called "messengers," to the alliance's formal meetings. The UBC values its alliances with larger Baptist affiliations because they provide an avenue for UBC to contribute financially to larger missions.

In December 1997, UBC's denominations committee voted to dedicate $4,500 to each of the following: American Baptist churches, the Alliance of Baptists, Cooperative Baptist Alliance, and the Baptist General Convention of Texas (BGCT). Of these, the first three are national organizations, while the last is statewide and, consequently, its contributions are largely funneled into local missions. UBC greatly valued its relationship with BGCT because it is the only statewide organization, and UBC members have a strong dedication to giving to projects within their region.

❖ ORDINATION OF A GAY DEACON

In 1995, UBC chose to ordain as deacon a church member who was openly, though quietly, known to be gay. He was one of six deacons ordained that year. The issue of his homosexuality was addressed only briefly. The decision to ordain him was based on his contributions as an individual and the church did not see itself as making a political statement or taking a specific stand on the issue of homosexuality. There was little, if any, dissension or discussion among the majority of church members regarding the ordination of a gay deacon.

Bob Price,[2] the leader of the student ministry group, however, was upset over the ordination because he believed that homosexuals should not serve as leaders in the church. He felt that this issue could invite negative perceptions of the church and negatively affect his standing in the community. Price sent copies of two letters to Bethune and the chair of the board of deacons. The first was a standard letter of resignation, and the second a letter of condemnation of both Bethune and the church. Bethune and the chair accepted the first letter and announced it to the congregation. Within the next month, Price told the student group and several conservative Baptist leaders in the Austin community of the gay deacon and of his decision to resign.

The students expressed anger about the gay deacon's ordination and demanded Bethune address it immediately. Bethune reacted by preparing a sermon on the history of homosexuality in the church, which he presented to the student group in three segments, on three consecutive Sundays. Soon thereafter, the majority of students (45 out of 50) left the church. Bethune then presented the same sermons to the congregation over a series of Wednesday-night discussion groups. Over the next several months, about 10 families quietly left the church.

At this time, the Austin Baptist Association (ABA), spurred on by its conservative leadership, met and voted to disassociate from UBC because the church had ordained a gay deacon. ABA is a local association of over 200 Southern Baptist churches and missions. UBC had been a member of the association for 44 years. Because of the controversy involving the local Austin Baptist Association, UBC leaders decided to stop sending messengers to BGCT state conventions. Bethune and the congregation felt that sending messengers would only rock a political boat; instead, they would focus on strengthening the church and its missions.

After a time, UBC leaders hoped that the issue of homosexuality had died down for them. In fact, they were considering sending messengers to upcoming BGCT conferences. Some moderate members of the BGCT, however, warned Bethune not to send messengers, as there were members of BGCT who were waiting for an opportunity to be able to confront UBC. Specifically, one preacher from Lubbock attended each annual convention prepared to motion that UBC be disassociated from the BGCT if they attempted to seat messengers.

❖   EARLY SIGNS OF TROUBLE

In mid- to late January of 1998, Bethune received a series of email messages from several pastors in West Texas. These emails questioned Bethune and the congregation's beliefs about homosexuality and sought confirmation that the church had indeed ordained a gay man as deacon. Bethune felt as if he was being set up, and that his answers would be copied and used against him in some way. At the same time, he felt that he should be open about his views and responded to each message. Bethune believed UBC's Web site (www.ubcaustin.org) to be the impetus for the emails. The Web site included two references that suggested the church's openness toward homosexuals. First, the Web site included a historical section, which mentioned the church's ordination of a gay man as deacon. Second, the Web site advertised an invitation to "gays, lesbians, transgender, bisexual, and straight persons" to Open Circle, the church's ministry for homosexuals. Bethune believed that the West Texas pastors were responding to the Web site due to not only its public nature, but also the fact that the BGCT was mentioned on the same page. This suspicion was confirmed when Davenport was quoted in a national publication as saying, "We've been aware of the situation in the University Church [sic] and the homosexual issue. When they went public on their Web page, we had to take a stand" (Tucker, 1998, p. 22).

The argument of BGCT against the church's ordination of a gay deacon rested primarily on their interpretation of biblical scripture. Reverend Russell Dilday, the Texas convention's president, was quoted in the *Austin American-Statesman* as saying, "I believe strongly the Bible is clear that the homosexual lifestyle is contradictory to God's plan . . . and therefore should not be condoned as a legitimate lifestyle" (Perkes, 1998). Bethune, meanwhile, offered his own interpretation of the scripture, arguing, "The Bible has not changed, but our understanding of it changes as our knowledge of the world changes" (Tolley, 1998, p. A16). Bethune also argued that Baptists have changed their viewpoints on slavery and the spiritual equality of women: "So we have to remain constantly open to what the scripture says."

Despite his public arguments, Bethune admitted feeling immense pressure from a variety of sources as the issue continued to brew in the media. First, there were financial concerns. UBC was located in an urban area of Austin, a city that was growing outward into the suburbs. Therefore, membership, the lifeblood of the church, was declining. If additional members were to leave over the current flap, UBC's already shaky financial status could worsen. Staff members, including Bethune, were concerned they would lose their jobs and become "un-hirable." Safety concerns arose after the church received "hate mail." Bethune wondered if it would be wise to soak mailed packages in water before opening them, just in case they were letter bombs. There were also family concerns. Bethune worried how the church's stance would affect his relationship with his own Baptist parents and his immediate family. He questioned, "How do my new wife and I make sure this pressure draws us closer together instead of dividing us?" Indeed, Bethune felt quite a bit of individual concern: "[H]ow does this controversy and my allowing it to happen reflect on my leadership and effectiveness as a pastor? Am I going to be responsible for the decline and death of this congregation? Am I up to the task of leading these people through this?" He addressed the pressures he felt:

Theological pressure. Am I right about my interpretation and application of scripture . . . or am I mistaken and leading these people into damaging error? Pastoral pressure. Dealing with corporate grief over long-time members leaving while dealing with personal grief over the same loss of members and personal friendships. Giving pastoral grief at hospitals and gravesides to people who are angry with me.

Added to this conflux of influences was the fact that much of the UBC–BGCT rift was being played out in the local and state media.

On Wednesday, January 28, leaders of BGCT met to discuss how they wanted to respond to the situation with BGTC. It was decided that the issue of disassociating University Baptist Church from the BGTC would go before the executive board on February 24 for a final vote. At this meeting, the church would be allowed 10 minutes to present its case before the vote was taken. UBC at this point had not been informed of these activities.

❖ SUNDAY, FEBRUARY 1

Just two days after receiving the messages from Davenport, Bethune carried on with his normal pastoral duties. During his Sunday sermon, he informed the congregation of the situation. In what he described as an "aside" comment, Bethune told the church members of the BGCT's actions. He added that he would provide further information as soon as it became available. That evening, church member Dr. George Alexander[3] sent an electronic mail message to the church's listserv, informing members of the situation.

❖ MONDAY, FEBRUARY 2

Bethune wrote Davenport a letter complaining that there had been no due process. He added that he was concerned that the motion was approved without meaningful prior notice or a chance for UBC leaders to be heard by the committee. Bethune also mentioned concerns that UBC has been made a "political scapegoat in the ongoing battle between moderates and liberals" in the BGCT. Also mentioned in his reply was "grief" over how homosexuals as a group would perceive this issue.

❖ WEDNESDAY, FEBRUARY 4

The following Wednesday night church service fell on Bethune's wedding anniversary. He had planned to spend most of the evening with his wife. Still, he spoke for about 20 minutes at the church on the issue and took about 10 minutes of questions. He then said, "It's my anniversary and I'm not going to let this keep me from celebrating." Members continued discussing the situation after Bethune left. The church would not meet formally again on this issue until February 18.

Over the next 10 days, Bethune and other church members spent much time communicating to the news media. Bethune estimated that he did about 20 radio talk shows and about the same number of newspaper interviews. A wide range of newspapers, including the *New York Times, Chattanooga Free Press, Austin American-Statesman,* and the *Baptist Standard,* reported the story. Television crews also visited the church, setting up cameras in the sanctuary and interviewing both church leaders and members.

❖ FRIDAY, FEBRUARY 13

One of the church's younger couples decided to conduct a town hall meeting on February 16 at their home and invited a select group of people they labeled as "progressive" to discuss how they thought the church should respond at the February 24 meeting. Bethune told the couple that he would not attend the meeting and would request that no other staff attend because the church has a history of "little political groups polluting democracy by trying to set an agenda before they go into a church meeting." The couple assured Bethune that that would not be the case and the meeting was held on February 16 as planned.

❖ WEDNESDAY, FEBRUARY 18

All members of the congregation were invited to a meeting held to determine how the church would respond to the BGCT at the February 24 meeting. At this meeting, Bethune explained that the church would be given 10 minutes to speak on its behalf. There was never any discussion about whether UBC should change its beliefs regarding homosexuality. Instead, the conversation focused on communicating to the BGCT that University Baptist Church be allowed to remain affiliated. Bethune also informed members that anyone could represent the church on this matter. The members agreed that he should represent UBC and present their side of this issue. It was also decided by the group to hold another church conference one week after the BGCT voted.

❖ TUESDAY, FEBRUARY 24

Several UBC members attended the BGCT meeting with Bethune. He spoke for 10 minutes, presenting UBC's statement. He urged the executive board not to pass the motion because there had been a lack of due process. Bethune also emphasized that the executive board had no authority over an autonomous local church; for example, one of the BGCT's tenets, as posted on UBC's Web site, read:

> One of the most important issues is that the BGCT continue to function as a servant, not an authoritarian, organization. Texas Baptists must continue to embrace historic Baptist principles that honor local church decisions and individual religious freedom. . . . Ordination is strictly a local church decision.

Several women not affiliated with UBC reiterated Bethune's trepidation concerning due process, emphasizing that Baptists should practice more compassion toward the gay community and their families. A vote was then taken by members of the BGCT to decide whether to disassociate the church. The vote was characterized as an "overwhelming majority" with 2/3 voting against UBC with several abstentions. Bethune then attended a press conference, presented his opinion of the issue, and answered questions from the media.

❖ CONGREGATION UNDER STRESS

After the media attention, Bethune knew that the stress put on the congregation would rise and that anxieties would surface. The church did not have a good business meeting following the events of the previous day. David Spalding,[4] the church's usual moderator, could not attend the meeting. Without his guidance, the meeting got bogged down into discussions of Robert's Rules of Order and how fairly they were being applied at the meeting. Some heated discussions ensued and the meeting became unproductive. Instead of formulating a response to the BGCT's actions, the meeting became convoluted with personal disagreements. Bethune would later say that he "felt good" about this meeting. "This is the grief being expressed," he said. He felt this meeting allowed members to vent their frustration and anger over events of the previous month. At this meeting, the members did decide to acquiesce to BGCT's demands and remove references to BGCT from their Web site. However, they also decided to retain the BGCT name on any historical elements of the Web site and in documents that explained the events that had occurred from January 30 until February 24. After the February 24 meeting, Bethune said he worked very hard to get the church to be active in other areas such as racial reconciliation, Christian social ministries, and building partnerships with area community churches and other congregations.

❖ AFTERMATH

It is helpful to analyze UBC's ethical dilemma with a "crisis communication" framework. A crisis is a "major occurrence with a potentially negative outcome affecting the organization, company, or industry, as well as its publics, products, services, or good name" (Fearn-Banks, 2002, p. 2). Crises are generally thought of as the domain of for-profit corporations, and case studies of companies such as Exxon, Intel, and Tylenol provide "good" and "bad" examples of crisis-management strategies. However, a review of UBC's experience provides an illuminating example of a nonprofit, religious organization having to navigate its own crisis situation.

Uzumeri and Snyder (1996) suggest that "characterization" is a milestone event within any given crisis situation. They conceptualize characterization as "a moment in time when the following criteria are met: someone has offered a reasonable explanation for the root causes of the crisis, someone has made a credible estimate of the expressed damage and risks, a critical mass of the key stakeholders in the crisis agree with the first two criteria" (pp. 44–45). Uzumeri and Snyder elaborate that this moment of characterization is important because it brings closure to a situation and allows participants to reallocate their attention toward remedies, or other elements of the future.

The way in which UBC met the first criterion of characterization is critical in the examination of how a potentially damaging situation was mitigated. An important element of crisis management entails examining the root cause of crisis, placing it within a framework of internal versus external causes. Despite the fact that his church had ordained a homosexual deacon, Bethune clearly attributed the cause of UBC's crisis as external, caused by BGCT actions. He did not perceive that UBC's position on homosexuality or any actions that the UBC had taken were grounds for disassociation. He believed that political motives were behind the issue. This perspective affected the way UBC discussed the matter within the congregation and responded to BGCT and the public.

The second step in characterization involves assessing the expected damage and risks of the crisis. Two factors that expedited this process for UBC were experience gained from a similar past event and immediate public feedback. UBC leaders and members were concerned about three issues: potential loss of membership, image preservation, and being labeled a "gay" church. These concerns were mitigated by the church's involvement in a similar situation three years before, when ousted from the ABA. Indeed, the past crisis with the Austin Baptist Association provided such a learning experience for UBC leaders to gauge the current issue. In addressing the possible loss of members, Bethune articulated that losing members from the ABA event had been painful, but ultimately had led to a more cohesive body that eventually regained its numbers. Based upon past experience, he felt confident that UBC's numbers would not be affected in the long term.

Immediate and generally positive feedback via the Internet and accurate portrayal by the news media helped alleviate fears that the church's image was being damaged. UBC received hundreds of "log-ons" to its Web site offering support for the church. Bethune said that the church received about 10 positive responses for every negative one. A review of news stories collected from the Lexis-Nexis database revealed generally positive coverage on UBC's behalf. "Letters to the editor" in the Austin newspaper commonly showed support for UBC and Bethune. Such feedback helped calm concerns that UBC would be labeled a "gay" church. The media accurately reported that homosexuals comprised just 10 percent of UBC's congregation.

Overall, the quick assessment of risks allowed UBC members to develop a shared understanding of the crisis. A thorough characterization brings critical closure to the situation and allows the focus to turn to possible remedies, remedial actions, and future plans (Uzumeri & Snyder, 1996). Because a critical mass of UBC stakeholders appeared to agree on the issue and received feedback to support their beliefs, they were able to immediately formulate responsive action, and carry on with business. Even if some members privately protested the recent actions of the church, UBC was able to portray a strong united front to the public.

❖ EXTERNAL RESPONSE STRATEGY AND RESULTS

Coombs (1995) suggests that categorizing a crisis affects how you position yourself within the crisis and how you respond. He categorizes crises along two dimensions: whether the crisis was intentional or unintentional, and whether it was caused by an organizational member (internal) or non-organizational member (external). According to Coombs's typology, UBC had suffered an act of "terrorism"—an intentional event, caused by an external party. Coombs identifies three common strategies or reactions that are associated with terrorism: suffering, distance, and ingratiation. Bethune attempted to use at least two of these response strategies, suffering and ingratiation.

In *suffering*, the organization attempts to use the crisis to win sympathy from the public and manipulates the crisis to achieve positive, rather than negative effects. Bethune attempted this strategy when he highlighted the "unfairness" of the situation in terms of its violation of the concept of local church autonomy, the lack of due process they had received, and by suggesting that UBC was being made a political scapegoat. With this strategy, UBC may have been seen as a "victim" by some of its key stakeholders.

Ingratiation involves seeking public approval for the organization by connecting it to things that are valued by the public. This strategy can be accomplished through *bolstering* and *transcendence*. Bolstering involves reminding the public of the many positive elements associated with an organization, while transcendence moves the crisis from a specific incident to a broader positive framework. UBC leaders reminded the public that the church had served the community for 90 years through charities and missions, and was the first in Austin to racially integrate. Evidence of transcendence was exhibited when Bethune consistently referred to the church's long-standing policy of inclusivity. He shifted the specific issue of ordination of a gay deacon to a higher plane, focusing on the church's open-door policy that existed for everyone.

❖ INTERNAL COMMUNICATION ISSUES

In addition to external communication strategies, UBC leaders also concentrated on internal dialogue. Bethune used face-to-face communication, group meetings, public-speaking opportunities, and an email listserv as communication channels to keep the congregation informed of the situation with BGCT. All members were allowed an equal voice in helping shape responses to BGCT and the news media, though it was obvious that some members spoke out a great deal more than others. UBC members demonstrated at least three communication strategies that helped maintain unity and communication within the church. First, they used technology as an invaluable communication tool. Next, Bethune continually framed the situation as a minor disruption rather than as a major crisis. Finally, UBC leaders focused on remaining "business-as-usual" throughout the crisis.

UBC's Web site had been an impetus for the crisis because it was the vehicle through which external parties had learned of the ordination of the homosexual deacon. This, however, did not prevent church members from realizing the benefits that accompany this unique communication tool. The church listserv was used initially to inform the members of the issue. Subsequently, the Internet was used to announce meetings, provide updated information, and provide moral support for an occasionally stressed church body. Members expressed an appreciation for the technology as it provided them up-to-date feedback from both internal and external actors. Verbal communication was increased as church members with access to the Internet provided verbal updates to those without access to the Web site.

Throughout the crisis, Bethune used two strategies that seemed to prevent the issue from disrupting and dividing the congregation. First, he attempted to prevent the development of factions within the church. This was exhibited when he reacted to the young couple's meeting by advising the staff not to attend as well as suggesting to the individuals themselves that they not formulate an agenda or make decisions for the church. Still, a large number of college-aged members did leave the church in a mass exodus.

Bethune also realized that there was danger in focusing too much on the crisis, or in allowing the drama of the crisis to control emotions. Through verbal messages and action, Bethune consistently communicated that the issue at hand did not define who the church was or how it should be behaving. An example of how Bethune implicitly communicated the above message occurred during the January 4 meeting. By leaving the meeting after 20 minutes in order to keep his anniversary date with his wife, Bethune intended to convey the image that the crisis was not so grave that it should alter and control their lives.

❖ RECOVERY AND PROFITABILITY

After the media frenzy died down, Bethune immediately dedicated attention to encouraging the church to revisit its mission and goals, and direct its energies toward realizing and enacting these goals. Thus, an attempt was made to shift the focus away from what they had lost toward what they stood to gain. Bethune tried to communicate a consistent, positive message during this time. Appearing both in a Sunday sermon and a published newsletter, located on the church Web page, Bethune wrote,

> We're having a revival. . . . What else can you call it when people feel excited about being in church together? When our attendance is up and our spirits are high. . . . When God plants a new vision in our souls in the urban church on the cutting edge of a mission in the heart of the city.

❖ CONCLUSION

Overall, UBC emerged from this ethical dilemma and crisis relatively intact. Though the church lost a vast majority of its college-student congregation, the more established membership remained. Another area in which UBC lost concerned their inability to reverse the decision of the BGCT, which meant UBC could no longer channel money directly into Texas missions. UBC responded to this sense of loss by focusing on ways in which they could work within their community as well as establish new ties. As of this writing, Bethune remains as pastor of UBC. For more information about the church, please see its Web site at http://www.ubcaustin.org/ubc.htm.

Discussion Questions

1. What would you identify as the difference between morals and ethics? Do you believe this situation was one of moral consideration or ethical consideration?

2. What special ethical considerations was Larry Bethune, the pastor of UBC, faced with in this situation? What ethical considerations do leaders face when confronted with potentially polarizing controversial issues?

3. It seems the church never openly discussed whether they should continue to allow the gay deacon to serve. Instead, discussion was centered solely on how to respond to the BGCT. Could this have fostered a climate of "groupthink" within UBC such that some alternative responses were not even considered?

4. Do you believe the members and leaders of both UBC and BGCT behaved ethically in this situation? Why or why not? Do you believe the actors in this case displayed ethical decision making? What would you do differently or the same in this situation?

5. Do you think Bethune made a good decision when refusing to attend the meeting arranged by the younger couple and held on February 16? Why or why not?

6. Did UBC and BGCT have competing ethical systems? If so, identify and contrast the two systems. If not, what commonalities did UBC and BGCT share?

7. Stout, in the *Journal of Religious Ethics,* asserts that "discussions of controversial issues among religious organizations should include the full range of theological opinion" (2003, p. 180). Do you think UBC and BGCT each considered the full range of theological opinion when faced with this decision-making dilemma?

❖ NOTES

1. Information for this case was collected through semi-structured interviews with Pastor Larry Bethune and four additional church members, by accessing newspaper articles with Lexis-Nexis, and reviewing the University Baptist Church Web site.

2. This individual's name has been changed.

3. This individual's name has been changed.

4. This individual's name has been changed.

❖ REFERENCES

Coombs, T. W. (1995). Choosing the right words: The development of guidelines for the selection of the "appropriate" crisis-response strategies. *Management Communication Quarterly, 8,* 447–476.

Fearn-Banks, K. (2002). *Crisis communications: A casebook approach* (2nd ed.). Mahwah, NJ: Erlbaum.

Perkes, K. S. L. (1998, February 23). Church faces ouster over gay members. *The Austin American-Statesman,* p. A1.

Stout, J. (2003). How charity transcends the culture wars: Eugene Rogers and others on same-sex marriage. *Journal of Religious Ethics, 31,* 169–180.

Tolley, L. (1998, February 26). Despite rejection, reverend plans to keep Austin church open to gays. *San Antonio Express-News,* p. A16.

Tucker, E. (1998, February 13). "Jewish Community Hour" hits milestone. *Chicago Sun-Times,* p. 22.

Uzumeri, M. V., & Snyder, C. (1996). Information technology and accelerated science: The case of the Pentium flaw. *California Management Review, 38,* 44–63.

CASE STUDY 21

Purifying an Image

Baxter International and the Dialyzer Crisis

Julie A. Davis

This case examines product liability regarding a blood filter produced by Baxter International, a medical supply company. Acting quickly, Baxter used rhetorical strategies of compensation and corrective action to strengthen the company's image. The case poses several challenging issues regarding a company's duty to inform patients of a product's risks and the patients' right to know. In this case, Baxter accepted responsibility without concern for possible litigation over the product, even in the absence of conclusive evidence of fault.

Health and safety are the main products medical supply companies have to sell. However, when these organizations face product liability problems, instead of offering improved health, the products leave death and disability behind them. This is the type of crisis Baxter International, a medical supply company based in Deerfield, Illinois, faced in the summer and fall of 2001.[1] By the time this crisis was resolved, 53 dialysis patients had died, two lines of dialyzers (a type of blood filter) were discontinued, two plants that manufactured the filters implicated in the deaths were closed, and Baxter took a charge to earnings of $189 million. Despite the high number of deaths, the company's quick actions, along with outside circumstances, kept the story from receiving the quantitative and qualitative amounts of press coverage endured by organizations facing crises with much lower death and injury rates.

The patient deaths placed Baxter in an ethical morass, seeking answers to a variety of questions: When should an organization inform customers of potential problems with a product? When should an organization act in the face of incomplete information to accept responsibility for a problem? How much responsibility should an organization take on for a crisis that could have plausibly been the result of several organizations' actions? What are the ethical implications of an organization's actions to prevent a tragedy's reoccurrence if those actions cause harm to innocents, including their own employees and customers? Can an organization attempt to be too ethical? To understand Baxter's attempts to answer these ethical questions, an examination of the organization and the dialyzer crisis, Baxter's responses to the deaths, and circumstances that allowed the organization to avoid negative media attention about the crisis and its aftermath is in order.

❖ ORGANIZATIONAL HISTORY OF BAXTER INTERNATIONAL

Before a discussion of the dialyzer crisis can be undertaken, a brief overview of the organization as a whole will be helpful. Baxter International is a $7.7 billion healthcare products organization headquartered in Deerfield, Illinois, outside Chicago. The company began in 1931, founded by Dr. Don Baxter, as a manufacturer and distributor of intravenous solutions (Hammonds, 2002). Its product line is divided into three divisions: Bioscience, which produces vaccines and biopharmaceuticals; Medication Delivery, focusing on dispensing medications to patients; and Renal, where Baxter is the leading supplier of products assisting patients with kidney disease. At this writing, the company employs approximately 50,000 people in over 100 countries worldwide (Baxter International, n.d.).

As best as can be determined, Baxter's problems began on August 15, 2001, when two dialysis patients in Spain died within hours of receiving treatment using dialyzers produced by Althin, one of Baxter's subsidiaries. At first, these deaths, while tragic, did not receive undue attention. The patients had been elderly and ill before beginning treatment. However, within a week, a total of 11 patients died in Spain soon after using the filters. A few weeks later, 21 people died in Croatia. By mid-October, when Baxter issued a worldwide recall of the devices, the deaths of 53 people in seven countries, including 4 in the United States, were linked to the filters ("Baxter's Harry Kraemer: 'I don't golf,'" 2002; Hammonds, 2002; Peterson & Daly, 2001). Criminal investigations into Baxter's role in the deaths were opened in Spain, Sweden, and Croatia. By November, Baxter faced what it called "the worst crisis in its 80-year history" (Firn, 2001, p. 34).

Within days of the first reported deaths in Spain, Baxter began an investigation into the filters and possible causes of death and issued a recall for the lot of filters implicated in the deaths. New products were not shipped to suppliers after these deaths (Greising, 2001). On October 9, Baxter announced the results of internal tests and those of an independent group of analysts, neither of which provided conclusive evidence about why the patients died.

Yet, later that week nearly two dozen deaths in Croatia were being blamed on the devices. Renal Division president Alan Heller feared a problem with the filters. "I knew that there was too much there to be a coincidence" (Hammonds, 2002, n.p.). Immediately, a team of Baxter investigators flew to the scene. The next day, the company issued a worldwide recall for these lines of filters and a distribution hold for filters already produced. Anyone possessing these filters was asked to return them for credit, at a cost to Baxter of about $10 million (Greising, 2001; Hammonds, 2002).

Continued investigation found the presence of a perfluorohydrocarbon-based fluid in some of the dialyzers ("Baxter's A and AF series dialyzers," 2001). This fluid was used to test filters that required leak repairs. Although the fluid was supposed to be removed from filters before shipping, dialyzers from the Romney Plant in Sweden had left the plant containing trace amounts of the fluid. While nontoxic at room temperature, when heated to body temperature in a patient's bloodstream, the liquid turned into a gas, causing fatal pulmonary embolisms. By early November, Baxter's internal tests indicated that the fluid in the filters caused the deaths. Baxter CEO Harry Kraemer decided to permanently discontinue making the filters and close the Romney Plant as well as another Althin plant in Florida, taking a charge of $189 million to cover settlements to the victims' families and close the plants. This charge lowered Baxter's 2001 net income 17% from the previous year ("Baxter's Harry Kraemer: '"I don't golf,' 2002).

When facing attacks from the Croatian press and the victims' families, coupled with its own sense of ethics, Baxter relied on image restoration strategies to solve the problem and maintain its reputation. The following section will examine Baxter's rhetoric during this time to determine which image restoration strategies the organization chose, or declined, to use.

❖ BAXTER'S RESPONSE TO THE DIALYZER DEATHS

When faced with a public threat to it reputation, as Baxter did in 2001, an organization must use crisis response strategies to defend itself. Much of modern crisis response theory stems from Ware and Linkugel's (1973) discussion of the apologetic genre. These authors argue that *apologia,* or speeches of apology, occur during "the questioning of a person's *moral nature, motives, or reputation*" (p. 274, emphasis in the original). They delineate these types of ethical questions from mere attacks on an individual's policies. Over time, other theorists have added to Ware and Linkugel's typology.

Apologia, Benoit's (1995, 1997) extensions of it, and Coombs's (2000) adjustment of the categories, need not be limited to individuals speaking to clear their reputations of allegations of moral wrongdoing. McMillan (1986) posits that while organizations lack human attributes such as thinking, abstracting, and feeling, "there is a social presence about an organization to which it is possible to assign definite traits and qualities that are readily verifiable" (p. 22). These traits are revealed through symbol use, which "presents an image of the organization that its constituents have come to know and recognize" (p. 22). This image, just like an individual's face or reputation, can be attacked and is vigorously defended. Benoit and Brinson (1994) comment:

> There can be no doubt that government agencies, corporations, and other bodies are as concerned as individuals with their image or reputation, and for good reason. Since the early 1970s, organizations have become more aware of their responsibility for contributing to society in economic, social, environmental, and political ways. (p. 76)

Benoit (1995) argues that while individuals and organizations may use different image restoration strategies, use different combinations of strategies, or expend different amounts of resources on the strategies, "the basic options are the same for both individual and corporate image repair efforts" (p. 177). The following sections will examine both the crisis response strategies that Baxter chose to use and the strategies it rejected when purifying its image in the aftermath of the dialyzer deaths.

Crisis Response Strategies Baxter Used

Baxter International was forced to choose from a variety of crisis response strategies to explain both the dialyzer crisis itself and its actions during it. In this situation, Baxter selected two strategies from the category of crisis response strategies designed to reduce the perceived offensiveness of the event (Benoit, 1997; Benoit & Czerwinski, 1997). While these strategies accept responsibility for the event, they attempt to convince audience members that the event was not as serious as originally thought. Specifically, Baxter used the strategies of compensation and corrective action to purify an image polluted by patient deaths.

The first of these strategies, *compensation*, offers the victims some form of reparation to repay them for the offensive action (Benoit & Czerwinski, 1997). This strategy hopes that "offering to compensate the injured party may function to reduce the act's offensiveness, and the damage to the accused's image" (Benoit & Brinson, 1994, p. 77). Compensation attempts to right a wrong by providing restitution for the victims' loss.

Baxter immediately pledged to compensate the victims' families for the deaths of their loved ones. Once the problem with the fluid came to light, Baxter immediately took a charge to earnings, in part to pay settlements to the families of patients who died. As early as November, a Baxter spokesperson was quoted as saying, "Baxter will compensate those families affected by this incident" (Japsen, 2001a, n.p.).

By the end of 2001, Baxter had made good on this promise, settling with the families of Spanish victims for approximately $292,000 apiece (Daly, 2001). An attorney representing some of these victims' families also applauded Baxter's actions, saying,

We feel that the settlement each family reached with Baxter is fair and reasonable. Baxter has treated the families with great respect during this unusually difficult time. The families are comforted in knowing that Baxter continues looking into the science surrounding these tragic events to ensure it will never happen again. (Baxter International Inc., 2001, n.p.)

Baxter refused to release the terms of this settlement, or the settlement it made with the Croatian victims. The only lawsuit involving an American victim had also settled. The plaintiff's attorney in this case said that Baxter "behaved responsibly and appropriately" (Hammonds, 2002, n.p.). Plaintiffs' lawyers in these cases were satisfied with the compensation Baxter offered.

While monetary settlements in product liability suits are nothing new, Baxter's statements surrounding these settlements were. Baxter chairman and CEO, Harry Kraemer, commented in the November 28, 2001, release announcing the Spanish settlement:

> Our goal is to do the right thing. While nothing we do will replace the loss these families have experienced, we understand their need to bring closure to this tragedy. Our hope is that this settlement helps to minimize the distress to the families involved. (Baxter International, 2001d, n.p.)[2]

This statement recognizes that while compensation is a relatively weak strategy in situations where people are killed, as it cannot return to the situation as it existed before the offensive act, it nonetheless provides some respite to those affected by the offensive act.

Another strategy accused individuals and organizations may use is *corrective action,* which occurs when the "accused promises to correct the problem" when faced with threats to their image (Benoit & Czerwinski, 1997, p. 44). This strategy can take two forms: (1) the accused attempts to return the situation to the state it was in before the offensive action, or (2) the accused takes steps to prevent the offensive action from recurring. Benoit and Czerwinski (1997) differentiate this strategy from compensation, arguing, "Unlike compensation, which seeks to pay for a problem, corrective action seeks to prevent or correct it." (p. 77). Since Baxter could not return the patients who were killed by the defective dialyzers to life, it used the second set of corrective action strategies to convince its audience that no other patients would be injured by the dialyzers.

Throughout the entire crisis, from the first press release issued following the Croatian deaths to the recent retrospective articles on the crisis published by the business press, Baxter officials have emphasized the process aspect of their investigations and their attempts to prevent future deaths, not only for their own customers but also for their competitors. For instance, the October 15, 2001, release about the Croatian deaths stresses how Baxter's concern for safety drives its actions:

> All testing by Baxter, as well as independent testing by TÜV Product Service, has continued to demonstrate the safety of these dialyzers. Nevertheless, in an abundance of caution, Baxter has put a global hold on distribution of this series of dialyzers and is advising customers worldwide to temporarily discontinue use, pending the evaluation by an expert commission. Baxter will work with customers to find suitable alternative dialyzers to use in the interim. (Baxter International, 2001a, n.p.)

This quotation talks about how Baxter, in the absence of compelling evidence, voluntarily asked its customers to stop using its products, and switch to those of its competitors, until the original dialyzers can be proven safe. This strategy sought to protect Baxter's patients at its own expense. Rarely will organizations voluntarily help their customers shift to competitors' products.

Baxter also aided its competition by informing them of the reason for the deaths. After the dialyzer crisis, Baxter not only explained its investigation and findings to the Food and Drug Administration and regulatory agencies in the affected countries, but also apprised 3M, the manufacturer of the fluid left in the filters, and rival competitors that could use the same manufacturing process that could leave them vulnerable to the same problems (Hammonds, 2002). Not only did Baxter take steps to ensure that a similar crisis never affected them again, they also attempted to keep a related problem from affecting their competitors.

Yet, Baxter went one step further, ceasing production of the entire line of filters implicated in the deaths. Baxter CEO Harry Kraemer commented in a November 5 press release that

> We are greatly saddened by the patient deaths and I would like to extend my personal sympathies to family members of those patients. We have a responsibility to make public our findings immediately and take swift action, even though confirmatory studies remain under way. . . . While a small number of our A and AF dialyzers appear to have played a role in some of these tragic events, we believe there remain substantive gaps in information about the facts associated with many of the patient deaths. Therefore, we have decided that in the interest of patient safety, the most

prudent course of action is to permanently cease manufacturing these dialyzers. (Baxter, 2001b, n.p.)

While some industry analysts considered closing the plants "overkill" (Birchard, 2002, p. 38), Baxter's emphasis on safety and on keeping the problem from recurring required that the filters be discontinued. Kraemer stated, when asked if the filters could have been produced safely, "Were we 100% confident? . . . No. We didn't know" (Hammonds, 2002, n.p.). One of the lead investigators in Spain and Croatia summed up Baxter's investigation this way: "This made us second-guess systems that we'd used for 20 years and that had always worked." Another investigator concluded, "What we know for sure is, this problem will never happen again" (Hammonds, 2002, n.p.). While they may never understand why the problem arose when it did, they took steps to prevent its recurrence, which is a clear example of corrective action. In this case, Baxter jettisoned a product that accounted for 30% of its dialyzer sales, and the $20 million in revenue it brought in, which likely could have been salvaged, to protect its customers.

Another way Baxter used the strategy of corrective action involved the extent of the investigation it pursued into the problems. As one of Baxter's investigators explained in the October 15 release, "Patient safety is our highest priority. . . . That is why we feel it is critical that all aspects of the hemodialysis treatment be thoroughly investigated" (Baxter, 2001a, n.p.). Although earlier tests had exonerated the filters, Baxter continued to investigate its products in an effort to prevent the problem from recurring. In the November 5 letter to customers, Baxter also emphasized the importance of safety, and how it used its investigation to guarantee it:

> Given our utmost concern for patient safety, we continued our intensive investigation, even after exhausting all standard internationally recognized safety and toxicity tests. We diligently pursued every potential lead based on the facts available to us and even began pursuing other less obvious courses of investigation in search of what could be the cause of the unexplained deaths. (Baxter International, 2001c, n.p.)

The investigative process Baxter used to find the cause of the problem and prevent future instances was so thorough that it continued the investigation past the limits normally imposed on organizations.

When discussing the dialyzer crisis with the media, Baxter decided to use strategies aimed at reducing the offensiveness of the event—compensation and corrective action. However, the strategies Baxter decided to use were not the only interesting decisions it made. Equally important are the strategies the company decided *not* to use.

Crisis Response Strategies Baxter Did Not Use

During its crisis response rhetoric, Baxter chose not to use a variety of tempting and common strategies. At no time did Baxter deny either that the dialyzers were responsible for the patient deaths or claim that other actors could have contributed to the crisis. Both of the strategies fall within a category of strategies that Benoit (1997) labels *denial.* This category is divided into two separate strategies: *simple denial,* where the "firm may deny that the act has occurred, that the firm performed the act, or that the act was harmful to anyone" (p. 179); and *shift the blame,* which argues "that another person or organization is actually responsible for the offensive act" (p. 180).

Despite plausible arguments, Baxter refused to engage in the strategy of shifting blame. They could easily have blamed 3M, who made the fluid used in testing the filters; or Althin, the filters' producer, which Baxter had acquired the March before the crisis began. They also did not blame Croatian and Spanish officials who opted not to cooperate with the investigation; Baxter never received the Croatian filters for testing (Greising, 2001). Baxter refused to use these strategies, because as Kraemer stated, "If you live in a world of let's find somebody to blame, then you're into a Ford-Firestone thing. . . . The reality of it is, we're responsible" (Greising, 2001, n.p.). In taking responsibility for the incidents, Baxter limited itself to strategies that would reduce the offensiveness of the original act (compensation) and attempt to prevent future problems (corrective action).

In sum, Baxter used corrective action and compensation to rebuild its image both during and after the dialyzer crisis. Equally as important are the available strategies it decided not to use. In accepting responsibility for this event, Baxter declined to shift the blame to 3M, maker of the fluid found in the dialyzers, or Althin's original management. After evaluating these strategies, this paper will examine how the circumstances surrounding the crisis and Baxter's responses to it helped the company avoid the withering public scrutiny common to many fatal-product liability cases.

❖ HOW BAXTER AVOIDED NEGATIVE MEDIA COVERAGE

Most of the image restoration cases researchers study involve widely publicized events where an organization faces a serious threat to its reputation, if not its continued existence (Benoit & Brinson, 1994; Benoit & Czerwinski, 1997; Boyd, 2001; Sellnow, 1993; Sellnow & Ulmer, 1995; Sellnow, Ulmer, & Snider, 1998). However, the organizations would, in most if not all of the cases, have considered that their crisis responses were more successful had they been able to limit the media coverage of the events in the first place. Baxter reached this goal of avoiding media coverage of the dialyzer crisis through a combination of its situation and its use of crisis response strategies.

Several situational variables prevented the media from paying close attention to this situation. Early in the crisis, the deaths occurred overseas—the first cluster of deaths took place in Spain. By the time the filters were recalled in mid-October, all but four of the deaths had taken place outside the United States. Under the best of circumstances, American media sources subscribe to the "all news is local news" motto and lavish attention on stories occurring in the United States or that affect large numbers of Americans. The four American deaths, two each in Texas and Nebraska, were not enough to catch the press's attention.

Part of the reason the American news media did not spend much time or ink on the Baxter case was due to other news stories. Less than one month after the first death on August 15, 2001, the World Trade Center attacks consumed the media's, and much of the news-consuming public's, attention. Fifty-three deaths caused by medical devices suddenly seemed less important, by comparison. By the time the media returned to business news, Baxter had completed its investigation, accepted responsibility, and begun settlements with victims. There was little left to report.

As well as paling beside the September 11, 2001, tragedies, Baxter also paled beside the size and scope of the domestic corporate scandals making headlines. The Enron, Adelphia, Global Crossing, Anderson, and WorldCom scandals had a greater impact on the pocketbooks and consciousness of the American public. Hence, the media devoted more attention to the larger business stories.

However, Baxter's successful navigation of the crisis cannot be credited entirely to the media's divided attentions. Its investors, and certainly its employees, paid close attention to the crisis. Baxter's strategic choices, in many ways, kept the story from escalating. The speed of

Baxter's response and its reliance on corrective action helped it recover from the crisis. Benoit and Brinson (1994) highlight the importance of a speedy response to crisis situations. In Baxter's case, the speed with which it began the investigation, issued the hold, and ordered the recall may have saved more lives and limited the corporation's potential liability: "They didn't look like they were trying to hide anything. . . . The recall was last month . . . and that is moving fairly quickly for an international company" (Japsen, 2001a, n.p.). Rather than waiting for conclusive evidence of responsibility from an independent agency, which they never received, and risking more deaths in the meantime, Baxter took immediate steps to solve the problem and protect patients.

In moving quickly, Baxter implemented corrective actions designed to prevent future occurrences of the dialyzer contamination. Closing the plant and discontinuing the production of an entire line of products were actions designed to "correct the problem" (Benoit, 1997, p. 181). However, corrective action can also leave an organization vulnerable to lawsuits. Chicago-area attorneys commented that Baxter "has sort of confessed" and this action "makes it [litigation] easier, but also brings in more competing firms" (Klein, 2001, n.p.). Benoit (1997) noticed this contradiction between image restoration and limiting liability when he stated, "image restoration concerns may, admittedly, conflict with a desire to avoid lawsuits, and the firm must decide whether it is more important to restore its image or avoid litigation" (pp. 183–184). Sellnow, Ulmer, and Snider (1998) admit, "we do [not] assume that corrective action should be taken without consideration of the legal consequences" (p. 64). Despite this concern, Baxter seems to have settled the lawsuits related to this case in spite of its early acceptance of responsibility.

Benoit (1997) affirms that accepting responsibility quickly when at fault is "morally the correct thing to do" (p. 184). Without concern for litigation, Baxter used this strategy, even in the absence of conclusive evidence, and won admirers for its crisis management. Lawsuits were settled, stock prices went up soon after the crisis, renal product sales rose, and members of the public familiar with the situation were impressed by Baxter's performance. Hammonds (2002) commented, "The message to CEOs: Investors like honesty, including public apologies. (Kraemer visited New York to apologize in person to the president of Croatia.) So, it turns out, do employees" (n.p.). Owning up to a problem and taking quick action to lessen its impact and prevent its recurrence allowed Baxter International to defuse a potentially devastating crisis and emerge stronger than ever.

❖   AFTERMATH OF DIALYZER CRISIS

Despite facing potential legal liability and damage to its reputation, in the short term Baxter seemed to have weathered the storm of the dialyzer crisis successfully. Both the finances and the prestige of the organization improved after the crisis, and Baxter's response to it, became public. This section will examine Baxter's reputation after the crisis by studying its stock price and its standing in the medical supply community.

In one of the most widely recognized measures of organizational success, stock price, Baxter initially suffered a loss as news of the charge against earnings and potential lawsuits rattled investors. However, as the company began to settle the lawsuits and amid assurances that the initial charge against earnings would cover any potential liability, stock prices began to rebound (Japsen, 2001b). By the end of 2001, Baxter's stock had risen 23% while its companions on the Standard and Poor's health care index dropped 13% ("Baxter's Harry Kraemer: 'I don't golf.'" 2002). The dialyzer crisis did not prevent Baxter from outperforming similar health care stocks operating in the same economic environment.

Stock prices jumped and Baxter's standing in the medical community scored its greatest coup in late November 2001, when the Bush administration awarded the company, in a joint contract with Acambis PLC, the $428 million contract to be the federal government's sole provider of 155 million doses of smallpox vaccine. This contract not only provided a financial boon for the organization, but also a rhetorical shot in the arm, as Baxter was selected over pharmaceutical giants Merck and GlaxoSmithKline. Baxter was moving up in the pharmaceutical market and closer to its goal of becoming a worldwide producer with $1 billion in annual sales by the end of the decade (Japsen, 2001b).

Despite the crisis, and the loss of a $20 million product, Baxter remained number one worldwide in renal care products with sales of $1.94 billion ("Baxter's Harry Kraemer: 'I don't golf,'" 2002). Not only did Baxter rise above other renal care providers, it was also recognized by industry publications for ethical behavior. For instance, *Business Ethics* awarded the company spots on its list of "100 Best Corporate Citizens" in 2001 and 2002. Baxter's environmental policies also earned it head-of-the-class honors in service to the environment.

However, recent years have been more difficult for Baxter. It has repeatedly lowered and often fallen short of its earning projections, eliminated thousands of positions, and faced tumbling stock prices.

In mid-March 2003, the Justice Department subpoenaed Baxter's records about the dialyzer crisis, possibly reopening the issue. These problems led Kraemer to resign his position as chairman and CEO in January of 2004 (Japsen & Miller, 2004). While Baxter initially ended the dialyzer crisis with its reputation intact, these later financial problems indicate that organizations cannot rest on past ethical behavior, but must constantly continue to update and revise their practices to remain viable.

Discussion Questions

1. What responsibilities do organizations have to consumers who rely on a line of products, one of which has exhibited a fatal, but potentially solvable, defect?

2. Did Baxter accept responsibility for the deaths too quickly?

3. How personally responsible is a CEO for a localized product-liability issue?

4. Was Baxter ethically obligated to close the Romney Plant?

5. Could Baxter have ethically attempted to shift blame for the dialyzer defects to 3M or to the organization that owned the Romney Plant a few months before the crisis?

6. What ethical responsibility did Baxter owe to the employees at the Romney Plant that it closed in the wake of the dialyzer crisis?

❖ NOTES

1. The information for this case came from publicly accessible news accounts, press releases, statements available on Baxter International's Web site, and published statements from its officers.

2. This and other releases from Baxter International were accessed from the organization's Web site, www.baxter.com. While these documents are no longer available online, the author has retained copies and would be happy to share them as requested.

❖ REFERENCES

Baxter International. (2001a, October 15). *Baxter urges comprehensive scientific analysis of hemodialysis treatment safety* [Press Release]. Retrieved November 11, 2002, from www.baxter.com/utilities/news/releases/2001/10–15.croatia. html

Baxter International. (2001b, November 5). *Following extensive investigation, Baxter identifies probable cause of recent hemodialysis patient deaths* [Press Release]. Retrieved November 11, 2002, from www.baxter.com/utilities/news/releases/2001/11–05dialyzer.html

Baxter International. (2001c, November 5). *Stop manufacture letter.* Retrieved November 7, 2001, from www.baxter.com

Baxter International. (2001d, November 28). *Baxter announces agreement with families affected by recent hemodialysis deaths in Spain* [Press Release]. Retrieved November 11, 2002, from www.baxter.com/utilities/news/releases/2001/11–28spsettlement.html

Baxter International. (n.d.). *Corporate overview.* Retrieved March 29, 2004, from http://www.baxter.com/about_baxter/company_profile/sub/corporate_overview.html

Baxter International Inc. (2001, November 29). Agreement with families affected by recent hemodialysis deaths—in Spain. *Market News Publishing.* Retrieved July 10, 2005, from General Business File ASAP database.

Baxter's A and AF series dialyzers linked to over 50 deaths. (2001, Fall). *Journal of Clinical Engineering,* pp. 241–242.

Baxter's Harry Kraemer: "I don't golf." (2002, March 28). *Business Week Online.* Retrieved March 29 2002, from www.businessweek.com.

Benoit, W. L. (1995). *Accounts, excuses, and apologies: A theory of image restoration strategies.* Albany: State University of New York Press.

Benoit, W. L. (1997). Image repair discourse and crisis communication, *Public Relations Review, 23*(2). 177–186.

Benoit, W. L., & Brinson, S. L. (1994). AT&T: Apologies are not enough. *Communication Quarterly, 42*(1), 75–89.

Benoit, W. L., & Czerwinski, A. (1997). A critical analysis of USAir's image repair discourse. *Business Communication Quarterly, 60*(3), 38–57.

Birchard, B. (2002, February). Citizen Kraemer. *Chief Executive,* pp. 34–38.

Boyd, J. (2001). The rhetoric of arrogance: The public relations response of the Standard Oil Trust. *Public Relations Review, 27,* 163–178.

Coombs, T. W. (2000). Designing post-crisis messages: Lessons for crisis response strategies. *Review of Business,* pp. 37–41.

Daly, E. (2001, November 29). Baxter settles dialysis deaths in Spain. *New York Times,* p. C4. Retrieved January 14, 2002, from the InfoTrac Custom Newspapers Database.

Firn, D. (2001, November 6). Baxter faces crisis over blood filters. *The Financial Times.* Retrieved November 11, 2002 from InfoTrac Expanded Academic Index.

Greising, D. (2001, November 7). Baxter gets grip on crisis, responsibility. *Chicago Tribune.* Retrieved November 7, 2001, from http:chicagotribune. com

Hammonds, K. H. (2002, November). Harry Kraemer's moment of truth. *Fast Company.* Retrieved November 6, 2002, from www.fastcompany.com

Japsen, B. (2001a, November 6). Baxter links its filters to deaths. *Chicago Tribune*. Retrieved November 7, 2001, from http://chicagotribune.com

Japsen, B. (2001b, November 30). Smallpox pact may invigorate Baxter. *Chicago Tribune*. Retrieved November 7, 2001, from http://chicagotribune.com

Japsen, B., & Miller, J. P. (2004, January 27). Chief stepping down at Baxter. *Chicago Tribune*. Retrieved March 22, 2004, from http://chicagotribune.com

Klein, S. A. (2001, November 26). Legal eagles eye wounded Baxter; lawyers scouring globe to find more filter victims. *Crain's Chicago Business*, p. 4. Retrieved November 11, 2002, from InfoTrac Expanded Academic Index.

McMillan, J. J. (1986). In search of the organizational persona: A rationale for studying organizations rhetorically. In L. Thayer (Ed.), *Organization communication: Emerging perspectives I* (pp. 21–45). Norwood, NJ: Ablex.

Peterson, M., & Daly, E. (2001, November 21). Baxter finds possible link in 53 deaths. *New York Times*. Retrieved November 7, 2001, from http://nytimes.com

Sellnow, T. L. (1993). Scientific argument in organizational crisis situations: The case of Exxon. *Argumentation and Advocacy, 30*(1), 28–43. Retrieved November 15, 2002, from InfoTrac Expanded Academic Index.

Sellnow, T. L., & Ulmer, R. R. (1995). Ambiguous argument as advocacy in organizational crisis communication. *Argumentation and Advocacy, 31*(3), 138–151.

Sellnow, T. L., Ulmer, R. R., & Snider, M. (1998). The compatibility of corrective action in organizational crisis communication. *Communication Quarterly, 46*(1), 60–74.

Ware, B. L., & Linkugel, W. A. (1973). They spoke in defense of themselves: On the generic criticism of the apologia. *The Quarterly Journal of Speech, 59*, 273–283.

Afterword

Casework and Communication About Ethics

Toward a Broader Perspective on Our Lives, Our Careers, Our Happiness, and Our Common Future

George Cheney

Philosophers often ask scholars in communication about what the field of communication studies offers to the discussion of ethics today. After all, if ethics is *grounded* in philosophical positions and then *applied* to various contexts—like work, science, and politics—what is the need for special attention to communication about ethics? Isn't that just talk, or simply a vehicle for transmitting ideas? We know that talk *is* often cheap, as when a promise is broken by a friend or a nation professes peace on the one hand and then acts militaristically on the other. Does the *expression* of an ethical position deserve attention as much as the position itself? The philosophers have a point in that except for occasional forays into ethics by scholars of rhetoric and persuasion, relatively little attention has been given to ethics in our field. And, as we see in most of our textbooks, ethics appears a bit like an afterthought:

"Oh, and by the way, if we have time, we'll talk about this last chapter—it's about ethics" (a major exception is Johanessen, 2002).

Still, the studies of rhetoric and persuasion have shown us how ethics is implied by the very capacity for choice: that is the *framing* of choice in language and with other symbols has an inherent ethical dimension. As just one example, consider how commercial advertising and political campaigns often create what some call "the illusion of two alternatives" by presenting the reader, listener, or viewer with a choice framed like this: "If you don't buy this facial cream or support this candidate, really bad things are going to happen." Thus, the very *definition* of a situation, as any debater knows, really makes a difference in the course of a discussion—and helps to define not only practical choices but also what we consider to be things of value or goodness.

So when I'm teaching ethics and communication, I ask students to consider not only cases where the role of communication is obvious—as in issues of lying, or professional confidentiality, or the sharing of information, or individual privacy—but also the ways communication is central to discussions of material-ethical issues such as genetic modification, global warming, or the end of life. For instance, just shifting terminology from "global warming" to "climate change" in public discourse can suggest less urgency and, therefore, affect public perceptions and ultimately public policy. Words matter.

❖ HOW TO CONNECT THESE CASES WITH BROADER ISSUES

This book offers you an array of current cases, ranging from consumer protection regarding harmful products to the very ways that the culture of an organization either encourages or discourages ethical reflection. Issues of ethics, work, and organizations are popping up in all sorts of ways these days; to notice that, you need only turn on the TV or pick up a newspaper. Some examples are controversies over executive salaries and "golden parachutes" (or sweet deals for departures); the changing roles of physicians and nurses within HMOs (health maintenance organizations); insider trading on Wall Street; the pricing and labor practices of Wal-Mart and other commercial giants; the use of performance-enhancement drugs in U.S. baseball; the sexual abuse crimes by priests in the Roman Catholic Church; the length of the work week and the distribution of work in Western Europe; the widespread use of deception/propaganda by the Pentagon; the organizational communication constraints within NASA; the outsourcing of sweatshops to poorer countries; and of course, the Enron, etc., scandals. A number of such cases are analyzed in this book, and we hope that they help you to think of still other cases. If there is one broad trend we see here, it is perhaps that the importance of ethics in business and other sectors is coming into the spotlight in a way that has not happened in a long time. So, while scandals are not a good thing, reflection and delibera- tion are. If something's rotten beyond "a few bad apples," then it's important to consider what's going on in the larger society that makes, for example, academic dishonesty something to which up to two thirds of college students admit when surveyed (Callahan, 2004).

❖ REVISITING ETHICAL THEORY
    IN LIGHT OF CONTEMPORARY CASES

Applied ethics has come a long way in recent years, as you can see not only with this book but also from the many practical discussions of the relevance of fields as diverse as engineering and interactive media. Until roughly 1990, there were not a lot of "middle-level" discussions of applied or practical ethics that bridged the abstract theories of, say, Aristotle, Kant, and John Stuart Mill (to name a few), with day-to-day pressures, concerns, and decisions of all of us. What's more, writings on applied ethics—especially in business—tended either to sound so idealistic as to set unattainable standards or to be uninspired in their treatment of ethical practice as simply a matter of working within the boundaries of the law. Today, there is a much wider range of writings, videos, and speeches that offer us realistic and inspiring assessments of ethical practice. For making stronger linkages between cases and theory, we can thank feminist ethicists, notably Carol Gilligan (1982); ethicists concerned with democracy, community, and difference like Selya Benhabib (1996); and environmental ethicists such as Andrew Light (Light & Rolston, 2003). I mention these three perspectives in particular because of the ways they are helping us to grapple with how today's ethical dilemmas are both timeless and distinctive. Environmental ethicists, for instance, aid us in rethinking our place in the world, our goals for the world, and our relations to other creatures and the entire biosphere. These discussions are valuable, regardless of what conclusions any of us may draw. In addition, when we start taking the environment, aspects of difference, and democracy seriously, we can see how very specific issues like the types of people favored in typical executive recruitment (or the type of policies perpetuated by them) can be cast broadly.

❖ THE NEED FOR BROADER REFLECTION

A few years ago, I was teaching an executive MBA leadership seminar in New Zealand to a group of middle–high level Chinese executives. As I was presenting both traditional and new conceptions of leadership to the class, one of the managers raised his hand and hesitatingly asked,

> Professor Cheney, we appreciate hearing about all these ideas, and we do want to cover them at some point. But, I was talking to some of my colleagues on the break. And, what we most want today is a chance to talk about ethical dilemmas and work and how to deal with them. You see, we have very few people to confide in, and our work schedules don't give us the time to think and talk about these things.

At that moment, I put down my notes, sat down in a circle with the students, and we began discussing the cases that they each were facing. I was reminded about the need to be flexible with pedagogy (or teaching philosophy and strategy) while the need for an open space of reflection was pressed upon me.

I have found much the same need for reflection by my students at home, and it comes to the foreground every time I teach a class on quality of work life or on communication ethics. This is why I have revised my courses over the years from a largely deductive (theory→principle→ application) model to one where theoretical discussions arise out of consideration of cases as much as they come out of the foundational readings by Aristotle and Co. But, the conversation doesn't end there because an individual case doesn't mean very much until it is tied to other cases and we talk about wider lessons. To demystify theory a bit, just remember that it is all about thinking across cases and situations. And, whether you realize it or not, you already have lay or implicit theories of important matters like work, love, family, friendship, power, money, and probably also career, success, and productivity. These "theories" almost always suggest ethics, even when we're not paying attention to that side of things. For example, if we buy the maxim that

"Time is money," this may mean that we evaluate many or all activities in terms of very specific notions of efficiency and worth. But, what are the blind spots associated with this saying and its associated worldview?

❖ BRINGING ETHICS TO LIFE, FOR US AS INDIVIDUALS AND FOR OUR SOCIETY

What does it mean, then, to bring ethics to life—and to work? In a recent discussion in my communication ethics class, the students offered insights on why the term "morality" is more compelling than "ethics" to the U.S. public today. They explained how the latter term seems dry, abstract, without passion, and removed from our most cherished concerns. On the other hand, "morality" seems full of life and passion, and it relates to both religious and secular perspectives that are being hotly debated in politics and the mass media. For my students, as well as for many leaders today, the phrase "moral values" carries with it a lot of significance, emotion, and concern. This is an interesting observation. Not only does it highlight the importance of language, of communication, but it also reminds us that people want very much to engage questions of "the good." So, I suggest that we bring ethics out of its little box, in our classes, our textbooks, and our lives. Ethics should not be something that involves only abstract general rules or guidelines but something that connects what is "the good" with living "the good life" (Solomon, 1999).

❖ TOWARD NEW UNDERSTANDINGS OF CAREER, SUCCESS, PRODUCTIVITY, AND HAPPINESS

One topic that I am coming to include in nearly every one of my classes these days is the transformation of the citizen to the consumer over the past century. Now, why would this topic deserve so much attention? And, what does it have to do with communication, work and ethics? Why should we care? I begin with the connotations and practices associated with each of these terms and how it is that the word "consumption" has come to have a very different cluster of meanings at the beginning of the 21st century than it did at the start of the 20th. In 1900, consumption referred to use, waste, and to the disease of tuberculosis.

It had both neutral and negative connotations. Today, consumption is elevated as a principal goal of individuals and our society. We see this in seemingly innocuous things, from the bumper sticker that says, "I'd rather be shopping" to the treatment of China in the news mainly as an emerging market of 1.25 billion consumers. "Consumer" has a very different ring than "citizen" and, curiously, the term citizen now sounds out of date to many of my students, just as it does to larger publics in North America, Europe, East Asia, Australasia, and beyond. Many members of our society readily announce, "But I *am* a consumer!" Of course, you and I are. But, the problem with "the consumer" is that the term and the role do not readily suggest responsibilities; the emphasis is on rights and demands. Typically, when we hear the word "consumer," we think mainly of what we want *from* and not what we might give *to* society. This means that we're less likely to think about ethical issues when we are thinking or acting with our consumer "hats" on than when we consider ourselves first of all as citizens.

A 1997 *New Yorker* cartoon captures the problem perfectly. It shows one political leader seated side by side with another, saying, "My government is concerned about your government's torture and maiming of potential consumers." We laugh at such a frame because it sounds odd, but underlying the irony is the fact that when we think about the consumer role, ideas of responsibility, political engagement, and ethical choices often seem to disappear. This is true even for many people who consider themselves "socially responsible": while they may consciously choose to buy a car that gets good gas mileage, they will at the same time not even think about where their investments are directed. All of us—and I do mean all of us—compartmentalize, or contain, our ethical positions and our values in certain ways.

With the consumer in mind, I now move into issues of the market and happiness. Recent research on happiness and the consumer society is telling. Some surveys of life satisfaction in the United States show that happiness may have peaked in the year 1957! Understandably, this is disheartening to many of today's college students. Another study shows that when the *Forbes* list of the 100 richest U.S. citizens was compared with a random sample from metropolitan phonebooks, the rich group came out only slightly happier on average than the randomly selected group. Finally, international surveys of more than 100 countries show that after a certain level of income—adjusted to about US$10,000—increased affluence did not yield increased happiness (see Hamilton, 2003). The title of one book that summarizes this kind of research makes the point well: *The Loss of Happiness in Market Democracies* (Lane, 2000). So, what's going on?

When I ask students to write vision statements of their ideal careers in my quality of work life class, or their main ideals or values, in the ethics class, there's an interesting convergence. Upon reflection, students realize that our consumer society doesn't necessarily deliver what it promises. While it pretends to be purely democratic in "giving 'em what they want," in some ways it diverts people from the things that really make them happy, beyond material subsistence: satisfying relationships with family and friends, meaningful work, and transcendent goals (Gilbert & Wilson, 2000). So, it may be that living "the good life" is not the same as living "a good life"—at least as we typically define things like wealth and success and being productive in our society. When many of us begin to reflect deeply on these things, we find that what advertising presents as solid and sure—a new car or a promotion as the path to happiness—is actually pretty fleeting.

❖ THE WAY WE TALK, AND THE WAY WE ARE

This is why I spend so much time in class on aphorisms or maxims like "Get a real job" (see Clair, 1996), "Act like a professional" (Cheney & Ashcraft, in progress), and "It's just business" (Cheney, 1998). These sayings express deep commitments of our culture that often go unquestioned. For example, by proclaiming "It's just business," a person is basically saying that certain activities—including harmful ones—shouldn't be evaluated by ethical standards outside of commerce as a justification in itself. This is part of the illusion of an amoral market, based on a faulty interpretation of Adam Smith's 1776 book *Wealth of Nations* (Werhane, 1991). In fact, Smith never imagined a market without emotions and values such as sympathy, compassion, and justice. Making these kinds of assumptions obvious or transparent can lead to some productive reflections on who we are, what we really want, and how we can make a better society.

Interestingly, it was Aristotle (1980 trans.), more than 2,400 years ago, who linked "the good life" and "a good life." His concept of *eudaimonia* was, until fairly recently, translated into English from the ancient Greek simply as "happiness." But, scholars now agree that he meant something more than that: the idea of "flourishing," which takes into account not just individual life satisfaction but also one's role in the world. In other words, true happiness involves something much more than individual life satisfaction: the upgrading of one's audio equipment, the bigger house, or the status associated with a high-end brand. Ethics is ultimately not something we keep in a box but rather have woven throughout our lives. But, this is not usually how ethics is taught or discussed or imagined, especially when it comes to business and professional activities (Cheney, 2004, in progress).

❖ MAKING ETHICS COUNT

As you reflect on the cases and issues discussed in this book, try to make connections not only to other cases, and to foundational theories of ethics (such as those discussed in the first two chapters), but also to your life commitments and life path. While you may not have to face certain issues—say, whether to report malfunctioning O-rings—you will inevitably face ethical choices about what kind of professional and what kind of person you want to be. And, better to think about that consciously, along the way, than to wonder later, "How did I get here?"

❖ REFERENCES

Aristotle. (1980). *The Nichomachean ethics* (D. Ross, Trans.). Oxford, UK: Oxford University Press.

Benhabib, S. (Ed.). (1996). *Democracy and difference.* Princeton, NJ: Princeton University Press.

Callahan, D. (2004). *The cheating culture: Why more Americans are doing wrong to get ahead.* Orlando, FL: HarcourtBrace.

Cheney, G. (1998). "It's the economy, stupid!" A rhetorical-ethical perspective on today's market. *Australian Journal of Communication, 25,* 25–44.

Cheney, G. (2004). Bringing ethics in from the margins. *Australian Journal of Communication, 31,* 25–40.

Cheney, G. (in progress). *Communication and professional ethics: How we talk about who we are at work and why it matters.* New York: Oxford University Press.

Cheney, G., & Ashcraft, K. L. (in progress). *The meanings and practices of professionalism.* Unpublished paper, University of Utah.

Clair, R. P. (1996). The political nature of the colloquialism "a real job": Implications for organizational socialization. *Communication Monographs, 63,* 249–67.

Gilbert, D. T., & Wilson, T. D. (2000). Miswanting. In J. P. Forgas (Ed.), *Feeling and thinking* (pp. 178–197).

Gilligan, C. (1982). *In a different voice.* Cambridge, MA: Harvard University Press.

Hamilton, C. (2003). *Growth fetish.* Sydney: Allen & Unwin.

Johanessen, R. (2002). *Ethics in human communication,* 5th ed. Prospect Heights, IL: Waveland Press.

Lane, R. E. (2000). *The loss of happiness in market democracies.* New Haven, CT: Yale University Press.

Light, A., & Rolston, H., III. (2003). *Environmental ethics: An anthology.* Malden, MA: Blackwell.

Smith, A. (1976). *Wealth of nations.* Oxford, UK: Oxford University Press (originally published, 1776).

Solomon, R. (1999). *A better way to think about business: How personal integrity leads to corporate success.* New York: Oxford University Press.

Werhane, P. (1991) *Adam Smith and his legacy for modern capitalism.* New York: Oxford University Press.

Index

About the Editor

Steve May (Ph.D., University of Utah, 1993) is associate professor in the Department of Communication Studies at the University of North Carolina at Chapel Hill. He is also currently a Leadership Fellow at the Institute for the Arts and the Humanities, an Ethics Fellow at the Parr Ethics Center, and a researcher and ethics consultant for the Ethics at Work program at the Kenan Institute for Ethics. His current research focuses on the relationship between work and identity, as it relates to the boundaries of public/private, work/family, and labor/leisure. His research has explored the role of corporate counseling programs during organizational change and crisis, including downsizing, labor strikes, and accidents. Most recently, he has studied the challenges and opportunities for organizational ethics and corporate social responsibility. His most recent book project was *Engaging Organizational Communication Theory and Research: Multiple Perspectives*, coedited with Dennis Mumby. His next book, *The Debate Over Corporate Social Responsibility*, coedited with George Cheney and Juliet Roper, will be published in 2006 by Oxford University Press. His organizational communication research has been published in journals such as *Management Communication Quarterly*, *Journal of Applied Communication Research*, *Rhetoric and Public Affairs*, *Public Policy Yearbook*, and *Organizational Communication: Emerging Perspectives*. He is a past forum editor of *Management Communication Quarterly* and associate editor of the *Journal of Applied Communication Research* and the *Journal of Business Communication*.

About the Contributors

Mohammad Auwal (Ph.D., Ohio University, 1994) is associate professor of Communication Studies at California State University, Los Angeles. His research interests include organizing for social change, communication ethics, and mythologies of extremism, tyranny, and terrorism. His coauthored and sole-authored articles have appeared in *Knowledge: Creation, Diffusion, & Utilization* (currently, *Journal of Science Communication*), *Communication Theory, Journal of Business Communication, Communication Monographs, Discourse & Society,* and *Kentucky Journal of Communication.*

Nicola Berg (Ph.D., University of Dortmund, 2002) is assistant professor and the Chair for Strategic and International Management at the University of Dortmund in Germany. She has made several research trips to China, France, India, Russia, Thailand, and the United States. Her research interests are in international management, human resource management, and public affairs management. She has published articles in journals such as the *Journal of Business Ethics, Journal for East European Management Studies, Zeitschrift für Wirtschafts- und Unternehmensethik (Journal for Business, Economics & Ethics),* and in edited books. At present she is preparing her post-doctoral thesis ("Habilitation").

Edward C. Brewer (Ph. D., Bowling Green University, 1995) is associate professor of Organizational Communication at Murray State University. Brewer has published articles concerning organizational communication and free speech issues in *The Free Speech Yearbook, Journal of Public Advocacy,* and *Iowa Journal of Communication.* Before he received his Ph.D., he worked in sales and banking and served as a pastor for 10 years.

Larry Davis Browning (Ph.D., The Ohio State University, 1973) is a professor of Organizational Communication and director of Graduate Studies in the Department of Communication Studies at the University of Texas at Austin. Larry's research on organizations is published in a variety of communication and management journals including *Communication Monographs, Academy of Management Journal, Communication Theory, Journal of Management, Communication Studies, Communication Education, Journal of Organizational Change Management, Journal of Applied Communication Research, Electronic Journal of Communication, Handbook of Organizational Communication,* and *Communication Yearbook 13.* He has recently coauthored a book titled *Information and Communication Technologies in Action: Linking Theory and Narratives of Practice* (2004).

Lori Byers (Ph.D., Ohio University, 1997) is assistant professor at the University of North Texas. Her research interests include communication in the family, gender and communication, and communication during times of crisis. In addition to several book articles, she has recently published in *Alzheimer's Care Quarterly.*

Paula Cano completed an M.A. in Communication Studies at the University of Kansas.

George Cheney (Ph.D., Purdue University, 1985) is professor in the Department of Communication at the University of Utah and adjunct professor in Management Communication at The University of Waikato, Hamilton, New Zealand. His interests include organizational communication, quality of work life, professional ethics, employee rights and participation, organizational identity, power in organizations, the marketization of society, the rhetoric of war, and issues in globalization. Recognized for both teaching and research, George has published over 75 journal articles and book chapters, along with four books. He has lectured in North America, Western Europe, and Latin America. He is at work on two books for Oxford University Press: an edited volume, *The Debate over Corporate Social Responsibility* (with Steve May and Juliet Roper), and a solo-authored text on new approaches to communication and professional ethics.

Teresa L. Clounch is a doctoral student in the School of Education at the University of Kansas.

Elise J. Dallimore (Ph.D., University of Washington, 1998) is an assistant professor of Communication Studies at Northeastern University. She teaches organizational and instructional communication courses and conducts research on organizational socialization, quality of life, and the impact of various pedagogical approaches on teaching and student learning. She has published work in journals such as *Women's Studies in Communication, Communication Education, Journal on Excellence in*

College Teaching, and *Business Communication Quarterly.* Further, she has been affiliated with the Centers for Teaching and Learning at two major research institutions and currently does instructional consulting work.

Julie A. Davis (Ph.D., University of Kansas, 2000) is an assistant professor of Communication at the College of Charleston in South Carolina. She teaches classes in Business Communication, Organizational Communication, and Crisis Communication. Dr. Davis's research interests include organizational image maintenance strategies and comic art exemplars of organizational life.

Jeanette Wenig Drake (Ph.D., Bowling Green State University, 2004) is an associate professor of Communication at the University of Findlay in Ohio, where she has taught public relations since 1998. Prior to teaching, she managed corporate communications for various organizations in Columbus, Ohio, for 13 years. Her research interests include social marketing, environmental communication, social protest, and media framing.

Scott C. D'Urso (Ph.D., University of Texas at Austin, 2004) is an assistant professor of Communication Studies at Marquette University, where he teaches courses focused on organizational communication and new communication technology. Scott's primary research interests include organizational use of communication technologies such as e-mail, instant messaging, and chat. He is currently preparing several manuscripts for publication on subjects such as the digital divide in organizations, virtual team decision making, the impact of intention of channel choice in relationship communication, and electronic monitoring/ surveillance in the workplace. Prior to a career in academia, Scott worked for several years as a multimedia specialist/manager of a multimedia production department for a government defense contractor in the southwest United States.

Stuart L. Esrock (Ph.D., Bowling Green State University, 1995) is an associate professor in the Department of Communication at the University of Louisville. His research focuses on strategic communication and the use of new media technologies. Beginning in the summer of 2001, Professor Esrock spent a year with the Kentucky ACTION cigarette excise tax campaign as a communication consultant while on sabbatical.

Carl E. Fischer is a doctoral student in the School of Education at the University of Kansas.

Bethany Crandell Goodier (Ph.D., University of South Florida, 2002) is an assistant professor in the Department of Communication at the College of Charleston. Her research interests include spirituality in the workplace, collaboration, and health communication, and her most recent publication appeared in *Popular Communication.*

Joy L. Hart (Ph.D., University of Kentucky, 1988) is a professor in the Department of Communication at the University of Louisville. Her research and teaching interests center on organizational and interpersonal communication. For the last four years, she has studied the campaign to increase the cigarette excise tax in Kentucky.

Penny Holmes has been employed as a consultant with Introspect, a fire and explosion investigation firm, since completing her MBA at the University of Texas at Austin. Her career focuses are failure analysis, problem resolution, and strategic planning. Prior to receiving her MBA, she worked in manufacturing-related industries for over five years. Ms. Holmes received a Bachelor of Science degree in mechanical engineering from Texas A&M University.

Catherine Howard is a doctoral student in Communication Studies at the University of Kansas.

Joann Keyton (Ph.D., The Ohio State University, 1987) is professor of Communication Studies at the University of Kansas where her coauthors are students in the graduate program. This case was developed as an assignment in a gender and organizational communication seminar. Dr. Keyton has published numerous scholarly articles on sexual harassment and serves as a consultant to organizations and counsel regarding sexual harassment issues.

Toru Kiyomiya (Ph.D., Michigan State University, 2000) is assistant professor in the Business English and Communication Course at Seinan Gakuin University, Japan. His master's degree is in Labor Relations and Human Resources (Michigan State University), and he previously taught at the University of Tulsa and the University of Texas at San Antonio. His major field of study is organizational communication and cross-cultural management. Current research interests include critical management, deception in group contexts, industrial and organizational democracy, crisis management, and theories of change.

Greg Leichty (Ph.D., University of Kentucky, 1986) is a professor in the Department of Communication at the University of Louisville. His research focuses on argumentation theory, public relations, and activist communication.

John Llewellyn (Ph.D., University of Texas, 1990) is associate professor of Communication at Wake Forest University in Winston-Salem, North Carolina. His research interests include organizational communication, rhetorical criticism, freedom of speech, and urban legends. His work has appeared in the *American Journal of Communication, Journal of Communication,* and *Public Relations Quarterly,* as well as in *Research in Corporate Social Performance and Policy, Psychology of Political Communication, Public Relations Inquiry as Rhetorical Criticism,* and *Case Studies in Sport Communication.*

Kaori Matake (M.A., Seinan Gakuin University, 2004) is currently teaching at Chikushi Jogakuen Senior High School. Her major field of study is interpersonal and organizational communication in educational settings.

Masaki Matsunaga (M.A., Seinan Gakuin University, 2004) is a Ph.D. candidate in Communication Arts and Sciences at Pennsylvania State University. After the completion of his master's, he was awarded a Fulbright Scholarship by the Institute of International Education, for graduate studies in the United States. His major fields of study include communication theory and intercultural/interpersonal communication.

Caryn E. Medved (Ph.D., University of Kansas, 1999) is an assistant professor of Communication Studies at Ohio University. Her research explores the discourses of work and family in relation to gender, power, and identity. Her work has been published in outlets such as *Management Communication Quarterly, Applied Journal of Communication, Communication Studies, Communication Education,* and *Communication Yearbook,* and has earned a top paper award from the organizational communication division of the NCA (National Communication Association) and the Organization for the Study of Culture, Language, and Gender. She was awarded the University Professor distinction at Ohio University in 2001 for excellence in undergraduate education.

Rebecca Meisenbach (Ph.D., Purdue University, 2004) is an assistant professor at Concord University in Athens, West Virginia. Her research focuses on organizational rhetoric, ethics, identity negotiation, and nonprofit organizing. She was a college admissions counselor at Wake Forest University during the NCRB (National College Registration Board) controversy.

David R. Novak (M.S., Illinois State University, 2001) is a doctoral student, and the 2004–2005 Assistant Basic Course Director in the School of Communication Studies at Ohio University. His research focuses on communication; "alternative" and feminist organizations; and the processes of community, democracy, and social change. He has journal articles published or in press in the *Journal of Applied Communication Research,* the *Basic Communication Course Annual,* and the *Journal of the Illinois Speech and Theater Association.*

Heather Osterman (M.A., University of Texas, 2000) is manager of Curricular Support and Professional Development at Ignite! Learning in Austin, Texas. Her professional interests include integrating technology into the middle school classroom, focusing on theories of multiple intelligences and constructivist theory.

Patricia Parker (Ph.D., University of Texas, 1997) is associate professor of Communication Studies at the University of North Carolina at Chapel Hill. Her research interests include critical and feminist studies of race, gender, class, and culture in organization processes, with a central focus on career socialization, leadership, and empowerment. Her research has appeared in *Leadership Quarterly, Management Communication Quarterly, Communication Yearbook,* and the *Electronic Journal of Communication,* and she has a recently published book, *Race, Gender, and Leadership: Re-envisioning Organizational Leadership From the Perspectives of African American Women Executives* (Erlbaum, 2005).

Brian K. Richardson (Ph.D., University of Texas, 2001) is an assistant professor of Communication Studies at the University of North Texas. His research interests include employees' responses to organizational wrongdoing, sexual harassment, and organizational change. He has published research in *Human Communication Research* and *Management Communication Quarterly.*

Alf Steinar Sætre (Ph.D., University of Texas at Austin, 1997) is an associate professor with the Department of Industrial Economics and Technology Management at the Norwegian University of Science and Technology in Trondheim, Norway. Dr. Sætre's research focuses on innovation and ICT use in organizations, new venture financing, and organizational communication. Dr. Sætre's research is published in a variety of journals including *Venture Capital,* the *International Journal of Entrepreneurship and Innovation,* and *Informing Science.* He has recently coauthored a book entitled *Information and Communication Technologies* *in Action: Linking Theory and Narratives of Practice.* He has a Ph.D. in Organizational Communication from the University of Texas at Austin, and a master of science degree from the Norwegian School of Economics and Business Administration.

Jan-Oddvar Sørnes (Ph.D., Norwegian University of Science and Technology, 2004) is an associate professor at Bodø Graduate School of Business at Bodø University, Norway. Jan's research focus is on organizational communication, specifically how ICTs are used in organizations. He has 10 years of experience with e-learning and ICT use in higher education. Jan teaches introductory courses in organizational communication and technology management, and graduate courses in qualitative research methods. He has a master's degree from Michigan State University in telecommunications management and an undergraduate degree from University of Idaho in broadcast journalism. Jan has published articles in journals such as *Informing Science,* has several book chapters, and has coauthored a book titled *Information and Communication Technologies in Action: Linking Theory and Narratives of Practice* (2004).

Keri K. Stephens (Ph.D., University of Texas at Austin, 2005) is an assistant professor at Texas State University where she teaches organizational communication and research methods. Keri's research focuses on how people use technology to communicate within and between organizations. Her published work has appeared in *Journal of Health Communication, Journal of Business Communication, Informing Science,* and several other edited books. She is also a coauthor on the book, *Information and Communication Technology in Action: Linking Theory and Narratives of Practice,* and she has received several teaching awards. She has a B.S. in biochemistry from Texas A&M University and prior to returning to academia, Keri worked in technology-related industries for eight years.

Jennifer Anne Thackaberry (Ph.D., University of Colorado, 2000) is an assistant professor of Communication at Purdue University. This case was developed as part of a larger project examining the historic role of the 10 Standard Fire Orders in the management of wildland firefighting safety. An article from that project recently appeared in the journal *Management Communication Quarterly.*

Sarah S. Topp completed a master's in Communication Studies at the University of Kansas.

Michelle T. Violanti (Ph.D., University of Kansas, 1995) is an associate professor in the School of Communication Studies at the University of Tennessee. Her research interests include interpersonal relationships in organizational settings (e.g., mentoring, socialization, and friendships), textual analysis of organizational documents and responses to crisis situations, how our communication is gendered, and instructional communication. She has published articles in *Journal of Applied Communication Research, Management Communication Quarterly, Human Communication Research,* and *Women's Studies in Communication.* Her favorite courses to teach are communication theory, research methods, and organizational theory and application.

Martin K. Welge (Ph.D., University of Cologne, 1973; Habilitation, 1978) is professor, department head, and chair for Strategic and International Management at the University of Dortmund in Germany. His research interests include international management and strategic management. His recent books include the third edition of *Internationales Management* (coauthor), and *Strategisches Management* (coauthor). He is actively involved in teaching in executive programs.

Michaella M. Zlatek is a student in the master's program in Communication Studies at the University of Kansas.